EMPOWERMENT OF WOMEN
IN
INDIA

EMPOWERMENT OF WOMEN
IN
INDIA

Edited by

Dr. M. Koteswara Rao

LLB., M.A., M.D., M.A., Ph.D.

Professor of Economics

Acharya Nagarjuna University

Nagarjuna Nagar–522 510

DISCOVERY PUBLISHING HOUSE

NEW DELHI-110002

First Published-2005
Reprinted: 2013
ISBN 81-7141-983-6

Published by

DISCOVERY PUBLISHING HOUSE
4831/24, Ansari Road, Prahlad Street,
Darya Ganj, New Delhi-110002 (India)
Phone: 23279245 • Fax: 91-11-23253475
E-mail:dphtemp@indiatimes.com

Printed at:

Dynamic printers, Delhi

Contents

Introduction

The section of Gender Development focuses on the gender dimension of development process. For a long time gender aspect of development process has been neglected. Until recently, there is very scant attention paid to these aspects by both the practitioners as well as scholars. During 1980s, as a result of the rapid growing feminist movement the gender role in the development has come into focus first in the West followed by the developing World. Since then, there has been serious debate going on, on the gender perspective of development. The issues like the role of women in the development process, the impact on the development on the conditions of women, the focus of development initiatives and studies on women, contribution of women to the development process, all such other issues are subjected to critical analysis from different perspectives. The advent of globalization and economic liberalization process have further intensified the on going intellectual discussion on the gender development interface.

There are three papers in this section, which address the theme of gender and development. Dr. Kuruba in his paper on "Gender Dimensions in Economic Reforms Programmes: Implications for policy", attempts critical analysis on the gender dimension of economic reforms programmes at macro level. His paper focuses on the initiatives aimed at promoting gender consideration in the formulation of economic reform policies along with the mechanisms needed for incorporating gender concerns in these reform initiatives. He explores the means to eliminate the constraints on the way of economic reform reaching the women with special focus on social security and safety needs. He pleads emphatically that there is an urgent need to integrate gender issues with the economic reforms process for empowering women all over the world.

In the insightful study on the gender related issues to urban labour market in the particular context of Kavali Town (AP) Raghava Reddy and Vbinodini probes the working of urban informal labour markets in the selected town of Kavali, on the basis of their empirical study conducted for this purpose. This study discusses the extent and nature of women labour, effects of state and intervention on the conditions of these labour and finally suggests the policy choices to improve the living conditions of the women labour. The significant feature of this study is the application of certain statistical test for the measuring the impact of policy interventions on the select women labour.

Rajasekhar's article on "Gender Discrimination and Poverty" is a macro exposition on inequalities suited out to women in different fields in different countries in the South Asian region. Adopting a broader perspective, the author analyses the different dimensions of vulnerability suffered by these women. He concludes that problems of gender inequalities can be resolved by means of suitable state interventions, individual as well as group based.

The pre-requisite for the growth and development of any economy in the provision of gainful employment to the labourforce. The developing economies all characterised by continuous population pressure, declining land-man ratio, small and fragmented land holdings highly inequitous land distribution structure, increasing application of labour saving farm production techniques etc., can not provide the ultimate solution to the problem of unemployment, underemployment prevailing in the farm sectors. Hence, it is inevitable for any country to expand the non-farm sector.

The second section presents the studies on the employment of farm and non-farm sectors of India. Brahma Prakash study entitled "Women's Participation in Rural Non-farm Employment", highlights the vital issue of women employment and its complications for development, using the census and NSSO data. Broadly the paper emphasises the current status of women in Rural Non-farm sector, responsible constraints for low level participation of female workforce in non-farm rural sector, legal provisions for women workers and finally the plausible suggestions for increasing the participation of female workforce in non-farm sector employment.

K. Srinivasa Rao paper as "Factors Influencing the Participation of Females in Rural Non-farm Employment" identifies the type of non-agricultural activities that are pursued by female workers and also identifies the factors facilitating the participation of females in RNFE. Both on the study of two delta villages of Andhra Pradesh the study finds the female work participation rates. The variables chosen to explain the participation of females in RNFE are caste, women dependency ratio, education above 5th standard and land.

K. Pazhani's study entitled "Women in Farm and Non-farm Employment is Tirunelveli District, Tamil Nadu", emphasises the growth of employment in the Indian context. Further, the study attempts to throw light as the various possibilities of employment of women in farm and non-farm sectors to improve the income and thereby economic dependence of workers, by conducting a survey in Radhapuram taluk of Tirunelveli district of Tamil Nadu. The study has effectively drawn the meaningful influences as the issue like factors leading to employment of women, factors preventing employment of women and problems faced by women in employment.

Silvia Maria de Mendonca Noronha's study on "Employment of Women in the Farm and Non-farm Sectors in Goa", explains the employment position of women based on census data for the period 1961-91. Broadly the study finds that women are by and large employed in the farm sector. Within the farm sector, they are employed largely as agricultural labourers, and a large percentage of them work as marginal labourers. In case of non-farm sector more male are employed than female which indicates that activities outside the farm sector are more favourable for employment of male workers.

Shakuntala Gupta and Disha Mittal's paper entitled "Women Enterprises in the Informal Sector in Punjab", analyses the actively status of women enterprises and use of finances and power in the women enterprises. This study confines to urban Punjab, particularly, the three big cities normally Ludhiana, Amritsar and Patiala. The data is collected from the records pertaining to the 4th Economic Census collected during April, 1998, by the office of the Economic Advise to the Government of Punjab, Chandigarh.

The third section emphasis the issue of women empowerment in India. Empowerment of women in the prerequisite for the sustainable development of any economy. Empowerment requires a fundamental and dynamic change in the perception of women, expectations from women in the society and a scientific and national understanding of women's problems and needs. Empowerment is an active multidimensional process which should enable women to realise their full identity and powers in all spheres of life. This section provides ten papers on various issues of empowerment of women in India.

Leela's paper entitled "Globalisation and Empowerment of Women" examines the impact of all-encompassing phenomenon of globalization on the empowerment of women, with particular reference to India. She analysed both the positive and negative impact of the globalization on women employment and proposed the alternative options for a better employment opportunities of women with high standard of living and better quality of life.

A. Sailaja Devi and M. Sunder Rao's paper entitled "Need for Empowerment of Women", examines the current status of tribal women in Srikakulam district of A.P. The study analyses the demographic features, health conditions, educational aspects, occupational pattern and levels of living of tribal women in the study area. Iyyam Pillai's study on Endowment, Entitlement and Empowerment of Women in Tamil Nadu consists of two sections. The study reveals that the endowment in the form of education and employment is found to be a strong determinant empowerment status. According to him, Government aims at providing higher level of education and job to its people.

N. Narayana's paper highlights the issue of gender equality and empowerment of women in the emerging information economy, especially in the developing countries. This paper emphasises that information and communication systems in penetrating into all aspects of human life. Knowledge and information and communication systems are interdependent drivers of economic growth. The author categorically emphasises the role and prominence of information economy is promoting women empowerment. To enhance the economic empowerment of women, the author suggests some measures which have to be incorporated in the information communication system policy in developing countries.

K. Sreelakshmamma's article on "Views and Perceptions of DWCRA Beneficiaries: A case study" analyses various issues of sample DWCRA women in Prakasam district of A.P. the author examines the socio-economic characteristic features of beneficiaries in terms of age, religion, educational qualification, residential accommodation, group formation and identification, group dynamics, motivation, reasons for joining group, distribution of revolving fund, training, supervising and monitoring and marketing of product etc. In her other paper entitled "Empowerment of Women through DECRA Programme in A.P.: A case Study" examined both the trends of DWCRA programme in A.P. According to this study the man day for women are increased after joining the DWCRA group, which improved their level of earnings, savings and levels of living considerably. Apart from economic empowerment, political empowerment of beneficiaries is also observed since majority of the beneficiaries are not only the members of the political parties but also participated in various activities of these parties.

P. Vanugopal's article on Empowerment of Women" SWOT analysis explains different components and categories of women empowerment. The internal and external aspects of empowerment in terms of SWOT analysis viz-a-viz strength, weakness opportunities and threats are examined.

M. Bapuji and M. Koteswara Rao's paper entitled "Welfare and Empowerment of Women in India Some Reflections", analyses the women welfare schemes incorporated in different five year plans of India along with various rural development schemes launched for the welfare of women. The authors highlighted the neglected issue of political empowerment of women in India.

S.. Murthy's paper as "Conditions of Scheduled Castes Women in Social Sector: A case study of Ujjain division of M.P", examines the condition of SC women in social sector of the economy. The study covers five districts viz., Ujjain, Dewas, Shajapur, Mandsaur and Ratlam of Ujjain districts in U.P. The condition of SC women are examined effectively in terms of educational status, health status and housing status.

—Editor

1

Gender Dimension in Economic Reform Programmes

Implications for Policy

Dr. Kuruba, G

Economic reforms in many developing countries have been associated with stabilisation and structural adjustment programmes supported by international financial institutions (IMF and World Bank). As these reforms have become more widespread and long term, concern has grown about the impact of economic reform policies on poverty and empowerment of women. Even though early results of structural adjustment programmes have highlighted the potentially negative effects, particularly on women, but the programmes have not been focusing on the issues of empowering women in developing countries.

In Sub-Saharan Africa and Latin America, particularly, Structural Adjustment Programmes (SAPs) have dominated economic policy-making in the 1980s and early 1990s. Some East Asian countries have undergone the processes of adjustments and recently countries in Indian sub-continent. The experience of structural adjustment is highly varied although, broadly, in Asia,

* Senior Lecturer, Centre for Continuing Education, University of Botswana, Private Bag–0022, Gaborone, Botswana.

it has been associated with continuing growth, while in Latin America and particularly Africa, it has been associated with negative growth and increasing poverty and gender inequalities. There are a number of exceptions to these overall trends.

Early objectives of structural adjustment were principally concerned with short-term stabilisation and macroeconomic aggregates. It was only in 1987, with the publication of UNICEF's *Adjustment with a Human Face* (Cornia *et al.* 1987), that the debate on gender issues in structural adjustment programmes gained some prominence. The international financial institutions have, by and large, tended to disassociate poverty in countries with adjustment policies, arguing that either pre-adjustment economic crises or government policies are mainly responsible for increases in poverty or the failure to address poverty. Adjustment policies, it is argued, would improve the situation of the poor in the longer term, through labour-intensive growth and providing new opportunities and increased incomes for the poor, especially women in rural areas.

Economic Reforms and Poverty

In recent years, however, it has become evident that the poverty in countries undergoing economic reforms is not temporary in nature. Moreover, there is considerable evidence that adjustment policies themselves have contributed to increasing poverty. Growth has not occurred as fast or as much as predicted in adjusting economies, and, where it has occurred, it has not, in general, been 'pro-poor', and tended to benefit higher income groups more. Not only has adjustment often been associated with worsening income distribution, but the majority of adjusting countries have also seen increases in levels of absolute poverty. Trends in social indicators have been more mixed, with infant and child mortality rates often continuing to fall, but in some places, educational enrolment has fallen and maternal mortality rates have worsened (Stewart, 1995).

Evidence on poverty is mixed: in some countries there has been a fall, in others results are mixed where income distributive effects of reform are regressive but targeted programmes have been effective in reducing absolute poverty, and in some others adjustment is associated with increases in poverty (Killick, 1995).

Those countries that have done relatively well under adjustment are the East Asian and middle-income heavily indebted countries, which are now recovering. The urban working poor are especially vulnerable under adjustment, through price rises, increased indirect taxation, job losses, and reduced real wages. However, the poor, especially in rural areas, have to benefit from adjustment and the positive impact of reforms depends on factors such as land distribution and on the proportion of cash crops being produced by small holders.

Since the late 1980s, the international financial institutions have acknowledged the need to reconsider adjustment policies in the light of poverty reduction concerns. The core of the World Bank's approach to poverty reduction—set out in the *World Development Report* of 1990—is the promotion of labour intensive growth, investment in basic services (health, education) and the provision of safety nets (or targeted schemes to assist the vulnerable). These objectives are reflected in changes in approaches to adjustment in the early 1990s, with increased emphasis on greater flexibility about the timing and phasing of subsidy removals and price reform, reallocation of social investment towards basic services used by the poor (e.g. primary education and health care systems); and the development of compensatory programmes, mainly employment schemes or social funds, in conjunction with reform programmes.

The extent to which these changes have made an impact is unclear. The limited evidence is not encouraging but perhaps there has been insufficient time for changes in policy emphasis to make a significant impact. In the 1980s, adjusting countries' spending on the social sector and priority to pro-poor services worsened compared to non-adjusting countries, in part because of stronger pressure to meet debt service obligations of the former (Stewart 1995). Social programmes introduced in conjunction with adjustment programmes have reached only a small percentage of the potential target group. Although some progress is reported in including poverty and gender concerns in adjustment documents, there is no evidence that poverty and gender sensitivity is applied to the formulation of macroeconomic stabilisation policies (Foster and Lee, 1996).

Gender Dimensions in Economic Reform Programmes

In structural adjustments programmes, there is still a tendency to ignore gender aspects of vulnerability (Stewart, 1995). The World Bank's own poverty assessments have, until recently, paid very little attention to gender issues (Hamner *et al.* 1996). Initially, the concern with gender issues in relation to economic liberalisation and adjustment emerged as a subset of the debates on poverty. Poor women were seen to carry the major burden of adjustment through increased demands on their reproductive labour, as well as falling social services provision (UNICEF's *Invisible Adjustment*, 1989).

The study *Engendering Adjustment* (Chinery-Hesse, 1989) argued that women bear the major burden of adjustment, in their four 'roles' as producers, mothers, home managers and community organisers. There is pressure for women to earn incomes when there is decreasing social services provision and community infrastructure. There is still considerable disagreement as to whether it is adjustment policies, which have negatively affected women, or the pre-existing conditions (Moghadam, 1997). More recent arguments for consideration of gender in structural adjustment have focused on efficiency questions. These perspectives that have proved influential in mainstream policy debates on women's empowerment.

A series of measures taken by the World Bank and donor agencies in the last two to three years have, in part, stimulated by external pressure from NGOs as well as researchers, to give a higher profile to the gender differentiated impacts of economic policy reform and to modify policies on this basis. However, despite the fact that 'macro-economics is gender biased, other growth related policies such as public expenditure allocation, tax policy, deregulation/price liberalization and even privatization are all highly amenable to gender analysis (Foster and Lee, 1996).

Gender is a key determinant of vulnerability (others are like age, class, region etc.), so that in periods of economic transition, women are likely to be especially vulnerable to increased poverty or insecurity. While job losses may affect men and women, women may find it harder than men to regain employment or become self-employed, due to relative lack of education and skills, and lack of independent access to capital. Poor women are more likely to have no other adult earners in the household and to have a higher dependency ratio (Tanski, 1994).

Poverty reducing benefits of economic reform may not reach women. For example, benefits to poor rural farmers from increased prices of cash crops accrue directly to men with limited positive, or negative impact on women. Although women labour is intensified to increase production, but the women are not always recompensed for this additional effort. In addition, reduced direct control over incomes undermines women's bargaining power in the households and influence over economic decision-making, as found with the intensification of traditional cash crops like tobacco in Uganda (Elson and Evers 1997).

Even though women do benefit directly from economic reform and liberalization with in the expansion of female intensive export manufacturing and earning a higher income than would be available in alternative forms of employment, these gains often disappear in the context of discriminatory practices in labour markets and often harsh working conditions (Moghadam 1997). Also, these benefits do not accrue to poor women (those most likely to be employed are younger, more educated women).

A failure to consider the systemic barriers to increased production faced by women, in response to price incentives, may lead to over-optimistic assumptions about their impact (World Bank 1996). A variety of interlocking, gender-related constraints limit the extent to which women are willing, or able, to increase the output, or to market the increased output. These include lack of command over productive resources (land, capital, labour) because of limited property rights, household power relations, and high market transactions costs as well as gender biases in marketing systems.

Time constraints are a major limiting factor for poor women, who cannot afford to hire in labour, and are occupied with meeting immediate survival needs. A recent study of farming households in Zambia showed that discrepancies in time use between men and women were particularly marked in subsistence level households. In general, poor women are concentrated in low profit; petty trading segments of agricultural marketing and often barely able to generate enough income.

Costs on Human Development

Often, the costs of economic transition are 'hidden' because they are absorbed by increases in poor women's unpaid labour, intensity of work, reduced nutrition or energy depletion. This has severe potential costs in terms of women's own health and well-being, and girls' education may suffer due to mothers drawing heavily on girls' labour in informal sector activity, agricultural work and in the household work. For example, in Uganda, women and girls are employed in the production of non-traditional exports and seasonal peaks in demand for their labour were known to affect girls' school attendance (Elson and Evers 1997).

Some social programmes associated with economic reform packages have a poor record on women's participation. This is because of preferential treatment given in recruitment procedure for retrenched workers from privatised industries, more likely to be men. Some times, the design of programmes builds in barriers to female participation (e.g.: project site a long way from the household, or markets, lack of child care facilities; heavy men's work required, such as construction). Indirect beneficiaries of social programmes are often assumed to be household members of the main earner (by implication usually women and children), which fails to consider inequalities in intra-household resource allocation. The benefits from social infrastructure provision through public works have a gender differential impact. Local community facilities (e.g. wells, schools, nurseries, sanitation provision etc.) are likely to be of much greater benefit to women, than, for example, roads, airport runways etc.).

Gender-oriented Economic Policy

A variety of tools are being developed to make economic policy and planning more gender-sensitive. This includes, for example, macroeconomic models, which take account of women's unpaid, labour and thus are able to factor this into attempts to predict the impact of policy reform. Public expenditure reviews (PERs) can incorporate a gender dimension. Underpinning these approaches, there is a need to refine methodologies, and improve the collection, analysis and use of gender-disagreegated data for policy and planning. Various initiatives have been taken to promote the consideration of gender perspectives in economic policy formulation. The World Bank has piloted 'gender-aware' adjustment operations in countries of the Sub-Saharan Africa, attempting to ensure that gender-based constraints are taken into consideration when adjustment policies are being devised (World Bank, 1996).

A second and equally important mechanism for incorporating gender concerns into the design of economic reform is to make the processes of economic policy more accountable to women and their organisations through consulting with women's groups, economic literacy work, women's budget campaigns etc. Changes to economic legislation in the context of financial sector reform should be introduced to ensure that they do not institutionalise discrimination or biases against poor women who are the main beneficiaries of non-formal microenterprise finance (Kiggundu 1998). The setting up of consultation mechanisms during the process of formulating economic policy is also important and, alongside this, raising gender issues during policy dialogue with government and stockholders.

The gender-disagreegated impacts of economic policies require monitoring to inform future policy development. One mechanism for this is gender-sensitive incidence analysis of public expenditure. Women's budget exercises, notably that in South Africa which has gained considerable support both within the Parliament and beyond, are also possible leverage mechanisms to raise awareness of the implications of public expenditure decisions, and their impact on women development. Other mechanisms are also required which institutionalise capacity for monitoring adjustment impacts, e.g. the collection of indicators via development programmes, social sector service provision or community-based initiatives.

Reducing Barriers to Women's Response to Economic Opportunities

A number of measures can be adopted to reduce or remove the constraints to women's response to economic opportunities. Some of these relate to reducing the time burden on women through improvements in the provision of social infrastructure, such as water supply, child-care facilities etc. In order to improve direct returns to women's labour, there is a need to secure their property rights through legal reforms although these often have limited effectiveness at local level, unless women develop bargaining power to assert their claims.

Gender biases in financial and agricultural markets need to be tackled. In the financial sector, support to the development of non-bank financial institutions is needed, as they are successful in reducing transactions costs of lending to women as well as providing credit and mobilizing savings of women. The reforming of banking institutions and bringing legislation to remove discriminatory practices are all some of the important measures in this direction. The financial sector should be flexible enough to ensure that institutions lending to women are not negatively affected.

Social Security and Safety Nets

Social safety nets by and large have not yet taken up the gender issues and, more broadly, wider social security and welfare provisions have not taken account of changes in social relations, which are occurring as a result of economic restructuring, as well as political and social conflict.

There is now considerable experience of the gendered impact of safety nets and of measures which can be taken to ensure greater participation of women, such as decentralised location of work sites, near homes and markets, provision of child care and health facilities, use of women's networks to publicise schemes, improved recruitment practices, hiring of women in supervisory positions. Programmes, which specifically target women, may have drawbacks in that they can institutionalise gender divisions of labour and discriminatory payment practices.

There is a need for greater recognition of the increasing variety of household forms, and associated patterns of vulnerability. It is also needed to move away from the male breadwinner model underlying social security and welfare systems, as well as for legal and institutional changes which strengthen the rights of women in non-formal unions, or who are not living with, or supported by, male partners. At the same time, the coping strategies of poor women, as well as men, need to be better understood, and supported, as alternatives to top down provision of safety nets.

Conclusions

Gender dimensions are to be more seriously considered while formulating and implementing economic reform programmes. Women are likely to find it more difficult to escape poverty. Poor women may be particularly vulnerable to deepening poverty under adjustment. Any poverty reducing effects which structural adjustment programmes may bring, through renewed stimulus to small scale agriculture, may not reach women directly, due to their lack of command over productive resources and control over output. Poor supply response, observed in some adjusting economies may be linked to constraints to women's ability or willingness to increase production including gender biases in financial markets, and marketing systems. The costs of economic restructuring are often disproportionately borne by women with severe human development consequences for women themselves and, potentially, for children, especially girls, who may be drawn into household or income earning labour. The existing safety net programmes have tended to target men, explicitly or implicitly, and wider social security and welfare provisions have not taken account of changes in social relations including gender gap, which are occurring as a result of economic restructuring.

Policy responses are required to incorporate gender concerns into the design of economic reform programmes, both through gender-aware economic planning and through increasing the accountability of policy-making to women. Monitoring the gender-differentiated impacts of economic policies is also important, using women's budgets and gender-disagreegated expenditure incidence analysis. Measures to remove the constraints to economic opportunities for women include reforming the marketing systems by creating infrastructure and financial institutions to help women. Useful conceptual frameworks are now in place, which can assist understanding of the linkages between economic policy, gender and poverty concerns. There are also a number of initiatives, which have attempted to influence policy in this area from a gender perspective.

In spite of mounting evidence, the economic reform programmes still pay little attention to the issues of women development. Wherever people are disagreegated, it should not be in terms of gender differences by treating women as most vulnerable group. There is an urgent necessity to integrate gender dimensions into many aspects of economic reform programmes. A comprehensive economic policy needs to be formulated taking into account the gender dimensions in order to empower women in all societies.

REFERENCES

Chinery-Hesse, M., *Engendering Adjustment for the 1990s: Report of a Commonwealth Expert Group on Women and Structural Adjustment*, London: Commonwealth Secretariat.

Cornia, G.A., Jolly, R. and Stewart, F., 1987, *Adjustment with a Human Face*, Oxford: Clarendon.

Elson, D. and Evers, B., 1997, 'Uganda,' *Gender Aware Country Economic Papers*, Manchester: University of Manchester, GENECON Unit, Graduate School of Social Sciences.

Hamner, L., Pyatt, G. and White, H., with Pouw, N., 1996, *Poverty in Sub-Saharan Africa: What Can we Learn From the World Bank's Poverty Assessments?*, The Hague: Institute of Social Studies Advisory Service.

Kiggundu, R., 1998, 'Loosening the Purse Strings: Financial Sector Reform in Uganda,' *Development and Gender in Brief*, No. 6: 2.

Killick, T., 1995, 'Structural Adjustment and Poverty Alleviation: An Interpretative Survey,' *Development and Change*, Vol. 26: 305-31.

Moghadam, V., 1997, 'The Feminisation of Poverty: Notes on a Concept and Trends', *Women's Studies Program Occasional Papers* No. 2, Illinois State University.

Stewart, F., 1995, *Adjustment and Poverty: Options and Choices*, London: Routledge.

Tanski, J.M., 1994, 'The Impact of Crisis, Stabilisation and Structural Adjustment on Women in Lima, Peru', *World Development*, Vol. 22, No. 11: 1627-42.

UNICEF, 1989, *The Invisible Adjustment: Poor Women and the Economic Crisis*, 2nd Revised Edition, Bogota: UNICEF Regional Office.

World Bank, 1990, *World Development Report*, Washington DC: World Bank.

World Bank, 1993, 'Paradigm Postponed: Gender and Economic Adjustment in Sub-Saharan Africa', *AFTHR Technical Note* No. 13, Washington DC: World Bank.

World Bank, 1996, 'Gender in the Special Program of Assistance for Africa (SPA): A Compilation of the Principal Documents', Gender Team, Africa Region, September.

2

Gender Related Issues of Urban Informal Labour Market

A Case Study of Kavali Town

*Prof. G. Radhava Reddy**

J.M.J. Vinodhini

1. Introduction

The role of the informal sector in the urban economy of the developing countries is well recognised and the literature on the subject is burgeoning. The informal sector of the urban economy provides as easy access to opportunities of work and thereby the means of livelihood for the deprived segments of the urban society as well as the migrants from the rural sector. The informal sector activity, its nature, character and structure has received greater attention than the labour component of it. It is also rather difficult to segregate the economic activities of persons who are self-employed such as petty traders, street-hawkers, piece-workers from their labour component. Since the informal sector is generally outside the regulatory framework of the government, labour laws

* Director and Research Associate of Rural Development Academy, Tirupati-2.

are hardly enforced. Gender discrimination and gender gap in wages and earnings are quite common. Issues of exploitation of women and child labour in the urban informal labour market are receiving greater attention in recent years at all levels because of the realisation that they have been bypassed in the process of development. There is a reorientation in the development strategies and models being formulated at the national and global level. Women's work escapes computation in home-based production, family concerns or on land owned by kin. World wide estimates show that at least one-fourth of women are neither housewives nor in paid employment. Thus, a substantial number of women are invisible or at home in a sporadic and informal manner in unpaid jobs. Gender discrimination and gap in wage employment are widely reported in Human Development Reports of the UNDP. The structural adjustment policies of the Fund-Bank being implemented in the developing world also seem to worsen segmentation and discrimination in the informal labour market. Due to the dynamics of the labour market over time and space, there is a need for region/area specific studies to diagnose the labour situation and to formulate appropriate policy choices by those who are operating in such markets as well as policy makers.

2. Role of Women in the Urban Informal Sector

The role of women in economic activity has been underestimated in the past for a variety of reasons. However, the contribution of women to work at home as well as outside the home is receiving greater attention and recognition, especially since the advent of the Human Development Reports. The burden of work on the part of the women is higher in developing countries. The empirical literature suggests that there is a positive correlation between economic development and female labour force participation rates. However, the gender gap in labour force participation rates persists and it is significant in the Islamic countries. It is also noticed that economic development and urbanisation go together due to interlinkage between industrialisation and urbanisation. It is widely reported that urban based industrialisation and commercialisation introduce the polarisation and hirerarchisation of mens' and women's roles and relationships. In the informal labour market women's choice of activity is determined by norms of female seclusion and not by economic rationality. Poverty weakens traditional seclusion and strengthens economic rationality. In this sense poverty acts as an instrument of social change for economic betterment. No wonder, women workers in several developing countries are concentrated in non-wage employment. The persistence of discrimination in employment and disparity in wages and earnings tends to deprive women workers and marginalise their contribution. The concept of work participation rate has undergone a complete change in the Census Reports of India since 1961. A trichotomy of persons into mutually exclusive groups of main workers, marginal workers and non-workers was introduced in 1981 and continued in 1991 also. In 1981 as well as 1991 the gender gap in work participation rate hovered around 37 and 36 per cent respectively. Trends in usual status work participation rates indicate a remarkable stability highlighting the persistence of gender gap.

The size of the urban informal sector differs based on the concept followed and the size varies significantly across the major urban centres of/the country ranging from a low of 28 per cent to a high of 75 per cent of labour force in the respective locations. More than 50 per cent of workers are women and therefore, their importance in the urban informal sector. Purely economic reasons account for nearly 1/3 of male migrants and hardly 2 per cent of female migrants. Among others the persistence of discrimination and disparity based on sex constraints mobility of female labour and thereby minimise their contribution to the world of work.

3. The Purpose of the Present Study

The purpose of the present study is to probe into some technical aspects of gender issues in the informal sector of Kavali town of Andhra Pradesh. In other words, it is proposed to comprehend and analyse the structure and working of the urban informal female labour market in terms of its segmentation and competitiveness. A wide variety of data were collected from different agencies and sources for fulfilling the specific objectives and testing the corresponding hypotheses.

As far as the primary data are concerned a 5 per cent stratified random sample was chosen covering 218 respondents. These 218 workers also represent 218 households wherever the household concept is applicable.

4. Employment, Earnings Indebtedness

The average size of household of 122 residents and 96 migrants was found to be 5.7 and 5.5 respectively. This finding is in correspondence with the size of rural labour households. 56 per cent of workers among residents are married while this figure stands at 67 per cent in the case of migrants. Unmarried workers constitute hardly 13 per cent among migrants which is understandable due to the vulnerability of unmarried workers in the urban setting for different risks that are ever present.

The nexus between caste and occupation and religious seclusion is getting marginalised in the case of our respondents. In other words we notice "Extensity—refers to the total volume of goods and services available for sale and purchase. Purity refers to the market principle unhampered by non-market considerations such as for example, friendship, kinship, caste and class. The perfectly pure and extensive market is, of course, only an ideal. It does not exist even in the most industrialised and commercialised societies", and purity is penetrating into the female labour market of our samples. Our analysis of the reasons for migration of our respondents enables us to accept the expected income model of Todaro Harris. Migrants are mostly (52 per cent) from within a radius of 15 to 20 Kilometres of Kavali. Nearly 2/3 of migrants have entered the town during the past 4 to 7 years. The average duration of migration works out to 4.5 years. Surprisingly the correlation between level of education and average earnings of our respondents is negative though insignificant and is contrary to the general situation in the sphere of the economics of education. In the light of our findings on the composition, sources and causes of migration and the link between education and earnings of our samples we reject our first hypothesis namely, there is no correlation between migration of male and female labour, level of education and earnings.

We incorporate the principal findings and statistical results of our empirical study regarding employment earnings and indebtedness and the causative and allied structural features in Table—2.1.

Table—2.1 Major Findings and Results

Variable	Reference group/category	Statistical measure/test	Finding/ Results	Remarks
Age of samples	(a) Residents	Chi-square test	Chi-square = 26.80 DF = 6 Critical value = 12.592	Significant at 5 per cent level
	(b) Migrants	Chi-square test	Chi-square = 9.98 DF = 6 Critical value = 12	Not significant
WPR of samples	(a) Residents	T-test	T-value = 1.1854 t–critical value = 2.0738	Not significant
	(b) Migrants	T-test	T-value = 2.53 t–Critical value = 2.0738	Significant at 1 per cent level
LFPR of samples	(a) Residents	T-test	T-value = 1.6655 T–Critical value = 2.0738	Not significant
	(b) Migrants	T-test	T-value = 1.0974 T-critical value = 2.0738	Not significant
Work experience and earnings	Respondents	r	0.9983	

(Table Contd…)

1	2	3	4	5
Work experience and mobility	Respondents	Chi-square test	Chi-square = 15.14 D.F. = 9 Critical value = 16.919	Not significant
Average wage and incomes	(a) Residents	ANOVA	F-value = 87.9940	Significant at 1 per cent level
	(b) Migrants	ANOVA	F-value = 84.5472	Significant
Income by location of occupation	Respondents	Chi-square test	Chi-square = 24.6951 D.F. = 12 Critical value = 12.592	Significant at 1 per cent level
Wage disparity between men and women workers	Respondents	T-test (Paired t-test)	T-value = 10.4354	Significant at 1 per cent level
Share of women's income in household income	Respondents	r	0.2817	Not significant at 5 per cent level
Indebtedness by location of occupation	Respondents	Chi-square Test	Chi-square = 27.6042 D.F. = 12	Significant at 1 per cent level
Incidence of poverty	Respondents	Head come Ratio	71 per cent for home-based workers 52 per cent for non-home based workers	

Source: Tables 4.4, 4.7, 4.8, 4.10, 4.11, 4.12, 4.13, 4.15, 4.16, 4.17 of the Ph.D thesis of Vinodini, SV University, 2000.

Our statistical analysis of work participation rates, labour force participation rates, work experience and earnings, work experience and mobility wage levels of migrants and residents (serial No. 1 to 6 in table 2.1) provide us enough evidence to partly accept our second hypothesis namely there is no significant difference in the participation rates between workers in different occupations, experience and mobility. Issues of poverty and indebtedness are inextricably interwined as well as the low economic status of women and their marginalisation in the household arena. We have incorporated the major statistical results on this front and these findings (serial No. 7 to 12 in table 2.1) enable us to reject the third hypothesis namely the incidence of poverty and indebtedness are not significantly different between categories of home-based and non-home-based women labour households.

5. Effects of State Intervention on Labour and Living Conditions

The concern of the state for the poor is as old as the rise of utilitarianism. Welfare economics provides a strong foundation for advancing the cause of the poor on grounds of equity and efficiency. The Directive Principles of State policy of the Indian Constitution offers a tremendous challenge for the State to intervene in the labour market on behalf of women and child workers. In recent years, provision of micro-credit for gainful employment and empowerment of women is widely followed. We notice that 26 per cent of current borrowings of our respondents are drawn from institutional agencies at an average rate of interest 12.5 per cent per annum. T-test and paired t-test indicate a significant difference in current borrowings from formal and informal sources by residents and migrants (Table—2.2).

Table—2.2 Effect of State Intervention on Selected Aspects of Samples

Variable	Reference group/ category	Statistical measure/ Test	Finding/ Results	Remarks
Average borrowing	Respondents	T-test (paired t-test)	T-value = 0.0779	Insignificant
Child population and child labour	(a) Residents	r	0.9636	Significant at 1 per cent level
	(b) Migrants	r	0.8844	Significant at 1 per cent level
Incidence of child labour	Respondents	Chi-square Test	Chi-square = 2.1932 D.F. = 7	Not Significant
Disparity in earnings	Child labour	Percentage of girls earnings to boys	Lowest = 71 ..	In beverages
Government subsidy for pucca houses owned	132 samples	Percentage subsidised	36	–
Income contribution to household	Child labour	percentage	16	–

(Table Contd...)

1	2	3	4	5
Access to fair price shop	(a) Residents	Percentage	62	There is a significant price difference in the items between the FPS and open market
	(b) Migrants	Percentage	44	There is a significant price difference in the items between the FPS and open market
Income range level and proportion of expenditure on food	Respondents	r	-0.713	It is in line with Engle's law

Source: Tables 5.1, 5.4, 5.5, 5.7, 5.9, 5.10, 5.12, 5.14, Ph.D thesis of Vinodini, SV University, 2000.

The Child labour situation of our respondents and our statistical findings in this regard are indicated in Table—2.2, child population and child labour, incidence of child labour among residents and migrants, disparity in earnings are indicated. These results provide us arms and ammunition to hypothesise a significant positive relationship between child population and child labour and an insignificant association between the incidence of child labour and residential status of respondents as well as the persistence of disparity in their earnings. Child labour's contribution to household income stands at 16 per cent of our samples. The other elements of welfare promotion such as access to fair price shop, pucca houses with sanitation, access to electricity, health, water supply differ significantly across categories. We find that the proportion of household expenditure on food of the samples to be broadly in conformity with the Engle's law of consumption.

6. Policy Choices

Women workers of our sample constitute the hard core of the informal female labour market of Kavali town. Whether they are resident or migrant they are deprived of education and training and therefore, they are crowded in low income economic activities and burdened with household work. They are also constrained by seclusion in some cases and are therefore marginalised. They are hardly conscious, of their fundamental rights let alone human rights. Their children are trapped in the world of work and are deprived of education and therefore future earnings. Most of our respondents live in semi-permanent thatched houses without basic civic amenities. They are the cause as well as victims of urban pollution and insanitation. State intervention to improve the educational status of their children, provide health, sanitation and civil supplies to the respondents as well as housing amenities and work opportunities is necessary to alleviate the poverty and bring them into the mainstream of civil life. It must be noted as Mabub-ul-Haq stated that poverty is not due to lack of income but lack of opportunity to earn income.

A determined, purposeful, result-oriented goal directed time-bound action is necessary to safeguard the interests of vulnerable groups like our samples in the era of market driven, market-guided, market-friendly policies being pursued by the State in India. Economic policy without social content and labour orientation might prove to be counter-productive. Therefore, labour oriented, equity-based, welfare-guided State policy is to be harmonised with growth–oriented market driven policies. The case for protection and promotion of the cause of the economically deprived, socially excluded and politically marginalised is as old and as strong as welfare economics, which should be pursued at the micro level as well as at the macro level by the respective governments.

REFERENCES

1. J.M.J. Vinodini's Ph.D Thesis, *Role of Women in Urban Informal Sector: A Case Study of Kalvali Town*; A.P. S.V. University, 2000.
2. The World Development Report, Oxford, 1995, 2000.
3. The World Bank, *Women in Pakistan*, 1989.
4. UNDP, *Human Development Reports*, Oxford 1990 to 2001.
5. ILO *World Labour Reports*, 1990-94.
6. GoI, *Report of the Committee on the Status of Women in India*, 1974.
7. Malavika Karlekar, *"Poverty and Women's Work: A Study of Sweeper Women in Delhi"*, Shakti Books, New Delhi, 1987.
8. World Bank Country Study, *"India Reducing Poverty, Accelerating Development*, Oxford, 2000.
9. World Bank Country Study, *"Gender and Poverty in India*, Oxford, 1991.
10. UNICEF, *The Progress of Nations*, Oxford, 1997.

3

Gender Discrimination and Poverty

Dr. A. Rajasekhar

Even though, we are in 21st century, Socio Economic evils like Gender Discrimination and Poverty are the two social banners ruling the community today. Social institutions—kinship systems, community, organisations and inform networks—greatly effect poverty outcomes. They do so by affecting the productivity of economics assets, the strategies for coping with rick, the capacity to pursue new opportunitics and the extent to which particular voices are heard when important decisions are made. Social institutions can help poor people get by and get ahead. But they can also place favours between poor people or the socially disadvantaged and the opportunity and resumes they need to advance their interests. Discrimination on the basis of gender, ethnicity, race, religion or social status can lead to social exclusion and look people in long term poverty traps.

Human values, norms and social institutions may reinforce persisting inequalities between groups in the society—as with gender based prejudice through out the world, the caste and creed

* Reader and Head, Department of Economics, Hindu College, Guntur, Andhra Pradesh.

system in India and racial problems in south Africa and United States. To the extreme, the social evils may lead to severe deprivation and conflict. To over come these inequalities, the legal and other measures must be accompanied by efforts to raise awareness about culturally based attitudes towards women and people of different races, religion or ethnic origin or else these measures will be unable to produce real change. Social barriers can be of any form. Here, the focus is on key barriers arising from Gender inequalities, social stratification and social fragmentation.

To the extent and manifestations of gender inequality vary among societies, shaped to a considerable degree by kinship rules. Rules of inheritance determine ownership of productive resources. Rules of marriage determine women's domestic autonomy: if these rules require that women join their husband's family, women have far less autonomy than if they are able to form a new household or live with their own family (which is uncommon). The most pervasive forms of gender inequality appear where both inheritance and marriage rules are heavily weighted in favour of men. By contrast, where such rules are more gender balanced, women have greater voice in the household and in public spaces and face fewer constraints on becoming independent economic and social actors.

Norms for gender roles and rights form part of the moral order of a community and permeate other institutions, including those of the state. This further reinforces gender inequalities, unless conscious efforts are made to avoid it. Legas systems play a key part, either reinforcing customary gender rights and roles—or deliberately seeking to alter them. Also, important is the provision of public goods and services, which often by pass women unless specific efforts are made to reach them.

Inequalities in Voice and Access to Resources

Customary gender norms and values can lead to political, legal, economic and educational inequalities that perpetuate women's lack of access to resources, control over decision making, and participation in public life. Greater political representation could help to change this—in no country do women hold more than a very small share of the seats in parliament.

Some countries use the legal system to formalize customary rules that explicitly limit women's rights. In the Republic of Korea, for example, customary laws restricting women's rights were formalized in the Civil Code of 1962, and women's legal rights have been very slow to improve. After decades of struggle by women's organisations, key amendments in 1990 gave women the right to inherit their parents and husband's property. Divorce laws were changed to allow women equal rights to property acquired during marriage, and child custody is no longer granted automatically to the father. But the law continues to insist on male household headship, which women's organisations see as the main source of gender inequality in the family and in other social institutions. So while women in Korea have become educated and participate actively in the labour force, their unequal status serves to maximize their economic contribution while minimizing advances in gender equity.

It is true for credit and agricultural extension services: unless strong countervailing measures are taken, the poor receive less than the non-poor; and women receive the least. Studies from many countries show that agricultural extension agents focus on male farmers, even through women are often the primary cultivator because husbands work off the farm. So women face disadvantages not only in land ownership, but in gaining access to the resources and information that would improve yields.

The Toll of Gender Inequality on Society

If the rights of men and women are flagrantly unequal, it is very difficult to establish a democratic and participatory socio-political order and an environment of equal opportunity. Moreover, the more extreme manifestations of power inequality between men and women constitute gross violations of human rights.

Gender inequality also has strong repercussions for human capital in the next generation, because the burden of bearing and rearing children falls largely on women. Women deprived of education and decision making power in the home face serious constraints in rearing healthy, productive children, they also tend to have more children than they wish, compounding the pressures on themselves and their family. Better-educated women are able to communicate better with their spouse about family size decisions, use contraception more effectively and have higher aspirations for their children.

Studies consistently show that women's education improves child survival. Among children of women who have greater financial autonomy, either because they earn cash incomes of their own or have a greater role in domestic decision making, nutrition and education are higher. Studies in Brazil show that more income in the hands of mothers is associated with better nutritional outcomes and physical development of children. Micro credit programmes in Bangladesh find that giving income-generating loans to women improves the nutritional status of their children, a result that does not hold for men.

Low education and low autonomy make it more difficult for women to obtain medical care, to obtain health care information, prevent illness, and care for the sick. More equitable distribution of opportunities and resources between men and women also leads more directly to higher economic growth and productivity. Cross country analysis indicates that countries that invest in girl's education have higher rates of economic growth. Country studies show the benefits of increasing women farmer's access to agricultural extension, credit services, and other productive inputs.

Discrimination Against South Asian Women

At fourth World Conference on Women in Beijing which was held in 1995, the situation of South African Women was one of bleakest faced by women in any part of the World. Srilankan President Chandrika Bandaranaike Kumara Tunga asserted that women should be empowered to share equal roles with men in holding position of power in participationing in decision making processes, in controlling and managing scarce resources and also in sharing the incomes and benefits. As 2000 year's Human Development in South Asia Report—the fourth Annual report by the Mahbub-ul-Haq Center for Human Development makes women in south Asia work from dawn to dusk, but their economic contribution is scarcely acknowledged at the national level and their access to health, educational and other facilities lags far behind that of men.

As a region, South Asia has both the lowest literacy rates and the largest gap between the rates of male and female literacy 64.1 per cent and 37.2 per cent respectively in 1992. Discrimination against South Asian women begins at, or even before, birth, Female foeticide and infanticide, neglect of health, and gender-biased feeding practices combined with heavy work burdens, all are manifestations of conferences and the patriarchal structures which prevail across the region. South Asia has one of the most distorted sex ratios in the world—therc are only 940 females for every 1000 males. Official statistics in South Asia show women's economic putrefaction as a mere fraction of that of men.

Women's political representation is very poor in South Asia: only 7 per cent of South Asian parliamentarians are women. South Asian women's real GDP per capita at US $ 874 is lower than any other region in the world, including sub-Saharan Africa. It is clear that women participate in and contribute to household and market economies; it is also clear that women's contributions are rendered invisible. Although women perform some of the heaviest, dirtiest and most labour-intensive work, much of the labour remains invisible as it occurs either within the household or in the unregulated informal-sector. The vast majority of South Asian women work in the informal sector or in unpaid family assistance, with the informal sector accounting for the employment of 96 per cent of economically-active women in India, 75 per cent in Nepal and Bangladesh and nearly 65 per cent in Pakistan. Women also endure a heavy workload in the agricultural sector, notably in crop farming, livestock husbandry and off-farm activities, but even in these activities, much of their work is not recognized. Women are not counted as agricultural workers. Nor do they have an appropriate legal share in ownership of the means of production.

Human Development in South Asia the Report proposes that women's labour be included in systems of national accounting. Until that happens, the true impact of their labour will never be fully compensated, nor will development strategies accurately account for the work that is actually being done by women in South Asia. Women have a right to equal recognition, opportunity and compensation; the continued economic marginalization of women and their work retards the economic progress of the region.

Meanwhile, South Asian girls and women continue to lack what they need for basic nutrition, with a majority of women in the region suffering from chronic energy deficit because their daily caloric intake is well below the daily adult minimum requirement of 2250 calories.

At the turn of the last century, South Asia was just beginning the battle that eventually freed the region of British colonialism. Now, at the turn of this century, South Asians—men and women alike—must break the shackles of gender inequality and free themselves from centuries of patriarchy. Otherwise, the years ahead will be just as desolate for millions upon millions of South Asians as those that followed the end of colonialism, with true freedom and prosperity still out of reach.

Helping Poor People Manage Risk

Poverty means more than inadequate consumption, education and health. As the voices of the poor cry out, it also means dreading the future—knowing that a crisis may descend at any time, not knowing whether one will cope. Living with such rick is part of life for poor people, and today's changes in trade, technology, and climate may well be increasing the riskiness of everyday life. Poor people are often among the most vulnerable in society because they are the most exposed to a wide array of risks. Their low income means they are less able to save and accumulate assets. That in turn restricts their ability to deal with a crisis when it strikes.

Economic growth is one way of reducing the vulnerability of poor people. As their incomes rise, they are better able to manage risks. However, at any point in time those who are poor will see their vulnerability licensed if mechanisms to reduce mitigated cope with risks are available to them.

Poor people have developed elaborate mechanisms for dealing with risk. But the mechanisms are far from capable of eliminating vulnerability. Many of the mechanisms offer short-term protection at long-term cost, preventing any escape from poverty.

The policy response to vulnerability must be aimed at helping poor people manage risk better by reducing and mitigating risk and lessening the impact of shocks. Such policies address the immediate problems of shocks and the inability to cope with them. But they also lay the foundations for investment by poor people that can take them out of poverty. They report advocates a modular approach to risk management that adopts safety nets to the specific pattern of risk in each country and complements existing risk management arrangements.

Table—3.1

	IDIOSYNCRATIC	COVARIANT	
Type of risk	Risks affecting an individual or household (micro)	Risks affecting groups of households or communities (meso)	Risks affecting regions or nations (macro)
Natural		Rainfall Landslide Volcanic eruption	Earthquake Flood High winds
Health	Illness Injury Disability Old age Death	Epidemic	
Social	Crime Domestic violence	Terrorism Gang activity	Civil strife War Social upheaval
Economic		Unemployment Resettlement Harvest failure	Changes in food prices Growth collapse Hyperinflation Balance of payments, financial, or currency crisis Technology shock Terms of trade shock Transition costs of Economic reforms
Political		Riots	Political default on social programmes Coup d'etat
Environmental		Pollution Deforestation	

Source: World Development Report (2001-01)–Attacking Poverty.

One way to understand risks better and design appropriate policy response is through a typology of risks and shocks to which people are vulnerable. Risks can be classified by the level at which they occur (micro, meso, and macro) and by the nature of the event (natural, economic, political, and so on) (Table—3.1). Micro shocks often referred to as idiosyncratic, affect specific individuals or households. Meso shocks strike groups of households or an entire community or village. These shocks are common to all households in the group. Shocks can also occur at the national or international level.

This distinction by level of risk is critical. A risk that affects an entire village, for example, cannot be insured solely within the village. It requires pooling with areas not subject to the risk. In practice, many shocks have both idiosyncratic and covariant parts, though most empirical studies find that the idiosyncratic part of income risk is large.

The extent to which a risk is covariant or idiosyncratic depends considerably on the underlying causes. For example, job loss can be an individual risk, or it can be common to most workers in a country if it is the result of a macro economic crisis. The risk of becoming ill can be idiosyncratic, or it can have a large common component if there is an epidemic. The HIV/AIDS pandemic is a health risk at the global level, with devastating effects on poor people and poor countries.

The Nature and Magnitude of Vulnerability

Vulnerability affects everyone. Even well-paid civil servants are vulnerable to losing their jobs and sliding into poverty. For the poor, and for people just above the poverty line, vulnerability is a graver concern because any drop in income can push them into destitution. As a result, poor people are highly risk averse and reluctant to engage in the high-risk, high-return activities that could life them out of poverty. One slip could send them deeper into poverty.

Furthermore, because poor people have fewer assets and less diversified sources of income, these fluctuations affect them more than other groups. In South Indian villages an increase in risk (from the monsoon arriving too soon or too late) reduced farm profits for the poorest quarter of households by 35 per cent but left the wealthiest farmers nearly unaffected. In Vietnam participants in the Voices of the poor study said of harvest losses due to floods.

Responses to Risk by Households and Communities

For poor people, dealing successfully with the range of risks they are exposed to is often a matter of life or death. To manage risks, households and communities rely on both formal and informal strategies. Informal strategies include arrangements that involve individuals or households or such groups as communities or villages. Formal arrangements include market-based activities and publicly provided mechanisms. Informal and formal strategies are not independent: public policies and the availability of formal mechanisms heavily influence how extensively informal arrangements are used and which kinds are used.

Table—3.2

	INFORMAL MECHANISMS		FORMAL MECHANISMS	
OBJECTIVE	INDIVIDUAL AND HOUSE HOLD	GROUP BASED	MARKET BASED	PUBLICITY PROVIDED
1	2	3	4	5
Reducing risk	Preventive health practices Migration More secure income sources	Collective action for infrastructure, Dikes, terraces Common property resource management		Sound macro economic policy Environment policy Education and training policy Public health policy Infrastructure (dams, roads) Active labour market policies
Mitigating risk Diversification Insurance	Crop and plot diversification Income source diversification Investment in	Occupational associations Rotating savings and credit associations	Saving accounts in financial institutions Microfinance Old age	Agricultural extension Liberalized trade Protection of

(Table Contd...)

1	2	3	4	5
	physical and human capital Marriage and extended family Sharecropper tenancy Buffer stocks	Investment in social capital (networks, associations, rituals, reciprocal gift giving)	annuities Accident, disability, and other insurance	property rights Pension systems Mandated insurance for unemployment illness, disability and other risks
Coping with shocks	Sale of assets Loans from money-lenders Child labour Reduced food Consumption Seasonal or temporary migration	Transfers from networks of mutual support	Sale of financial assets Loans from financial institutions	Social assistance Workfare Subsidies Social funds Cash transfers

a. Publicly provided coping mechanisms can also serve risk mitigating purposes if they are in place on a permanent basis.

Source: World Development Report (2000-01)—Attacking Poverty

Risk management strategies can be further classified as risk reduction and mitigation measures (actions in anticipation of a shock) and coping measures (actions in response to a shock). Risk reduction aims at reducing the probability of a shock or negative fluctuation. Individuals or households can sometimes take such action themselves (digging wells, getting vaccinated). But to reduce most risks effectively, action is also needed at the meso or macro level. The risk of flooding can be reduced if the community builds a dike or the government builds a dam. Sound economic and environmental policies, education and training, and other measures can also reduce a wide variety of risks.

Risk mitigation aims at reducing the impact of shocks. Households mitigate risk through diversification (acquiring assets whose returns are not perfectly correlated) and insurance. Common diversification strategies are planting different crops and plots, combining farm and non-farm income in rural areas, and combining wage income and income from household enterprises in urban areas. Households can take most of these actions on their own—though group or government action (agricultural extension, infrastructure) can sometimes facilitate diversification. Households also mitigate risk through insurance, including self-insurance, informal insurance, and formal insurance—though market-based formal insurance plays a minor role for poor people.

Coping strategies aim to relieve the impact of a shock after it occurs. Actions by individuals include drawing down savings or selling assets. Borrowing, and calling on support networks. Actions by government include activating the transfers or workfare mechanisms that constitute the social safety net. If these measures prove insufficient, households may need to reduce consumption or increase labour supply. Many of these coping responses force a high long-term cost on households for a short-term benefit.

REFERENCES

1. World Development Report 2000/2001, *Attacking Poverty—World Bank*—Oxford University Press.
2. India Reducing Poverty, *Accelerating Development and World Bank Country Study*, Oxford University Press.
3. Human Development Report 2000, Oxford University Press.
4. Human Development Report 2001, Oxford University Press.
5. South India Human Development Report NCAER—Oxford.
6. Human Development in South Asia 2000, Oxford University Press.

4

Women's Participation in Rural Non-Farm Employment

Brahm Prakash

Unemployment has always its roots much deeper in the economic system than is commonly supposed. There is no problem so fundamental to economic development as the problem of unemployment. So long as the satisfaction of human needs is the prime objective of all economic activity, the prevalence of unemployment and underemployment will stand as an index to economic distress and primary poverty. The larger the opportunities of employment, the greater the scope for the people to increase their prosperity and augment production of goods and services thereby national welfare. Industrialisation was the answer to problems of economic backwardness, unemployment and poverty in the developed countries. However, since the less developed countries depend much more heavily on agriculture and are faced with much faster growth of population and labour force than the industrialised countries faced in their pre-industrial phase. It is widely maintained that higher priority must be given to agriculture and agro-based industries in order to provide not

* Indian Institute of Pulses Research, Kanpur 208 024.

only adequate food and fibre but also sufficient employment and income to the poor. But the recent studies revealed that though the new technology in agriculture did need more labour, the increase was less than proportionate to the increase in yield. As such, the growth of agricultural employment, both in absolute terms and relative to increase in agricultural output was far less than expected. It is also evident that in peasant economies, typically characterised by continuing population pressure, an ever declining land-man ratio, small and fragmented agricultural holdings, highly iniquitous land distribution structure, increasing application of labour saving farm production technologies etc., agriculture alone can not provide the ultimate answer for rural unemployment and under employment. That underscores for employment generation in the rural areas. This brings the development of non farm sector into focus.

The problem of unemployment is worst in females than males. Women constitute one half of our population but they still continue to languish far behind. The fundamental challenge that women's development now face is to ensure economic empowerment and self reliance for women. In a situation characterised by deep rooted age old sex discrimination, economic oppression and social stratification, women have occupied a place much below to men and are still deprived as the gains of development have not been shared proportionately. It may be surprising to note that women contribute two third of total human labour hours but they get one tenth of the world's property and income. The Constitution of India enjoys upon every citizen of India the duty to promote the common brotherhood of all the people of India and renounce any practice derogatory of the dignity of women. But it is amazing to note that the services of women are not properly utilized even today after fifty five years of the independence of the country.

1. CURRENT STATUS OF WOMEN IN NON-FARM RURAL EMPLOYMENT

(a) Growth Rate of Population and Sex Ratio

Data embodied in Table—4.1 clearly reveals that except for one decade (1911 to 1921), the population of both females and males have shown a continuously increasing trend from 1901 to 2001. But it is disturbing to note that the sex ratio, i.e. females per one thousand males have declined in almost each decade from as high as 972 in 1901 to as low as 927 in 1991. It is worth to mention here that sex ratio has increased to 933 during 2001. But it was quite low in comparison to sex ratios of average of the world (i.e. 986 females per 1000 males) and the ten most populated countries of the world (Table—4.2). Although there was disparity in sex ratio among different states of the country. While in Kerala, there were 1058 women per 1000 men and in Pondicherry, there were 1001 women per 1000 men. But, there were 773 women per 1000 men in Chandigarh, 811 in Dadar Nagar Haveli, 821 in Delhi, 861 in Haryana, 874 in Punjab and 875 women per 1000 men in Sikkim. Census of India 2001 revealed that sex ratio has further declined in comparison to 1991 Census in the states of Maharashtra, Goa, Himachal Pradesh, Haryana, Punjab and Sikkim. While sex ratio has increased in rest of the states. Among Union territories, sex ratio has declined in Delhi, Daman and Diu and Dadar Nagar Haveli during last decade. Five leading states with the highest sex ratio were Kerala (1058), Chhatisgarh (990), Tamil Nadu (986), Andhra Pradesh (978) and Manipur (978). Five major states with the lowest sex ratios were Haryana (861), Punjab (874), Sikkim (875), Uttar Pradesh (898) and Jammu and Kashmir (900). The highest increase in sex ratio in all states and union territories during the period between 1991 and 2001 was recorded in Uttaranchal where it has increased to 964 from 936. While the highest decline in sex ratio was noticed in Daman and Diu where it has declined to 709 from 969. According to Census of India 2001, while adult sex ratio has been improving in India but sex ratio of children less than 6 years of age has been declining. This ratio was 945 per 1000 male children during 1991 which has further been declined to 927 during 2001. The causes of low sex ratio are our socio economic system which considers the girl as a liability and is discriminated right from the cradle to the crematorium. There are instances when female babies are punished to death as soon as they are born or they are denied proper health care like immunization against various diseases at the proper time and proper nourishment. Among the more sophisticated and educated class of the society, the pregnancy test for sex determination has made it easier to get rid of unwanted female foetus.

The Pre-Natal Diagnostic Techniques (Regulation and Prevention of Misuse) Act 1994 was intended to regulate the use of pre-natal diagnostic techniques only for detecting genetic or metabolic disorders. There were provisions for punishment for doctors and the family members involved for sex determination test of the child. The amended Act 2002 has now diluted the stringent measures and paved the way for doctors to resort to unethical practices and kill the girls, in the womb itself. Interestingly, the amended Act has excluded men from the pre-natal diagnostic procedures. One of the methods to detect the sex of the child is to remove samples of fluid from the Act. Under the amended Act, women too, will henceforth be punished with 3 years imprisonment and a fine of Rs. 50,000, if they undergo a sex determination test. However, more than 98% of the cases, the pregnant women is forced by her family to terminate or abort the foetus, if it is a girl child.

The progress of urbanisation of a country is an indicator of economic development. Urbanisation and economic development are closely associated with each other. A country with high ratio of urbanisation will be more developed. In 1901, 10.8% of the total population of our country reside in urban areas. This figure has increased up to 27.8% in 2001 (Table—4.3). Although there was disparity among different states of the country (Table—4.4).

Thus, 72.2% of the population of our country still reside in rural areas. Low employment opportunities in rural areas is one of the major reasons for urbanisation. For mitigating the rural urban migration, we will have to create enormous employment opportunities in rural areas with facilities of medical, education, recreation and training. It is also worth to mention here that most of the rural men move to the cities in search of employment leaving their families at villages only. Even after getting the employment, they don't afford their families at the cities. Thus, most of the females remain unemployed wasting enormous precious manpower. It will not be out of context to note that 33.4% of rural population and 20.1% of the urban population was below the poverty line in 1987-88 (Table—4.5). The persons below the poverty line were identified as persons who get less than 2400 calories from food in rural areas and less than 2100 calories from food in urban areas. Planning Commission on 11 March 1997 accepted the Lakadawala formula (1993) for determining poverty line. According to new approach, poverty ratio in India has been estimated and shown in Table—4.6. Current estimates of poverty accepted by Planning Commission based on the recommendations of Expert Group reveal that 27.1% of Indians living in rural areas and 23.6% of the people living in urban areas were below poverty line during 1999-2000 (Table—4.7). Population below poverty line in important states of the country during 1999-2000 embodied in Table—4.8 clearly shows that 47.15% of the population of Orissa and 42.60% of the population of Bihar were below poverty line. Although separate data for females below poverty line has not been mentioned, but it is easily understood that the states with higher percentage of the population below poverty line has higher number of females too below poverty line.

(b) Occupation Structure in India

Occupation can be broadly divided into three sectors. Primary sector includes employment related to agriculture, agricultural labourers, livestock, forestry, fishing, plantation etc. Secondary sector includes employment in mines, household industries, large industries, gas and power production, while tertiary sector includes the employment related to commerce and trade, transport, storage, communication, financial management and banking. Thus, the tertiary sector helps in the activities of primary and secondary sectors. Data of occupational structures of Indian population embodied in Table—4.9 revealed that dependence on primary sector has declined slightly. The data also reveal that our economy is still backward due to heavy dependence on primary sector. According to World Development Report 1995, 72.1% of labour force in Canada, 71.3% in United States of America, 69.3% in United Kingdom and 58.8% in Japan was involved in tertiary sector during 1991 (Table—4.10).

(c) Economically Active Population

Economically active population of a country depends upon life expectancy, availability of employment opportunities and interest of the people in work. Data of economically active population embodied in Table—4.11 revealed that percentage of economically active female population which was 31.7% in 1901 has been reduced to 22.73% in 1991 while the figure of male population has been reduced to 51.56% in 1991 from 61.11% in 1901. This reveals that males are more economically active than females. On classifying the population into rural and urban category, it was found that work participation rate in the rural areas are high in comparison to urban areas. Data embodied in Table—4.12 indicate that work participation rate in rural females increased more in comparison to the participation rate in urban females. Although the female work participation rate has increased during 1981-91 but it is still below the participation rate in 1901-31. The reasons for declining female work participation rate could be various i.e. increase in population, reduction in traditional industries, urbanisation, industrialisation, mechanisation of production process, etc., also with the coming of night shift, many factories women have been displaced. The work participation rate of the different states of the country has been depicted in Table—4.13.

(d) Workers Population Ratio of the Rural Population

Data embodied in Table—4.14 summarizes the available data on worker population ratio starting with the 1951 Census. It includes the census based estimates as well as the results of four large quinquennial surveys of employment and unemployment conducted by National Sample Survey (NSS) during 1971-73, 1977-78, 1983 and 1987. The estimates based on the subsequent annual surveys of a relatively small sample are also reported in the Table. The NSS surveys on employment and underemployment conducted between 1958-59 and 1967-68 were based on a short reference period of one week. The two large surveys conducted during 1960-61 and 1961-62 had reported markedly lower worker population ratios than the 1961 Census, particularly for rural areas. Beginning with 1972-73, the NSSO surveys began to estimate the level of employment according to the three alternative reference periods of the last year, the week preceding the data of survey and each day of reference week. The four surveys of 1972-73, 1977-78, 1983 and 1987-88 have shown a remarkable stability in worker population ratios based on the usual status approach. The later are also similar to those reported by 1961 census. These estimates confirm that despite substantial growth in population since 1951, the worker population ratios have not really declined. While the contrary results from 1971 and 1981 censuses must be attributed to the difficulties of obtaining dependable counts of female workforce through honorary enumerators with only a limited interest in their assignment.

When the workers' population ratios are not quite comparable, the underlying industrial distribution of workers can not be presumed to reflect the reality because the excluded workers are not necessarily distributed at random over different industrial divisions or groups. However, the share of the agriculture sector in total employment was remarkably similar according to both the 1961 census and the 16th round of the NSS.

(e) The Share of Agriculture in the Workforce

The data embodied in Table—4.15 clearly revealed that after 1972-73, the share of agriculture seems to have declined by almost 8 per cent to 65 per cent by 1987-88. The share of agriculture in rural workforce in 1987-88 was 78 per cent which was higher than in the urban workforce (14 per cent). Urbanisation has thus been a factor contributing to the process of diversification of the pattern of economic activities in the country as a whole.

The share of male workers engaged in agricultural activities in rural India which was 83.3% during 1972-73, reduced to 74.6% during 1987-88. While the share of female workers engaged in agriculture activities reduced to 84.2% during 1987-88 from 89-7% during 1972-73. When we combine both the sexes, we observe a decline of 7 per cent in agricultural activities. With the continuous growth in population, the absolute number of agricultural workers as well as male and female workers continued to grow during 1972-73 to 1987-88 except the period 1983 to 1987-88, when number of rural females engaged in agricultural activities declined due to decline in rural female workers population ratio and rise in the construction sector employment.

(f) Growth of Non Agricultural Employment

As evident from Table—4.15, the non agricultural employment among rural males of India has expanded at an annual rate of 4.7 per cent while agricultural employment has expanded at an average annual rate of only 1 per cent. The corresponding rate of growth of rural female employment were 4.6 and 1.5 per cent, respectively.

The sectorial distribution of workforce in rural India by sex both in percentage and absolute numbers have been depicted in Table—4.16. The average annual growth rates during 1972-73 to 1987-88 and three quarters between the mid points of the initial and the last survey years have also been presented in the Table.

The data embodied in Table—4.16 clearly revealed that electricity, gas and water sector recorded maximum growth rate with annual growth rate in employment of more than 11 per cent in rural India. Only male workers are engaged in this sector. The next highest rate of growth in employment (7.9%) was recorded in construction sector. The data recorded through different NSS rounds on percentage of workers employed in construction industry embodied in Table—4.17 revealed that the volume of rural female employment in construction has declined considerably after 1987-88 while the proportion of rural males engaged in this sector has remained quite high. This can be attributed to large scale public sector expenditure on rural and urban employment schemes as well as public and private investment in construction.

Transport, storage and communications, trade and commerce, and mining and quarrying were other sectors with relatively high rate of growth of employment.

For rural females, mining and quarrying sector recorded maximum annual growth rate of employment of 9.9% during 1972-73 to 1987-88 followed by construction sector with annual growth rate of 8%. Manufacturing sectors and trade and hotels, etc. recorded 4.6 and 3.8 per cent growth rate per annum for rural female employment.

Employment of women in non-agricultural sector has been increasing since last two decades (Table—4.18). It is seen that non-agricultural women workers as a percentage to rural workforce in India has been increasing from 12.96% in 1971 to 13.10% in 1991. The share of non-farm women workers as percentage to total workforce has decreased in Andhra Pradesh, Haryana, Karnataka,

Madhya Pradesh, Orissa, Punjab and Rajasthan, while there is substantial growth in states like Bihar, Gujarat, Himachal Pradesh, Kerala, Maharashtra, Tamil Nadu, Uttar Pradesh and West Bangal.

Data embodied in Table—4.19 reveals the rural population and their engagement in different sectors as per different censuses. Data on population by category of workers as per 1991 census depicted in Table—4.20 revealed that there were 31.49 crore people as total workers. Out of this, there were 24.93 crore rural workers. A worker was defined as one who has worked at least for a day in the last one year. Out of total 24.93 crore rural workers, there were 2.77 crore rural marginal workers and 22.16 crore rural main workers. Marginal worker is one who works for less than 183 days during the preceding year, while main worker is a worker who works for 183 days or more. Out of these, 22.16 crore rural main workers, there were 10.74 crore rural cultivators, 7.04 crore rural agricultural labourers, 0.68 crore household industry workers and 3.7 crore other rural workers. Among the females, 44.23% workers were working as agricultural labourers and 34.57% as cultivators (Table—4.21). Thus, only small percentage of female workers were engaged in non farm activities.

Planning Commission, Government of India (1978) stated in the Draft Five Year Plan, 1978-83 it is a historically unique fact that over the last six decennial census, in spite of impressive development of the large scale manufacturing and infrastructure sectors, the share of agriculture in the workforce has not diminished at all. It was 73% in 1921, 73% again in 1961 and 73.8% in 1971. The figure for 1971 is, in fact, slightly higher than for 1961. In almost all countries, economic development is associated with a significant decrease in this share. Even during the decade 1965-75, the share declined in thirteen Asian countries. But in India fairly rapid growth in the non agricultural sector in the last 25 years of planned development has completely failed to make any noticeable impact on the industrial distribution of the workforce. This constancy noted by Professor Raj Krishna and Professor Y.K. Alagh, however, changed in the seventies and eighties.

Table—4.22 reveals that the share of the male rural labour force in the agriculture sector fell from 83.2% in 1972-73 to 74.5%

in 1987-88. The fall in the share of female labour force in the rural areas in the agricultural sector was lower. Thus, structural change started in the rural labour force also. These changes were first documented by Sheila Bhalla (1983). According to her views, the structural changes were pronounced in Gujarat, Haryana, Karnataka, Maharashtra and Tamil Nadu. In Gujarat, Maharashtra and Haryana, the rise in the share of non-agricultural workers (between 4.92% and 5.58%) was much higher than national average of 3.26%. In Karnataka and Tamil Nadu, the decline was 5.29% and 3.52, respectively. Thus, in states, which account for about a quarter of the country's population and labour force, a fairly systematic and persistent trend of structural change and labour reallocation has been achieved during 1960-80.

The regional structure of the workforce embodied in Table—4.23 shows considerable variations. It reveals that the status in which male workers in rural areas have both a lower percentage than the national level in the agriculture sector (i.e. less than 74%) and higher percentage and in manufacturing sector (i.e. higher than 7.6%) are Kerala, Jammu and Kashmir, Tamil Nadu, Rajasthan, Gujarat, Punjab, Haryana and West Bengal. Of these states, only Tamil Nadu, Gujarat, West Bengal and Haryana have over 30% of the male labour force in urban areas engaged in the manufacturing sector. These regions have a diversified structure of the labour force by the end of nineties. For the country as a whole, the percentage of workers dependent on agriculture has fallen from 70.7 to 63.9 in 1977-78.

(g) Agro-industry and Non-farm Employment

During 1987-88, non-agricultural sector as a whole accounted for a little over one fifth of rural employment in India. Out of this, manufacturing sector accounted for 7.3%. Distribution of non-agricultural rural enterprises in 1980 showed that 39% were engaged in manufacturing and repair services. The distribution of rural males and females employed by industry sector has been depicted in Table—4.24.

Between 1972-73 and 1987-88, employment in the rural manufacturing sector has shown a growth rate of 3.95% per annum and against 1.1% of agriculture sector and 1.75% of the rural employment sector as a whole. The labour force is presently growing at the rate of 2.4% per annum. On the other hand, contribution to the employment growth from agriculture is placed at 0.7 per cent only. Thus, the non-agricultural sector will have to contribute to the remaining if full employment is to be achieved.

There are two types of village and small industries viz., traditional and modern. Khadi and Village industries, handlooms, handicrafts, sericulture, coir etc., are examples of traditional industries. These industries are generally artisan-based located mostly in rural and sub urban areas and involve lower level of investment in machinery are in the small scale industrial sector. Traditional industries are characterised by low level of technology resulting in poor productivity and low returns. Most of the activities of non-farm enterprises are carried out in small enterprises and a majority of these are unorganised in nature. It has been proved by successive censuses that employment in household industries is declining and such declines are more pronounced in traditional industries like processing of cereals and pulses, jaggery and *khandsari*, edible oils, wool and silk spinning and curing and tanning of hides and skins. There are also evidence that the decline is much sharper in female employment.

The other group of industries viz., modern small scale industries, employs slightly higher levels of technology and has been the main source of employment growth in the industrial sector. The non-traditional industries coming up in rural areas are both agriculture related as well as not related with agriculture viz., agro-based and food processing, textile based industries and those producing construction material viz., bricks, tiles etc. Although their location may not be strictly rural in the sense as they are tending to get located in smaller towns, they provide employment to rural workers.

(h) Income Distribution and Non-farm Employment

In rural areas, the levels of productivity of all the crops are low which lead to poverty and malnutrition. Non-farm work opportunities supplement income. This feature of economy is evident from the data collected by N.S.S.O. which is depicted in

Table—4.25. It is clear that in the consumption classes above Rs. 110 to Rs. 125 the percentage of workers working in non-farm sector is higher than in consumption classes below the poverty line i.e. Rs. 110 to Rs. 125 per month. It also highlights the importance of non-farm employment for supplementing income in rural areas.

(i) Determinants of Rural Non-farm Employment

(a) Local Rural Demand

Non farm employment is greatly influenced by local rural demand of the material used in agriculture and livestock, commodities manufactured for final consumption, capital formation, consumer services of different types, trade, transport and related services of non-farm produce. Traditional cultivation is done mostly by the materials produced locally. With the invent of new technology, the dependence on non-local material like fertilizers, insecticides and mechanical implements, like pumps and tractors has been increased. Except for repairing services of the machines, all the material is developed by industries situated far away from villages. Therefore, demand for material produced by non-farm sector increases more than proportionate to increase in agricultural production. The demand for the materials of non-farm sector is more in the areas with high per capita income of the farmers or unequal distribution of income. It has been noticed during the past few decades that more opportunities of employment has been provided to the non-farm sector like education, public health and public administration. The level of local demand in case of trade, transport and finance depends upon the per capita income and level of commercialization of rural economy.

(b) Additional Local Demand

Although in most of the cases, the market of products of non-farm rural sector has been limited to villages only, but in some cases, the products of rural industry like earthen pots, leather goods, processed agricultural produce like jaggery, sugar and cloth etc., are also sold in nearby cities.

(c) Planning Results and Technology

The technology used for a level of demand and types of producing a thing can vary the level of employment. Less labour will be employed in a modern rice mill than the traditional system of beating the paddy manually. The level of commercialization of rural economy is the major determinant of influencing results and techniques in non-farm rural activities. Traditionally, village community is self-dependent. Trade and transport activities are limited. Ox-driven carts and animals are the major source of transport. The level of development of network of transport along with density and size of rural residences also determine the intensity of rural non-farm employment.

2. CONSTRAINTS RESPONSIBLE FOR LOW PARTICIPATION OF FEMALE WORKFORCE IN NON-FARM RURAL SECTOR

Although, equal opportunities are available at every level in the country, a limited portion of total female, workforce is being utilized and that too, in a low profitable sector like agriculture makes the matter of great concern. It is difficult for a country to progress unless it utilizes each and every available resource including labour force. If a country of enormous population like China is economically strong and highly developed, its credit goes to a large extent to about cent per cent utilization of their female workforce. Same is the case in the countries of USA, Britain, Germany, France, Japan and Korea.

Following are some of the major constraints responsible for low participation of female workforce in non-farm rural sector.

(a) Low Female Literacy Rate

Today, nobody may deny the need for women's education. But still, there is a feeling that providing education for women is luxury which the rich may afford for their girls and the poor do not bother to provide the facilities of education for their girl children. Educated females play an important role in the development of society and the country where is high literacy ration among females, birth and death rates are also low there and there is no problem of population explosion. Educated and trained women taken an active part in economic activities and help in accelerating the process of development, while illiterate women are an evil for the society and they cannot raise the voice against oppression and exploitation. The same is the case with India. According to 2001 census, there were only 54.16% literate females (above 7 years) in the country (Table—4.26). While the highest literacy rate (90.92%) was recorded in Kerala and the lowest literacy was recorded in Bihar (47.53%). While in case of female literacy, the highest literacy (87.86%) was recorded in Kerala and the lowest literacy (33.57%) was recorded in Bihar (Table—4.27). Education broaden the mental horizons, give her access to information and make her aware of her rights as an individual. In absence of education, there is no way for the rural women to participate in non-farm employment and they underutilize and waste their manpower in activities associated with the farm.

(b) Marriage

One of the characteristics features of our rural society is to get the girls married at an early age. Rajasthan is the leader in this case where hundreds of girl babies are married annually. Marriage may be an inseparable institution, for the furtherance of the family and society. It is the mean by which womanhood is fully realized by girl. Right to marry and to have a family is firmly established in the International Human Rights Law. Article 6 of the Universal Declaration of Human Rights (1948) provides that men and women of full age, without any limitation due to race, nationality or religion, have the right to marry and found a family. Similar rights are guaranteed under the International Covenant on Civil and Political Rights 1966. Law has always respected marriage as the foundation of family life subject to certain well-founded rules restricting marriage in blood relationships or offensive to the conscience. It is universally accepted legal proposition that there can be no direction so far as to completely deprive a person of the right to marry (Article 12-Convention). Marriage is a sacrament amongst Hindus and most significant amongst other religions. As such any bar against marriage or prohibition against marriage is devoid of any sanction social or legal. But forcing the girls into the marriage is violation of their rights. If that is necessary to provide security to her in life, then she should be made to realise it and then enter it, knowing fully well th e implications of the act. Forcing her into early marriage against her wishes, denying her freedom to marry outside the caste, forcing repeated pregnancies on her, compelling her to continue to live in matrimony even when her husband happens to be a drunkard, a sick or a womanizer, denying her the right to remarry in the case of her husband's death—all these constitute oppression and have been heaped on women since time immemorial. The state has brought forth to several pieces of legislation to curb these forms of oppression—Child Marriages Restraint Act, the Age of Marriage Act, Special Marriage Act, The Medical Termination of Pregnancy Act, The Widow Remarriage Act and many more. By themselves, these acts cannot transform the realities for women. Tampered by the forces of habit and socially conditioned to accept a secondary role, women continue to devalue themselves and have not benefited from the rights and privileges conferred on them by these Acts. They hesitate to accept social change since still subordinate their rights to life for fear of losing their social status, religious sanctions being imposed against them of bringing a bad name to themselves and their family and for fan of being ridiculed by their own kith and kin. They do not opt for change, worse still condemn those who opt for such change.

In the early days, relationship within the family between husband and wife were based on love and trust. Further the earnings were rather low and just enough to meet the family needs. There was not much of a question of surplus of wealth. In such a simple life, when wants were also limited, the issue of rights did not figure much. But in the modern context, where the woman works as much as man, competing with him effectively in all walks of life, she has recognised the institutions which subtly and sometimes explicitly deny her the basic rights. Denial of rights does not employ lack of employment opportunities for rural women but that through opportunities exist, women are denied the right to avail of these opportunities in non-farm sector and are restricted with agriculture sector with their families.

(c) Pregnancy

Right to marriage having been established as inherent in everyone by necessary implications, includes right to the family and stroke or to conceive a child in utero or even to have an abortion, subject to statutory restrictions. None can prescribe against pregnancy-which is purely personal privilege and the most endeared right of a woman. Hon'ble Supreme Court of India in Nagesh Meerza (an air hostess) case, struck down the provision of termination of services at attaining the age of 35 years or on marriage or on first pregnancy as manifestly unreasonable or absolutely arbitrary". In an old case, Hon'ble High Court of Madras held that the right to conceive and give birth were personal rights inherent to a woman. Even a rule which requires teachers to quit their jobs before pregnancy were severely criticized by US Courts and in India, the Supreme Court struck down a rule (Bombay Labour Union Vs. International Franchise Pvt. Ltd. 1966).

As there is a provision for maternity leave up to 12 weeks with salary for women under Factories Act 1948, Maternity Benefits Act 1961 and Employees State Insurance (General) Regulation 1950, a large number of the employers do not provide employment to the women on one or other ground.

(d) Social Values

In the male dominated society, women are supposed to remain in the four walls of their households or help in husband's jobs particularly at firm. Woman has been subject to inequalities and subsidiary status relative to man, within the family and outside in the society. The difference in age between husband and wife may account partially for the higher status enjoyed by the man in the family in respect of decision-making and other roles. Since time immemorial, man was acknowledged as the head of the family as the bread winner, as the guardian of the family, entitle to education, acquiring the skills and to practice professions. Since he was acknowledged as the leader in all aspects, he became the custodian of the family property too. Women because of their innate interest in nurturing the children and taking care of the members of the family willingly acquired and recognised the importance of security provided by the husband, never questioned his leadership nor made any efforts to change the situation in their favour. If they dare to come out of the four-walls of their households, women are subject to different kinds of harassment and atrocities. Even the slightest aberration on their part becomes a subject of criticism, calumny and condemnation, as if all the morals were meant exclusively for women, men giving scot free of all blame even in cases in which the alleged depravity of women is the consequence of men's seduction, rape or molestation. Moral or spiritual exploitation of women also obstacles their participation in non-farm employment.

(e) Unfavourable Attitudes of Employers

In most of the cases, employers in private sector adopt policy of biasedness in providing employment to the women. Even having some academic and technical qualification, women are not offered the employment equal to the status of the men. Any work associated with higher responsibility is never offered to them. Some of the employers only employ unmarried girls and they are retrenched after getting married. As most of the non-farm activities in the rural areas are existing in the unorganised sector, the employers of this sector still engage women on low wages in comparison to their male counterpart.

(f) Lack of Organisation

As far as organisations for woman workers are concerned, no separate organisation has grown up in the country among the woman workers. The woman workers have also to attend to their household duties and as such have got no time to take active interest in the organisations. They also do not stick to a job permanently and also lack initiative and organising capacity. Traditions have also grown up in the country, which make women always dependent upon men and the illiterate woman workers cannot even think of having a separate organisation. As we are aware, when the trade unionism is not strong and healthy even among the male workers, women workers cannot be blamed, if they have not paid much attention towards their own organisation. It does not mean that women have not taken interest in the labour movement of the country. The membership of women in trade unions have increased significantly over time. But they could not organise any trade union. The already existing trade unions are dominated by males which generally neglect the interest of women labour. It has also been observed that the women's participation in the top or middle level leadership in these trade unions is almost negligible.

(g) Establishment of Factories/Industries etc. in the Urban Areas

As most of the factories/workshops, offices, schools etc., are located in urban areas, the rural women get less opportunities due to their limited mobility and family cases as in the cases with men. Rural women have no option except for activities associated with farm or cottage industries. Due to rapid industrialisation and entry of foreign companies in the domestic market, the cottage industries are also struggling for their existence, reducing the employment opportunities particularly for rural women.

(h) No Legislation Regarding Reservation of Women in Government/Semi-Government/Autonomous Organisations

There is no legislation regarding reservation of women who constitute a major economically and socially backward group in Govt./Semi-Govt./Autonomous Organisations like other backward groups. This does not pave the way for women to engage them in any activities, associated other than farm.

(i) No Incentive for Self-employment

Although Government has launched a number of schemes for providing financial assistance for self-employment of the unemployed youths irrespective of sex, education and rural background, hardly few rural women could have availed this opportunity due to lack of incentive from the Government, the family and the society as well as lack of education, vocational training, the entrepreneurship, etc. In absence of any job, they underutilize their services in various farm operations or allied activities.

3. LEGAL PROVISIONS FOR WOMEN WORKERS

A number of legal provisions have been made for the interest of women workers. Every woman is entitled to be treated with equality, regard and dignity as there can be no discrimination against her only on the ground of sex. Indian Constitution prohibits all sorts of discrimination against women (Article 14, 15 and 16). While laying down the fundamental duties, the Constitution of India [Article 51 (A)] clearly prescribes that it shall be the duty of every citizen to renounce practices derogatory to the dignity of women. In the International scene also, we find that almost all around the globe, barring some exceptions, women are treated equally with dignity and respect. The Conference Against Elimination of Discrimination Against Women (CEDAW) in its recommendation No. 17 defined gender based violence as "the form of discrimination which seriously inhibits women's ability to enjoy rights and freedom on the basis of equality with men". Violence against women in any form is prohibited on the premises of her basic or fundamental rights, rights to life, the right to liberty and security of the person, right to physical and mental health and the right to just and favourable conditions at work. In the CEDAW and Vienna Declaration (1993), sexual harassment of women at work place was clearly prohibited. In the absence of any such law in India, our Hon'ble Supreme Court has inducted the guiding principles of CEDAW in the Indian Judicial System as well and thereby completely prohibits sexual harassment at work which may be physical, mental or even psychological.

Article 39(A) of the Directive Principles of the State Policy under Part IV also contained in the Constitution clearly states that "State will implement its policy in such a way that it may be helpful in providing the right to get employment to men, women all the citizens". Under article 39 (D), there is a provision of equal pay of equal work to men and women both. Article 39(E) ensures that the manpower and health of men and women workers and childhood of children are not mis-utilized and they are not compelled for such employment which may not be appropriate according to their age and strength. Provision for ensuring justified and humanitarian working conditions and maternity benefits have been made under Article 42.

It may be mentioned that the legislative provisions for protection and welfare of woman workers are largely inspired by the ILO Conventions. The Conventions concerning women are on (1) Maternity Protection 1919, Revised in 1952; (2) Night Work (Women) 1919, Revised in 1934 and 1948; (3) Underground Work (Women) 1935; (4) Equal Remuneration (1951); (5) Discrimination (Employment and Occupation) 1958. There are two ILO recommendations also concerning women namely (1) Lead Poisoning (Women and Children) Recommendations of 1919 and ratified all the Conventions except of Maternity Protection but the

1	2	3	4	5	6	7
Nagaland	5.21	40.04	0.28	7.47	5.49	32.67
Orissa	143.69	48.01	25.40	42.83	169.09	47.15
Punjab	10.20	6.35	4.29	5.75	14.44	6.16
Rajasthan	55.06	13.74	26.78	19.85	81.83	15.28
Sikkim	2.00	40.04	0.04	7.47	2.05	36.55
Tamil Nadu	80.51	20.55	49.97	22.19	130.48	21.12
Tripura	12.53	40.04	0.49	7.47	13.02	34.44
Uttar Pradesh	412.01	31.22	117.88	30.89	529.09	31.15
West Bengal	180.11	31.85	33.38	14.36	213.49	27.02
Union Territories						
Andaman & Nicobar Islands	0.58	20.55	0.24	22.11	0.82	20.99
Chandigarh	0.06	5.75	0.45	5.75	0.51	5.78
Dadar & Nagar Haveli	0.30	17.57	0.03	13.52	0.33	17.14
Daman & Diu	0.01	1.35	0.05	7.52	0.06	4.40
Delhi	0.07	0.40	11.42	9.42	11.49	8.20
Lakshadweep	0.03	9.38	0.08	20.27	0.11	15.60
Pondicherry	0.64	20.55	1.77	22.11	2.41	21.60
All India	1932.43	27.09	670.07	23.62	2602.50	26.10

Source: NSSO (2001).

Table—4.9 Occupation Distribution of Population (%) in India

Year	Primary Sector	Secondary Sector	Tertiary Sector
1901	71.7	12.6	15.7
1921	76.0	10.4	13.6
1931	74.8	10.2	15.0
1951	72.1	10.6	17.3
1961	72.3	11.7	16.0
1971	72.0	11.2	16.8
1991	63.2	14.2	22.6

Source: Different Censuses of India.

Table—4.10 Occupational Distribution of Population (%) in Different Countries

Status of economy	Countries	Year	Primary Sector	Secondary Sector	Tertiary Sector
Developed	Canada	1991	3.5	24.4	72.1
	France	1991	5.7	28.8	65.5
	Italy	1991	8.4	32.0	59.5
	Japan	1991	6.7	34.5	58.8
	United Kingdom	1991	2.1	28.7	69.3
	USA	1991	2.9	25.8	71.3
Developing	Brazil	1988	24.2	23.4	52.4
	India	1991	63.2	14.2	22.6
	China	1993	61.0	18.0	21.0
	Pakistan	1992	47.4	19.9	32.7
	Indonesia	1993	50.4	15.8	33.8
	South Korea	1991	16.7	35.6	47.7
	Nigeria	1986	45.0	6.6	48.7

Source: World Development Report, 1995.

Table—4.11 Percentage of Economically Active Population

Year	Males	Females
1901	61.11	31.70
1911	61.90	33.73
1921	60.52	32.67
1931	58.27	27.63
1951	54.05	23.30
1961	57.10	27.96
1971	52.75	14.22
1981	52.62	19.67
1991	51.56	22.73

Source: Different Census of India.

Table—4.12 Work Participation Rate in India

(in Percentage)

Year		Total	Male	Female
1971	Gross	34.17	52.75	14.22
	Rural	35.33	53.78	15.92
	Urban	29.61	48.88	7.18
1981[1]	Gross	36.70	52.62	19.67
	Rural	38.79	53.77	23.06
	Urban	29.99	49.06	8.31
1991[2]	Gross	37.68	51.56	22.73
	Rural	40.24	52.50	27.20
	Urban	30.44	48.95	9.74

Note: 1. Excluding Assam.

2. Excluding Jammu and Kashmir.

Source: Annual Report (1993-94), Ministry of Labour, Govt. of India.

Table—4.13 Work Participation Rate (Total Workers as Percentage of Total Population) in the States/Union Territories of India

State/Union Territories	Work Participation Rate (in percentage)
1	2
States	
Andhra Pradesh	45.05
Arunachal Pradesh	46.27
Assam	36.09
Bihar	32.16
Goa	35.28
Gujarat	40.23
Haryana	31.00
Himachal Pradesh	42.83
Karnataka	41.99
Kerala	31.43
Madhya Pradesh	42.82
Maharashtra	42.97

(Table Contd...)

1	2
Manipur	42.18
Meghalaya	42.67
Mizoram	48.91
Nagaland	42.68
Orissa	37.53
Punjab	30.88
Rajasthan	38.87
Sikkim	41.51
Tamil Nadu	43.31
Tripura	31.14
Uttar Pradesh	32.20
West Bengal	32.19
Union Territories	
Andman & Nicobar Islands	35.24
Chandigarh	34.94
Dadar and Nagar Haveli	53.25
Daman Diu	37.63
Delhi	31.64
Lakshadweep	26.43
Pondicherry	33.08

Source: Census of India (1991).

Table—4.14 Crude Worker Population Ratios by Sex and Rural—Urban Residence in India (1951 to 1952)

Yours/Source/ (NSS Round)	India		Rural areas		Urban areas	
	Persons	Females	Persons	Females	Persons	Females
1	2	3	4	5	6	7
1951 Census	39.1	23.4	39.5	25.0	37.1	14.7
1955 NSS (9)	–	–	43.2	26.6	32.4	11.6
1960-61 NSS (16)	–	–	40.3	25.9	33.2	13.2
1961-62 NSS (17)	–	–	35.6	20.3	31.2	10.5
1961 Census	43.0	28.0	45.1	31.4	33.5	11.1
1971 Census	34.0	13.9	36.1	15.5	29.6	13.2

(Table Contd...)

1	2	3	4	5	6	7
1972-73 NSS (27)	40.7	27.8	42.8	31.4	32.6	13.2
1977-78 NSS (32)	41.6	28.9	43.8	32.6	33.9	15.3
1981 Census @	36.8	19.8	38.9	23.2	30.0	8.3
1983 NSS (38)	41.8	29.3	44.2	33.7	34.0	14.9
1987-77 NSS (43)	40.9	28.0	43.3	32.3	34.0	15.2
1989-90 NSS (45)	41.5	27.9	43.7	31.9	33.7	14.6
1990-91 NSS (46)	40.4	25.4	42.7	29.2	33.8	14.3
1991 Census*	37.5	22.3	40.0	26.7	30.2	9.2
July-Dec. 1991 NSS (47)	40.1	25.3	42.4	29.4	33.4	13.2
Jan-Dec. 1992	41.2	27.2	43.7	31.3	33.6	14.6

@ Excluding Assam.

* Excluding J & K.

Source: Different Reports of NSS and Census.

Table—4.15 Number (in millions) and Percentage of Workers in the Agricultural and Non-Agricultural Sectors during 1972-73 to 1987-88 in India

Sector/Sex/Industry	1972-73		1977-78		1983		1987-88	
	No.	%	No.	%	No.	%	No.	%
	Rural India							
1	2	3	4	5	6	7	8	9
Persons								
Agriculture	169.1	85.6	183.5	83.4	198.9	81.5	201.8	78.3
Non-agriculture	28.5	14.4	36.5	16.6	45.1	18.5	55.9	21.7
All	197.6	100.0	220.0	100.0	244.0	100.0	257.7	100.0
Male								
Agriculture	105.9	83.3	113.0	80.7	119.4	77.8	112.9	74.6
Non-agriculture	21.2	16.7	27.1	19.3	33.9	22.2	41.8	25.4
All	127.1	100.0	140.1	100.0	153.3	100.0	164.7	100.0
Female								
Agriculture	63.2	89.7	70.5	88.2	79.5	87.8	78.9	84.2
Non-agriculture	7.3	10.3	9.4	11.8	11.0	12.2	14.1	15.8
All	70.5	100.0	79.9	100.0	90.5	100.0	93.0	100.0

(Table Contd...)

Urban India

1	2	3	4	5	6	7	8	9
Persons								
Agriculture	5.8	14.8	7.4	15.2	8.7	14.8	9.1	13.6
Non-agriculture	33.3	85.2	41.4	84.8	50.1	85.2	57.9	86.4
All	39.1	100.0	48.8	100.0	58.8	100.0	67.0	100.0
Male								
Agriculture	3.4	10.7	4.1	10.6	4.8	10.3	4.8	9.1
Non-agriculture	28.4	89.3	34.4	89.4	41.8	89.7	48.1	90.9
All	31.8	100.0	38.5	100.0	46.6	100.0	52.9	100.0
Female								
Agriculture	2.4	32.9	3.3	31.9	3.9	32.0	4.3	30.5
Non-agriculture	4.9	67.1	7.0	68.1	8.3	68.0	9.8	69.5
All	7.3	100.0	10.3	100.0	12.2	100.0	14.1	100.0
India								
Persons								
Agriculture	174.9	73.9	190.9	71.0	207.6	68.6	210.9	65.0
Non-agriculture	61.8	26.1	77.9	29.0	95.2	31.4	113.8	35.0
All	236.7	100.0	268.8	100.0	302.8	100.0	324.7	100.0
Male								
Agriculture	109.3	64.8	117.1	65.6	124.2	62.6	127.7	58.7
Non-agriculture	49.6	31.2	61.5	34.4	79.2	37.4	89.9	41.3
All	158.9	100.0	178.6	100.0	200.1	100.0	217.6	100.0
Female								
Agriculture	65.6	84.3	73.8	81.8	83.4	81.2	83.2	77.7
Non-agriculture	12.2	15.7	16.4	18.2	19.3	18.8	23.9	22.3
All	77.8	100.0	90.2	100.0	102.7	100.0	107.1	100.0

Source: Visaria (1995).

Table—4.16 Number (in millions) and Percentage Distribution of Workers (Usual Status) by Sex 1972-73 to 1987-88, and Average Annual Growth Rate (Per cent) over the 15 Year Period

Sector/Sex	1972-73		1977-78		1983		1987-88		Growth rate
	No.	%	No.	%	No.	%	No.	%	
1	2	3	4	5	6	7	8	9	10
Rural India									
Persons									
Agriculture	169.1	85.6	183.5	83.4	198.9	81.5	201.8	78.3	1..2
Mining & quarrying	0.6	0.3	0.8	0.4	1.2	0.5	1.5	0.6	6.4
Manufacturing	10.6	5.4	13.7	6.2	16.6	6.8	18.6	7.2	3.9
Electricity, Gas & Water	0.1	0.1	0.3	0.1	0.3	0.1	0.5	0.2	11.5
Construction	2.8	1.4	2.9	1.3	4.0	1.6	8.6	3.3	7.9
Trade, Hotels etc.	5.0	2.5	7.2	3.3	8.4	3.4	10.3	4.0	5.0
Transport & Storage	1.3	0.6	1.8	0.8	2.7	1.1	3.4	4.3	6.7
Services	8.1	4.1	9.8	4.5	11.9	4.9	13.0	5.1	3.3
All	197.6	100.0	220.0	100.0	244.0	100.0	257.7	100.0	1.8
Males									
Agriculture	105.9	83.3	113.0	80.7	119.4	77.8	122.9	74.6	1.0
Mining & quarrying	0.5	0.4	0.7	0.5	0.9	0.6	1.1	0.7	5.5
Manufacturing	7.3	5.7	9.0	6.4	10.8	7.0	12.2	7.4	3.5
Electricity, Gas & Water	0.1	0.1	0.3	0.2	0.3	0.2	0.5	0.3	11.5
Construction	2.0	1.6	2.4	1.7	3.4	2.2	6.1	3.7	7.9
Trade, Hotels etc.	3.9	3.1	5.6	4.0	6.7	4.4	8.4	5.1	5.3
Transport & Storage	1.3	1.0	1.7	1.2	2.6	1.7	3.3	2.0	6.5
Services	6.1	4.8	7.4	5.3	9.4	6.1	10.2	6.2	3.5
All	127.1	100.0	140.1	100.0	153.5	100.0	164.7	100.0	1.8

(Table Contd...)

1	2	3	4	5	6	7	8	9	10
Females									
Agriculture	63.2	89.7	70.5	88.2	79.5	87.8	78.9	84.8	1.5
Mining & quarrying	0.1	0.2	0.1	0.2	0.3	0.3	0.4	0.4	9.9
Manufacturing	3.3	4.7	4.7	5.9	5.8	6.4	6.4	6.9	4.6
Electricity, Gas & Water	–	–	–	–	–	–	–	–	–
Construction	0.8	1.1	0.5	0.6	0.6	0.7	2.5	2.7	8.0
Trade, Hotels etc.	1.1	1.5	1.6	2.0	1.7	1.9	1.9	2.1	3.8
Transport & Storage	–	–	0.1	0.1	0.1	0.1	0.1	0.1	–
Services	2.0	2.8	2.4	3.0	2.5	2.8	2.8	3.0	2.3
All	70.5	100.0	79.9	100.0	90.5	100.0	93.0	100.0	1.9

Source: Visaria (1995).

Table—4.17 Percentage of Usual Status Workers Employed in Construction Industry in India during 1972-73 to 1992 (NSS Results)

NSS Round/ Year	Rural			Urban		
	Persons	Males	Females	Persons	Males	Females
27 (1972-73)	1.4	1.6	1.1	4.1	4.4	2.7
32 (1977-78)	1.3	1.7	0.6	3.7	4.2	2.2
38 (1983)	1.6	2.2	0.7	4.8	5.2	3.3
43 (1987-88)	3.3	3.7	2.7	5.4	5.9	3.5
45 (1989-90)	3.3	4.2	1.7	5.7	6.3	3.2
46 (1990-91)	2.2	2.7	1.3	5.0	5.4	3.6
47 (July-Dec. 1991)	3.1	3.6	2.1	5.5	6.0	3.6
48 (1992)	2.1	2.7	0.9	5.7	6.2	3.6

Source: NSSO.

Table—4.18 Non-farm Female Workers as a Percentage of Rural Workforce: Census 1971-91

State	Census		
	1971	1981	1991
Andhra Pradesh	12.96	12.27	12.20
Bihar	6.10	7.66	6.80
Gujarat	7.24	11.42	14.60
Haryana	23.06	14.89	13.70
Himachal Pradesh	5.12	5.91	7.60
Karnataka	19.17	16.60	14.80
Kerala	41.17	46.09	51.50
Madhya Pradesh	6.05	7.32	6.00
Maharashtra	5.94	6.70	6.50
Orissa	23.02	16.53	14.70
Punjab	67.15	17.69	37.90
Rajasthan	9.95	11.27	6.40
Tamil Nadu	15.47	13.43	15.50
Uttar Pradesh	7.86	9.55	10.40
West Bengal	30.56	33.46	34.30
All India	**12.96**	**12.73**	**13.10**

Source: Different Censuses of India.

Table—4.19 Rural Population and Agricultural Workers

(Millions)

Year	Rural Population	Rural Workers			
		Cultivators	Agricultural	Others	Total
1951	298.6	69.9 (49.9)	27.3 (19.5)	42.8 (30.6)	140.0
1961	360.3	99.6 (52.8)	31.5 (16.7)	57.6 (30.5)	188.7
1971	439.1	78.3 (43.4)	47.5 (26.3)	54.7 (30.3)	180.5
1981	525.5	92.5 (37.8)	55.5 (22.7)	96.6 (39.5)	244.6
1991	627.1	110.6 (38.8)	74.6 (26.1)	100.2 (35.1)	285.4

Figures in parenthesis shows percentage to total rural population.

Source: Different Censuses of India.

Table—4.20 Population by Category of Workers during 1991

(Millions)

Category of workers	Population		
	Rural	Urban	Total
Total workers	249.3	65.6	314.9
Marginal workers	27.7	1.7	29.5
Main workers	221.6	63.8	285.4
Cultivators	107.4	3.2	110.6
Agricultural labourers	70.4	4.2	74.6
Household industry workers	6.8	3.6	10.4
Other workers	37.0	52.8	89.8

Source: Census of India (1991).

Table—4.21 Distribution of Female Workers by Industrial Category

(Percentage)

Category	Years		
	1971	1981	1991
Cultivators	29.84	33.20	34.57
Agricultural labour	50.86	46.18	44.23
Livestock, forestry & fishing	1.91	1.85	2.07
Mining and quarrying	0.40	0.36	0.33
Manufacturing, processing, service, repairs, household	4.24	4.59	3.51
Other than household	2.77	3.55	3.81
Construction	0.65	0.80	0.65
Trade and Commerce	1.78	2.04	2.24
Transport, storage and communication	0.47	0.38	0.32
Other services	7.08	7.05	8.27

Source: Different Censuses of India.

Table—4.22 Structural Change in Indian Rural Workforce

Sector	Rural Labour Force			
	Male		Female	
	1972-73	1987-88	1972-73	1987-88
Agriculture	83.2	74.5	89.7	84.7
Industry and Mining	6.5	8.4	4.9	7.3
Services, Trade Transport and Construction	10.3	17.1	5.4	8.0
Total	100.0	100.0	100.0	100.0

Source: NSSO (1990).

Table—4.23 Industrial Distribution of the Rural Workforce by States of India during 1987-88

States	% distribution of workforce					
	Rural				Urban	
	Agriculture		Manufacturing		Manufacturing	
	Male	Female	Male	Female	Male	Female
All India	73.9	82.5	7.6	7.5	26.0	26.7
Tripura	43.7	48.6	5.5	11.5	6.1	1.8
Kerala	52.2	53.7	10.7	23.7	20.7	20.3
J & K	61.0	83.5	9.2	9.4	24.0	38.0
Tamil Nadu	64.7	74.9	13.7	14.1	31.1	41.2
Rajasthan	64.9	83.0	7.9	4.0	19.5	18.0
H.P.	66.4	96.0	7.2	1.8	11.6	7.7
Gujarat	67.7	72.1	9.5	3.6	33.4	22.1
Punjab	68.1	74.4	9.8	5.5	29.8	14.0
Manipur	68.4	78.5	3.2	10.1	7.8	17.6
Haryana	69.8	88.6	8.7	2.6	30.9	19.8
W.B.	70.8	56.7	9.6	27.3	32.8	25.1
Sikkim	73.5	85.7	1.8	0.4	4.4	2.8
A.P.	73.9	80.7	7.9	8.1	20.0	28.3
Orissa	74.4	74.1	6.3	13.4	15.8	24.3
Maharashtra	75.1	90.7	7.4	2.8	29.4	21.6
Assam	75.2	77.2	2.1	4.5	9.3	5.8
U.P.	78.4	90.5	7.3	3.9	23.0	22.6
Karnataka	79.3	83.9	6.3	9.6	24.6	30.5
Bihar	79.6	89.3	5.0	3.9	21.2	21.8
M.P.	85.1	90.5	4.9	5.2	21.7	21.5

Table—4.24 Distribution of Persons Normally Employed by Rural Industry Section (1987-88)

(per 1000)

Males/Females	Agriculture	Manufacturing	Services	Others
Rural Males	739	76	64	121
Rural Females	825	75	37	63

Source: Sarvekshana (September 1990).

Table—4.25 Income Distribution of Persons/days Worked by Rural Males in 1987-88

(% of total persons/days)

Sl. No.	Sector	Consumption levels per capita worked per month	
		Below poverty level consumption classes (Rs. 125)	Above poverty level consumption classes (Rs. 125)
1.	Workers in agricultural sector	17.28 to 22.9	24.5 to 27.9
2.	Workers in Non-agricultural sector	3.5 to 6.1	6.9 to 8.6

Source: NSSO.

Table—4.26 Literacy Rate Among Males and Females in India

(Percentage)

Year	Male literacy	Female literacy	Total literacy
1901	9.83	0.60	5.35
1911	10.56	1.05	5.92
1921	12.27	1.83	7.16
1931	15.59	2.93	9.50
1941	24.90	7.30	16.10
1951	24.90	7.93	16.69
1961	24.44	12.95	24.02
1971	39.44	18.69	29.45
1981	46.89	24.82	43.56
1991	64.13	39.29	52.21
2001	75.85	54.16	65.38

Source: Different Censuses of India.

Table—4.27 Literacy Rate Among Males and Females in Different States of India

(Percentage)

State/ Union Territories	Male literacy	Female literacy	Total literacy
State			
Kerala	94.20	87.86	90.92
Mezoram	90.69	86.13	88.49
Goa	88.88	75.51	82.32
Maharashtra	86.27	67.51	77.27
Himachal Pradesh	86.02	68.08	77.13
Tripura	81.47	65.41	73.66
Tamil Nadu	82.33	64.55	73.47
Uttaranchal	84.01	60.26	72.28
Gujarat	80.50	56.60	69.97
Punjab	75.63	63.55	69.95
Sikkim	76.68	61.46	69.68
West Bengal	77.58	60.22	69.22
Manipur	77.87	59.70	68.87
Haryana	79.25	56.31	68.59
Nagaland	71.77	61.92	67.11
Karnataka	76.29	57.45	67.04
Chhatisgarh	77.86	52.40	65.18
Assam	71.93	56.03	64.28
Madhya Pradesh	76.80	50.28	64.11
Orissa	75.95	50.97	63.61
Meghalaya	66.14	60.41	63.41
Andhra Pradesh	70.85	51.17	61.11
Rajasthan	76.46	44.34	61.03
Uttar Pradesh	70.23	42.98	57.36
Arunachal Pradesh	64.07	44.24	54.74
Jammu & Kashmir	65.75	41.82	54.46
Jharkhand	67.94	39.36	54.13
Bihar	60.32	33.57	47.53
Union Territories			
Lakshadweep	93.15	81.56	87.52
Delhi	87.37	75.00	81.82
Chandigarh	85.65	76.65	81.76
Pondicherry	88.89	74.13	81.49
Andaman & Nicobar Islands	86.07	75.29	81.18
Daman and Diu	88.40	70.37	81.09
Dadar and Nagar Haveli	73.32	42.99	60.03

Source: Census of India (2001).

5

Factors Influencing the Participation of Females in RNFE

*K.Srinivasa Rao

1. Introduction

Women in general spend a lot of time performing domestic chores and this is more so in the case of rural women. Considerable part of their time is spent in fetching water, collecting fuel, cooking, laundering, attending to children, rearing cattle etc. Therefore not much time is left to women in the so called productive work. However we notice that rural women participate in productive activities. The data at the all India level show that the percentage of female workers in total rural labour force is 36.43 per cent according to 1987-88 NSS and 27.20 per cent according to 1991 census. Among the females participating in work in rural areas 15.3 per cent are engaged in non-agricultural work as per the 43rd round of NSS (1987-88). According to the census 1991 the females in rural non-agricultural work form 13.1 per cent of total female rural workers. Though the census data does not suggest any

* Senior Research Officer, IAMR, Planning Commission, Govt. of India, New Delhi.

significant increase in the proportion of female workers employed in non-agricultural activities, the NSS data show a substantial rise in the ratio from 10.3 per cent in 1972-73 to 15.3 per cent in 1987-88. In the state of Andhra Pradesh where the survey villages are located the percentage of female non-agricultural workers among the rural female workers constitutes 17.9 per cent in 1987-88 (NSS) and 12.2 per cent in 1991 (Census). Later on we will note whether the proportion of rural female non-agricultural workers is higher in the survey villages or not.

Our concern in this paper is not so much to comment on the level and the changing level of participation of females in rural non-agricultural work, but to analyse the factors that influence the participation of females in RNFE. This is done with the help of the village survey data of two villages in the Godavari delta region of Andhra Pradesh. The primary data that we are working with facilities a study of these factors. The specific objective of this paper is one of identify the type of non-agricultural activities that are pursued by female workers and two to identify the factors facilitating the participation of females in RNFE.

2. Female Participation in Rural Non-Agricultural Activities

As noted already the non-agricultural activities provide sizeable employment in the survey villages both males and females. As may be seen from Table 5.1 the female headed households participating in non-agricultural activities are very low. Only 5.05 per cent of all households constitute females. However among other workers females out number males in non-agricultural activities. 59.40 per cent of all other workers are females. Taking heads and other workers together we notice that the males engaged in the non-agricultural activities comprise 64.35 per cent of all workers and females engaged in non-farm work constitute 35.65 per cent among all workers. Therefore the participation of females in non-farm work is lower than males. However, the female participation in the study villages at 35.65 per cent is higher than the national average of 22.35 per cent.

Table—5.1 Distribution of Heads and other Workers in Non-agricultural Activities by Sex

Heads	Male	Female	Total
Heads	639	34	673
	(94.94)	(5.05)	(100.00)
Other workers	352	515	867
	(40.60)	(59.40)	(100.00)
Total	991	549	1540
	(64.35)	(35.65)	(100.00)

Those participating in non-agricultural work pursue both traditional and non-traditional activities. The composition of these activities will be noted later in this paper. For the present we note that non-traditional activities provide employment to a lower percentage of non-agricultural workers than traditional activities. Of the total number of 673 workers 60.77 per cent are engaged in traditional activities. Whereas 39.23 per cent are engaged in non-traditional activities. It is important to note that females participation in non-traditional, non-agricultural work is rather low. Only 8.82 per cent of female heads are reported to be participating in non-traditional non-agricultural work. While the rest i.e., 91.18 per cent are participating in traditional work. In contrast to this the rate of males participating in non-traditional activities is quite high i.e., 40.84 per cent. Two views may be put forward based on the low participation of females in non-traditional work. One, since their participation rate in this work is very low it is possible to absorb more females into this sector, and two, since the participation rate of females in this sector is low, there are no great prospects for females to great absorbed in this non-traditional sector. Probably non-traditional sector in the non-agricultural sphere requires greater skills which the females do not possess under the present socio-economic setting, acquiring skills is beyond the reach of the females.

Table—5.2 (A) Heads of Households Participating in Non-agricultural Activity Classified by the Nature (Traditional/Non-Traditional) of Activity

Sex	Traditional	Non-traditional	Total
Male	378	261	639
	(59.15)	(40.84)	(100.00)
Female	31	3	34
	(94.18)	(8.82)	(100.00)
Total	409	264	673
	(60.77)	(39.23)	(100.00)

We considered the classification of males and females other than heads participating in non-agricultural work, and we classified them by nature of activity.

We notice from Table 5.2 (B) that female participation in the non-traditional sector is again lower than that of males. Of the total females participation in non-agricultural activity 27.57 per cent are engaged in the non-traditional work. Whereas the remaining 72.43 per cent are engaged in the traditional work. In the case of males those engaged in the non-traditional work comprises 58.81 per cent of all workers participating in non-agricultural work. So the general conclusion stands, i.e., female participation in non-traditional non-agricultural activities is lower than that of males. Since it is only the non-traditional activity which may prosper in future the females must be equipped to absorb into this sector.

It is possible to further classify non-traditional activities of the non-agricultural sector. These may be classified into activities which are related to agriculture sector and the activities which are not related to the agricultural sector.

Table—5.2 (B) Other Workers Participating in Non-agricultural Activity Classified by the Nature (Traditional/ Non-traditional) of Activity

Sex	Traditional	Non-traditional	Total
Male	145 (41.19)	207 (58.81)	352 (100.00)
Female	373 (72.43)	142 (27.57)	515 (100.00)
Total	518 (59.75)	349 (40.25)	867 (100.00)

As may be seen from the panel A of Table 5.3 the non-agricultural activities that are not related to agricultural employ 94.45 per cent of all non-traditional workers. Only 5.55 per cent of these workers are employed in the activities related to agriculture. Between males and females we do not find much of a difference as regards the participation in activities that are not related to agriculture. Of the total male workers in the non-traditional non-agricultural activities 93.38 per cent are engaged in activities not related to agriculture. In the case of females 97.73 per cent are engaged in non-traditional activities that are not related to agriculture.

3. Characteristics of Non-agricultural Workers Engaged in Non-traditional Activities

It is possible that those participating in non-traditional activities possess certain special characteristics. It may be that the caste base, land base, and education of these people may be occupation specific. We will examine below whether it is in deed so.

Panel B in Table 5.3 provides details on the caste wise classification of workers engaged in non-traditional occupations separately for activities related to agriculture, and the activities not related to agriculture. Considering the activities related to agriculture we notice that 61.29 per cent of males belong to forward caste, 35.48 per cent to backward caste B group, and 3.22 per cent

Table—5.3 Characteristics of Non-traditional Workers

	A				A.R	B			A.N.R		C			
Sex	**A.R**	**A.N.R**	**Total**	**FC**	**BCB**	**SC**	**Total**	**FC**	**BCA**	**BCB**	**BCC**	**BCD**	**SC**	**Total**
Male	31 (6.62)	437 (93.38)	468 (100.00)	19 (61.29)	11 (35.48)	1 (3.22)	31 (100.00)	168 (38.44)	20 (4.58)	159 (36.38)	7 (1.60)	–	79 (18.08)	437 (100.00)
Female	3 (2.06)	142 (97.73)	145 (100.00)	3 (100.00)	–	–	3 (100.00)	69 (48.59)	10 (7.04)	29 (20.42)	6 (4.22)	1 (0.07)	27 (19.01)	142 (100.00)
Total	34 (5.55)	579 (94.45)	613 (100.00)	25 (75.53)	11 (32.35)	1 (2.94).	34 (100.00)	237 (40.93)	30 (5.18)	188 (32.46)	13 (2.24)	1 (0.001)	106 (18.31)	579 (100.00)

			Land	D					Education		E
Sex	**L.L**	**S & M**	**Total**	**L.L**	**S & M**	**M**	**L**	**Total**	**A.R**	**A.N.R**	**Total**
Male	24 (77.42)	7 (22.58)	31 (100.00)	355 (81.23)	74 (16.93)	5 (1.14)	3 (0.006)	437 (100.00)	20 (5.86)	321 (94.13)	341 (100.00)
Female	2 (66.66)	1 (33.33)	3 (100.00)	120 (84.51)	22 (15.49)	–	–	142 (100.00)	2 (1.98)	99 (98.02)	101 (100.00)
Total	26 (76.48)	8 (23.53)	34 (100.00)	475 (82.03)	96 (16.58)	5 (0.008)	3 (0.005)	579 (100.00)	22 (4.98)	420 (95.02)	442 (100.00)

to scheduled caste and scheduled tribes. The 3 males who are engaged in these agriculture related activities belong to the forward castes. Generally speaking 73.53 per cent of all workers engaged in agriculture related activities are from forward castes. Among the workers engaged in non-traditional non-agricultural activities 40.93 per cent belong to forward castes and 32.46 per cent belong to backward caste B group. Among the females 48.59 per cent are engaged in these non-traditional non-agricultural occupations. The corresponding figure for men is 38.44 per cent. Thus females of forward castes seem to be participating actively in these activities.

The land base of these non-traditional non-agricultural workers may differ as between agriculture related and agriculture not related activities as may be seen from panel D of Table 5.3. In the case of activities related to agriculture 76.48 per cent are landless. The figures for males and females respectively are 77.42 per cent and 66.66 per cent. Thus these activities are predominant among the landless. Even in respect of activities not related to agriculture land less people predominate. They constitute 82.03 per cent of all workers who are engaged in non-traditional non-agricultural activities that have no relation with the agriculture sector. Male workers in this category belong predominantly to landless (81.23 per cent). Even females constitute a large proportion (84.51 per cent). The main conclusion that emerges from panel D of the Table 5.3 is that the non-traditional activities in the non-agricultural sector are generally pursued by landless and to some extent by the small and marginal farmers. Medium and large farmers rarely participate in these activities.

Panel E of Table 5.3 provides details in the educational status of those engaged in non-traditional non-agricultural activities by the nature of activity. It is interesting to notice that 95.02 per cent of workers employed in the non-traditional non-agricultural sector are found in activities that are not related to agriculture. Only 4.98 per cent are in agriculture related activities. There is not much of a difference between males and females in this respect. So one important characteristic that is necessary for securing employment in non-traditional non-agricultural activities that are not related agriculture is education.

We have provided a detailed activity-wise classification of non-traditional non-agricultural activities that are (a) related to agriculture and (b) not related to agriculture in Appendix Table 5.1 and 5.2.

As may be notice from the table Appendix-5.I the non-traditional non-agricultural activities that are related to agriculture and providing employment to the village workers are tobacco shops, vegetable vending, fair price shops, rice business and rented cart which is used mainly for transport of agriculture commodities such as coconuts and paddy. Even at this disagreegated level we notice that forward caste people predominate in the activities that are listed above. Further they are mainly landless and have educated above 5th standard.

Appendix Table 5.2 provides activity wise details for workers engaged in non-traditional non-agricultural activities that are not related to the agricultural sector. The most important among these agriculture not related activities are (1) employment in government services, (2) petty business and (3) tailoring and (4) lace and sewing. A large number of male workers are employed in the first 3 activities. Whereas in the 4th activity females predominate. Caste wise classification shows that among the 142 male workers serving in the government, 49 workers are of forward caste and 55 workers of backward caste B group and scheduled caste and scheduled tribe number is 31. The female workers serving in the government number is 24 and 14 of them are scheduled caste and scheduled tribe. And the rest are distributed among other castes. Landless workers predominate in this activity and most people have education above 5th standard. Petty business is again the mainstay of the forward castes. 51 of the 83 male workers engaged in this business belong to forward castes. In case of females 8 out of 16 belong to forward castes. The land base of those engaged in the petty business is almost nil. And they have education above 5th standard.

Tailoring and lace and sewing are very important activities in the villages. Female participate very actively in lace and sewing and tailoring. They belong to backward caste B group and forward caste. And have no land base of significance, but have education above 5th standard.

Disaggregated data presented in Appendix-5.I and Appendix-5.II show that the non-traditional non-agricultural occupations are highly diversified. It is no doubt true, it is only a few activities account for majority of the workers, but all the same those are many activities which are found in the villages. There are 13 agricultural related activities and 39 agricultural not related activities.

Earnings in Traditional and Non-traditional Activities

Average daily earnings of male and female by occupation are shown in Table-5.4. These details relate to the earnings of workers in both traditional and non-traditional occupations by sex. The earnings are arrived at each occupation and averaged for males and females. There are occupations like weaving and petty trade where both the male and female participate in work. In such cases it is difficult to distinguish between the earnings of the male and female members. Therefore while calculating the average daily wage received by female workers we considered only those females who are performing to non-agriculture activity on their own without the assistance of male members. We have put together the average daily wage received by male workers and female workers by occupation. There is a problem in putting this data together because in many instances male workers are helped by female members of the family in undertaking work. In cases where females assist males in their work, the wages earned by the males need to be treated as those received for the labour of both males and females. In as much as this is true, it is very difficult to the actual wage received by the male members. This is particularly true in weaving where the female members, not to speak of children actively assist in the weaving activity of males. But even here it is quite likely that they are helped by children. Among the males the earnings of those received by employees is the highest at an average of 50 rupees per day. In the case of females also employees are receiving the highest earnings at 44.47 rupees. Next to employment the earnings in Kirana business are the highest both in case of males and females. Males earn 33.50 rupees, females secure 30.83 rupees per day. Both these activities fall in the category of non-traditional occupation. Which are not related to agriculture. Tailoring is another non-traditional occupation which is not related to agriculture which fetches substantial earnings males engaged in tailoring earn 25 rupees per day. Whereas females earn 21 rupees.

Table—5.4 Average Daily Earnings Received by Males and Females by Occupation (Rs)

	Traditional						Non-traditional					Agriculture	
Sex/ Occupation	1	5	7	8	9	10	2	3	4	6	11	12	13
Male	22.50	–	25.00	15.00	20.00	15.00	25.00	33.50	5.00	50.00	30.00	25.00	20.00
Female	17.44	12.75	15.29	10.00	-	13.50	21.00	30.83	14.64	44.57	23.33	20.00	17.54

Legend: Traditional Non-agriculture: 1 = weaving; 5 = cooking and cleaning; 7 = coconut and cashew nut workers; 8 = basket making; 9 = goldsmiths; 10 = washerman.

Non-traditional Non-agriculture: 2 = tailoring; 3 = kirana; 4 = lace and sewing; 6 = teachers, and doctors etc.; 11 = other non-agricultural workers; 12 = fishermen; 13 = agricultural labourers.

Weaving is a traditional activity and is the mainstay of many workers. Males engaged in this activity earn 22.50 rupees whereas females earn 17.44 rupees, cashew nut and coconut activity is another important activity which secures reasonable incomes to both males and females. The males in this activity have an average daily earnings of 25 rupees and females 15.29 rupees.

Notwithstanding these limitations in assessing the wages of males (and even females), we have obtained and put together the data on wages. The intuitive belief is that females participate in inferior and less paying work gets support from a couple of occupations like sewing, females earn much less than males.

Changes in the Relative Significance of Traditional and Non-traditional Non-agricultural Activities Related to Sex

Traditional occupations may decay in course of development for instance handloom weaving which is pursued in this region may have suffered a sét back overtime because of the fact that the handloom cloth produced in this sector is treated as an inferior good as the levels of income of people increases. Conditions therefore are not favourable for the growth of employment in this sector. Competition from the mill sector also is responsible for the decay of the handloom sector in many places. It is with this background we try to examine whether the significance of traditional and non-traditional activities are undergoing change. We examine change by comparing the significance of non-traditional at two points of time i.e., 1981 and 1991. Data pertaining to 1981 are collected based on the recall method. Data presented in Table 5.5 show that 24.50 per cent of all non-agricultural workers are engaged in non-traditional activities. In the case of males this percentage is slightly higher at 29.21 per cent and lower for females at 15.64 per cent. This situation in 1991 is quite different from that 1981. In 1991 the ratio of non-agricultural workers engaged in non-traditional activities amounts to 54.55 per cent. This is much higher than the corresponding figure (24.50 per cent) of 1981. Both males and females reported a higher percentage of non-agricultural workers in non-traditional activity during the year 1991. There is an unquestionable increase in the significance of non-traditional activities among the non-agricultural activity.

Data presented in Table-5.5 is shown slightly different in Table-5.6 to sharply bring out the male, female differences. In 1981 38.77 per cent of females were engaged in the traditional activities and this percentage increased to 51.26 per cent in 1991, i.e., the relative significance of females in traditional non-agricultural activities increased between 1981 and 1991. In the case of non-traditional non-agricultural occupations, females constitute at 22.16 per cent in 1981, whereas in 1991 their proportion increased to 245.30 per cent. In other works the relative significance of females in non-traditional activities did not show much change.

We have attempted X^2 test of significance in order to study whether there is any association between traditional and non-traditional occupations in the matter of sex. This test is conducted for two points of time i.e. 1981 and 1991.

Table—5.5 Changes in the Non-agricultural Occupations Over the Period by Sex

Sex	1981 Traditional	1981 Non-traditional	1981 Total	1991 Traditional	1991 Non-traditional	1991 Total
Male	349 (70.79)	144 (29.21)	493 (100.00)	174 (34.94)	324 (65.06)	498 (100.00)
Female	221 (84.35)	41 (15.64)	262 (100.00)	183 (63.76)	104 (36.24)	287 (100.00)
Total	570 (75.49)	185 (24.50)	755 (100.00)	357 (45.48)	428 (54.55)	785 (100.00)

Table—5.6 Changes in the Relative Significance of Traditional and Non-traditional Non-agricultural Activities Related to Sex

Sex	Traditional 1981	Traditional 1991	Non-traditional 1981	Non-traditional 1991
Male	349 (61.23)	174 (48.73)	144 (77.84)	324 (75.70)
Female	221 (38.77)	183 (51.26)	41 (22.16)	104 (24.30)
Total	570 (100.00)	357 (100.00)	185 (100.00)	428 (100.00)

Calculated value of X^2 for 1981 is 2.97 and it is lower than table value of 3.84 at 5 per cent level of significance. Therefore the hypothesis that nature of occupation is related to sex is not valid. The same test is conducted with 1991 data. And if yields 14.01 as the value of X^2 and it is statistically significant at 5 per cent level. Therefore we accept the hypothesis that there is an association between the nature of occupation and sex.

4. Factors Influencing Female Participation in RNFE

A priori one may say that rural females participate in work generally under distress conditions. For instance, when the land base of the household is small, females may be forced to seek employment outside the farm. We may therefore expect a negative relationship between the proportion of female non-agricultural workers in a family and the size of operated land per worker in the family.

Caste of the household is another factor which may influence the participation of females in work in general and non-agricultural activities in particular. Females of socially forward castes may refrain from working on the farm or outside. So if caste is defined as a dummy variable, taking values 1 or 0 depending on whether a family belongs to a forward caste or otherwise, it will have negative relationship with the ratio of females in the non-agricultural workers of the family.

Occupation	Sex	1981 O	E	O-E	(O-E) 2	1991 O	E	O-E	(O-E) 2
Traditional	Male	349	372	23	529	174	227	53	2809
Traditional	Female	221	197	24	576	183	131	52	2704
Non-trad.	Male	144	120	24	576	324	272	52	2704
Non-trad.	Female	41	64	23	529	104	157	53	2809
	Total		753		2210		787		11026

$$X^2 = \frac{(O\text{-}E)2}{E} \qquad 1981 = \frac{2210}{753} = 2.93; \qquad 1991 = \frac{11026}{787} = 14.01$$

The worker-dependent ratio is another factor that may influence female participation in RNFE. Households with more dependants relative to workers will tend to participate actively in RNA work. The dire need to maintain the family drives the females into taking up some work. We therefore except a negative relationship between the worker-dependent ratio and the ratio of females in the non-agricultural workers of the family.

Yet another factor influencing the participation of females in RNA work is the level of education of females. Education in general facilitates females to take up non-agricultural work. Education increases the awareness of the females as regard, the work opportunities outside agriculture and there by induces them to pursue such activities for a livelihood. However, those with education of the marginal kind, let us say, with education of 5th standard and below may not really facilitate female participation in RNA work. It is only when females receive education, above, for instance, 5th standard, it may favourably influence female participation in RNF activities. One therefore excepts a positive relationship between the ratio of females workers with education above 5th standard, to total number of female workers in the family and the ratio of females in the non-agricultural workers of the household.

5. Regression Results

Based on the above understanding we have tried to identify the factors that may influence female participation in RNF activities employing the household level data. In the process we have employed a multiple linear regression model. The independent variables in the regression exercise are (1) the size of the operated land per worker in the household, (2) Caste (as defined by a dummy variable which takes values 1 or zero depending on whether a household belongs to a forward caste or otherwise), (3) worker-dependent ratio in the family, and (4) the ratio of female workers with education above 5th in the household to total number of female workers. The dependent variable in the regression is the proportion of female non-agricultural workers in the family. The causal relationship between the dependent variable and the independent variables is already established. The results of the regression exercise are presented in Table 5.7. As may be noted from the table, the number of observations in the regression is 1801.

It may be noted from the table that the independent variable farm size per worker has the expected negative sign and statistically significant. The smaller the availability of land per worker the larger is the ratio of female workers participating in RNA activities.

The caste variable also has the expected negative sign. It is also significant statistically. This result indicates that females workers of forward castes generally refrain from entering into RNA activities.

Table—5.7 Regression Results of Factors Determining the Level of Female Rural Non-farm Employment

Definition of dependent variable	Operated land per worker	Caste	Worker dependent ratio	Ratio of female workers with above 5th class	R2	F-Value
Proportion of Female Non-agrl. workers in the family	-0.0341* (4.46)	-0.1659* (7.89)	0.6901* (17.27)	0.3001* (11.76)	0.2978	190.46

* Indicates 1 per cent significance level.

Figures in parenthesis indicate 't' values.

Next, we have the worker-dependent ratio as another independent variable. In this case, contrary to expectation, the regression coefficient has turned out with a positive sign. The more the workers relative to dependents, the greater is the proportion of female workers in RNA activities. In expecting a negative sign to this regression coefficient we implicitly assumed that only under distress conditions, such as when there are few workers relative to dependents, will the proportion of female workers in RNA activities will be high. In other words we expected that female workers take up non-agricultural work under distress conditions. But this point of view is not validated by our empirical evidence. The evidence presented in the table shows that a higher worker-dependent ratio is accompanied by a higher ratio of female workers in RNA activities. The emergence of demand led non-traditional occupations in the 1980s gave an opportunity for entry of women into RNFE. In the put out system practice in such non-traditional occupations such as lace making, beedi making, etc. women are preferred. This explains the higher rate of growth of female in the RNFE.

The last of the four variables employed in the regression in the ratio of females with education above 5th standard to total female workers. It has the expected positive sign. Education of females throws open their employment in RNA activities.

It is to be noted here that the explanatory power of the regression model is about 30 per cent. All the four factors viz., farm size per worker, caste, worker-dependent ratio, and education, included in the regression model have turned out to be statistically significant in influencing the participation rate of females in RNA activities.

6. Summary

The data at the national level show that the percentage of female workers is 36.43 per cent in 1987-88 according to the NSS. Among the females participating in work 15.30 per cent are engaged in rural non-agricultural activities. This is an improvement over 1972-73 when only 10.3 per cent of the female workers are engaged in rural non-agricultural activities. With the help of primary data we try to examine the factors that influence the participation of females in RNFE.

Non-agricultural activities provide sizeable employment in the survey villages. Females engaged in the non-farm work constitute 35.65 per cent among all workers. The participation of females in non-farm work is lower than that of males. However, the participation rates of females in study villages is higher than the national average of 22.35 per cent. Females participate both in the traditional and non-traditional forms of non-agricultural work. But their participation in non-traditional non-agricultural work is rather low. Only 8.82 per cent of female heads and 27.57 per cent of other female workers are engaged in non-traditional non-agricultural work. These participation rates of females are lower than the general participation rate of females in non-agricultural work. Two views may be put forward based on the low participation of females in non-traditional work. One, since their participation rate in this work is very low it is possible to absorb more females into this sector, and two, since the participation rate of females in this sector is low, there are no great prospects for females to great absorbed in this non-traditional sectors. Probably non-traditional sector in the non-agricultural sphere requires greater skills which the females do not possess under the present socio-economic setting, acquiring skills is beyond the reach of the females.

We can readily think of 3 factors which may influence the participation rates of workers engaged in non-traditional non-agricultural activities. These are caste, land and education. Non-traditional non-agricultural activities are further divided into agriculture related activities and agriculture not related activities. Females of forward castes seem to be participating actively in these non-traditional non-agricultural occupations which are not related to agriculture. Considering land base of the workers in non-traditional activities that are not related to agriculture. We notice that, these activities are generally pursued by the landless and to some extent by the small and marginal farmers. Medium and large farmers are rarely participate in these activities. Our analysis has revealed that one important characteristic that is necessary for securing employment in non-traditional non-agricultural activities that are not related to agriculture is education. Education above 5th standard seems to be a prerequisite for an entry into this segment of non-agricultural sector.

We try to examine the earnings of workers in traditional and non-traditional activities. Estimating, the earnings were not easy, because males and females and even children help each other in securing wages. Nevertheless, we put together some data of males and females. Weavers constitute an important force among the workers. Males engaged in weaving earn 22.50 rupees. Whereas females earn 17.44 rupees. Thus, females earn less than males per day on an average. Even in other activities the earnings of females are much lower than those of males. Thus the belief, that females participate in inferior and less paying work gets support from our data.

Over time we notice that there is an unquestionable increase in the significance of non-traditional activities in the non-agriculture. This is evident from our data relating to 1981 and 1991. In 1981 there does not seem to be any barrier to the entry of females into this non-traditional non-agricultural sector. But as the sector expanded it has become more and more confined to males. This may be one reason why X^2 test of significance conducted to find out the association between the nature of occupation and sex has turned out to be significant at 5 per cent level in 1991. That is there is an association between the nature of work and sex of the workers.

We attempted a regression analysis to identify the factors influencing participation of females in RNFE. The independent variables chosen to explain the variations in the dependent variable are caste, worker dependent ratio, education above 5th standard and land. The dependent variable is the proportion of female non-agriculture workers in the family. Caste variable has turned out to be negative and significant as expected i.e., female workers of forward caste generally avoid taking up non-agricultural activities. Worker dependent ratio is associated with a positive coefficient. This has a wrong sign. Farm size per worker has to expected negative sign. And finally an education has expected positive sign. The explanatory power of the regression model is about 30 per cent.

The above analysis reveals that entry to females is generally restricted to females in the non-traditional sector. It is the females of those who possess some basic education who seem to be preferred in non-traditional non-agricultural occupations. One need not possess any land and need not belong to any forward caste to gain entry into the non-agricultural sector. What seems important is education. Some basic education has to be important to those seeking employment in the non-agricultural sector.

Appendix—I Workers Engaged in Non-traditional Non-agricultural Activities Related to Agriculture by Sex, Caste, Land held and Education

S. No.	Name of the activity	Participation			Caste						Land								Education		
		Male	Female	Total	Male				Female		Male				Female			Grand total	Male	Female	Total
					FC	BCB	SC	Total	FC	T	g.t	1.1	s & m		Total	1.1	s & m		Total		
1.	Tobacco shops	3	1	4	3	–	–	3	1	1	4	2	1	3	1	–	1	4	2	1	3
2.	Veg. vending	5	1	6	3	2	–	5	1	1	6	2	3	5	1	–	1	6	3	1	4
3.	Fair price shops	3	–	3	1	1	1	3	–	–	3	2	1	3	–	–	–	3	3	–	3
4.	Rice business	3	–	3	2	1	–	3	–	–	3	2	1	3	–	–	–	3	1	–	1
5.	Oil business	1	–	1	–	1	–	1	–	–	1	1	–	1	–	–	–	1	1	–	1
6.	Prawn business	1	–	1	–	1	–	1	–	–	1	1	–	1	–	–	–	1	1	–	1
7.	Timber merchant	1	–	1	1	–	–	1	–	–	1	1	–	1	–	–	–	1	1	–	1
8.	Fertilizer business	1	–	1	–	1	–	1	–	–	1	1	–	1	–	–	–	1	1	–	1
9.	Flower business	1	–	1	–	1	–	1	–	–	1	1	–	1	–	–	–	1	1	–	1
10.	Banana business	1	–	1	1	–	–	1	–	–	1	1	–	1	–	–	–	1	1	–	1
11.	Eggs business	1	–	1	–	1	–	1	–	–	1	1	–	1	–	–	–	1	1	–	1
12.	Rent cart	7	–	7	6	1	–	7	–	–	7	6	1	7	–	–	–	7	2	–	2
13.	Mill workers	4	–	4	3	1	–	4	–	–	4	4	–	4	–	–	–	4	2	–	2
	Total	32	2	34	20	11	1	32	2	2	34	25	7	32	2	–	2	34	20	2	22

Appendix—II Workers Engaged in Non-traditional Non-agricultural Activities Related to Agriculture by Sex, Caste, Land, Held and Education

S. No.	Name of the activity	Land									Education		
		Male					Female						
		L.L	S & M	M	L	T	L.L	S & M	T	G.T	Male	Female	Total
1.	Teachers, doctors and govt. servants	118	16	5	3	142	24	–	24	166	142	24	166
2.	Petty business	77	6	–	–	83	16	–	16	99	57	10	67
3.	Tea shop & hotel	4	–	–	–	4	15	6	21	25	–	7	7
4.	Biscuit business	3	–	–	–	3	1	–	1	4	2	–	2
5.	Kirana	3	1	–	–	4	22	–	22	26	3	14	17
6.	Book shop	–	1	–	–	1	–	–	–	1	1	–	1
7.	Wine shop	2	–	–	–	2	–	–	–	2	2	–	2
8.	Cycle shop	9	2	–	–	11	–	–	–	11	8	–	8
9.	Chit fund business	1	1	–	–	2	–	–	–	2	2	–	2
10.	Sweet stall	1	–	–	–	1	–	–	–	1	1	–	1
11.	Medical shop	2	–	–	–	2	–	–	–	2	2	–	2
12.	Ration shop clerks	3	–	–	–	3	–	–	–	3	3	–	3
13.	Metal shop	1	–	–	–	1	–	–	–	1	1	–	1
14.	Fancy shop	3	1	–	–	4	–	–	–	4	2	–	2
15.	Retail shop	1	–	–	–	1	–	–	–	1	1	–	1
16.	Cloth business	2	2	–	–	4	–	–	–	4	4	–	4
17.	Cement business	1	–	–	–	1	–	–	–	1	1	–	1
18.	Iron foundry	1	–	–	–	1	–	–	–	1	1	–	1
19.	Tailoring	18	30	–	–	48	13	3	16	64	42	13	55
20.	Hotel workers	11	–	–	–	11	–	–	–	11	7	–	7
21.	Cinema hall work	5	1	–	–	6	–	–	–	6	4	–	4
22.	Road workers	2	1	–	–	3	–	–	–	3	3	–	3
23.	Cycle shop workers	14	1	–	–	15	–	–	–	15	5	–	5
24.	Biscuit selling	3	–	–	–	3	–	–	–	3	1	–	1

(Table Contd...)

25. Arackshop clerk	1	–	–	–	1	–	–	–	1	1	–	1
26. Painting	4	1	–	–	5	–	–	–	5	1	–	1
27. Lorry workers	2	–	–	–	2	–	–	–	2	1	–	1
28. Moneylending agent	2	1	–	–	3	–	–	–	3	2	–	2
29. Paper agent	–	1	–	–	1	–	–	–	1	1	–	1
30. Health village ser.	1	1	–	–	2	–	–	–	2	1	–	1
31. Kirana shop worker	13	–	–	–	13	–	–	–	13	2	–	2
32. Chit fund employee	5	–	–	–	5	–	–	–	5	1	–	1
33. Lace & sewing	8	6	–	–	14	27	13	40	54	10	31	41
34. Construction work	13	–	–	–	13	–	–	–	13	2	–	2
35. Company workers	3	–	–	–	3	–	–	–	3	2	–	2
36. Trainees	1	–	–	–	1	–	–	–	1	1	–	1
37. Rickshaw pullers	20	–	–	–	20	–	–	–	20	3	–	3
38. Sweepers and cleaner	–	–	–	–	–	2	–	2	2	–	–	–
39. Peerless agent	–	1	–	–	1	–	–	–	1	1	–	1
Total	355	74	5	3	437	120	22	142	579	321	99	420

Appendix—II Workers Engaged in Non-traditional Non-agricultural Activities Related to Agriculture by Sex, Caste, Land held and Education

Name of the activity	Participation			Caste													
				Male						Female							
	Male	Female	Total	FC	BCA	BCB	BCC	SC	T	FC	BCA	BCB	BCC	BCD	SC	T	GT
1. Teachers, doctors and govt. servants	142	24	166	49	3	55	4	31	142	2	2	5	1	–	14	24	166
2. Petty business	83	16	99	51	3	23	–	6	83	7	1	4	3	1	–	16	99
3. Tea shop & hotel	4	21	25	2	–	2	–	–	4	4	2	10	–	–	5	21	25
4. Biscuit business	3	1	4	1	–	1	–	1	3	–	1	–	–	–	–	1	4
5. Kirana	4	22	26	1	1	1	–	1	4	19	2	1	–	–	–	22	26
6. Book shop	1	–	1	–	–	–	–	1	1	–	–	–	–	–	–	–	1
7. Wine shop	2	–	2	1	–	1	–	–	2	–	–	–	–	–	–	–	2
8. Cycle shop	11	–	11	2	1	2	1	5	11	–	–	–	–	–	–	–	11
9. Chit fund business	2	–	2	2	–	–	–	–	2	–	–	–	–	–	–	–	2
10. Sweet stall	1	–	1	–	–	–	–	1	1	–	–	–	–	–	–	–	1
11. Medical shop	2	–	2	2	–	–	–	–	2	–	–	–	–	–	–	–	2
12. Ration shop clerks	3	–	3	3	–	–	–	–	3	–	–	–	–	–	–	–	3
13. Metal shop	1	–	1	1	–	–	–	–	1	–	–	–	–	–	–	–	1
14. Fancy shop	4	–	4	3	–	1	–	–	4	–	–	–	–	–	–	–	4

(Table Contd...)

1	2	3	4	5	6	7	8	9	10	11	12	13	14	15	16	17	18	19
15.	Retail shop	1	–	1	1	–	–	–	–	1	–	–	–	–	–	–	–	1
16.	Cloth business	4	–	4	2	–	2	–	–	4	–	–	–	–	–	–	–	4
17.	Cement business	1	–	1	1	–	–	–	–	1	–	–	–	–	–	–	–	1
18.	Iron foundry	1	–	1	1	–	–	–	–	1	–	–	–	–	–	–	–	1
19.	Tailoring	48	16	64	14	3	26	2	3	48	4	1	5	2	–	4	16	64
20.	Hotel workers	11	–	11	3	–	–	–	–	11	–	–	–	–	–	–	–	11
21.	Cinema hall workers	6	–	6	3	–	3	–	–	6	–	–	–	–	–	–	–	6
22.	Road workers	3	–	3	3	–	–	–	–	3	–	–	–	–	–	–	–	3
23.	Cycle shop workers	15	–	15	3	2	6	–	4	15	–	–	–	–	–	–	–	15
24.	Biscuit selling	3	–	3	–	–	3	–	–	3	–	–	–	–	–	–	–	3
25.	Arackshop clerk	1	–	1	1	–	–	–	–	1	–	–	–	–	–	–	–	1
26.	Painting	5	–	5	1	–	2	–	2	5	–	–	–	–	–	–	–	5
27.	Lorry workers	2	–	2	2	–	–	–	–	2	–	–	–	–	–	–	–	2
28.	Moneylending agent	3	–	3	–	–	3	–	–	3	–	–	–	–	–	–	–	3
29.	Paper agent	1	–	1	–	1	–	–	–	1	–	–	–	–	–	–	–	1
30.	Health village ser.	2	–	2	–	–	1	–	1	2	–	–	–	–	–	–	–	2
31.	Kirana shop worker	13	–	13	2	1	8	–	2	13	–	–	–	–	–	–	–	13
32.	Chit fund employee	4	–	4	1	1	2	–	–	4	–	–	–	–	–	–	–	4
33.	Lace & sewing	14	40	54	8	–	6	–	–	14	33	1	4	–	–	2	40	54

(Table Contd...)

1	2	3	4	5	6	7	8	9	10	11	12	13	14	15	16	17	18	19
34.	Construction workers	13	–	13	2	3	6	–	2	13	–	–	–	–	–	–	–	13
35.	Company workers	3	–	3	–	–	2	–	1	3	–	–	–	–	–	–	–	3
36.	Trainees	1	–	1	–	–	1	–	–	1	–	–	–	–	–	–	–	1
37.	Rickshaw pullers	20	–	20	3	1	12	–	4	20	–	–	–	–	–	–	–	20
38.	Sweepers & cleaner	–	2	2	–	–	–	–	–	–	–	–	–	–	–	2	2	2
39.	Peerless agent	1	–	1	1	–	–	–	–	1	–	–	–	–	–	–	–	1
	Total	437	142	579	168	20	159	7	79	437	69	10	29	6	1	27	142	579

FC = Forward Caste;

BC 'A' = Backward Caste 'A' Group;

BC 'C' = Backward Caste 'C' Group;

BC 'D' = Backward Caste 'C' Group;

BC 'B' = Backward Caste 'B' Group;

SC & ST = Scheduled Caste & Scheduled Tribe;

T = Total;

GT = Grand Total.

6

Women in Farm and Non-farm Employment in Tirunelveli District, Tamil Nadu

*Dr. K. Pazhani

"When the creative abilities and personal contributions of one half of the society are shifted by constant subjugation, in addition to the drudgery of constant domestic work and child bearing, social opportunities are suppressed in a wide range of domain, the progress will get restrained. Even the level of economic production is likely to be higher in the society where women are able to engage in a wide range of activities".

—Amartya Sen

The economic development of the Third World Countries has been characterised by mass unemployment and poverty. The Central as well as the State Governments have been taking numerous steps to eradicate poverty by reducing the problem of unemployment. Even after five decades of planned development, we are unable to frame a suitable policy to reduce the severity of these interrelated problems. Employment is a crucial link between

* Reader in Economics, T.D.M.N.S. College, T. Kallikulam, Tamil Nadu—627 113.

population growth and poverty. It provides the means to secure their entitlements by the people. Whatever may be social securities provided by the governments, absence of employment opportunities to a larger portion of the population will pave the way for unequal distribution of wealth and income and also social injustice.

Throughout history and in many societies inequalities of women and men were part and parcel of an accepted male dominated culture. One of the basic factors causing unequal share of women in development relates to the division of labour between sexes. This division of labour has been justified on the basis of child bearing function of women and this is basically important for survival. Consequently, distribution of tasks and responsibilities between men and women in a given society has mainly restricted women to the domestic sphere. Mass poverty and general backwardness has further aggravated the inequalities (Maithili, 1994).

Women in the rural areas are engaged in farm activities in addition to their household activities. Contrary to this, women in urban centres, if not qualified to get gainful employment are engaged in domestic employments. Domestic employment is such that it brings the employee in very close contact with the employer and his family. More often, the relationship is of dependency, exploitation and of quasi-bondage often referred as the "Cinderellas" of the Indian Economy, with low wages but work hard, the arm of the law does not protect them because they are unorganised and they have no contracts. Due to their lack of education, most of them cannot communicate with their parents or relations (Jessie, 1983).

The employment of women in an index of their economic status in the society, especially with reference to equality. It has been recognised as the critical entry point for their integration to the mainstream of development. Women's employment has a direct bearing on the improvement of the quality of life of the family. In poor households' the women's capacity to work, her health, her knowledge and her skill endowments are often the only measure resources to fall back upon for survival. The participation of women in economic activities is highest in poor households. Women are critical agents in the process of moving their families out of poverty (Yadappanavar; 2000).

The High Level Committee on Agricultural Credit through Commercial Banks (1977) remarked, "Although the population depending on agriculture countries to be around 62 per cent, the share of agriculture in national income has fallen from 50 per cent to around 30 per cent. This situation will have its direct impact on the employment generation in agriculture". Frequent failure of monsoon has also added fuel to the already existing problem of unemployment and underemployment of both men and women in the farm sector.

Women play a crucial role in the socio-economic development of any country. But they have been mostly neglected and overlooked by men in most of the developing countries like India. Margaret Mead (1950) has summarized the sex role as: "The home share by a man and female partners, into which men bring the food and women prepare it, is the basic common picture the world over. But this picture can be modified, and the modifications provide proof that the patter itself is not something deeply biological'.

The Problem

Unemployment, poverty and malnutrition are the three problems which hit severely both the rural and the urban poor of our country. Failure of monsoon has been affecting the Southern part of Tamil Nadu for more than a decade. It led to a considerable reduction in employment opportunities both from the farm and non-farm activities. This situation compelled the male workforce to find non-farm employment which is less remunerative. Considering the budget deficit in their daily household activities, even female members began to earn something to supplement the efforts taken by their counterparts in the family.

People's participation, especially women is essential for the rapid and sustainable development of our country. But, women are the victims of multiple socio-economic and cultural factors. They need to empowered and it can be achieved only by increasing the educational status of women, creating chances for their participation and also provision of social justice by providing equal opportunities at par with men. At this juncture, the following questions arise. Do we give importance in providing necessary education to women? If it is provided, is it helpful to make them to achieve economic independence? Do we create conditions to generate employment to women in rural areas? If it is provided, do we provide remuneration at par with men? What are the causes for gender discrimination in jobs and also giving remuneration?

In the present study an attempt has been made to find answers to the above questions in the light of the data collected and also to study the availability of employment for women in the farm and non-farm sector activities, the factors leading to employment of women, the factors preventing the employment of women, impact of women employment in household income and also its effect on income distribution in the study area.

Nature of Employment

According to Sen (1982), one is entitled to one's own labour power, and thus to the trade-based and production-based entitlements related to one's labour power. But, people in the rural areas have been labour to sell but very often fail to find a willing party to employ them. This situation has made the labour force to accept any type of work at very low wage. If there are more number of self-employed and regularly employed work force it will accelerate the growth of output, income and improvement in the standard of the living of the people.

Table—6.1 Sex-wise Distribution of Nature of Employment in Rural India

(Percentages)

Year	Male			Female		
	Self employed	Regular employed	Causal labour	Self employed	Regular employed	Causal labour
1972-73	65.9	12.1	22.0	64.5	4.1	31.4
1977-78	62.8	10.6	26.6	62.1	2.8	35.1
1983	60.5	10.3	29.2	61.9	2.8	35.3
1987-88	58.6	10.0	31.4	60.8	3.7	35.5
1993-94	57.9	8.3	33.8	58.5	2.8	38.7
1999-00	55.0	8.8	36.2	57.3	3.1	39.6

Source: Different Quinquential Reports on Employment and Unemployment of NSSO, G.O.I.

Table—6.1 reveals that the percentage of self-employed male and female shows a declining trend while the percentage of causal labour employed shows an increasing trend. Further, the percentage of regularly employed male and female workers also shows a declining trend. More self-employment and more regular employment means more food, clothing, housing, social amenities, increased education and welfare. But, trends in the nature and growth of employment depict an unhealthy development of the economy. The percentage of male causal labour had increased from 22 per cent to 36.2 per cent whereas female causal labour increased from 31.4 during 1972-73 to 39.6 per cent during 1999-2000. This indicates that fall in the employment opportunities of male workers had influenced female workers to work whether in causal or in self-employment.

Growth of Employment and GDP

The Central and State Government of India have been taking strenuous efforts through various plans to implement self-employment schemes such as TRYSEM (1970), IRDP (1980), DWCRA (1983), wage employment schemes like JVVT (1989) EAS (1993), IAY (1996), MWS (1996), CRSP (1986) and also Special Area Development Programmes (SADP) such as DPAP (1973) and WGDP/HADP (1975) to generate more employment to improve the economic conditions of the poor. These programmes will act as inducing factors for the rapid economic development of India, if the growth of GDP is having a corresponding increase in the growth of employment opportunities.

Table—6.2 Growth of Employment and GDP during the Five Year Plans

Plans	I	II	III	IV	V	VI	VII	VIII	IX
GDP*	3.7	4.2	-3.8	3.4	5.0	5.5	6.7	6.5	7.3
Growth of employment	0.39	0.85	2.03	1.99	1.84	1.89	1.38	1.13	1.14

Source: Plan Documents.

* Annual Growth Rate at Constant Price.

Table 6.2 reveals that there has been fluctuations in the growth of employment and acceleration in the growth of GDP from the Fourth Five Year Plan Period. This situation may be attributed to factors such as, rapid mechanization of agriculture after the Green Revolution, rapid industrialization to produce export surpluses, improvement in the productivity per unit of labour, establishment of export-oriented unit to produce on a large scale unaccompanied by generation of employment, adoption of labour-saving devices in manufacturing, mining and construction industries.

The process of economic changes through various Five Year Plans has not resulted in appropriate and necessary structural changes in the economy. Agriculture still remains as the key sector and there are no significant shifts in the sectorial composition of labour force in different regions of our country. Rapidly growing population and absence of industries viz. small, medium and large scale industries, have contributed much for the over dependence on agriculture and the resultant unemployment and underemployment irrespective of sex. According to Desai (1983), successive plans of development have not generated gainful employment for all the net addition to the labourforce and continue to add to the backlog of unemployed persons. This may be attributed to the failure of the content and manner of implementation to make the maximum impact on employment and absence of additional programmes for making an effective use of the available manpower resources.

It is the employment of workforce which stimulates economic activities in different angles and helps to faster the economic development of any country. But a vast majority of workers, both men and women remains without gainful employment. Therefore, developing countries like India should frame suitable policies for the fuller utilisation of its own human resources since labour is abundant in both rural and urban areas. Employment is the bedrock of both development and social upliftment, particularly in the rural sector. As such, each country must concentrate on evolving an effective employment policy. The International Labour Organisation (ILO) has therefore argued that employment should become the target and overall growth, the by-product of rural development, rather than the other way round (Satya Sundaram, 1999).

Table—6.3 Population, Labour Force and Employment

(in million)

Particulars	1st July 1983	1st January 1994	1st April 1997	IX Plan (1997-02)
Population	725.8	893.7	949.9	N.A
Labour force	289.1	367.4	397.2	423.4
Employment	283.2	360.0	389.7	416.4
Unemployment	5.9	7.4	7.5	7.0

Source: Tata Services Limited, Statistical Outline of India 2000-01.

Note: . Estimates of labour force and employment, etc. are on "usual status" concept and relates to 15 years and above.

Table 6.3 reveals that there has been an increasing trend in the growth of population, labour force and employment generation in the succeeding years. But, unemployment grows steadily upto 1st April 1997 and has fallen afterwards. This situation may be attributed to the steps taken by the Central as well as the State Governments by introducing reforms in different sectors, reducing the role of public sector and encouraging investment by private entrepreneurs through liberal credit policies. The decrease in unemployment from 7.5 million to 7.0 million at the end of the Ninth Plan is only estimation. But, failure of monsoon and continuous drought in different regions of the country has made the unemployment problem still worse than before.

Table—6.4 Employment During 1991 to 1997

(in million)

Year	Public Sector	Private Sector	Total
1991	19.06 (1.5)	7.68 (1.3)	26.74 (1.4)
1992	19.21 (0.8)	7.85 (2.2)	27.06 (1.2)
1993	19.33 (0.6)	7.85 (0.1)	27.18 (0.40)
1994	19.45 (0.6)	7.93 (1.0)	27.38 (0.7)

(Table Contd...)

1	2	3	4
1995	19.47 (0.1)	8.06 (1.6)	27.53 (0.5)
1996	19.43 (-0.2)	8.51 (5.6)	27.94 (1.5)
1997	19.25 (-0.3)	8.66 (1.8)	27.91 (1.1)

Source: R.B.I., Report on Currency, 1997-98.

Note: Figures in brackets indicate annual growth rate (Percentage)

Table 6.4 shows an increasing trend in employment in both public sector and private sector undertakings. But employment in public sector began to decrease from 1996 onwards. This situation may be attributed to the government policy of closer of many sick industries and go for privatisation to cope with the on going process of globalisation. This has paved the way for a steady increase in employment opportunities in the private sector during the reform period.

Table—6.5 Employment in Organised and Unorganised Sectors

(in millions)

Year	Organised Sector	Unorganised Sector	Total
1988	25.7 (1.4)	296.3 (1.3)	322.0 (2.1)
1991	26.7 (1.3)	315.2 (2.1)	341.9 (2.1)
1994	27.4 (0.9)	344.6 (3.1)	372.0 (2.9)

Source: Tata Services Limited, Statistical Outline of India 1998-99

Note:
1. Data in this table cover all the establishment in public sector and non-agriculture establishments in private sector employing 10 or more persons.
2. Figures in brackets indicate average annual growth rate (percentage).

Table 6.5 reveals that employment in the organised sector has declined over the years whereas it shows an increasing trend in the unorganised sector. This situation may be attributed to absence of industries in majority of the rural areas and also increasing number of temporary and causal labourers who work for a minimum wage because of the absence of trade union to save their interest.

Employment Opportunities in Tamil Nadu

The working population in Tamil Nadu had increased from 202 lakhs in 1981 Census to 242 in 1991 Census. It had shown an annual compound growth rate of 1.82 per cent per annum against the population growth rate of 1.44 per cent per annum. But the ratio of organised sector employment to total workers (as per 1991 Census) was only 9.5. This may be attributed to the over dependence on agriculture for employment and also the policy of privatization followed by the State.

Tamil Nadu had the highest work participation rate (WPR) for men (56.4 per cent) in the country. The female WPR has also been substantially higher (29.9 per cent) than that of several States. Between 1981 and 1991, the WPR for rural areas had increased at a faster rate from 46.48 per cent to 48.49 per cent as compared to that of urban WPR. This situation may be attributed to an increase in the number of women employed in the rural areas.

The striking feature of the 1991 Census estimates is that the WPR for female, both in the rural and urban areas, had increased at a faster rate than that of the males which had even declined. Consequently, the proportion of female workers to total workers in the State had increased from 31.4 per cent in 1981 to 34.04 per cent in 1991. The WPR for female was more than twice than that of the corresponding national rates both in rural and urban areas of Tamil Nadu.

Women account for 39.2 per cent of the total workers in the State. The women applicants on the 'Live Register' account for about one-third of the total registrants. In the organised sector employment, the share of women had increased from 15.9 per cent in 1980 to 21.2 per cent in 1990 and further to 28.1 per cent during 1996-97. A total of 7.3 lakh women were employed in the organised sector as on 31st December 1998.

II

The present study is an attempt to throw light on various possibilities of employment of women in farm and non-farm activities to improve the income and thereby the economic dependence of women with the following objectives.

1. the study the socio-economic conditions of the sample households;
2. to know the nature and type of employment available to women in the study area;
3. to examine the extent of employment and income generated in farm and non-farm activities during the study period;
4. to measure the impact of women employment on the income of the households and also income distribution; and
5. to examine the possibilities of generation of farm and non-farm employment to the unemployed women.

Methodology

The study was conducted in Radhapuram taluk of Tirunelveli district in Tamil Nadu. The district includes eleven taluks of which Radhapuram taluk was selected purposively. This taluk consists of two blocks, i.e. Radhapuram and Vallioor. Out of these two blocks, Radhapuram block was selected to know the employment opportunities available for women workforce. Five villages namely, Anaikulam, Kovankulam, Perungudi, Koodankulam and Terkku Villioor were selected randomly for the present study.

A random sample of 20 households was taken from each of the selected villages to get a total of 100 sample households. All the required information were collected from the households through personal interview of the year 2001-2002. Simple techniques of percentages and averages were used to examine different objectives of the study. To test the significance of income from employment of women on the household income t-test is also conducted.

Description of the Study Area

Tirunelveli district is on the southeastern part of Tamil Nadu. It covers an area of 6823 sq. kms. Out of the total population of 25,01,832 in the district, as per 1991 census, 1,70,86,556 (68.3 per cent) live in rural areas and 7,93,176 (31.7 per cent) live in urban areas. The density of population per sq. km. was 367 as against 429 for the State.

Agriculture is the main source of income of the people in this district. Ninety one per cent of the total working population is cultivators. Out of the total area of 1,43,691 hectares in the district 33,472 hectares were cultivated more than once. Among the total irrigated areas, well irrigation covers 40,061 hectares (39.58 per cent), tank 43,758 (43.24 per cent) and canals 17,384 (17.18 per cent) hectares. Cement, cotton textiles, wheat products and manufactures of chemicals are large-scale industries. Important village industries are handloom, poultry farming, brick-making, lime-burning, mat-weaving and jaggary production. This district is famous for the production of varieties of handloom clothes, fine mats of Pathamadai.

Out of the 19 Blocks in this district, Radhapuram Block, the drought prone area, has been selected for the present study. Eighty four per cent of the population is living in the rural areas. This Block is having 11,175 (15.54 per cent) hectares of cultivable land, of which only 3,778 (33.8 per cent) hectares are net area sown. The normal rainfall for this district for the year was 888.7 mm whereas in Radhapuram it was 463.7 mm. This is one of the important reasons for the fall in the employment opportunities both in the farm and non-farm sectors.

III

Employment of Women

Employment status of members in a family influences the income of the household and thereby determines their standard of living. But, people in most of the village areas of Tamil Nadu fail to get employment in major part of a year due to factors like frequent monsoon failure, fall in the labour absorbing capacity of the agricultural sector, absence of small, medium and large-scale industries. This situation paved the way for unemployment, under employment and insufficient income even to meet their daily expenses. This necessitated the need for the employment of female members of the family to go for another employment in addition to their domestic work.

The rural economy comprises two sectors, i.e. farm and non-farm sector. In the farm sector, mostly the uneducated and people lack, skill and training and involved. The payment is very meager since it has been done arbitrarily. This situation paves the way for the employment of more members including women to earn their livelihood. Non-farm employment has not expanded adequately to absorb the rapidly growing workforce. However, more than 20 per cent of the rural workers are engaged in non-agricultural activities (Ghose, 1993).

The level, composition and growth of non-farm employment in rural areas are derived from three sources (a) non-food goods and services for rural population which rise with rural income levels; (b) inputs and services to agriculture which rise with agricultural development; and (c) manufactured and handicraft goods, stemming from external markets in other regions or abroad (Reddy, 2000). But in the study area, employment from the third source is completely absent because of absence of industries of different size.

Factors Leading to Employment of Women

Economic development is concerned with improvement in the standard of living of human beings and neglect of people at the bottom of the ladder would indicate a failed economy. This statement necessitates policies to improve the standard of living of people irrespective of their sex, caste, religion, education and also change in the old tradition of keeping women only in kitchen. Women should be brought to the mainstream by giving them proper education to stand on their own legs to achieve development with equity and social justice. The researcher has identified the following as the important factors influencing employment of women.

1. Family size;
2. Composition of the family;
3. Members employed;
4. Cheap labour;
5. Unorganised labour;
6. Dowry;
7. Self-help groups;
8. Nature of industries;
9. Household income;
10. Nature of employment.

1. Family Size

Family size is an important factor influencing employment of women in activities which provide some amount of income. Higher the family size greater will be the inclination to do some job whether permanent, temporary or causal, to meet their basic necessaries. Larger the size of family greater will be the amount required to purchase at least the necessaries for life. This situation compels women to work in any types of work according to their ability to earn something to support their family.

Table—6.6 Sex-wise Classification of Sample Respondents

Sex	Number of persons	Percentage
Male	283	57.64
Female	208	42.36
Total	491	100.00

Source: Survey data.

Table 6.6 reveals that male population outnumbers female population. But it was reported that there were no incidence of female infanticide as seen in the case of some other districts of Tamil Nadu. Since the total number of sample households is 100 the average family size came to 4.91 (approx. 5 members).

2. Composition of the Family

Every family is having old people, adults and younger ones. Old and younger people are in general composition units and are burden if the household income is insufficient. This situation couples women to do some job, mostly on temporary basis to earn an income to share the burden of his better-half. If there is no old people and one or two children, provided the head of the family earns sufficiently, generally women are restricted within household activities. But, if women are better qualified to get an employment this problem would not arise at all.

Table—6.7 Age-wise Classification of Sample Respondents

Age	Number of persons	Percentage
Below 15	57	11.61
15-60	422	85.95
Above 60	12	2.44
Total	491	100.00

Source: Survey data.

Table 6.7 shows that only 14.05 per cent of the sample population is children and old people. Out of 491 persons 422 (85.95 per cent) are adults. They can work to improve the economic condition of their families if they are provided with employment.

3. Number of Members Employed

Larger family size, composition of family, general rise in the price of consumer goods and also many other reasons necessitate the need for the employment of more number of members in the family. Income earned by the head of the family may not be sufficient to meet the changing expenditure pattern of their households. If there are more number of adults to go for some employment women are not permitted to do any job except their household activities. If there are older and school going children, out of necessity, women prefer to do some job to earn an income to supplement the income earned by their life-partner.

Table—6.8 Sex-wise Classification of Number of Persons Employed

Persons employed	Number of families	
	Male	Female
1.	22	15
2.	33	52
3.	31	5
4.	10	1
5.	4	–
Total	100	73

Source: Survey data

Table 6.8 shows that out of the 100 sample households only 73 have women in employment other than household activities and in 27 families women were engaged in household activities only. It also reveals that higher the number of male members lower will be the number of women in employment.

4. Cheap Labour

Gender discrimination in the payment of remuneration is a normal feature prevalent in the unorganised labour market. For instance, in agriculture, female labourers are paid 2/3 or ½ of the payment made to male workers. That is why, in many cases, women are preferred for employments, which require less skill, both in the rural and urban areas.

5. Unorganised Labour

Women labour is mostly unorganised. They have no trade unions to fight for fewer hours of work and equal pay in par with men for the same job in the unorganised rural labour market. That is why, women are compelled to work from dawn to dusk in the agricultural sector. The profit motivated private entrepreneurs prefer to employ more women than men to accumulate more and more wealth through the exploitation of poor women, who remain unorganised.

6. Dowry System

Though the Government has been taking numerous steps for the elimination of the deep-rooted dowry system, it has been remaining as a normal custom in most of the communities in Tamil Nadu in general and the study area in particular. Dowry system is also a cause for female infanticide and school drop-outs, especially, female children since they are made to work for their survival and also for future life. It is one of the important causes of the employment of female children in beedi-making activities in the study area.

7. Self-help Groups (SHGs)

Failure on the part of the Government to provide employment as a source of living has brought to light the importance of SHGs to uplift the socio-economic conditions of the rural poor. They first create awareness among the public about the factors contributing to their low economic status; their power to do things which improve not only their economic status but also helps them to contribute to the national development, form SHGs; arrange credit facilities to start self-employments; arrange market facilities and also make them to save to settle their loan and for their future.

8. Rural Industries

Though much is talked about rural industrialization for the rapid economic development of our country very little has been done in this regard. Out industrial policies are urban-centred and pro-rich. Industries, small, medium and also large are conspicuous in their absence in the rural villages of our country. A considerable fall in the labour absorbing capacity of agricultural sector due to vagaries of monsoon necessitate the need for creating non-farm sector employment in the rural areas to utilise the locally available raw material to productive purposes which otherwise will be wasted. If there exist few industries, especially agro-based industries, they too are very small in nature, which is insufficient to meet the growing employment needs of the poor masses. Moreover, they also aim to provide employment to women and female children. For instance, Khadi and village industries employ mostly women in most of their production activities.

9. Household Income

Different families get income from different sources. Some get income from more than one source while others get income from only one source, i.e., from selling their labour power. If the family size is greater and the composition of the family increases daily expenditure, then income from only one source will not be sufficient enough even to meet their consumption expenditure. In most cases, especially in the rural areas, people are not having properties, if they have properties; they too remain unutilized due to seasonal failure of monsoon. Even male members fail to get gainful employment for a major portion of a year. At this juncture, employment of women, though temporary and poorly paid, becomes pertinent to save the family from stress and strain due to inadequate household income for its maintenance.

10. Nature of Employment

Women in both rural and urban areas are mostly employed in low paid activities. Most of the women in the rural areas are engaged in farm works like planting, weeding, harvesting and in many agriculture related activities. They remain scattered and have no organisation to protect their interest and fight for more pay and regularising their job opportunities.

Table—6.9 Sex-wise Classification of Nature of Employment

Sl. No.	Sex	Nature of Employment			
		Permanent	Self-employed	Temporary	Total
1.	Male	12 (9.38)	27 (21.09)	89 (69.53)	128 (100.00)
2.	Female	8 (5.80)	28 (20.29)	102 (73.91)	138 (100.00)
	Total	20 (7.52)	55 (20.68)	191 (71.80)	266 (100.00)

Source: Survey data.

Table 6.9 reveals that out of 266 employed 138 (51.88 per cent) are women and 128 (48.12 per cent) are men. This situation will depict a backward sloping supply curve since more number of women is employed to get additional income in addition to the income earned by the head of the family. 92.48 per cent of the employed are in self-employment and temporarily employed. More than 80 per cent of the female workforce is engaged in beedi-making since it provides regular employment of at least 5 or 6 days work per week, provident fund provisions, bonus, medical care and also scholarship to their children who are studying in schools and colleges.

Table—6.10 Women in Farm and Non-farm Employment—2002

Sl. No.	Category	No. of women employed: Permanent	Self-employed	Causal labour	Percentage to total
A.	FARM SECTOR				
1.	Agricultural labour	–	–	20 (80.00)	20 (14.5)
B.	NON-FARM SECTOR				
2.	Beedi-making	–	98 (97.03)	–	98 (71.0)
3.	Tailoring	2 (16.67)	3 (2.97)	–	3 (2.2)
4.	Teaching	10 (83.33)	–	–	2 (1.5)
5.	Others	–		5 (20.00)	15 (10.8)
	Total	12 (100.00)	101 (100.00)	25 (100.00)	138 (100.00)

Source: Survey data

Note: Figures in parentheses indicate percentage to total

Table 6.10 indicates that more than 85 per cent of women employed are in the non-farm sector. Out of the 138 women in employment only 8.7 per cent are in permanent employment, 73.18 are self-employed and 18.12 per cent are causal employment. This situation may be attributed to the existing drought condition in the study area and also the decline trend in the labour absorbing capacity of the farm sector.

Factors Preventing Employment of Women

Though liberalisation, privatisation and globalisation (LPGs) are policies widely discussed and being practised by most of the developing countries like India without considering the status of their economy and also the evil effects of these policies, we are not free from the good old tradition of keeping women within the kitchen. Even after five decades of planned economic development we are unable to provide economic independence by providing enough gainful employment to the female workforce. Many factors may be mentioned as the cause for this state of undesirable situation, which is not conducive for the development of developing countries like India. The important factors are:

1. Traditional attitude;
2. Composition of the family;
3. Prestige;
4. Education;
5. Skill and training;
6. Ignorance;
7. Monsoon failure;
8. Banking policies;
9. Absence of SSIs;
10. Psychological factors.

1. Traditional Attitude

Traditionally, procreation, child-care and maintenance of the family are considered as the important duties of women in most of our Indian societies. But, the economic backwardness of their family compels them to do some employment outside their house in addition to their household activities. Even today, in many communities sending women for outside employment is a bad practice of men. Women have to depend completely on men for each and everything. This traditional attitude is a major factor preventing employment of women.

2. Composition of the Family

All families cannot have more number of adults. Moreover, having more number of adult males unemployed will create more problems than the unemployed female members. If there are too many small children and old people to look after, women could not find time to go for yet another employment to support her family. Under such circumstances, male members are put under pressure which paves the way for national and international migration in search of jobs which are more remunerative than the jobs available in our country.

3. Prestige

Many families irrespective of their economic conditions consider employment of women will reduce fame and name of their family. They consider that it is the responsibility of the head of the family (usually men) to earn for the subsistence of the family members. This paves the way for inadequate income for the maintenance of the family, loss of properties and indebtedness of many families.

4. Education

Education is a powerful and pervasive agent for all-round development, individual and social transformation. Generally, female population gets only primary education in the past due to various reasons. But they are also getting higher education according to their economic status. The education they get is of little use to get gainful employment to support their family.

5. Skill and Training

Most of the female population has enough skill and training in the preparation of tasty food, making dresses to their kids and old people and also management of other household activities. But, they don't have skill and training essential to get a job in this competitive world. At present, the female population in the study are is mostly engaged in beedi-making since it requires not much technical knowledge and expensive training. Lack of skill in modern production techniques and absence of training facilities prevents women from entry into the labour market even for a minimum wage for their subsistence.

6. Ignorance

Most of the female population is busy in the household activities. They don't have time to contact people from outside to know what is going on around them. A pitiable condition is that most of the villages don't have even daily newspapers. If they get it, they are mainly used by male population. Absence of proper information ›ut the availability of jobs also prevents women from getting employment.

7. Monsoon Failure

Agriculture is the main source of income and livelihood to a major percentage of the people living in the study area. But frequent failure of monsoon has reduced the labour absorbing and income generating capacity of agricultural sector. For instance, in the last 10 years (upto 2001) the average rainfall in Radhapuram Taluk shows only less than 500 mm. This undesirable situation has not only reduced employment of women in the farm activities but also farm related activities such as agro-based industries. Thus, nature has its role to play in preventing women from getting employment.

8. Banking Policies

Banking policy of our nation is framed in such a way to help mainly the rich or those who have properties of their own. Most of the loan facilities are security-oriented. Securities such as properties and other costly assets are in the name of men which cannot be used for the economic independence of women. Further, absence of activities of NGOs and SHGs in most of the villages prevents rural women from getting their entitlements, especially bank loans, like their counterparts in the urban centres. It prevents women even from generating their own employment by starting very small production units using locally available resources economically.

9. Absence of Small Scale Industries

Small, medium and large-scale industries are mostly established in and around urban centres. Cottage and small scale industries are meant to generate employment mainly to the female population, who cannot do hard job like men in other industries. But they are conspicuous in their absence in the study area. This situation paves the way for the entitlement deprivation of women in the rural areas who constitute almost 50 per cent of the population in Tirunelveli district.

10. Psychological Factors

In the modern world, women are also equally efficient and qualified to get remunerative employments. But they hesitate to move or migrate to other places if job is not locally available. Further female workforce has to face many sufferings in work-spot because of gender discrimination with regard to hours of work, reward for work and also promotion in their employment. They are bound to take more leave and loose salaries after marriage due to pregnancy and child-care period. Sometimes, women in temporary or even permanent employments are made to resign from their employment due to family problems and health problems after marriage.

Impact on Income Distribution

Employment of women either in farm activities or non-farm activities has a positive impact on the income of the households. It depends on the job in which they are employed and also the number of women employed per family. Out of 138 female workers in the sample households 21 (15.22 per cent) are engaged in household activities only. While the overall average of the families with women in employment come to Rs. 40,400, it is Rs. 31190 in the case of families without women employment. Thus the study reveals that employment of women has paved the way for an increase in the average income per family.

Table—6.11 Classification of Households on the Basis of Income Before and After Women in Employment

Income (Rs. '000)	Number of household	
	Before women employment	After women employment
Below 10	7	3
10-20	17	8
20-30	20	19
30-40	25	22
40-50	17	20
50-60	8	16
60 & Above	6	12
Total	100	100

Source: Survey data.

Table 6.11 reveals that out of 100 households, 69 households comes under the category of income below Rs. 40,000/- before the employment of women in activities other than household activities. But employment of women in different activities, whether permanent, causal or self-employment have changed the situation completely. Employment of women has decreased the number of households below Rs. 40,000/- increase from 69 to 52 and increased the households above Rs. 40,000/- from 31 to 48.

To find the impact of women in employment on the income distribution, we worked out the Gini-coefficients before and after women in employment. The Gini-coefficient of families without women in employment is 0.5974 while the inclusion of income from the employment of women, it has come down to 0.5284. Further, the t-test conducted to know whether income from employment of women influences the family income or not also reveals that the t-value (t = 3.53) is significant at one per cent level. Thus, the study reveals that employment of women in farm and non-farm activities has contributed income to minimize the magnitude of income inequalities among the sample households.

Problems Faced by Women in Employment

Lack of skill, adequate education and training in anyone of the available jobs restricted the employment of women either in household activities or unorganised sectors or both. Female workforce, whether employed in household activities or in self-employment have to face many problems. Self-employed women have to face the following problems:

(i) they have no access to formal credit;

(ii) they find it difficult in getting raw materials for the production of different product;

(iii) they are not having adequate skill in production and lack management capacity in most cases;

(iv) they do have problems related to marketing of their produce;

(v) the existing social structure impedes the formation of SHGs to make use of the opportunities created by the Government and many voluntary agencies for rural development;

(vi) the restrictions imposed by their husbands and in-laws.

On the other hand, women engaged in household activities have to face different type of problems:

(i) they cannot mostly act on their own. They have to follow the words of either their husbands or in-laws;

(ii) they feel monotonous in doing household activities since they have no leisure, no recreation and appreciation for what valuable services they have been rendering daily;

(iii) they are not getting due respects from other members of the family and often ill-treated;

(iv) they cannot look after their physical and mental health.

IV

Policy Implications

In order to bring women into mainstream of economy and society, the Central as well as the State Governments have been launching different development programmes for women. Special emphasis has been given for employment and income generating activities for women in succeeding Five Year Plans. But the benefits of these programmes have not reached the targeted female population. The following are the policy implications emerging out of the present study which needs speedy actions by the Government.

1. The most important single factor that contributes much for the existing unemployment in the rural and urban areas is the problem of population explosion and the resultant increase in the average family size. Both the Central and the State Governments have to take necessary steps to curtail the rapidly growing population. The services of voluntary social organisation and the schools and colleges. NSS volunteers may also be better utilized to create awareness among the people about the evils of larger family size.

2. There exists interlinkage between the farm and non-farm sectors in the developmental process. To develop the farm sector, especially in the drought prone areas, the Central as well as the State Governments have to take the following steps:

   (i) Establishing basic infrastructures like dams, tanks and canals after linking the rivers all over the country.

   (ii) Bunding, desilting and deeping of tanks should be undertaken by using more labour-intensive techniques rather than the present system of using more machines which helps the rich to accumulate more wealth and paves the way for furthering inequalities in the distribution of income.

   (iii) The Government of Tamil Nadu should take necessary steps to simplify the formalities with regard to getting electricity connections for agricultural purposes. The present system of asking huge amounts as deposits should be scrapped instead of supplying clectricity free of cost.

   (iv) The National Bank for Agriculture and Rural Development (NABARD) should instruct the Primary Co-operative Agriculture and Rural Development Banks to lend liberally for the development of farm sector instead of lending more to non-farm and small road transport operators to achieve their objectives.

   (v) The on-farm employment may be increased sufficiently by constructing necessary irrigation infrastructures for increasing area under cultivation by introducing systems like wasteland development with an aim of increasing employment and increasing the share of agriculture to the Gross Domestic Product.

(vi) The employment of women in non-form activities is very low mainly because of their educational status, lack of skill and training and also long distance to be covered for such works.

(vii) To make the employment of women in the farm and non-farm activities attractive, the authorities concerned have to take necessary and sufficient steps to fix minimum wages to women labour who are mostly employed in the unorganised sectors.

(viii) As the employment of women in different activities reduces income disparities of households, while framing employment policies the Government must give due consideration to the employment opportunities of women.

Conclusion

To conclude we can quote Nowiki: "How the economic, social and cultural developments of the country is realised where half of its population (women) is in such great dependency on the other half." Development programmes for women such as Development of Women and Child in Rural Areas (DWCRA), Support to Training and Employment (STEP) and Training-cum-Employment and Production Centres under NORAD Scheme cover only a small margin of women leaving others unemployed and underemployed. A permanent solution to the problem of employment of women can only be achieved through the reduction of family size, improvement in the quality of education imparted to female population, growth of new skill, the development of a system of scientific, diversified and assured agriculture, the building of a wide range of small scale processing industries in the rural areas, rural electrification and general industrial development. Therefore, it is the responsibility of the Central and State Governments to frame suitable employment policies which will pave the way for the economic independence of women and contribute much for the rapid development of the economy.

REFERENCES

Amartya Sen (1982), *Poverty and Famine: An Essay on Entitlements and Deprivation*, Oxford University Press, Delhi.

Ghose, B (1993) The Challenges of Unemployment, *Yojana*, Vol. 37 (17).

Jessie B. Tellis Nayak (1983), *Indian Womanhood Then and Now—Situations, Efforts, Profile*, Satprakashan Sanchar Kendra, Indore.

Jozef Nowki (1973), *Some Contradictions and Barriers of Development in Bangladesh*, The Ford Foundation, Dacca.

Kumar, S. (2001) Amartya Sen's Economic Philosophy and Education, *University News*, Vol. 30. No. 26.

Maithili Vishwanathan (1994), *Women and Society* Vol. III Printwell, Jaipur.

Margaret Mead, *Male and Female*, London (1950) Stated in *Women's Role in Economic Development* by Easter Boserup, George Allen and Unwin Ltd., London, 1970.

Satya Sundaram, I (1999), *Rural Development*, Himalayan Publishing House, Delhi.

Sudhakar Reddy, E (2000), Rural Non-farm Employment in Developing Economies—Theoretical Formulation and Empirical Evidence, *Journal of Rural Development*, Vol., 19 (1).

Vasant Desai (1983), *A Study on Rural Economics*, Himalayan Publishing House, Bombay.

Yadappanavar (2000), Role of Banks in Women's Development, *Land Bank Journal*, Vol. XXXIX Issue I.

Tamil Nadu—Economic Appraisal 1997-98, Government of Tamil Nadu, Chenni, 2000.

Statistical Outline of India 2000-2001, Tata Services Limited, Department of Economics and Statistics, Mumbai.

7

Employment of Women in the Farm and Non-farm Sector in Goa

*Silvia Maria de Mendonca-Noronha

Introduction

Women workers constitute an important component of the Indian labour force. An increasing number of women are today compelled to leave the security of their homes and venture out in search of work. The underlying factors are numerous, depending on their socio-economic status. We can divide working women into 3 categories on a socio-economic basis.

1. Agricultural workers and those engaged in traditional menial services. This group is the largest and the poorest. Their counterparts in urban areas include, construction labour, migrant labour, domestic servants, and self employed women in the formal sector.

2. The second category comprises women who work in offices or as professionals.

* (Ph.D), Reader & Head, Department of Economics, Goa University, Taliegao Plateau, Goa, 403 206, India. Ph. No. 0832, 2459453 (Res.), E-mail address: elgarnor@goatelecom.com.

3. In the third category are better educated women and those who have economic security. These women work to ameliorate their living standards and for self-actualisation.

A majority of working women fall in the middle and lower socio-economic class and they work mainly for economic reasons. These women would have preferred to remain at home and attend to household chores and their children, than offer themselves to work. Nath (1970), found in Rajasthan, that agricultural working women of both agricultural and non-agricultural households, expressed a strong desire to be able to afford the leisure of preparing two hot meals and looking after the health and personal hygiene needs of their children, as could the high caste, higher income group of women of the area, who were not working. It was further observed that, women of the non-agricultural group, in which both men and women were workers in a cement factory, withdrew from work, as soon as the husband, or one of the sons became a permanent worker with higher wages in the factory. This proves that women in the lower rungs of the economic ladder work due to economic necessity.

Significance of the Study

The Primary Sector still provides employment for a large percentage of the labour force in India. Since, Independence, while the composition of India's Net Domestic Product (NDP) has changed considerably, the composition of its workforce has altered very little. The share of agriculture and allied activities in the output declined from around 52 per cent in 1951 to be about 32 per cent in 1991, but their share in the workforce moved marginally from about 73 per cent to 65 per cent over the same period (Bhaduri, 1993).

We find that a large percentage of women are employed in the agricultural sector. The main reason why we find a large percentage of women in this sector is that, as employment in other sectors demand a certain level of skill which women lack, they have no option but to fall back on agriculture for employment.

Since a large percentage of women are found in the Primary Sector, it would be interesting to know the percentage of women employed in the primary sector viz a viz of men, if women in the primary sector are employed in the farm sector or in the non-farm sector, if within the farm sector they are employed as agricultural labourers or as cultivators and, if the percentage of women working as marginal workers in this sector is greater than that of men.

The paper has been divided into six sections along the following lines:

Section 1: Sex distribution of the total workforce in the primary sector as a whole, 1961-'91.

Section 2: Sex distribution of the total workforce in the farm sector, 1961-91.

Section 3: Sex distribution of the workforce in the farm sector as, (i) Cultivators and (ii) Agricultural Labourers, 1961-'91.

Section 4: Sex distribution of the workforce in the non-farm sector.

Section 5: Conclusion

Section 6: Policy Implications.

1. Sex Distribution of the Total Workforce in the Primary Sector As a Whole, 1961-91

This section discusses the sex distribution of the total workforce in the primary sector as a whole.

From table 7.1 we note a decline in the workforce in the primary sector both in absolute terms and in percentage (refer column 7) from 1961-91. However this decline has not been equal in male and female workers. The present section attempts to throw light on the trends in the sex distribution of the workforce in the Primary Sector during this period.

From columns 5, 6 and 7 in the table we observe the following:

1. A decline in absolute terms in the number of male workers in the primary sector from 88,546 (col. 5) in 1961 to 61,218 in 1991.

Table—7.1 Sex Distribution of the Total Workforce in Goa and in the Primary Sector

Year	Total workforce in Goa			Total workforce in the primary sector		
	Males	Females	Total	Males	Females	Total
1	2	3	4 (2 + 3)	5	6	7 (5 + 6)
1961	147,036 (100%)	97,225 (100%)	244,261 (100%)	88,546 (60%) (51%)	83,547 (86%) (49%)	172,093 (70%) (100%)
1971	192,624 (100%)	61,851 (100%)	254,475 (100%)	83,856 (44%) (67%)	41,692 (67%) (33%)	125,548 (49%) (100%)
1981 Main	234,975 (100%)	76,272 (100%)	311,247 (100%)	82,230 (35%) (67%)	40,270 (53%) (33%)	122,500 (39%) (100%)
Marginal	12,367 (100%)	32,595 (100%)	44,962 (100%)	8,974 (73%) (24%)	28,562 (88%) (66%)	37,538 (83%) (100%)
Total	247,342 (100%)	108,867 (100%)	356,209 (100%)	91,204 (37%) (57%)	68,832 (63%) (43%)	160,038 (45%) (100%)
1991 Main	287,154 (100%)	96,405 (100%)	383,559 (100%)	81,008 (28%) (65%)	42,853 (44%) (35%)	123,861 (32%) (100%)
Marginal	7,605 (100%)	21,572 (100%)	29,177 (100%)	4,734 (62%) (20%)	18,365 (85%) (80%)	23,099 (79%) (100%)
Total	294,759 (100%)	117,977 (100%)	412,736 (100%)	85,742 (29%) (58%)	61,218 (52%) (42%)	146,960 (36%) (100%)

Source: Census of India, 1961, 1971, 1981, 1991, Goa, Daman and Diu, Economic tables.

Note: 1. Percentages not underlined and percentages of figures in columns 5 and 6 respectively, with that of figures in column 7.

2. Underlined percentages are percentages of figures in columns 5, 6 and 7, with that of figures in columns 2, 3 and 4 respectively.

2. The female workforce also shows a decline in absolute terms in the primary sector from 83,547 in 1961 to 61,218 in 1991.
3. There has been a rise in the percentage of the male workforce in the primary sector viz a viz that of females, from 51% in 1961 to 58% in 1991, (refer Col. 5).
4. The percentage of the female workforce in the primary sector in Goa viz a viz the male workforce shows a fall from 49% in 1961 to 42% in 1991, (Col. 6).
5. We note a fall in the percentage of the male workforce in the primary sector to the male workforce in Goa from 60% in 1961 to 29% in 1991 (Col. 5).
6. The percentage of the female workforce in the primary sector in Goa declined from 86% in 1961 to 52% in 1991, (Col. 6, underlined percentages).
7. Although, the percentage of the total female workforce in the primary sector, to the total female workforce in Goa, declined from 86% in 1961 to 52% in 1991, it was higher than the percentage of the total male workforce in the primary sector to the total male workforce in Goa, which was 60% in 1961 and declined to 29% in 1991 (refer Col. 5 and 6).
8. The percentage of female marginal workers is higher than that of males both in 1981 and in 1991.

From the above observations we conclude the following:

1. The primary sector in Goa has been male dominated and this domination has increased from 1961-91.
2. More female workers out of the total female workforce in Goa (52% in 1991) are employed in the primary sector than males. This implies that the females have been getting employment mainly in the primary sector in Goa, though this percentage has decreased from 1961-1991.
3. The percentage of female marginal workers in the primary sector is greater than that of males, which implies that more female workers are employed as marginal workers in the primary sector than males.

2. Sex Distribution of the Total Workforce Employed in the Farm Sector, 1961-91

This section discuss the sex distribution of the total workforce in the farm sector. This sector includes cultivators and agricultural labourers.

Table—7.2 Sex Distribution of the Total Workforce Employed in the Farm Sector

Year	Total workforce in the primary sector			Total workforce in the farm sector		
	Males	Females	Total	Male	Females	Total
1	2	3	4	5	6	7
1961	88,546 (100%)	83,547 (100%)	172,093 (100%)	66,394 (75%) (47%)	75,702 (91%) (53%)	142,096 (83%) (100%)
1971	83,856 (100%)	41,692 (100%)	125,548 (100%)	61,975 (74%) (63%)	36,840 (88%) (37%)	98,815 (79%) (100%)
1981	82,230 (100%)	40,270 (100%)	122,500 (100%)	53,775 (65%) (60%)	35,157 (87%) (40%)	88,932 (73%) (100%)
Marginal	8,976 (100%)	28,562 (100%)	37,538 (100%)	7,959 (89%) (22%)	27,552 (97%) (78%)	35,511 (95%) (100%)
Total	91,206 (100%)	68,832 (100%)	160,038 (100%)	61,734 (68%) (50%)	62,709 (91%) (50%)	124,443 (78%) (100%)
1991	81,008 (100%)	42,853 (100%)	123,861 (100%)	54,370 (67%) (59%)	37,442 (87%) (41%)	91,812 (74%) (100%)
Marginal	4,734 (100%)	18,365 (100%)	23,099 (100%)	4,179 (88%) (19%)	17,420 (95%) (81%)	21,599 (94%) (100%)
Total	85,742 (100%)	61,218 (100%)	146,960 (100%)	58,549 (68%) (52%)	54,862 (90%) (48%)	113,411 (77%) (100%)

Source: Census of India 1961, 1971, 1981, 1991, Goa, Daman and Diu, Economic Tables.

Note: 1. Percentages not underlined and percentages of figures in column 5 and 6 respectively with that of figures in col. 7.

2. Underlined percentages are percentages of figures in columns 5, 6 and 7 with that of figures in cols. 2, 3 and 4 respectively.

From the above table we make the following observations:

1. The total male workforce in the farm sector declined in absolute terms from 66,394 in 1961 to 58,549 in 1991.

2. We also note a decrease in absolute terms in the total female workforce in the farm sector from 75,702 in 1961 to 54,862 in 1991.
3. The percentage of the male workforce in the farm sector to the total male workforce in the primary sector declined from 75% in 1961 to 68% in 1991.
4. The percentage of the female workforce in the farm sector to the total female workforce in the primary sector also declined from 91% in 1961 to 90% in 1991 a marginal decline over a period of 30 years.
5. The percentage of the male workforce to the total workforce (male + female) in the farm sector increased from 47% in 1961 to 52% in 1991.
6. The percentage of the female workforce to the total workforce (male + female) in the farm sector decreased from 53% in 1961 to 48% in 1991.
7. From 1981 to 1991 there has been a decline in the male marginal workers from 22% of the total workforce in the farm sector to 19% in 1991, whereas the female workers in the farm sector shows a rise from 78% in 1961 to 81% in 1991.

From the above observations we can conclude the following:

1. Less number of male workers are being employed in the farm sector both in absolute terms as well as in it's percentage to the total workers in the primary sector from 1961-91.
2. Most of the female workers in the primary sector are employed in the farm sector, (90% in 1991) which implies that other avenues of employment in the primary sector are more favourable for men.
3. More females are employed as marginal workers in the farm sector than males.

3. Sex Distribution of the Total Workforce Employed in the Farm Sector as Cultivators, 1961-91

This section discusses the sex distribution of the total workforce employed as cultivators from 1961-1991.

(i) **Cultivators**

(ii) **Meaning of 'cultivator'**: At the outset, it is appropriate to first define the term 'cultivator' as used in the various censuses.

The 1961 Census definition: In the 1961 census, the term 'cultivator' include both the owner cultivators, as well as tenant cultivator. Therefore, "as persons working in land, cultivation on which they had either ownership or tenancy rights were included in this category. 'Cultivation' according to this census involved ploughing, sowing and harvesting and did not include fruit growing, keeping of orchards or groves and working for plantations like coffee, tea, rubber, chinchona and other medical plantations."

The 1971 census definition: The 1971 Census says, "for purposes of the census a cultivator is one who is engaged in cultivation by oneself or by supervision or direction in one's capacity as owner or lesee of land held from private person(s) or institution(s) for consideration of payment in cash, kind or share. A person who merely owns land but has given out land to another person or persons for cultivation for money, kind or share of crop and who does not even supervise or direct cultivation of land, is not considered to be working as a cultivator. Similarly, a person working on another person's land for wages in cash, kind or share is also not considered as cultivator".

The 1981 Census Definition: According to the definition in the 1981 Census, "a person is working as cultivator if he or she is engaged either as employer, single worker or family worker in cultivation of land owned or held from Government or held from private person or institutions for payment in money, kind or share. Cultivation includes supervision or direction of cultivation. A person who has given out his/her land to another person or persons for cultivation for money, kind or share of crop and who does not even supervise or direct cultivation of land, will not be treated as cultivator. Similarly a person working in another person's land for wages in cash or kind or a combination of both (agricultural labourer) will not be treated as cultivator".

The 1991 Census definition: According to the definition in the 1991 Census, "a person is working as Cultivator if he or she is engaged either as employer, single worker or family worker in cultivation of land owned or held from Government or held from private persons or institutions for payment in money, kind or share. Cultivation includes supervision or direction of cultivation. A person who has given out his/her land to another person or persons for cultivation for money, kind or share of crop and who does not even supervise or direct cultivation of land, will not be treated as cultivator. Similarly, a person working in another person's for wages in cash or kind or a combination of both (agricultural labourer) will not be treated as cultivator".

Table—7.3 Sex Distribution of the Total Workforce in the Farm Sector Employed as Cultivators

Year	Total workforce in the primary sector			Total workforce employed as cultivators		
	Males	Females	Total	Males	Females	Total
1	2	3	4	5	6	7
1961	88,546 (100%)	83,547 (100%)	172,093 (100%)	54,161 (61%) (52%)	49,978 (60%) (48%)	104,139 (61%) (100%)
1971	83,856 (100%)	41,692 (100%)	125,548 (100%)	41,899 (50%) (69%)	18,620 (45%) (31%)	60,519 (48%) (100%)
1981 Main	82,230 (100%)	40,270 (100%)	122,500 (100%)	37,321 (45%) (64%)	21,055 (52%) (36%)	58,376 (48%) (100%)
Marginal	8,976 (100%)	28,562 (100%)	37,538 (100%)	4,236 (47%) (22%)	15,236 (53%) (78%)	19,472 (54%) (100%)
Total	91,206 (100%)	68,832 (100%)	160,038 (100%)	41,557 (46%) (53%)	36,291 (53%) (47%)	77,848 (49%) (100%)
1991 Main	81,008 (100%)	42,853 (100%)	123,861 (100%)	35,201 (43%) (62%)	21,327 (50%) (38%)	56,528 (46%) (100%)

(Table Contd...)

1	2	3	4	5	6	7
Marginal	4,734 (100%)	18,365 (100%)	23,099 (100%)	2,136 (45%) (18%)	9,972 (54%) (82%)	12,108 (52%) (100%)
Total	85,742 (100%)	61,218 (100%)	146,960 (100%)	37,337 (44%) (54%)	31,299 (51%) (46%)	68,636 (47%) (100%)

Source: Census of India, 1961, 1971, 1981, 1991, Goa, Daman and Diu, Economic tables.

Note: 1. Percentages not underlined are percentages of figures in cols. 5 and 6 respectively with that of figures in col. 7.

2. Underlined percentages are percentages of figures in cols. 5, 6 and 7 with that of figures in cols. 2, 3 and 4 respectively.

From the above table we make the following observations:

1. The number of male cultivators decreased in absolute terms from 54,161 in 1961 to 37,337 (Total figures) in 1991. The total female cultivators also declined from 49,978 in 1961 to 31,299 in 1991.

2. The percentage of the male workforce (underlined percentages) engaged as cultivators in the primary sector declined from 61% in 1961 to 44% in 1991. The percentage of female cultivators to the total female workforce in the primary sector also declined from 60% in 1961 to 51% in 1991. However, the decline is greater in the case of male cultivators (the percentage of male cultivators declined by 17% points from 1961 to 1991 and that of female cultivators declined by 9% points).

3. We note throughout that the percentage of females engaged as cultivators has always been lower than that of males except in the case of marginal workers where we find a higher percentage of females.

From the above observations we conclude the following:

1. There seems to be a general decline in the absolute number as well as the percentage of both male and female cultivators from 1961 to 1991 in Goa.

2. More males are engaged as cultivators than females.

3. There are more female cultivators who are marginal workers than males.

(ii) Agricultural Labourers

(iii) Meaning of Agricultural Labourers

The 1961 Census definition: According to the 1961 Census, "an agricultural labourer is one who works in another person's land only as a labourer (without exercising any supervision or direction in cultivation) for wages in cash, kind or share or produce. He should have been working as agricultural labourer in that last or in the current working season".

The 1971 Census definition: According to this census, an agricultural labourer was, "a person who works in another person's land for wages in money, kind or share. He has no risk in the cultivation but merely works in another person's land for wages. The labourer could have no right of lease or contract on land on which he works".

The 1981 census definition: The 1981 census definition is the same as the 1971 census definition. According to this census, "a person who works on another person's land for wages in money, kind or share should be regarded as an agricultural labourer. He or she has no risk in the cultivation be he/she merely works in another person's land for wages. An agricultural labourer has no right of lease or contract on land on which he/she works."

The 1991 census definition: According to the 1991 census, "A person who works in another person's land for wages in money, kind or share should be regarded as an agricultural labourer. He or she has no risk in the cultivation but he/she merely works on another person's land for wages. An agricultural labourer has no right of lease or contract on land on which he/she works".

We note that the definition of agricultural labourer in the last three censuses are the same.

Table—7.4 Sex Distribution of the Total Workforce Employed in the Farm Sector as Agricultural Labourers

Year	Total workforce in the primary sector			Total agricultural labourers		
	Male	Females	Total	Males	Females	Total
1	2	3	4	5	6	7
1961	88,546 (100%)	83,547 (100%)	172,093 (100%)	12,233 (14%) (32%)	25,724 (31%) (68%)	37,957 (22%) (100%)
1971	83,856 (100%)	41,692 (100%)	125,548 (100%)	20,076 (24%) (52%)	18,220 (44%) (48%)	38,296 (31%) (100%)
1981 Main	82,230 (100%)	40,270 (100%)	122,500 (100%)	16,454 (20%) (54%)	14,102 (35%) (46%)	30,556 (25%) (100%)
Marginal	8,976 (100%)	28,562 (100%)	37,538 (100%)	3,723 (23%)	12,316 (77%)	16,039 (100%)
Total	91,206 (100%)	68,832 (100%)	160,038 (100%)	20,177 (22%) (43%)	26,418 (38%) (57%)	46,595 (29%) (100%)
1991 Main	81,008 (100%)	42,853 (100%)	123,861 (100%)	19,169 (24%) (54%)	16,115 (38%) (46%)	35,284 (28%) (100%)
Marginal	4,734 (100%)	18,365 (100%)	23,099 (100%)	2,043 (43%) (22%)	7,448 (41%) (78%)	9,491 (41%) (100%)
Total	85,742 (100%)	61,218 (100%)	146,960 (100%)	21,212 (25%) (47%)	23,563 (38%) (53%)	44,775 (30%) (100%)

Source: Census of India 1961, 1971, 1981, 1991, Goa, Daman and Diu, Economic Tables.

Note: 1. Percentages not underlined are percentages of figures in cols. 5 and 6 with that of figures in col. 7 respectively.

2. Underlined percentages are percentages of figures in cols. 5, 6 and 7 with that of figures in cols. 2, 3 and 4 respectively.

From the above table we make the following observations:

1. There was an increase in absolute number in the total male as well as female agricultural labourers from 12,233 in 1961 to 21,212 in 1991, but a decrease in the case of female agricultural labourers from 25,724 in 1961 to 23,563 in 1991.

2. The percentage of both male and female workers employed as agricultural labourers from the total male as well as female workers employed in the primary sector has increased from 1961 to 1991. In the case of males it was from 14% in 1961 to 25% in 1991 and in the case of females it was from 31% in 1961 to 38% in 1991. The increase was greater in the case of male workers (by 11% points as against 7% points in the case of females).
3. We also note from the table that from 1961 to 1991 the percentage of females engaged as agricultural labourers is greater than that of males. However from 1961 to 1991 the percentage of males employed as agricultural labourers has increased while that of females has decreased. (Refer table).
4. The percentage of marginal workers in the case of female agricultural labourers is greater than that of males.

From the above observations we conclude the following:

1. A higher percentage of agricultural labourers are females in Goa.
2. The percentage of females viz a viz that of males, employed as agricultural labourers is declining.
3. A high percentage of the women employed as agricultural labourers in the primary sector from 1981 to 1991 are marginal workers.

4. Sex Distribution of the Total Workforce Employed in the Non-farm Sector

In this section we discuss the sex distribution of the total workforce employed in the non-farm sector.

Table—7.5 Sex Distribution of the Total Workforce Employed in the Non Farm Sector

Year	Total workforce in the primary sector			Total workforce in the non-farm sector		
	Males	Females	Total	Males	Females	Total
1	2	3	4	5	6	7
1961	88,546 (100%)	83,547 (100%)	172,093 (100%)	22,152 (25%) (74%)	7,845 (9%) (26%)	29,997 (17%) (100%)
1971	83,856 (100%)	41,692 (100%)	125,548 (100%)	21,881 (26%) (82%)	4,852 (12%) (18%)	26,733 (21%) (100%)
1981 Main	82,230 (100%)	40,270 (100%)	122,500 (100%)	28,455 (35%) (85%)	5,113 (13%) (15%)	33,568 (27%) (100%)
Marginal	8,976 (100%)	28,562 (100%)	37,538 (100%)	1,017 (50.2%)	1,010 (49.8%)	2,027 (100%)
Total	91,206 (100%)	68,832 (100%)	160,038 (100%)	29,472 (32%) (83%)	6,123 (9%) (17%)	35,595 (22%) (100%)
1991 Main	81,008 (100%)	42,853 (100%)	123,861 (100%)	26,638 (33%) (83%)	5,411 (13%) (17%)	32,049 (26%) (100%)
Marginal	4,734 (100%)	18,365 (100%)	23,099 (100%)	555 (12%) (37%)	945 (5%) (63%)	1500 (6%) (100%)
Total	85,742 (100%)	61,218 (100%)	146,960 (100%)	27,193 (32%) (81%)	6,356 (10%) (19%)	33,549 (23%) (100%)

Source: Census of India, 1961, 1971, 1981, 1991, Goa, Daman and Diu, Economic tables.

Note: 1. Underlined percentages are percentages of figures in cols. 5, 6 and 7 with that of figures in cols. 2, 3 and 4 respectively.

2. Percentages not underlined are percentages of figures in cols. 5 and 6 with that of figures in col. 7.

From the above table we make the following observations:

1. The total male workforce engaged in the non farm sector increased in absolute terms from 22,152 in 1961 to 27,193 in 1991, whereas there was a decline in absolute terms in the female workforce in these activities from 7,845 in 1961 to 6,356 in 1991.

2. The percentage of the total male workforce in the non farm sector to the total male workforce in the primary sector increased from 1961 to 1991 by 7% points, i.e. from 25% in 1961 to 32% in 1991, whereas the percentage of the total female workforce in the non farm sector to the total female workforce in the primary sector increased only marginally by 1% point from 9% in 1961 to 10% in 1991.

3. From 1961 to 1991 we note that the percentage of the male workforce engaged in the non farm sector was much higher than that of the female workers (refer percentages that are not underlined in cols. 5 and 6).

From the above observations we conclude that this sector is more conducive to the employment of men rather than women.

From the analysis of the above tables we conclude the following:

5. Conclusion

1. A higher percentage of female workers are engaged in the primary sector than males.
2. Compared to males there are more female marginal workers in the primary sector. This implies a greater casualisation of employment of women in this sector, which places the women workers in a more vulnerable position.
3. As compared to males, more females in the primary sector are engaged in the farm sector which implies that, the other areas in the primary sector were more favourable for men.
4. Female marginal workers form 81% of the total marginal workers in the farm sector in 1991. From 1981-91, there has been an increase in the percentage of female marginal workers in the farm sector from 78% in 1981 to 81% in 1991.
5. In the farm sector, a higher percentage of women workers are employed as agricultural labourers than

as cultivators from 1961 to 1991, whereas more males are employed as cultivators.

6. More males are employed in the non farm sector than females, indicating that activities outside the farm sector are more favourable for the employment of male workers.

Thus we conclude that in the primary sector, women are by and large employed in the farm sector. Within the farm sector, they are largely employed as agricultural labourers, and a large percentage of them work as marginal labourers. From the above conclusion we note that, though the primary sector is the largest employer of women, women are found at the lowest level of employment in this sector.

6. Policy Implications

From the above study, we find that the percentage of women employed in the primary sector is higher than that of men. Within the primary sector, women are largely employed as agricultural labourers and a much higher percentage of women are employed as marginal workers than men.

The primary sector being an unorganised sector, it increases the opportunities to exploit women. Therefore, the government should take extra precaution to protect the rights of women, who are easy targets for exploitation by their employers, by appropriate legislations to safeguard their interests. These legislations should be constantly monitored, to make sure that they are properly implemented.

Within the primary sector, more employment opportunities should be created in the non farm sector for women, as it is found that in this sub-sector, the percentage of women employed is very low. This will enable women to earn higher incomes. This will also enable them to be gainfully employed. These allied activities could be home-based, which will enable more women to take up such activities with ease. Training, programmes can be started for women in animal husbandry, rural crafts etc. However these training programmes, should be so designed, as to take account of the dual roles women play as producers and family nurturers.

Training should not involve long absences from home. With the onset of economic reforms in India, and the increasing importance given to informal sector activities, women can find themselves gainfully employed in such activities.

The government can also provide credit facilities on easy terms for women, so that they can be self employed.

Finally, the government should seriously implement the various schemes for self employment of women in rural areas such as DWCRA (Development of Women and Children in Rural Areas), IRDP (Integrated Rural Development Programme) etc.

REFERENCES

Anker R., Buvinic M. and Youssef N.H., (1982), *Women's Role and Population Trends in the Third World*, Croom Helm, London.

Anker R., (1983), "Female Labour Participation in Developing Countries", *International Labour Review*, Vol. 122, No. 6.

Banerjee, N., (1999), "Women in the Emerging Labour Market", *The Indian Journal of Labour Economics*, Vol. 42, No. 4.

Bhaduri, A. (1993), "*Structural Adjustment, Labour Market and Employment in India*", ILO-ARTEP.

Director of Census Operations, Goa, Daman and Diu, "*Census of India, 1961, Goa, Daman and Diu, Economic Tables*".

——, Goa, Daman and Diu, "*Census of India, 1971, Goa, Daman and Diu, Economic Tables*.

——, Goa, Daman and Diu "*Census of India, 1981, Goa, Daman and Diu, Economic Tables*.

——, Goa, "*Census of India, 1991, Goa, Economic Tables*.

8

Women Enterprises in the Informal Sector in Punjab

*Dr. Shankuntla Gupta
*Disha Mittal

Informal sector plays a significant role with regard to employment and income generation in developing economies. The present study analyses the activity status of women enterprises in the informal sector, employment in women enterprises and use of finance and power in the women enterprises. An attempt has been made to find out either the women owned enterprises are actually women operated enterprises or not.

Introduction

At least in one field women have attained equality with men i.e. micro-enterprises, this hypothesis is corroborated by UN estimates of micro-enterprises where women operate and employ approximately half or the world's micro-enterprises that comprise cottage crafts such as basketry weaving, the crafting of clay utensils

* Reader, Deptt. of Economics, Punjabi University, Patiala.

* Research Scholar, Deptt. of Economics, Punjabi University, Patiala.

for cooking and other hand made goods, still others are flourishing services such as trading useful goods, dress making operations and curbside beauty saloons (International Encyclopedia of women, 1998).

In developed countries, like United States and Canada, women own 30 per cent of the total business. In the U.S.A, women are forming small business at almost twice the rate of men. In fact, the number of self-employed women more than doubled during 1975-1990 (Murphy, 1992). Consequently the women own 7.7 million firms, employing 15.5 million workers and generate nearly $ 1.4 billion worth of sales. These firms collectively employ over one third (35%) more people in the United States than the Fortune 500 companies worldwide (National Foundation for women Business Owners, and Dun and Bradstreet Information Service, 1995).

In Latin America, women represent 15 to 20 per cent of all employers, which are primarily engaged in commercial and service sector activities, studies by Hisrich (1987), Cisneros (1987) and U.S. Small Business Administration (1985) corroborate these results.

The US-AID micro-enterprise stocktaking report (1989) characterises micro-enterprises being run primarily by family labour Harper and Ramachandran (1992), Sumel (1992) a report from Great Britain and a European commission's study observed similar results and U.S. Bureau of census data revealed that in 1982 only 9.8 per cent of all women owned business had employees (Gould 1987).

Studies by Sarngadharan and Risia (1985), Page (1979), Kilby et al (1984); Hammam (1989), Ramamurthy (1991), George (1992) revealed that women micro-enterprises mostly depend on entrepreneur's own savings rather than on borrowed funds i.e. there is preponderance of owned capital and loan capital is comparatively insignificant. This is true not only for the third world countries for e.g. in Amsterdam, the Netherlands, two-third of a group of 233 female entrepreneurs used their own savings or obtained loan from relatives and friends for initial investments (STEW, 1990).

Data Base and Methodology

The scope of this work is confined to state of urban Punjab, three big cities in general and in particular, namely Ludhiana, Amritsar and Patiala. The data of women enterprises located in urban areas, though engaged in agricultural and non agricultural enterprises has been culled from the records pertaining to the 4th Economic Census conducted during April, 1998, by the office of Economic Advisor to the Govt. of Punjab, Chandigarh.

Information regarding women enterprises records such attributes as registered/non-registered, agricultural/non-agricultural, location of the enterprise, nature of the activity, number of persons employed, type or ownership, social group and gender of owner, power/fuel used and loan/assistance dependence etc.

For the purpose of analysis, the activities of women enterprises in the informal sector are classified into three categories namely manufacturing, trading and servicing. For statistical analysis of the information frequency tables, percentages and simple averages have been calculated.

Results and Discussion

In the sampled cities of Punjab, Ludhiana, Amritsar and Patiala, 2906 women enterprises in the informal sector were reportedly functioned during 1998. Against the total of 127902 enterprises in these cities, share of women owned enterprises is just 0.023 per cent.

Conventionally economic activities are trifurcated as manufacturing, trading and servicing activities. From the functional perspective, 1030 (35.4%) units were engaged in manufacturing, 705 (24.2%) in trading and 1175 (40.4%) were engaged in servicing sector activities.

(Table 8.1) only a negligible number (2%) were engaged in the agricultural activity.

Owning to locational resource advantages of the state, in each of these three activity groups few activities will be dominating. In the context of women enterprises operated in the informal sector in Punjab it will be interesting to identify these. In manufacturing sector the activities that dominated (83.2%) the scene were engaged in the production of leather and rubber products and the textiles; those that dominated (81.5%) the trade sector were engaged in the retail trade in food, textiles and general items and those that dominated (84%) the service sector were engaged in providing services in the field of education, health and personal care (Table 8.1).

Table—8.1 Distribution of Activity in Women's Enterprises

Description of the activity	No. of units	%age out of the grand total
1	2	3
Dairy farm	52	1.70
Manufacture of food products	27	0.92
Cotton textiles	7	0.24
Wool, silk and man made fibre textile Jute	6	0.20
Textile products (including wearing apparel)	99	3.41
Wood and wood prod., furniture	24	0.82
Paper and paper prod. printing, publishing and applied industry	17	0.58
Leather and products of leather	555	19.08
Rubber, plastic, petroleum and coal products	203	6.98
Non-metallic mineral prod.	9	0.31
Basic metal and alloy	3	0.206
Metal products and parts	9	0.31
Machinery and Equipment	5	0.17
Other than transport equipment, scientific, photographic and clocks	10	0.34
Transport equip. and parts	4	0.13
Total	1030	35.4
Trade in		
Wholesale trade in Agricultural, raw materials, live animals, food, beverages, intoxicants and textiles	30	1.02

(Table Contd...)

1	2	3
Wood, paper, skin, leather, for fuel, petroleum, chemicals	4	0.13
Ceramics, glass, ores and metals	1	0.03
All types of machinery equip. including transport equipment	8	0.27
Commission agent	2	0.06
Retail trade in		
Food and food articles Beverages, tobacco, intoxicants	287	9.87
Textiles	143	4.92
Fuels and other household utilities and durables	48	1.65
Departmental stores, general stores	145	4.98
Restaurants and Hotels	37	1.27
Total	705	24.2
Servicing		
Communication	89	3.06
Banking and financial	2	0.06
Legal	1	0.03
Renting and leasing	7	0.24
Business services	20	0.68
Education	279	9.60
Health	123	4.23
Community	17	0.58
Recreational and cultural	16	0.51
Personal	584	20.09
Repair	24	0.82
Repair of capital goods	9	0.30
Storage and warehousing	1	0.03
Real estate activity	4	0.13
Total	1175	40.4
Grand total	2906	100.00

Source: Economic advisor to Govt. of Punjab, Chandigarh.

Are there any regional peculiarities? Yes, because, the informal activities cater to localised resource base. These enterprises rarely enjoy economies of scale advantage. In fact, the above proposition is supported by the distribution pattern that emerges from the data on women enterprises. Consequently we find that amongst the manufacturing activities, the manufacturing of footwear dominated in Ludhiana and Patiala and textiles products in Amritsar. Amongst the trading activities, retail trade in food articles dominated in all the cities and amongst the service sector, services in personal care and education dominated in Amritsar, whereas in health services Patiala and Amritsar had almost the same number of enterprises.

Are women enterprises activity specific? Yes, due to prior knowledge/understanding, traditionally service sector activity (particularly education and health) dominated among women. This fact has been strengthened by our study results also. As per the findings 57 per cent of the women entrepreneurs were engaged in the service sector activities, their employment in the manufacturing and trading sector activity was 29 and 14 per cent respectively. While child labour and male labour force was more engaged in the manufacturing sector (Table 8.2).

Do informal sector enterprises operated by women, hire any labour? Informal activities can not afford to have hired labour, therefore family members are involved in the activity. Enterprises run by women tend to be small even by the standards of the informal sector. Generally extra labour is not contracted and the enterprise depend heavily on the unpaid labour of family including children. Although child labour is prohibited by law, yet it prevails in the informal sector. Census data highlights this fact though its use was only 6 per cent in the women enterprises. (Table 8.2).

Do their financial needs are catered by informal sources? Yes, financial institutions/banks are not very responsive to women seeking financial assistance. Women enterprises are usually very small and therefore, women enterprises are usually very small and therefore, women seek to borrow very small sums; these loans are considered as unprofitable and too costly to administer by banks/ financial institutions, moreover lack of 'track record' or proven performance in dealing with these institutions is also a problem

Table—8.2 Employment in Women's Enterprises by Activity Group in Punjab, 1998

Description of activity	Total employment				Hired employment			
	Men	Women	Child	Overall	Men	Women	Child	Total
Manufacturing	1745 (52.42)	1441 (29.34)	372 (72.6)	3558 (40.65)	287 (25.51)	30 (1.67)	24 (32.43)	341 (12.20)
Trading	748 (22.46)	682 (13.68)	63 (12.30)	1493 (17.05)	307 (27.28)	40 (2.50)	30 (40.54)	377 (13.48)
Servicing	836 (25.11)	2788 (56.77)	77 (15.03)	3701 (42.28)	531 (47.2)	1526 (95.61)	20 (27.02)	2077 (74.31)
Total	3329	4911	512	8752	1125	1596	74	2795

Source: Economic advisor to Govt. of Punjab, Chandigarh.

Manufacturing includes: Food, textiles, wooden produces, leather, non-metallic, machinery equipments etc.

Trading includes: Wholesale and retail trade in raw materials, food articles, textiles, paper, leather, transport equipments, household goods etc.

Servicing includes: Communication, education, health, community, personal recreational repair etc.

for women. This may largely explains, why women enterprises are mostly self financed. As in our findings 83% women enterprises in the informal sector were self financed. (Table 8.3).

Table—8.3 Use of Finance in Women Enterprises

Source of finance	No. of units	%age
Self finance	2715	93.43
Borrowing from institution	61	2.10
Assistance under IRDP	8	0.27
Assistance under poverty alleviation programme (TRYSEM/DWCRA/Tool kits)	16	0.55
Borrowing from non-institutions	27	0.93
Others	79	2.72
Total	2906	100

Source: Ecónomic advisor to Govt. of Punjab, Chandigarh.

What is the technology level of these women enterprises? The technology level of women enterprises is quite poor, an indicator of technology base is use of power. As observed from the data that due to low technology base 84 per cent women enterprises did not use any kind of power/fuel at all. (Table 8.4).

Table—8.4 Power Used in Women's Enterprises

Power used	No. of units	% age
Without power	2453	84.41
Electricity	348	12.00
Coal	48	1.65
Petrol/Diesel	9	0.31
LPG/Natural gas	10	0.34
Fire wood	13	0.45
Kerosene	22	0.74
Animal power	–	–
Non-conventional energy	–	–
Other	3	0.10
Total	2906	100.00

Source: Economic advisor to Govt. of Punjab, Chandigarh.

Are the enterprises genuinely woman operated enterprises? In an imperfect market, to take advantages from, offered to a particular gender by the state or avoid the tax laws, it is possible that enterprises may be operated and owned by male members of the family but formally registered/designed in the name of women members. Our agenda reveals 8 per cent of the enterprises, where the women owner herself was not working.

Conclusions and Suggestions

The main attributes of women operated micro enterprises in the informal sector are (a) self operated; (b) self financed; (c) poor technology base; (d) dominant presence in the service sector.

Some specific changes that need to be implemented for women entrepreneurs to become more important and effective element in the business environment include:

All women entrepreneurs should join together and form co-operative societies to see their businesses run effectively and should avail themselves of all of the information, services now available and should seek assistance from experts in the field, from colleagues and from friends in order to establish both formal and informal networks that serve as support system. Experienced mentors could be drawn from these networks to act as advisors, particularly on financial matters.

To support and supplement women entrepreneurship, women organisations can arrange training programmes like skill up gradation, marginal skills, production, and marketing etc.

A collective effort on the part of women entrepreneurs to create new work structures and broaden the forms of solidarity is required.

REFERENCES

Agarwal and Patel. R. (1998). Paper Presented at 8th National Conference of *Indian Association for Women's Studies* held at SNDT University, Pune.

Baumback, C.M. and Mancuro, J.A. (1987) *Entrepreneurship and Venture Management*. New Jersy: Prentice Hall, Inc. Englewood Cliffs.

George, May (1986). *Role of Women Entrepreneurs in Indian Economy*. Report of a Dialogue on *Problems of Self-employed Women Workers* Organised by National Institute of Public Cooperation and Child Development, New Delhi.

Goffee, R. and Richard S. (1987). *Patterns of Femalê Entrepreneurship in Britain*. OECD Paris.

Gould, Sara K. (1987). Report of the National Strategy Session on *Women's Self-employment*, Cooperation for Enterprise Development, Washington, D.C.

Govt. of Punjab (1998). Survey for 4th Economic Census, by the Deptt. of Econ. Advisor. to Govt. of Punjab.

Moore, P. Dorothy and Buttner, Holly, E. (1997). *Women Entrepreneurs—moving Beyond the Glass Ceiling*. Sage Publication, Thousand Oaks, London.

Oppenoorth, H. and Hilhorst, T. (1992). *Financing Women's Enterprise Beyond Barriers and Bias*. Intermediate Technology Publications-UK.

Pinilla Cisneros, Susana. (1987). *Women in a Peruvian Experience in Support of the Informal Sector*. Lima, Peru: Instituto de Desarrollo del sector informal.

Ramamurthy, Savitri. (1991). *Women Entrepreneurs in Delhi: Their Motivations, Management Practices and Problems*. Univ. of Delhi. Unpublished Ph. D. thesis.

Sarngadharan. M., Beegam, Risia, S. (1995). *Women Entrepreneurship Institutional Support & Problems*, Discovery Publishing House, New Delhi.

U.S. Small Business Administration (SBA). (1985). *The State of Small Business* Report of the President, Transmitted to the Congress, Washington, D.C.: United States Government Printing Office.

Uschi Kraus-Harper, (1992). *What Makes Poor Women Start Micro Enterprises*. Paper Presented in Regional Workshop on the *Development of Micro Enterprises by Women*.

9

Globalisation and Empowerment of Women

*Prof. P. Leela

1. Introduction

Since a very long time, it is generally believed all over the world that, the place of a woman is at home. However, this institutional belief has been radically transformed, particularly since the beginning of the twentieth century, due to political, economic and social changes in the attitudes and outlook of the people towards women and their role in the society. Consequently, women are no longer exclusively confined to their homes alone. "The whirl of economic forces has lifted women from their old orbit. They have been slowly drawn into the economic arena in large numbers compared to earlier times" [Y. Shanmugasundaram 1993, p. 1]. While economic necessity has drawn women into labour force participation in sizeable degree, the concept of emancipation of women has over a period of time undergone a significant and meaningful shift towards the recent concept of empowerment of women. In this context, an attempt is made in the present paper to

* Professor, Dept. of Applied Economics, Andhra University, Visakhapatnam–530 003 (A.P.)

examine the impact of the all-encompassing phenomenon of globalisation on the empowerment of women, with particular reference to the Indian economy.

2. Globalisation Trends

In the post-independence era, the decade of 1990's marks a different development policy regime compared to the early planning era beginning in 1951. During the 1990's the Indian economy experienced a series of widespread economic reforms touching all major sectors of the economy like agriculture, industry, fiscal and financial institutions, foreign investment and technology, the most important above all being the foreign trade sector and the public sector. The establishment of W.T.O. in 1995, further integrated the Indian economy into the global economic system thus paving the way for globalisation of the Indian economy. "Every section of the Indian economy is now linked with the world outside, either through its direct involvement in international trade or through its indirect linkages with the export or import transactions of other sectors of the economy. The new policy regime is as much important, and relevant, to farmers, industrialists, traders and sundry service providers as to scientists, writers and singers" [G.K. Chadha, P.P. Sahu 2002, p. 1998]. In this era of globalisation, issues relating to the various marginalised sections of the society particularly women in the third World countries, demand added attention.

3. Concept of Empowerment of Women

"Empowerment is an active multidimensional process which should enable women to realise their full identity and powers in all spheres of life. It would consist of greater access to knowledge and resources, greater autonomy in decision-making, greater ability to plan their lives, have greater control over the circumstances that influence their lives and free them from shackles imposed on them by custom, belief and practice" [Balbir Soni (ed) 2001, p. 28].

Empowering women requires a fundamental and dynamic change in the perception of women, expectations from women in the society and a scientific and rational understanding of women's problems and needs. Empowerment of women is the prerequisite for the sustainable development of any country.

There are quite a number of indicators of the empowerment of women that are generally and widely adopted. These indicators relate to empowerment of women in the household, in the work and in the community. In the household, the indicators are the degree or influence in decision-making exercised by women. In the three different types of work viz. factory work, domestic work and home-based work, the indicators are the positive and negative reactions to work and to what extent work has a positive impact on the lives of women. In respect of community, the indicator is the involvement of women in political participation and in the occupational organisations. While these indicators may not capture the full range of the concept of empowerment, still they are generally employed to examine women's empowerment and under what conditions women feel more empowered and under what conditions women feel less empowered [Balbir Soni (ed) 2001, pp. 5-6].

4. Impact of the Policy of Globalisation

The policy of globalisation must be judged from the stand point of improving the quality of life of the people. It must be noted that globalisation has a varied impact on the different segments of the society and on the different sectors of the economy. Ensuring good quality of life depends on factors like food security, shelter and drinking water, access to health care and sanitation and the right to education and employment. It also depends on psychological factors like: self-reliance, self respect, dignity and confidence. Novel Laureate Amartya Sen explained a person's well-being in terms of the concept of 'capability', which represents "the alternative combination of things a person is able to do or be—the various 'functionings' he or she can achieve". The capability approach to the quality of life, thus, stresses on the person's ability to achieve various functioning and the selection of the best choice among the different alternatives in leading life.

Globalisation has multifarious characteristics. It influences not only the economy of a country, it also affects the culture of the country. There are people who strongly supported globalisation, as well as those who strongly oppose globalisation. Those who support globalisation maintain that globalisation accelerates economic development reduces poverty and increases general well-being. Those who oppose globalisation condemn it on the ground that it is a sure recipe for economic subjugation and a path leading to further exploitation of the poor and the defenceless [V.S Vyas 2002, p. 1109]. Either way, it is evident that globalisation which represents the trend towards integration of world economies, has an impact on the economies of the poor countries in particular on the poorer and vulnerable sections of the society like women.

The mainspring of globalisation, no doubt, is the development in information technology. Under the all pervasive influence of information technology, the aspirations of people in general and the aspirations of women in particular have undergone drastic changes. Even in the remote rural areas, there is a strong desire for a higher standard of living and better quality of life.

Liberalisation and privatisation are an integral part of the policy of globalisation. Liberalisation has created greater opportunities for educated and professional men as well as women [R. Bhatia 2002, p. 3464].

Women with the required skills, with access to resources and markets and with better links in the fast changing economic arena, have benefited from the opportunities for employment in diversified and emerging sectors like computers, information technology, fashion designing, engineering, electronics and communication and marketing. But a large majority of women in India are illiterate, poor, uneducated with meagre skills and knowledge. They mostly live in the rural areas and work in the unorganised informal sectors of the economy, like petty trading, household work, food gathering and processing. The impact of globalisation on the employment and income of the majority of women will be of greater interest for policy makers.

Liberalisation has increased employment opportunities for women in some sectors like the craft sector. There is an increase in the female work force the participation particularly in rural home-based craft sector [Maithreyi Krishnaraj, 1992, p. 2044]. There are large number of women artisans in embroidery and lace making, choir work, earthenware and printed textiles, cane and bamboo works, weaving, leatherware and reed mat making. Employment opportunities for women are also increasing in the services sector like domestic work, care of children, old age homes, cleaning and cooking services. But in most of these cases, working conditions of the women workers are poor, the pay is less than that of men, with no child care, or maternity benefits of sickness or unemployment benefits or other social security benefits.

Liberalisation has caused loss of employment in some sectors. For example in Bihar, women working as silk spinners and twisters lost their employment due to the import of 'China-Korea' silk yarn, which is preferred by weavers and consumers for its shine and relative cheapness. In Gujarat, women gum collectors lost employment due to the import of cheaper gum from Sudan.

Women are also affected by mechanisation. This has happened in the agricultural sector, in the textile and garment industry, in the hosiery industry. So is the case with construction industry, the food-processing industry and the screen printing industry.

Liberalisation and privatisation are leading to increase in casual labour force. Casualisation creates more employment opportunities particularly for the women workers, but all these are low-paid and insecure employment avenues. Female workers are joining the informal sector or casual labour force more than ever before. For example new rice technology has led to higher use of women workers, but most of their activities are often unpaid or underpaid. On the other hand, application of fertilisers and other plant treatments, which are essential for new HYV rice technology, are done exclusively by men. Further, in case of unemployment of men, women are being made to pay the social cost in terms of increased family violence and dowry deaths [Bharathi Ray]. Women are also unable to bear the extra burden necessary for health-care, educational expenses, better nutrition, physical care and skill improvements which are essential to cope with the emerging competitive environment associated with globalisation.

5. Alternative Options

Employment opportunities for women will be created with the opening up of new markets or extension of already existing markets either within the domestic market or in the export sector. The crafts sector witnessed a dramatic increase in the number of crafts persons from 48.25 lakh during 1991-92 to 81.05 lakhs in 1997-98 [G.O.I. 1998-99). This traditional sector from the rural economy has now developed direct links with metropolitan and global markets.

Similarly, globalisation has increased the export prospects for milk and milk products in the major dairy markets like West Asia, South-East Asia and North Africa. The dairy sector offers increasing employment opportunities for women as most of the dairy operations are carried out by women within the household. A survey of households conducted by NCAER for four villages in Punjab indicate that the share of women in dairy farming operations is around 64 per cent of the family labour and nearly 54 per cent of the total labour (R. Jhabvala and S. Sinha 2002, p. 2040).

Employment opportunities for women are increasing in the garments sector and related activities, consequent to the growth in demand in the domestic market as well as in the export markets. The expanding sector of modern health care in the rural areas is another important service sector offering good employment opportunities for women. The system of microfinance is also contributing to the increase in the opportunities for employment and livelihood for women in a large way.

Agricultural sector offers wide ranging opportunities of employment for women. While mechanisation may have a negative effect on employment opportunities for women, this can be more than compensated by the recent spurt in demand for agricultural commodities produced with organic fertilisers rather than chemical fertilisers. For example in more recent times, organic cultivation of spices has been gaining momentum. The country has developed national standards for organic production. Other certified organic products include: cardamom, black pepper, white pepper, ginger, turmeric, mustard and nutmeg. The Spices Board gives 75 per cent of the cost for securing organic certification. Training is also given to farmers for generating organic inputs such as manures, pesticides, vermi-compost etc. The Board provides financial and technical support for the project. Women play a predominant role in the preparation of organic manures and vermi-compost and hence will be able to have increased employment opportunities.

Similar is the case with livestock sector which offers increased employment and income earning opportunities for women from poor families in the rural areas. Similarly forestry sector offers substantial increase in the employment opportunities for women in the unorganised and informal sectors in terms of collection, processing and sale of minor forest produce. Reforestation programmes including nursery growing, plantations and tending of plants could be undertaken by women's groups.

6. Conclusion

Globalisation has opened up the frontiers of the Indian domestic economy to the opportunities and the challenges of the global economic system. The days of inward-orientation are over and the people of the country in general and the women who constitute fifty per cent of the population of the country in particular have to reorient themselves to the rapidly changing economic scenario.

Globalisation has brought about a change in the pattern and levels of employment for the women workers of the country and in the quality of their lives. There is a greater access to knowledge and resources and a better control over the circumstances that influence their lives. But this is mostly confined to the urban educated women. The majority of Indian women live in the rural areas and are engaged in agricultural operations.

Globalisation has had a varying impact on the employment opportunities for women, especially in the unorganised sector. In some sectors like textiles, construction, food-processing and screen-printing there has been a decline in employment opportunities and a trend towards casualisation and feminisation of the workforce.

Globalisation requires constant knowledge of the market conditions, continuous upgradation of skills and increasing levels of literacy. Women workers need to be provided with access to skills and technology and access to information regarding the new employment opportunities being opened up by the market economy. Women workers in the unorganised informal sector also need some safety nets and social security benefits like child care provisions, maternity benefits and better working conditions.

The need of the hour is globalisation with a human face and a greater role for women in shaping policies which affect their lives through employment opportunities and through poverty reduction policies. The future sources of rural employment expansion which offer increased opportunities for the poor and unskilled women to fulfil their aspirations for a higher standard of living and better quality of life need to be incorporated into the globalisation policy to make it more gender sensitive, and oriented towards greater empowerment of women.

REFERENCES

Bhatia, R (2002): "Measuring Gender Disparity using Time Use Statistics", *Economic and Political Weekly*, August 17-23, Vol. XXXVII, No. 33, pp. 3464-69.

Chadha, G.K and P.P. Sahu (2002): "Post-Reform Setbacks in Rural Employment: Issues That Need Further Scrutiny", *Economic and Political Weekly,* May 25-31, Vol. XXXVII, No. 21, pp. 1998-2026.

G.O.I. (1998-99): *Annual Report*, Ministry of Textiles.

Jhabvala, R. and S. Sinha (2002): "Liberalisation and the Women Worker", *Economic and Political Weekly,* May 25-31, Vol. XXXVII, No. 21, pp. 2037-2044.

Krishnaraj, M (1992)" "Women Craft Workers as Security for Family Subsistence", *Economic and Political Weekly,* Vol. XXVII, No. 17, April PWS 7-17.

Ray, B: Globalisation and Women in India: A Women's Studies Perspective.

Shanmugasundaram, Y (1993): *Women Employment in India,* Allied Publishers Ltd., Bombay.

Soni, B. (2001): *Reform Prospects for Rural Development*, Vol. 2, Chapter 1: Empowerment of Women, Dominant Publishers and Distributors, New Delhi.

Vyas, V.S. (2002): "Globalisation: Hopes, Realities and Coping Strategy", *Economic and Political Weekly,* March 23-29, Vol. XXXVII, No. 12, pp. 1109-1114.

10

Need for Empowerment of Tribal Women

Dr. (Mrs.) A. Sailaja Devi
Prof. M. Sundara Rao

Introduction

The State is expected to protect the special interest of women, and at the same time is seen to endorse the control of men over women. The concept of women's empowerment relates to fertility regulation, employment, health or social hygiene or modernization and decision making. It is appropriate time to control gender inequalities or to discuss about the role of the state in achieving women's empowerment as the Indian Government has declared 2001 as the year of women's empowerment.

* Dr. (Mrs.) A Sailaja Devi is UGC Project Fellow in the Department of Economics, AU. Dr. B.R. Ambedkar PG. Centre, Etcherla–532 402, Srikakulam District (AP).

* Prof. M. Sundara Rao is Head of the Department of Economics, AU. Dr. B.R. Ambedkar PG. Centre, Etcherla–532 402, Srikakulam District (AP).

The principles of gender equality and protection of women's rights have been the prime concerns in India from the days of independence. However, more than half a decade of independence and over a century of striving for a better status for women has still not produced results. Data by various agencies clearly indicates that empowerment of women is still a far away for the average Indian women, as they have not gained gender equality in development indices on par with men. The objective of empowerment policy is to empower women as the agents of social change and development. This process creates an enabling environment for women to exercise their rights both within and outside home, as equal partners along with men. The phenomenon of women's empowerment in the Indian context has been considered as an important variable for integration of women in development process. Enabling women to gain equal access to and control over resources, transforming the institutions and structures through which the ideology and practice of subordination is reinforced and reproduced.

The important studies on women empowerment are conducted by Batliwala, Srilatha, Hall, Stephen, Vijaya Lakshmi, Kate young. Some of the research studies analysed the term as a multi-faceted concept, in order to prepare ground for this process, the central and state government had been declared the policy for empowerment of women.

The studies of Uma Chakravarthy, Agarwal, Hasan, Kasambi analysed that the state is a major planner in the enterprise of women's empowerment and the role of the state is always a question. During the first 50 years after independence the question of bringing women into the mainstream through opportunities and capabilities has been considered from time to time. In recent years, there has been considerable work on the question of empowerment. The most notable contributions came from Sen and Gupta, Shama, Kabeer and others are with the view the empowerment aims to increase women's access to and control over social, economic and intellectual resources. However the debate on empowerment strategies have not sufficiently explored or analysed the role of the state.

Until the report of the committee on the status of women in India in the mid seventies, this neglect was invisible to policy makers as well as scholars. By the mid seventies and mid eighties, the women's movement had accelerated. Throughout eighties, women's groups kept addressing the state as their was a belief that only through public policy can the status of women be empowered. However, field experience reveal that women's empowerment process must take the form of social movement located within communities.

In this direction, the state of Andhra Pradesh has initiated a 'strategy paper on women empowerment' in 2001. In order to achieve of Swarna Andhra Pradesh of Vision 2020, a cabinet sub-committee was set up to give recommendations on the women empowerment policy. The main trust of the policy in convergent of all activities pertaining to the women in order to improve education, health's nutrition and overall development of the social and economic indicators for women and children in the state. The objectives of the policy are: reducing gender discrimination, address to gender inequalities in education and employment. Increase gender sensitivity to health, welfare programmes and prevent atrocities against women.

Andhra Pradesh is famous for its Anti-arrack Movement in 1990s and recent self-help group movement. The government has realised the potential of women power and encouraged their participation in developmental programmes. If women are to be empowered, it is necessary to provide an expending network of support services so that they are feed from some of their gender shackles. However, the variables live sex-ratio, literacy rate, work participation rate, health and nutrition and violence against women indicate low status of women in Andhra Pradesh. The government of Andhra Pradesh has initiated the political reservation policy three-tire system. The objective of the policy is implementation of 33.13 per cent reservation for women in employment by government departments, corporations and public sector undertakings by monitoring of reservations in all departments and institutions by regional deputy director and project director of WD & CW department by inspections.

The Government of Andhra Pradesh has announced 'A strategy paper or women empowerment' during the period January 2001. However it is very shortest period to evaluate the role of state in the process of women's empowerment. One must appreciate the approaches advanced by the Government of Andhra Pradesh. But still some criticism is there that the wide income disparities and gender gaps stay in the face of all societies. Hence moving towards women's empowerment is not a technocratic goal it is a political process. It requires a new way of thinking.

Against this background an attempt is made in the present study to highlight the need for empowerment of tribal women. At the outset the methodology and collection of data are presented (section 1.1) afterwards, the dimensions relating to the status of women in tribal society (section 1.2), demographic indicators (section 1.3), health indicators (section 1.4), education indicators (section 1.5) and occupational patterns of tribal women are discussed. The conclusions are presented at the end (section 1.6).

Methodology and Collection of Data

Multi stage stratified random sampling method is used in the present study. The selection process is carried out in four stages, they are relating to district, mandal, villages and households. The Srikakulam district is selected for the study due to the fact that the district has drawn worldwide attention through the tribal movement in the political upheaval of 1969-71. The Seethampeta mandal is selected for the study because it is the only tribal mandal that is having a high proportion of (89.54 per cent) tribal population and also the ITDA is placed at Seethampeta. The villages are selected depending upon the higher concentration of specific tribes. With a stratification procedure based on the specific tribe population concentration, the panchayats are classified into three categories. From the Konda Savara tribes concentrated panchayats the villages Vajjayyaguda and Mutyalu are selected from very interior hill areas are keesari jodu villages are selected and from Jatapu tribe concentrated panchayats Goidi and Gadiguddi villages are selected.

The Konda Savara and Jatapu tribes are equally proportioned in the Seethampeta mandal. To examine the inter tribe variations in the socio-economic conditions of tribal women 60 households are selected from each tribe from their concentrated selected villages based on the random sampling procedure. The eldest female member was treated as a unit of study. In this way we had 180 households who are equally proportioned from Konda Savara and Jatapu. Information relating to the selected households is collected while canvassing a prely designed and structured household schedule in the selected villages during April 1998 to March 1999 in different visits. The secondary data has been obtained from Annual Reports and Actions Plans of ITDA Seethampeta, District had book of statistics of different years published by the Chief Planning Officer, Srikakulam, MRO and MDO offices of Seethampeta Mandal.

Status of Women in Tribal Society

Generally, sex ratio, treatment of women, legal status, opportunities for public activity, taboos and traditional beliefs and practices and eligibility for equal share in family and ancestral property are followed as criteria for determination of the status of the women in any society.

Scholars to determine the status of women have also used sex ratio. It is generally believed that discriminatory practices against women, as well as a low age at first child birth result into high female mortality leading to a lower female sex ratio. The sex ratio of STs is almost equal in the districts of Srikakulam, Vizianagaram, Visakhapatnam, East and West Godavari. In this study it has been found that there were 927 females per 1000 males in the study area. However, the number of females were low in case of Jatapu tribe which indicate that women in Japatu tribe were better placed as compared with their counterparts of Konda Savara tribe.

Regarding treatment of women in tribal society, most of the tribal communities treat their sons and daughters equally and they rejoice at the birth of female child. The tribal communities usually do not face any problem in up-bringing the female child and for the marriagē at later stage. Unlike in the non-tribal caste groups there is no dowry system in the tribal communities and on the contrary the bridegroom has to pay bride price to the parents of the girl. The parents of girl never face any kind of difficulties in getting their daughters married. In all types of marriages including levirate type of marriage the will of women prevails over all other considerations. The women as daughter-in-law or wife is treated well and she is not put to any kind of hardships. In case of bad treatment by husband or parents-in-law in her family of procreation, she deserts her husband and goes to her parents divorce is granted by the tribal society at that moment the second husband pays compensation to the aggrieved husband. The woman is not put to many restrictions in tribal communities and she is treated well.

Customary laws in their ways of life largely govern the tribal societies. All the tribal communities in Andhra Pradesh are patriarchal, patrilineal and patrilocal. The property is distributed equally among the male members. The girls in the family may get ornaments of mother, few cattle etc. But in case of absence of male child, the daughter gets the property and husband generally lives in the house of his wife. After the death of the husband his wife gets the property and she can enjoy and control over the property if she does not marry another person. She is not entitled to any property of the decreased husband if she marries another person.

Regarding the opportunities to the tribal women for public activity, it is not a taboo for a tribal woman to participate in public life and religious activities of the community except during the period of her menstruation. Woman in tribal communities freely participate in all kinds of village and community festivals and fairs. They play dominant role in traditional colourful dances. Irrespective of age, all females spontaneously participate in the ethnic dances, which are performed on festive and marriage occasions. It is significant to note that women in certain tribal groups occupy a very important position as priestesses. It is believed that these priestesses are endowed with supernatural powers to heal the sick or to exercise the evil spirits. They often act as priestesses to the goddesses in tribal areas. But they neither indulge in witchcraft nor do any harm to individuals. The institution definitely indicates superior status of women in tribal areas when compared to the social status enjoyed by their counterparts in rural areas.

The tribal women folk suffer a number of disabilities like their counterparts in rural areas. Generally men impose more restrictions on their women folk. The parents do not take much care of their daughters are they do not send their girls to schools. The Grand women is not expected to go before elders with chappals and she is not allowed to sit on a cot before her elder brother-in-law and her elder sisters-in-law by names. She should not also call the children of her husband's elder sister by name. She can only mention them by her relationship. Parents settle the marriage of their daughters without least consideration for their preference of wishes of their daughters.

The women are not permitted to plough the lands. If she ploughs, it is believed that it does not rain. Even in the marriage by capture the girl can be reputed much against her will and she is forced to marry that particular boy only. This practice has a social sanction. The girl's education is totally neglected by the parents since they believe that investment on girl is not rewarding. Further, early marriage and various peculiar types of matrimony are great obstacles for the development of education among girls. Thus, women suffer because of traditional belief systems and tabboos.

As per the customary laws prevalent in all the tribal societies, except few matriarchal societies the women are not entitled for a share within the family's or ancestral property except in families where there are no male members. There are no matriarchal tribal societies in the study area and all the tribal communities are patriarchal and patrilineal. This customary law makes tribal women insecure in case of divorce or desertion by the husband. Moreover the Hindu social codes are not applicable to scheduled areas in the study area.

Demographic Indicators

With the help of certain demographic indicators, an attempt has been made to find out the presence or absence of discrimination against women as well as to find out the extent of change that has taken place in the status of women of the younger generation in the tribal economy. The demographic analysis pertaining to age composition of the selected households and their family members (Tables 10.1, 10.2, 10.3 and 10.4) indicate that nearly 60 per cent are within the working age of 15 to 55 years. The household average family size is 4.49, it is relatively higher among Konda Savara tribes.

Age at marriage has been taken as one of the indicators of the status of women. It is assumed that if woman is married at a younger age and there is wide age gap between the husband and the wife, she would have a lower status. In this study, it has been found that the average age at marriage for the respondents came out 13-25 and 14-17 years in Konda Savara and Jatapu tribes respectively. On the other hand, average age of the husband came out 19.7 years in Konda Savara tribe and 20.15 years in Jatapu tribe indicating a big age gap. The results clearly indicate that though the average age at marriage of the respondents of Jatapu tribe was relatively higher than that of Konda Savara tribe, nevertheless, the age at marriage of both the tribes was quite low in contrast with the national average. Secondly, the age gap between the husband and the wife has also been quite considerable, indicating the low status of women in both the tribes.

In order to find out the extent of change that has taken place with regard to age at marriage of women, the children of the respondents were taken into account and the average age at marriage has been worked out. It has been noticed that the mean age at marriage for daughters of Konda Savara tribe was 13.05 years and in Jatapu tribe it was 14.88 years indicating a slight increase in age at marriage. Nevertheless, the age at marriage of the younger generation still remains below the national average indicating that their status has not yet improved with regard to this variable. However, no marked difference has been found in the age at marriage of the younger generation of both the tribes. In addition to work out the mean age at marriage of the daughters of the respondents, the average age at marriage of their sons has also been worked out which came to 20-44 years of Konda Savara tribe, and 21-32 years in Jatapu tribe. It is clear from the analysis that so far as the male members of both the generations are concerned, their age at marriage is quite high in contrast with their spouses and the average age at marriage for the husbands and the sons is higher than the national average. It can be concluded that with regard to age at marriage, the women have lower status in both the tribes.

Fertility dynamics of the respondents of both the tribes was another indicator taken to gauge the status of women by taking into account the mean age at first child birth. It has been found that the mean age at first child birth for the respondents of Konda Savara tribe was 15.3 years, whereas it was 16.2 years in case of Jatapu tribe. Fertility dynamics for the younger generation were also considered to find out the trend of change. The mean age at the time of first child birth for the daughters of the respondents of Konda Savara tribe has been worked out 16.8 years, whereas in case of Jatapu tribe it was 17.9 years. The younger generation of Jatapu tribe had a higher mean age at first child birth in contrast with the younger generation of Konda Savara tribe indicating a slight improvement in the status of younger women of Jatapu tribe.

The fertility performance of the respondents has also seen with reference to the number of conceptions, miscarriages and live birth. On all the three counts no major difference came out among the respondents of both the tribes. When the fertility performance of the respondents was compared with that of their daughters, it was noted that the daughters had a lower fertility performance than their mothers, which was attributed to their higher mean age at first child birth. As the younger generation (daughters of the respondents) has not completed their fertility span, it is difficult to draw any conclusions. Nevertheless, it was noted that in case of Jatapu tribe the mean age at first child birth was higher. Even though the mean age at marriage of the younger generation of both the tribes was almost constant, indicating a slight improvement in the status of the younger generation of Jatapu women.

To find out the extent of discrimination against the women, infant and child mortality has been worked out for both the tribes. Some of the studies have indicated that due to discriminatory social practices, mortality is higher for the female children as compared to the male children. Data of the present study however, reveal the opposite trend. In both the generations, the male infant and child mortality was higher than that for the females in both the tribes. Further, the percentage of households experiencing infant and child mortality came out higher in Konda Savara tribe when compared with Jatapu. The results do not support the common contention that female child mortality is higher as compared with male child because of discriminatory social practices.

Health Indicators

In spite of good personal hygienic conditions among tribal female population health conditions found to be deteriorating due to inaccessibility of medical and health facilities. In modern times the traditional herbal medicines are being discouraged by agents of change and allopathic medicines and services are not available to them as these primary health centres are not catering to the needs of tribals living in interior hilly tracts. The maternity mortality rate (MMR) among ST females was around 8 per 1000 as per the studies conducted by TCR & TI in 1992. Among generation population MMR during that period was 4 per 1000 live births. The tribal women scantily dressed up because of their grinding poverty. Some of the women belonging to primitive tribal groups do not possess second sari for change. As they are not able to change their clothes regularly they are likely to be afflicted with skin diseases. In view of scarcity of water, the women folk are not able to take bath regularly. They sleep on the floor without any kind of mats during nights, some times sharing the space with goats, sheep which are considered as immovable property to them.

A few studies have indicated the existence of discriminatory practices with regard to providing health facilities to the women. In the present study, immunization and breast feeding have been taken as two health indicators to find out the presence or absence of sex discrimination. With regard to immunization, no discrimination has been established. More than four-fifth children of the first and second generation were immunized irrespective of sex in both the areas. Further, non-immunization was attributed to ignorance and non-availability of the facilities rather than sex discrimination. Hence, on this variable also we did not find the practice of sex discrimination in the tribal areas. Prior to advent of development in tribal areas, tribal societies were having their own herbal pharmacopoeia. The women folk were able to maintain reasonable health standards with administration of herbal medicines and by following certain productive and prohibitive taboos. A woman breast feeds the child till the baby begins to walk and till that time sexual relations are tabooed. Because of this taboo pre-natal and post-natal diseases among women folk are rare and this restriction automatically limits family size.

These rigid traditions are disappearing due to contacts with non-tribals. Large scale immigration of non tribals into tribal areas are also resulting in transmission of venereal diseases (VD) to innocent females. As the tribal settlements are found in the interior places, modern medical facilities are not accessible to them and women folk are the worst, sufferers. The healthy delivery system is paralysed in the study area and most of the posts of doctors, nurses, compounders are vacant. In case doctors are other medical staff are available the required medicines and transport which are essential are not available.

The survey conducted about the existing health facilities in the tribal area indicate that (Tables 10.5 and 10.6) the governmental and non-governmental agencies have been trying to intensify health facilities in the tribal areas during last few decades. In spite of the facilities the native doctor and medicine are still playing an important role in the health care of tribal people. Particularly tribals are prone to a variety of diseases due to their unhygienic living conditions. Drinking water is a serious problem in all-tribal villages. They have to drink highly contaminated water, which is with calcium deficiency and causes anaemia and other chronic diseases. Many tribals in the hill tracts reported that they use herbs and leaves for their diseases. The Primary Health Centres (PHCs) in these areas are under utilized due to its distance from villages and also due to non-availability of medicines in the centres. However 35 per cent of the households in plains reported that they are taking medical care from government PHCs and at their village health camps. The village health camps are creating awareness about the medical care among the tribal.

Similarly immunization of children against TB, BCG and small pox diseases is also not following by the tribals in the hill tracts only (22 per cent) responded positively for the immunizations care in these areas. The numbers of children vaccinated are found high in plain areas (43 per cent) rather than hill areas. These ANMs are performing excellent job in immunization of children. ANMs and other medical staff are propagating about medical care for children and pregnant women in the tribal villages.

The presented data on adoption of family planning by heads of households (Table 10.7) show that family planning has not become more popular in the traditional and remote hilly tribal areas. It is noticed that all most all the tribes in plains use some kind of native medicine, which is derived from herbs to control their size of families. However there is good feeling in the tribal plains regarding family planning. There are midwives and health workers posted in the villages who were trained to propagate the family planning programmes in the tribal areas. Though the family planning programmes are intensively campaigned in the tribal areas by ANMs and others, the tribal women are not showing interest in the family planning. It is indicated that though 90 per cent of the family members are aware of family planning only 42.77 per cent adopted it, 77 per cent of the tribal women in the hill tracts are still using a native medicine as a preventive alternative. The adoption is very limited among the Konda Savara tribe and marginal farms. However nearly 40 per cent of Jatapu women responded positively to the family planning programmes. There is need to strengthen the public health and family planning system particularly in the remote hill areas.

Breast feeding is another health indicator taken for the present study, it was assumed that a female child was likely to be breast fed for a lesser duration than a male child. In the present study, we noticed that on an average the respondents breast fed for 2.2 years for male children whereas their female children were breast fed on an average of 1.8 years in Konda Savara tribe. In case of Jatapu tribe, the duration of breast feeding was comparatively low. The respondents on an average breast fed their male children for a period of 1.5 years, whereas their female children were breast fed on an average for 1.1 years. However, in both the tribes either with regard to the respondents themselves or their children, no discrimination based on sex was practised. Hence, both at the inter-tribe and inter-generation levels, we found that the female children were not discriminated against.

Need for Promoting Health Conditions

In view of high incidence of maternity and infant mortality in tribal areas full-fledged maternity hospitals with a minimum 30 beds have to be started. The local traditional mid-wives have to be trained in safe delivery practices and they should be provided with safe delivery kits. Basic knowledge of health and hygiene have to be imparted to women through women's organisations in every village. As the tribal people including children and women suffer with a number of nutritional deficiency diseases, ICDS schemes have to be introduced in interior tribal villages/hamlets. The criteria and rules have to be relaxed in extending special nutrition programme to tribal children, pregnant and lactating mothers. Dietary pattern of all tribal communities has to be properly studied. Local dietary patterns, availability of low cost food items have to be taken into consideration while recommending nutritious diets to tribal clients.

Educational Indicators

The tribal women folk are stepped in ignorance and illiteracy. The ST female literacy rate in Andhra Pradesh is only 8.68 per cent which is less than half when compared to their counter parts at national level (18.19 per cent) as per 1991 census reports. The ST female literacy is less than one third of the ST male literacy in Andhra Pradesh (25.25 per cent) and further it is less than one fourth when compared to general female literacy (32.72 per cent) in Andhra Pradesh as per 1991 census.

Differential literacy rate, enrolment for higher education and drop out rates among males and females can help to find out the extent of sex discrimination that prevails in tribal society. The presence and absence of discrimination against women has been worked out in the present study based on education by sex and generation, drop out rate by sex and generation and studies outside the village by sex and generation. Education has been recognised as a key factor in tribal development to bring in economic and social transformation among the tribals. The government of Andhra Pradesh spends approximately 50 per cent of tribal sub-plan allocation on education. The ITDAs right from their inception has been putting tremendous effort in the provision and spread of both formal and non-formal education among tribal people.

The tribe wise distribution of head of the households literacy level (Table 10.8) reveal that only 32.22 per cent households are completed primary education and 6.11 per cent completed secondary education and 61.67 per cent are illiterates. Though majority of the households are illiterate (61.67 per cent) in the study area they care more for their word of promises than for any written document.

It is clear that majority of the educated heads of households are having education up to primary level only. Further there is considerable variation of the education status of the heads of households among the tribes. However, the literacy level of the heads of households partially reflects the status of tribal women. To have a complete picture, one has to examine the literacy levels among all the members of the family. The details of literacy level of all members of the family are examined (Table 10.9). Out of the total family members only 40.72 per cent are literates. The adult literacy rates are very low it is 36.12 per cent in case of male and only 6.27 per cent in case of women. However the children literacy rates are very encouraging in the tribal areas. In the total male children 70.07 per cent are literates and it is very interesting that in the total female children 60.74 per cent of female children are literates. The difference between the adult female literacy and female children literacy levels indicate the changing position in the tribal areas. The female literacy level is extremely low, particularly among the adults because in olden days in villages female members are not sent to school, due to social inhabitation.

A comparison of sex-wise literacy levels of children population shows a different picture that, the levels of literacy among the children are very high in both males and females. This reflects the change in the attitude of the elders towards education, which is the main reason for increasing the incidence of literacy among children. Increasing educational facilities particularly, separate Ashram schools for girls students scholarships to girl students coupled with favourable change in parental attitude has resulted in more and more girls attending schools.

Normally in the villages, the number of dropout children is expected to be more. Hence an attempt is made to study the pattern of dropouts and data are presented in (Table 10.10). It can be noticed from the table that among school drop-out children the proportion of female children is more than that of male children. Most of the children are dropouts at the primary education level. The number of dropout children is more in the remote hilly tracts rather than in plains. The dropouts are high among the children of Konda Savara and very less among the children of Jatapu. The positive change on education is very high in the plain tribes. Generally in the tribal economy children are used as wage earners. But in the present period, children are being sent to schools by foregoing the present income for their future prosperity. This is one important change in the value system of tribal economy that parents are accepting the importance of education of their children for the future prosperity of the children by diverting them from the traditional rural activity to other urban activities.

Measures to Improve the Levels of Literacy

Functional literacy has to be carefully formulated to suit changing scenario in tribal areas. The main objective of functional literacy in tribal areas is to empower local tribal communities and traditional institutions. Greater awareness has to be created in tribals about sustainable exploitation of forest resources and economic resources. In spite of comprehensive protective regulation available for the benefit of tribals they are not properly implemented as tribals are ignorant and illiterates. The men and women have to be enlightened about various protective legislation through functional literacy programmes. Adult literacy centres separately for males and females have to be started. At present literacy levels among ST females is extremely low and girls residential schools. Ashram Schools and hostels are only less than one third of boys educational institutions. This gap has to be filled up by establishing more number of residential schools, junior and degree colleges to promote education among girls.

Occupational Patterns

Women in tribal societies are more industrious compared to men. A tribal woman is considered was an economic asset. She attends to all kinds of economic activities except ploughing which is a taboo in most tribal societies. In addition to regular work of fetching water from distant streams, fuel from forest, grinding, cooking, collection of minor forest produce along with her husband and grown up children. The processing of minor forest produce is largely done by women folk. She carries heavy head loads of either minor forest produce or some items of agricultural produce and go to weekly markets along with her husband. It is significant to note that both wife and husband attend to weekly markets and sell whatever they brought to markets and purchase some items of their domestic necessities.

Woman plays vital role in all kinds of economic transactions along with her husband in selling or purchasing their essential items. Tribal woman plays crucial and vital role in all kinds of economic productive activities. They constitute more than half of the labour force. They are invisible potential workers. Declined from 59.9 per cent to 56.8 per cent. The occupational pattern of tribal women as per 1991 census reports reveals that 32.2 per cent are cultivators and 59.1 per cent are agricultural labourers, where as among males, agriculture labourers constitute only 37.2 per cent. These figures indicate that large number of women supplement their meager family income by wage income. This trend also reveals that 96.2 per cent of women are working in primary sector and rest are pursuing occupations in off farm sector. Occupational pattern may form basis for formulation of relevant specific schemes for economic empowerment of tribal women.

Female children from the tender age are assigned more duties by parents than male children, as female children are more obedient by nature. The grown up girls are not usually sent to schools but they are made to look after younger children and other household duties like cooking, cleaning of utensils etc., during the absence of parents in the day time. The girl in the tribal household around 10 days of age goes along with parents for collection of minor forest produce, agricultural operations and attend to other domestic chores.

Man in tribal areas attend to only ploughing of the land and collection of minor forest produce. Tribal woman not only assist the husband in all kinds of agricultural operations, collection processing and marketing of MFP in addition to her regular duties of bringing fire wood, water, cleaning of utensils, cooking, looking after children and all kinds of activities connected with maintenance and management of the house. The woman works in the fields and forest till the last days of her advanced pregnancy and again resumes her regular duties soon after purificatory bath is performed. In hunting and gathering societies, woman collects edible roots, tubers, wild fruits, leaves etc., to keep ready for household consumption at regular intervals. The man sits at home and looks after young children while woman goes to the forest for collection of MFP, fire wood etc.

(A) Work Participation Rates

The details pertaining to sex-wise distribution of workers indicate that (Table 10.11) though the male population is higher (61.86) than female population (48.14). Among the work force female participation is higher (50.10) than male population (49.92). Among the total female population 71.53 per cent are working and on the other hand in the total male population only 68.69 per cent are working population. This indicates that in tribal economy women does much work, she participates in agricultural operations, collection of minor forests produce and also in non-agricultural labour activity. The freedom to remarry and the bride price give her more or less equal status with men. This situation reveals a low dependency ratio among the tribal households. In the total population, workers are very high (70.42 per cent) than non-workers (29.38 per cent) and the extent of child labour is only 10.91 per cent of total population. Inter tribe worker participation rates indicate that except in case of Jatapu in all other tribes women work participation rates are very high. The data pertaining to non-workers among different tribes reveal that including school going children the male workers are only 29.38 per cent of total population of the households. Among the non-workers men are in higher proportion (56.49 per cent) than women (43.51 per cent). The male non-workers are higher in number rather than women. The non-workers are very less in number in case of Konda Savara tribe and very high in case of Jatapu tribe.

The tribe-wise distribution of child labour among the selected households shows that, the child labour are only 9.78 per cent of total population of the selected households (Table 10.12). Among the child labour female are higher (56.96 per cent) than men (43.04 per cent). The child labour are more in number among Konda Savara tribe residing in the hill and remote areas and the number of child labour are relatively low among the Jatapu tribe who are residing in the plain areas of the tribal economy. In the remote and interior areas tribal people used to engage their children in activities like cow hording, sheep rearing, crop guarding and other agricultural and household activities. As the tribal agriculturist cannot afford to employ wage labour because of poverty, he finds it easily and necessary to involve his children in some activity. The low rate of child women labour among the selected households indicate that more and more female children are being sent to schools rather than involving them in household activities. This is a good symptom of transformation of the tribal economy.

(B) Dependency Ratio

In the tribal economy in agriculture and non-agriculture activities most of the family members are involved. Hence we assume a low dependency ratio among the tribal households. The data on the dependency ratio shows (Table 10.13) that, it is ground 1:0:31 to 1:0:51 among different tribes and it is 0.42 when the two tribes put together. The size of dependency ratio depends upon the work participation ratio of the children and also of the adult above the age of 55 years. Though nearly 35.90 per cent of the children population are not in the effective work force, due to the existence of adults above 55 years of age is negligible (4.21 per cent) of total population. A high rate of the female work participation rates it is observed that the dependency ratio in general is relatively low among the tribal communities. It is interesting to note that the dependency ratio is relatively low among the hill tribes (Konda Savara) rather than the tribes in plains (Jatapu) because in the hill and remote areas the child labour is very high in Konda Savara, when compared to plain tribes.

(C) Nature of Different Occupations

Agriculture is the predominant occupation in the study area followed by labour works. Because of the subsistence nature of agriculture, the tribals are compelled to work as both agriculture and non-agricultural labour, to collect minor forest produce in the forestry to earn additional income. Though all the selected households are agriculturists most of them are forced to go with other occupations like labour works and forest produce collection. As all the selected households are agriculturists their main occupation is cultivation and they are owner cultivators. The occupational spread of women workers by participation in number of activities shows that (Table 10.14) in addition to their main occupation 52 households in the plain areas are participating in labour works both in agriculture and non-agriculture and forest produce collect as secondary occupations. On the other hand a number of 60 per cent households in the remote and hilly areas are considering labour works and forest produce collection as one of the secondary occupations. In the selected sample 36 per cent of the households are with more than two occupations.

Tribe wise occupational distribution of women workers according to their main occupation indicates that (Table 10.15), in the total workers 47.77 per cent are largely depending upon agriculture, 18.93 per cent of workers are relying upon labour works and the extent of women workers depending upon collection of forest produce is only 3.09 per cent. Out of 26.64 per cent of the non-workers, larger portion belongs to school going children (22.52 per cent). The Konda Savara women are relatively relying more upon minor forest produce. Jatapu women in plain are diverting towards non-farm occupations like other services, salaried services and non-form labour. The occupational distribution of family members ultimately reveal that all the tribals are relying more upon agriculture (47.77 per cent) and labour works (18.93 per cent).

(D) Measures to Improve the Levels of Living of Tribal Women

In development of women and children of rural areas programme (DWACRA), several income generating schemes are being introduced among women folk in order to make them real productive economic assets. Women folk among tribal communities are not equipped with necessary operational and managerial skills. Moreover several schemes such as horticulture, sericulture, soil and water conservation, improved varieties of crops, joint forest management, construction activities etc., are being introduced in tribal areas. It should be made as mandatory to all the departments to introduce all these schemes through participatory management. Tribal women folk have to be imparted skills in exclusive groups in management of various development activities. It is significant to note that women thrift societies in some tribal areas of Andhra Pradesh have taken up construction of school buildings, anganwadi centres, even check dams and these works are appreciated for their quality by both internal and external funding agencies. Women folk should be imparted skills in different occupations. As women folk possess innate skills in raising nurseries, grafting etc. they have to be entrusted with the responsibilities of raising plants required under joint forest management.

One of the important reasons for pauperisation of tribal societies is exploitation by money lenders, land lords and merchants. These exploitative agencies spread their debt traps in the tribal areas and made innocent and gullible tribals as permanent debtors by charging exorbitant rates of interest. In the past when transportation and communication facilities were not developed, tribal societies had full command over the resources available in their habitat. But in modern times tribals are gradually alienated from their own lands, forest resources and even from his own cultural moorings. All the exploitative and disruptive forces have to be totally eliminated to restore credibility and self reliance.

Conclusion

In view of various debilitating problems faced by women folk as discussed in the preceeding pages, empowerment of tribal woman is sine-quo-non for not only improving their quality of life styles but also improving the conditions of tribal families and tribal villages. Empowerment is the process of revitalisation of local people by giving more powers and responsibilities so that they can utilise the opportunities, resources available for sustainable development. This process encompasses social, cultural, financial, skill and knowledge empowerment. Unless all these vital aspects are integrated and greater vision is developed in local female population the sustainable development among tribals cannot ensured. The important areas to be considered for empowerment of tribal women in this study are identified as: functional literacy and education, health and nutrition, development of skills to take up new income generating schemes, social and cultural development and organisation of thrift, credit and processing societies.

It has been concluded after screening the theoretical controversies and establishes the empirical evidences with respect to the demographic, health, educational and economic indicators prevailing in the tribal economy. Economic development of a region alone does not help in the elevation of the status of women which is enshrined in the social and cultural values. For the removal of inequality based on sex and discriminatory practices against the women, we have to shift our focus on values of the society and culture. The status of women can be elevated only when they will be made economically, socially and psychologically independent in the society. It will provide an insight to the planners, policy makers, academicians and researchers about the grass-root relations prevailing in the tribal economy.

The tribal women should be allowed to use their full potential. Through adequate measures of health, education, skills and intellectual as well as moral capabilities, they should be equipped to raise the quality of life. Social change through equal treatment for the girl child and reducing son preference, schooling for both boys and girls, empowering women and providing them new skills for income generation is need of the hour. In view of fast changing scenario in tribal areas, a vision for self reliance and urge for development has to be inculcated in tribal societies especially in the women folk. These vital changes can be accomplished by establishing thrift and credit societies, grain banks, M.F.P. processing societies. Adult literacy centres, DWACRA groups have to be established in the interior tribal areas. These local organisations have to be empowered and guided properly in functioning and maintenance by women liaison workers and community coordinators.

REFERENCES

1. Agarwal. B (1998). Patriarchy and the Modernizing State: An Introduction; in Bina Agarwal (ed) *Structures of Patriarchy: State Community and house hold in Modernizing Asia*, New Delhi, *Kalifor Women*, pp. 1928.
2. Batliwala Srilatha (1997) "Empowerment Women", *Seminar No.* 449, New Delhi, p. 89.
3. G.O.I (1974) Towards Equality, New Delhi.
4. G.O.I (1989) National Perspective Plan for Women, New Delhi.
5. G.O.I. (1999) 9th Five Year Plan Document, New Delhi.
6. Government of Andhra Pradesh *(2001 'Strategy Paper on Women's Empowerment*, Department of Women Development and Child Welfare, Hyderabad.
7. Kate Young (1993) Planning Development with Women: Making a World of Difference, Mac Millian, p. 157.
8. Kosambi Meera (1997), "Gender Reform and Competing State Controls Over Women: *The Rakhmabai Lax (1884-1988) in Social Reform, Sexuality and the state (ed by) Patricia Uberoi*, New Delhi, Sage Publications.
9. Marilee Karl (1995) Women and Empowerment: *Participation and Decision Marking*, London, Zed Books Ltd.
10. Maithreyi Krishna Raj (2000) Public Policy: An Agenda, *IAWS*, Hyderabad.
11. Stephen. F. (1997) Women's Empowerment: A Process of Restricting Power Relations, *"Search Bulletin, XII, pp. 4-13*. Quoted by B.V. Jaya Lakshmi (2001) Women's Empowerment Published by IDPS, Visakhapatnam.
12. Uma Chakravarthy (1999) Whatever Happened to the Vedic Dasi? Orientalism, Nationalism and a Script for the Past *"in Kunkum Snayasi and Sudesu Vaid (eds) Recasting Women*, pp. 302.
13. Vidyarthi and Roy, *"Tribal Culture of India"*, Concept Publishing Company, New Delhi, 1977.
14. Nag, D.S., *"Tribal Economy—An Economy Study of the Baiga"*, Bharatiya Admmajati Sevak Sangh, Kingsway Camp, New Delhi, 1958.
15. Sexena, R.P., *"Tribal Economy in Central India"*, Calcutta.
16. Ramaiah, P., *"Tribal Economy of India"*: Light Life Publishers, New Delhi, 1981.

17. Chinnalabudu, "*A Socio-Economic Survey of a Multi-Tribal Village in Araku Valley Visakhapatnam Districts*", AER Centre, Andhra University, 1970.

18. Gopala Rao, Ram Gopal, N., "Chinnababudu Resurveyed", AER Centre, Andhra University, 1983.

19. Patnaik, N., "*Tribals and their Development*" National Institute of Community Development, Hyderabad, 1972.

20. Singh, S.K., "*Economics of the Tribals and their Transformation*", New Delhi, 1982.

21. Jain, L.C., "*Emancipation of Schedule Castes and Tribes*: Some Suggestions", *Economical Political Weekly*, February, 28, 1991.

22. Bhowmic, P.K., 1991; "Tribes in the Changing Circumstances of India", *Man in India, Vol. 71*, No. 1.

23. Imam Balu, 1993, "Cultural Spatial Concepts inflict in Tribal art and Identity in Hazaribagh District", *Man in India, Vol. 73 and No. 2*.

24. Janah, Sunil, 1993: "The Tribals of India", Calcutta, Oxford University Press.

25. Mohan Rao K. 1990: "*The Kolams a Primitive Tribe in Transition*", Hyderabad, Book Links Corporation, p. 57 and 58.

Table—10.1 Distribution of the Households by Age Composition Across Tribes/Size Groups of Farms

S. No.	Tribe	Below 25	25-35	35-45	45-55	above 55	Total
I	Tribes:						
1.	Konda Savara	13 (13.33)	18 (20.00)	27 (31.67)	25 (26.67)	7 (8.33)	90 (100.00)
2.	Jatapu	14 (15.00)	21 (23.33)	26 (30.00)	23 (25.00)	6 (6.67)	90 (100.00)
	All tribes	27 (15.00)	39 (21.67)	53 (29.44)	48 (26.67)	13 (7.22)	180 (100.00)

Table—10.2 Distribution of the Total Family Members by Age Composition

S. No.	Tribe	Age composition						Grand total	Family size
		0-15	15-25	25-35	35-45	45-55	Above 60		
I.	Tribes:								
1.	Konda savara	149 (33.36)	65 (12.29)	56 (14.64)	96 (24.43)	41 (18.93)	16 (5.36)	423 (100.00)	4.67
2.	Jatapu	141 (36.12)	68 (14.05)	53 (13.31)	90 (22.07)	45 (11.41)	18 (3.04)	385 (100.00)	4.38
	All Tribes	290 (25.90)	103 (12.74)	109 (13.50)	186 (24.26)	86 (10.64)	34 (9.21)	808 (100.00)	4.49

Table—10.3 Sex-wise Distribution of Family Members in the Sample Households

S. No.	Tribe	Male			Female			Grand Total
		Adult	Children	Total	Adult	Children	Total	
I.	Tribe:							
1.	Konda Savara	138 (34.74)	78 (18.57)	217 (53.61)	131 (33.57)	69 (16.74)	198 (46.79)	415 (100.00)
2.	Jatapu	134 (35.36)	69 (52.73)	202 (52.09)	123 (32.67)	66 (16.35)	191 (48.91)	393 (100.00)
	All tribes	272 (33.67)	147 (18.19)	419 (51.86)	254 (32.67)	135 (16.71)	389 (48.14)	808 (100.00)

Table—10.4 Distribution of the Households by Family Size

S. No.	Tribe	Family size			Total	Adoption of family planning by household
		Less than-5	0-7	7 and above		
I.	Tribes:					
1.	Konda Savara	25 (25.00)	45 (48.33)	21 (26.67)	90 (100.00)	36 (35.00)
2.	Jatapu	26 (28.33)	45 (50.00)	18 (21.67)	90 (100.00)	41 (48.33)
	All tribes	51 (28.33)	90 (50.00)	39 (21.67)	180 (100.00)	77 (42.78)

Table—10.5 Medical and Health Facilities in the Study Area and District

S. No.	Type of Institution	Seetharapeta Mandal		Srikakulurr District	
		Number	Percentage	Number	Percentage
1	2	3	4	5	6
1.	Government hospitals	01	1.30	12	9.84
2.	Dispensaries	–	–	14	11.48
3.	Mobile Medical Units	–	–	2	1.64
4.	Hospital for Special Treatments	–	–	7	5.74
5.	Primary Health Centres	02	2.60	51	41.80
6.	Ayurvedic Dispensaries	01	1.30	18	14.75
7.	Homeopathy	–	–	16	13.11
8.	Unani	–	–	2	1.64
9.	Integrated Child Development Centres (ICDS)	70	90.90	–	–
10.	Family Welfare Centres	03	3.90	–	–
11.	Total	77	100.00	122	100.00

Source: Chief Planning Officer, Srikakulam.

Table—10.6 Action Plan for 2000-2001, ITDA, SEETHAMPETA

S. No.	Item	Amount
1.	Community Health Workers Scheme Honorarium 348 x 300 x 12	12.528
	Supply of Medial Kit box to CHWs 348 x 200	0.690
2.	Training Programme to CHWs 248 x 40 x 4	0.550
3.	Other Training to the Medical Staff	0.500
4.	Financial Asst. to the Tribal Patients per month Rs. 5000/-(Roughly)	0.600
5.	Referral cases from the villages (like TB, Cancer and other diseases)	0.500
6.	Maintenance of vehicles (Six ambulance + 3 Zeeps) 5000 x 9	0.450
7.	For diesel oil and engine oil	1.944
8.	Non governmental organisation's consultancy and other expenditure	0.500
9.	Hospital equipments for the PHCs 500 x 6	0.030
	Total	18.292

Table—10.7 Awareness and Adoption of Family Planning by Sample Households

S. No.	Tribe	Awareness & responded	Not responded	Total	Adoption
I.	Tribe:				
1.	Konda Savara	77 (81.17)	13 (18.33)	90 (100.00)	31 (30.00)
2.	Jatapu	85 (96.67)	5 (3.33)	90 (100.00)	46 (53.33)
	All tribes	162 (90.00)	18 (10.00)	180 (100.00)	77 (42.78)

Table—10.8 Distribution of Head of the Households by Literacy Level

S. No.	Tribe	Literacy level				Total
		Primary	Secondary	Higher	Illiterates	
I.	Tribes:					
1.	Konda Savara	24 (23.33)	3 (3.33)	–	63 (13.33)	90 (100.00)
2.	Jatapu	33 (38.33)	8 (8.33)	–	49 (53.33)	90 (100.00)
	All tribes	57 (32.22)	11 (6.11)	–	112 (61.67)	180 (100.00)

Table—10.9 Sex-wise Distribution of Literacy Level of All the Family Members of the Households

S. No.	Tribe	Literates						Grand total
		Male			Female			
		Adult	Children	Total	Adult	Children	Total	
I.	Tribe:							
1.	Konda Savara	52 (37.65)	48 (32.94)	100 (70.59)	7 (4.71)	31 (24.71)	47 (29.42)	85 (100.00)
2.	Jatapu	69 (35.88)	55 (27.48)	124 (63.36)	14 (7.63)	51 (29.00)	56 (36.64)	121 (100.00)
	All tribes	121 (36.12)	103 (30.74)	224 (66.87)	21 (6.42)	82 (24.48)	103 (33.13)	206 (100.00)

Table—10.10 Distribution of School Drop-out of Children by Sex

S. No.	Tribe	School Drop-outs of children						Grand total
		Male			Female			
		Primary	Upper primary	Total	Primary	Upper primary	Total	
I.	Tribes:							
1.	Konda savara	20 (42.11)	3 (5.26)	23 (47.37)	22 (44.74)	5 (1.89)	26 (52.68)	50 (100.00)
2.	Jatapu	9 (29.41)	3 (11.76)	12 (41.18)	10 (35.29)	5 (23.30)	16 (52.82)	27 (100.00)
	All tribes	29 (37.66)	6 (7.79)	35 (45.45)	32 (41.56)	10 (12.99)	42 (54.55)	77 (100.00)

Table—10.11 Distribution of Workers by Sex

S. No.	Tribe	Male			Female			Grand total	Dependency ratio
		Adult	Children	Total	Adult	Children	Total		
I.	Tribes:								
1.	Konda Savara	125 (40.64)	24 (9.13)	153 (49.77)	121 (39.73)	29 (10.51)	154 (50.23)	303 (100.00)	1:0:31
2.	Jatapu	125 (47.22)	10 (3.33)	131 (50.55)	119 (43.89)	16 (5.56)	101 (49.45)	266 (100.00)	1:0:46
	All tribes	250 (43.48)	34 (5.91)	284 (49.39)	240 (42.78)	45 (7.83)	285 (50.61)	569 (100.00)	7:0:42

Table—10.12 Distribution of Non-workers Sex-wise

S. No.	Tribe size groups	Male			Female			Groand total	Dependency ratio
		Adult	Children	Total	Adult	Children	Total		
I.	Tribes:								
1.	Konda Savara	11 (3.11)	55 (30.07)	40 (49.18)	7 (11.48)	47 (39.34)	47 (50.82)	117 (100.00)	1:0:31
2.	Jatapu	11 (9.64)	58 (45.78)	66 (55.42)	7 (4.82)	53 (39.76)	57 (44.58)	132 (100.00)	1:0:46
	All tribes	22 (9.44)	113 (44.21)	135 (53.65)	14 (7.73)	90 (38.63)	104 (46.35)	239 (100.00)	1:0:42

Table—10.13 Distribution of Child Labour in the Sample Households by Sex

S. No.	Tribe	Male children	Female children	Total
I.	Tribes:			
1.	Konda savara	24 (46.51)	29 (53.49)	63 (100.00)
2.	Jatapu	1 (37.50)	1 (62.00)	26 (100.00)
	All tribes	34 (43.50)	45 (56.96)	79 (100.00)

Table—10.14 Occupational Spread of Adult Workers by Participation in Number of Occupations

S. No.	Tribe occupations	Single occupations	Two occupations	Three	Total
I.	Tribes:				
1.	Konda savara	59 (14.20)	138 (32.95)	118 (52.84)	257 (100.00)
2.	Jatapu	31 (18.90)	79 (50.00)	71 (31.10)	239 (100.00)
	All tribes	90 (18.15)	217 (43.75)	189 (38.10)	496 (100.00)

Table—10.15 Occupational Distribution of Family Members According to their Main Occupation

S. No.	Activity	Konda Sarava	Savara	Jatapu	Total
A.	**Workers:**				
1.	Agriculture	135	118	127	380 (47.77)
2.	Labour	64	45	44	153 (18.93)
3.	Collection of Forest Produce	20	3	2	25 (3.09)
4.	Artisans	–	2	2	4 (0.49)
5.	Services	–	1	1	2 (0.25)
6.	Employees	–	1	3	4 (0.49)
7.	Non farm labour	–	–	1	1 (0.12)
	A: Sub total	219	170	180	569 (70.42)
B.	**Non-workers**				
1.	Unemployees	3	3	2	8 (0.99)
2.	School going children	46	76	66	188 (22.52)
3.	Old agers	8	11	9	28 (3.46)
4.	Others	4	5	6	15 (1.86)
	B: Sub total	61	95	83	239 (29.58)
	Grand total	280	265	263	808 (100.00)

Note: **Figures in the brackets indicate percentage to total.**

11

Endowment, Entitlement and Empowerment

Concept and Evidences from Tamil Nadu

**S. Iyyampillai*

This paper consists of two sections. First section describes the possible meanings of the term empowerment and indicates the difficulty in meaningfully constructing the index of empowerment status [ES] suitable for different contexts. Levels of endowment and entitlement determine the ES. Taking the objective factors, women are less empowered comparing men in a given specific context. However, women are as heterogeneous as the other population groups are. Disparity among women is much worse in many respects. Hence, any programme for upliftment of women has to be properly targeted to avoid widening the existing inequality among them. Second section presents the empirical evidences of three studies on women' empowerment conducted at different points of time and with different groups of respondents. The endowment in the form of education and employment is found

* Professor of Economics, Bharathidasan University, Tiruchirapalli–620024.

to be a strong determinant of ES. Hence the governments, if interested in people's welfare, should aim at providing higher level of education and job to its people.

The Concept

In spite of the fact that the profitability of getting a female child is almost equal to that of a male child in every delivery of child, the sex ratio is favourable to female in almost all the age groups in many districts and States in India. The number of female per 1000 male has come down steadily in the last few decades, and fortunately got stabilized around 930 without further falling, in the recent years in India. The difference in adult sex ratio could be some times explained by the factors like in and out migration, but the gap in the child sex ratio clearly indicates the sex determination in the birth itself. Only a few States and a few districts are exceptional to this trend. This proves a clear discremination against female in the Bharatha Matha. This discrimination is traced in almost all the stages of life—womb to tomb. Birth of male child is preferred to that of girl child; and, health and educational facilities are discriminated against female. It has been observed [Duncan, 1989], "mothers prefer to devote resources to improving the nutritional status of their daughters, fathers to son" and mostly fathers are main earners. This is true in almost all the families, irrespective of region, religion, caste and class, barring some deviations, may be owing to some family specific differences. Thus, discrimination against women at specified levels is very clear. The women in general lag behind men in every specific context.

But at the macro level, however, intra-gender disparities, i.e., disparities among women is much wider. There is wide variation in the representation by women across different groups of women While women from higher strata of the society are able to take away greater portion of the resources and facilities available, the women from other groups lag far behind them. The data available from NSSO [2000] clearly show that in educational aspects the urban women are enjoying a significantly higher educational status comparing not only the rural women but also the rural men. It may be true in other aspects [eg. health] too. The upper caste rich women do enjoy greater ES than the lower caste landless men. Landless Scheduled Caste men have been badly treated by upper caste women in many Indian villages; the upper caste women have made the scheduled caste men to dance to their tunes, and, against the wishes of the scheduled caste men [Anandhi et al., 2002].

Like any other case, the group of women too is not a homogenous one. Generally the rural scheduled caste women form the most disadvantaged group in India. Hence, any specialized facility to women as a group, would certainly be gulped by some at the top, while majority of the women would be deprived of the benefits. The women empowerment programmes, unless suitably targeted, might further widen the existing disparity among the women groups.

A close look into the subject would show that ES for anybody for that matter is a function of endowment levels and entitlement to the endowments. Endowment could be in terms physical health and intellectual skills, economic assets including lands, monetary resources and social status or some other resources that could serve as a source of income. Sometimes it is argued that the social capital [Michael, 2000] and physical appearance [Daniel and Jeff, 1994] could also be good sources of earning, Daniel and Jeff state [p. 1174] "Plain people earn less than average-looking people, who earn less than good-looking". These physical, social and economic endowments, if not intellectual, are highly unequally distributed among the women of different castes and class in India, may be due to historical reasons.

Entitlement indicates the legal and/or social sanction to one to make use of or sell out or transfer the endowment one owns. Hence, the entitlement relations too can explain the relative ES of women or anybody for that matter. Hence, it becomes important to suitably correct the legal system if one wants to give greater relative ES to one group over the other. Normally, it is believed that to a large extent, barring some extreme cases, everybody is equal before law, which is, however, not true in the case of economic endowment.

As observed by Sen [1981, p. 1], in a private ownership market economy like India, an entitlement relation applied to ownership connects one set of ownerships to another through certain rules of legitimacy. Entitlement relations accepted in a private ownership market economy include, among others, the inheritance and transfer entitlement. That is, one is entitled to own what is willingly given to one by another who legitimately owns it. Encroachment into one's endowment is considered to be illegal. The scope of ownership relations can vary greatly with economic systems as well.

As explained above, the women with better endowment and entitlement certainly enjoy greater ES than the others who lack them. Thus, ES is a function of endowment and entitlement; and endowment and entitlement in majority cases are the function of ancestral endowment position, which is highly unequally distributed in country like India. It is this which explains the continued poverty of many and continued richness of a few for generation after generation in India. This is precisely the reason why some women enjoy greater ES while the others lag far behind them.

Health, education and employment are the three basic and essential endowments at personal level that influence the ES [here too, the influence by the past endowment levels cannot be ruled out]. Generally better health and education, if used in right manner would improve one's productivity levels and thus income and economic status, which would ultimately result in greater ES. Here, employment acts as the necessary link between productivity level and earning. Unless one makes use of or gets an opportunity to make use of the productive capacity, the productive capacity alone is one sufficient to earn income or improve economic status. Also, all those who are employed may not enjoy greater status. For instance, in the rural areas, a greater proportion of women [compared to urban women] are employed [in agricultural sector], but their economic or social status is poorer than the unemployed rich women. In this regard Sen [1975, p. 5] observes: "Employment can be a factor in self-esteem and indeed in esteem by others. Much, of course, depends on the class one comes from. To a member of the 'leisured class' the fact that one does not work for one's living may be, in fact, a source of pride, but for those who have to work for a living, lack of 'employment' is not only a denial of income, it can also be a source of shame". It is quite possible that some empowered women may long for more and hence may consider themselves to be not so empowered while the less empowered ones may consider themselves to be sufficiently empowered.

Therefore, it appears that if a person is able to obtain through legal means whatever he/she needs, he/she may be considered to have been adequately empowered. It is not necessary weather he/she is working or not, literate or not, and so on. In the present system, the children of rich people, irrespective of sex, do enjoy greater endowment, for they can inherit greater amount of wealth. Within a family, a boy may get greater or smaller share than a girl, depending upon many other factors operating at family level. But, still the richer girls do enjoy greater empowerment status than the poor girls who have no asset to inherit from their parents, [excepting perhaps some debt].

A macro level too, excepting some extreme cases, it is generally observed that there is a positive association between women's empowerment status and per capita income. Data on cross section of families and countries would show this trend. Barring some extreme cases, generally women in richer families and countries do enjoy greater empowerment status than the women in poor families and countries.

Another important point to be noted is that while assessing the empowerment status, it is necessary that the objective factors are considered for the purpose. Subjective feelings may not serve the purpose, for those who have tasted the power would always long for getting more and more power, while those who have not tasted the power may be contented with even little power. As stated by Robbins [1938], a Brahmin has said "I am ten times as capable of happiness as that untouchable over there". Eegeworth expressed the same point, "The Benthamite argument that equality of means tends to maximum happiness, presupposes a certain equality of natures; but if the capacity for happiness of different classes is different, the argument leads not to equal, but to unequal distribution [1897, p. 114]. Thus, it appears that as long as the capacity of happiness differs between women, even the equal amount of endowments need not necessarily bring equal empowerment status.

Let us now turn to answer another question. Why should the women be empowered at all? Why should their health, educational and employment status be improved? From the economic point of view, if every one of the men and women is empowered to take decisions, he/she would try to enhance his/her productive capacity, to participate in income earning activities and to endow oneself with greater wealth and welfare. This way, a country would be able to achieve higher economic growth rate. If the workforce participation rate [WPR] is higher and if the productivity is also higher, then obviously, per capita income would also be higher. In our country both WPR as well as productivity are lower for various socio-economic reasons, hence per capita income is also lower. These WPR and productivity levels could be improved if women are better endowed and empowered.

But here, the underlying assumption that 'production of more goods and services would improve the welfare of the people' has been frequently questioned, for the satisfying capacity of the goods and services depend not only on the nature of produce but also on the nature of the consumers/users. The utility patterns are different for different persons. Level of satisfaction is influenced very well by many other non-economic variables, besides income. Also, the cost of production should not be greater than the benefit from the produce. The costs are many—economic, environmental and psychological. Similarly the benefits are also many dimensional—direct, indirect, tangible, intangible, short term, long term, economic, social and phychic. The valuation of these items is a complex one. Hence, it is difficult to assess the welfare implications of the women's employment outside home. For some women their employment outside home may appear to be welfare reducing while for others it may appear to be welfare increasing.

To cite an illustration at this point, let us suppose that a woman is employed outside home, earns income and is also empowered to use her income as she likes. Another woman is similar to her excepting that she is working at home; therefore her work is neither paid nor enumerated in national income accounting; she does not earn income of her own and hence she has to depend on others for her expenses. In these two cases, normally the housewife is considered to enjoy lower ES than the employed woman. But it would be difficult to say which of the two women enjoys greater well-being. In majority of richer households, women, working outside for wage may not necessarily improve the well-being of the family members though it may empower the women, while in majority of poorly endowed households, women's earning might empower not only the women but also their wards.

Another problem is with the valuation of the non-market activities mostly performed by women folk at home. To some extent almost all the goods and services supplied by a housewife could be purchased in the market, the summation of the prices of them however, cannot be equated with the value of the labour supplied by the housewife. The quality difference certainly exists. Mother's care can hardly be compared with the care purchased in the market.

Therefore, raising the capabilities of all the members of a household is important. It however does not necessarily mean that all of them must be employed outside home for earning money. In our country about 25 per cent of able women are estimated to be free from domestic works and also not joining the usual workforce [Iyyampillai, 1989]. This is a real wastage of human power. The reason stated is that some of them are voluntarily unemployed while a majority of them are involuntarily unemployed. Hence, unemployment problem has also to be considered while making comments on women empowerment.

Thus, it is essential to give better education, health and employment to the women particularly at lower strata of the society to improve the women's ES.

Empirical Evidences

The evidences relating to women's empowerment and its determinants available for different caste and class groups are discussed in this section.

Study 1

This study [Iyyampillai, Bhuwaneswari and Rajeswari, 1998] was carried out to assess the endowment patterns of men and women of three generations in two areas with different levels of infrastructure, education, occupation and income. Required information on education—an important component of endowment in the present day world—were collected from 162 households in advanced area [KK Nagar and Anna Nagar in Tiruchirapalli town] and 130 households in backward area [a remote dry village, namely Suriyar, Tiruchirapalli district]. The evidences suggested that: (a) The educational status of women was lower comparing men within the area, but between the areas, the women of advanced area enjoyed greater educational status than that of women as well as men of the backward area [Table 11.1]. (b) The educational levels had improved over the generations in both areas for both male and female. But the striking difference was that the girls were normally sent for general education and that too only if they did not get married till then, whereas the boys were sent to the kind of education by their choice and as long as they could. Hence, very few girls manage to go for higher/professional education [Table 11.2]. There was a striking difference in the educational expenditure pattern too. The total private expenditure on education per students was lower for girls than for boys. Of the total cost, for girls 32 per cent went for dress and uniform followed by fees for regular courses [Table 11.3]. Whereas for boys the top two major expenditure items were fees for regular courses and hostel expenses in that order. Parents hesitated to send girls to outside the town for studies. This was the reason why many self-financing women's colleges were started and many men's colleges were also converted as co-educational colleges in Tiruchirapalli town.

Study 2

This study [Iyyampallai and Shanti, 1992] relates to two wards—one advanced and another backward in terms of literacy rates—in Tiruchirapalli town. Fifty households [proportionate to the population size] were randomly selected from each ward from their respective lists of households. Respondents were wives of the heads of the households or women who headed the households. *Decision-making status was considered to be one of the components of ES. Hence, the respondents' participation in household decision-making was assessed*. The number of decisions varied across the households; and, the economic importance and implications for the welfare of the households also varied across the decisions. As many as twenty decisions were identified to cover maximum proportion of the activities of the households. They included household management, children's education, medical care, presentation of gifts and donations, savings, investment, occupation and entertainment. In many cases decisions were made at different levels and some decisions had many sub-decisions. For instance, a decision regarding purchase of a consumer durable might include such sub-decisions as how to mobilize resources for the purchase; when to purchase; where to purchase; who should take the responsibility of selecting the brand, colour, model etc. and finally the actual purchase. A maximum of five points per decision were allotted to every decision. The points varied depending upon the level of participation. Equal weight was given to all the major decisions. Therefore, 100 points [20 x 5] of status score were to be awarded, if a woman had fully participated in all the decisions pertaining to all the 20 activities identified. Thus the decision-making status score ranges from 0 for complete absence to 100 for complete participation in decision-making. While assigning the score, the main consideration was to see whether a respondent participated or not in the decision-making. Questions such as whose suggestion was finally accepted or who executed the decisions were not considered for the purpose of assigning scores. This score for every respondent was associated with their respective endowment variables such as years of schooling of respondents and their fathers and husbands and the contribution of the respondents to the household income.

It was inferred from the evidences that the endowment levels of the respondents in terms of education and earning were higher in advanced ward than in backward ward [Table 11.4]. In the advanced ward, as much as 74 per cent of the respondents and 92 per cent of their husbands had college education, while in the backward ward, almost all the women and men had only education upto middle level; and, no women had college education. The respondents' parents too had good educational status in the advanced ward.

The absolute income levels of the respondents were very high in advanced ward, and, lower in backward ward. As much as 50 per cent of the respondents in advanced ward earned annual income of more than Rs. 15 thousand [in the year 1990] per year per head, while none of the respondents nor their respective husbands in backward ward earned so much. However, in backward ward, 14 per cent of the respondents contributed more than 80 per cent of their household income, as their men earned a little; no such case was reported in the advanced ward. In other cases too in the backward ward men earned less, hence, women's percentage contribution to household income was greater. In this analysis, women's contribution in terms of value of household production of goods and services [which was the major activity of women in majority households] was not included, mainly due to the following difficulties involved in assigning correct prices to the services provided by women at home. One, it was not appropriate to assign the market prices to the services provided by women at home as the qualities of those services differed significantly. Two, due to the existing wage differentials in the labour markets, it would not be proper to take the wages and salaries of the working women as a correct proxy for the value of the time of the women with same level of education and experience at home.

In the study areas, the level of endowment had significantly influenced the decision-making status. Higher the level of endowment in terms of education and earnings, the larger was the participation in decision-making. The women of the advanced ward had participated in economically crucial decision too, while the women in the other ward had largely participated in economically less significant decisions. In both the areas, the simple correlation coefficients worked out confirmed that the level of education and earning of the respondents, and the level of education of their respective husbands had positive association with the women's decision-making status. Hence, greater endowment in terms of education, occupation and income to women is the prerequisite for empowerment.

Study 3

This study [Iyyampillai and Kulandai Therasa, 2001] tried to assess the levels of freedom and ability the women had acquired in a small town namely Pudukottai. This town, as reported by

Athreya and Sheela Rani Chunkath [1996], had achieved 100 per cent literacy. Evidences were collected from 102 married women chosen randomly from eleven residentially predominant wards out of total 38 wards in the town. These women respondents were active participants in the household affairs.

Here the women's empowerment status [WES] was assessed by their economic status, educational status, health status; participation in household decision-making process; political awareness and psychological strength with the maximum score of 19, 13, 18, 19, 15 and 30 respectively. The ES was assigned to the woman respondents on the basis of their answers to the questions relating to each of the six fields mentioned above. The highly empowered woman had scored 80 per cent of the total score [92 out of 114]. The mean ES score was 53.87, which was slightly less than 50 per cent of the total score of 114. About 35 per cent of the respondents had scored more than 50 per cent of the score. A majority of young, educated, employed and Christian women had obtained higher WES, while, the aged, illiterate, domestically employed and Muslim women had poor scores. In the sample, a Christian woman had obtained the highest score [80%] and a Muslim woman had obtained the lowest score. Generally the Christian women had better education and occupational status and hence enjoyed greater ES too. The correlation analysis confirms the positive association of ES with the variables like religion, community, education, employment and respondents' mothers' education [Table 11.5].

Conclusion

The term ES has to be carefully defined to understand the women of cross section. Though women are generally less empowered compared to their men, a vast variation in the degree of empowerment among the women cannot be ruled out. Generally, women of upper communities and class enjoy greater status than the women as well as men of lower communities and class. The available studies show that education and employment are the two major endowments that have got strong influence over the women's empowerment status. Women of better off families and recent generation are better endowed than their respective counterparts. Hence, it becomes essential to focus attention on the education and employment of women, particularly at the lower strata of the society.

Table—11.1 Percentage Distribution of Children, Parents and Grand Parents by Level of Education and Gender

Level of schooling	Advanced area		Backward area	
	% Male	% Female	% Male	% Female
		Children		
No schooling	0	0	8	23
Upto school	22	15	90	77
Above school	78	85	2	0
Total	100	100	100	100
		Parents		
No schooling	0	6	36	62
Upto school	32	67	58	38
Above school	68	27	6	0
Total	100	100	100	100
		Grand Parents		
No schooling	49	81	60	87
Upto school	27	18	40	13
Above school	24	1	0	0
Total	100	100	100	100

Note: 1. Those who are aged more than 5 years, continuing study and unmarried are counted as children.

2. Parents are heads of the households and respective spouses.

3. Grand parents are the parents of the head of the households.

Table—11.2 Details of Courses taken up by Boys and Girls in the Advanced Area

Type of education		% Boys	% Girls
General	UG	35	62
	PG	18	19
Technical/	UG	37	13
Professional	PG	10	6
Total		100	100

Table—11.3 Private Expenditure [in Rs.] on Education in the Advanced Area

Expenditure head	Percentage of expenditure		Per student expenses	
	Boys	Girls	Boys	Girls
Transport	11.77	16.05	1316	1344
Hostel	24.20	7.19	2706	602
Dress/uniform	15.77	31.87	1763	2668
Notes and books	10.56	9.28	1181	777
Fees for regular courses	30.20	28.16	3376	2358
Others	7.50	7.45	836	621
Total	100.00	100.00	11178	8370

Table—11.4 Endowment Levels of the Respondents [Figures in Percentage]

Description	Advanced ward respondent	Advanced ward husband	Backward ward respondent	Backward ward husband
Educational Levels:				
Illiterate	0	0	20	10
School	26	8	80	82
College	74	92	0	8
Occupation				
Domestically employed	34	0	68	20
Employed in unorganised sector	0	6	14	54
Employed in organised sector	66	94	18	26
Annual income				
Below Rs. 5,000	34	0	86	60
Rs. 5,001- Rs. 15,000	16	0	14	40
Rs. 15,001- Rs. 20,000	20	24	0	0
Rs. 20,000 and above	30	76	0	0
Percentage contribution by respondents to household income				
0-40	64	NA	72	NA
41-60	28	NA	8	NA
61-80	8	NA	6	NA
81-100	0	NA	14	NA
Time spent by respondents on domestic chores per day				
Upto 6 hours	94	NA	76	NA
Above 6 hours	6	NA	24	NA

NA = Not applicable.

Table—11.5 Correlation Coefficients [n = 102]

Variables	'r'
Empowerment score and religion	0.45
Empowerment score and community	0.21
Empowerment score and employment	0.42
Empowerment score and education	0.67
Empowerment score and mothers' education	0.44

Note: All the correlation coefficients were statistically significant at 1 per cent level

Religion: Weights were assigned on the basis of the average Women Empowerment Score [WES] for the religions—Christian = 3, Hindu = 2 and Muslim = 1

Community: Weights were assigned on the basis of the average WES for the communities—Upper Castes = 3, Backward Castes = 2 and Scheduled Castes = 1

Employment: Organised sector employment = 3, informal sector = 2 and household employment =1

Education: Number of schooling years.

REFERENCES

Anandhi S, et al., Work, Caste and Competing Masculinities: Notes from a Tamil Village, *Economic and Political Weekly*, Vol. 37, No. 43, pp. 4397-4406.

Athreya V B and Sheela Rani Chunkath, 1996, *Literacy and Empowerment*, Sage Publications, New Delhi.

Daniel S. Hamermesh and Jeff E. Biddle, 1994, Beauty and the Labour Market, *American Economic Review, Vol. 84*, No. 5, December, pp. 1174-1193.

Duncan Thomas, 1989, Intra-household Resource Allocation: An Inferential Approach, *Economic Growth Center*, Yale University.

Edgeworth, F. Y, 1987, Papers Relating to Political Economy, Macmillan, London, Referred in The New Palgrave: *A Dictionary of Economics*, Ed. Y. John Eatwell et al., 1988, The Macmillan Press Limited, London, Vol. 2, p. 170.

Iyyampillai S, 1989, Leakages in Human Resources: Some Data and Speculations, *Peninsular Economist*, Vol. 2, No. 1, pp. 21-28.

Iyyampillai S. R.P Bhuwaneswari and K. Rajeswari, 1998, Women's Education: Investment or Ornament? *Social, Welfare, Vol. 45*, No. 3, June, pp. 10-14.

Iyyampillai S and Shanti Getzie Ranjini Devi, 1992, Decision Making in the Home, *Social Welfare, Vol. 39*, No. 3, June, pp. 23-26.

Iyyampillai S and Kulandai Therasa, 2001, Status Inside and Outside the Home: Co-related, *Social Welfare, Vol. 48*, No. 8, November, pp. 28-33.

Michael Woolcock and Deepan Narayan, 2000, Social Capital, Implications for Development Theory, Research and Policy, *The World Bank Research Observed, Vol. 15*, No. 2, August, pp. 225-249.

NSSO, 2000, *Sarvekshana, 82nd Issue*, [Results of 52nd Round], *Vol. 23*, No. 3, January-March.

Robbins L, 1938, Interpersonal Comparisons of Utility, *Economic Journal*, 48, 635-41.

Sen, A.K., 1975, *Employment, Technology and Development*, Clarendon Press, Oxford.

Sen, A.K., 1981, Poverty and Famines: *An Essay on Entitlement and Deprivation*, Oxford University Press, Delhi.

12

Information Economy and Empowerment of Women

*N. Narayana

The rapid growth of the information and communications systems is increasingly recognised as more important, in terms of its overall economic impact and spillover effects, than any of the major technological revolutions of the past two centuries. Information and Communications Technology (ICT) is permeating all aspects of business and, increasingly, the wider society. It is emerging as one of the major drivers of economic growth and wealth creation all over the world by raising productivity levels and allowing markets to work more quickly and efficiently. By reducing costs and increasing the speed of communications, it is now playing a major role in globalising production of goods and services as well as financial markets. Its broader adoption and application has already had a dramatic impact on employment patterns and skills requirements in the job market. In the long run, the significance of the new information system is likely to be even greater since it opens unprecedented opportunities for connecting and unleashing

* Department of Economics, University of Botswana.

the creative potential of much larger groups of people than has been the case up to now. This, in turn, is profoundly influencing the life styles of people in general and women in particular.

One important aspect of rapid changes in ICT is its impact on employment opportunities for women and achieving gender equality. This impact is significant in the context of understanding the likely employment challenges and opportunities that are emerging. Information and Communications Technology should not favour only men with the capabilities and resources to access it but should reduce the effects of the educational gap between men and women combined with increasing levels of skills of women and thereby promoting human development (UNDP, 1995). The process of human development in any country cannot be completed if equal opportunity for women in all social and economic activities of the economy is not ensured.

This paper examines the issues of gender equality and empowerment of women in the emerging information economy, especially in developing countries. Women must be regarded as agents and beneficiaries of change. Investing in women's capabilities and empowering them to exercise their choices is not only valuable in itself but is also the surest way to contribute to economic growth and all round development.

The international community has realised the importance of women's empowerment as a vital element in national development efforts. This is equally true in building the information system in developing countries, where wide technical and economic disparities exist between countries and within countries. Therefore, the process of development that shapes the information economy should cover the goals of achieving gender equality and women's advancement and sustainable human development. The information economy should be grounded on human rights approach as a means to ensure the rights of all, including the rights to non-discrimination and the right to communicate. Communication is a basic human need, indispensable for the organisation of societies, and should be the foundation for building the information society.

Women's effective participation in the information economy needs to be assured if countries have to successfully achieve their development goals and priorities. While there have been developmental efforts to increase the access and use of ICT in general, there is still a marked difference in their impact on the lives of men and women. While assessing the implications of ICT policies, programmes and projects for women and men, necessary measures have to be taken to ensure women's empowerment. It is evident that Information and Communications Technology (ICT) can positively contribute and facilitate women's economic, social and political participation. Women can be the best agents to transform the society, as they are not just consumers of information and information products, nor just users of these technologies. More importantly, women are producers of information as well as innovators in applying ICT and their convergence with traditional media.

Information Economy and Development

Information and Communications System is penetrating into all aspects of human life and everything seems to be happening much faster today (Pyramid Research 1999). Majority of the world's poor, living in rural areas, do not have access to a reliable information and communications infrastructure (DOT Force 2001). Those who suffer from chronic hunger and poverty are obviously not covered by these communication facilities (UNDP 2001). As we know, the poor need not only food but also a combination of basic education and skills together with information and communication infrastructure so as to derive the full effects of market forces that raise their income level.

Knowledge and information and communications systems are interdependent drivers of economic growth. The link between knowledge and its diffusion and growth are the subject of a large body of literature. Schumpeter made the distinction between the creation of knowledge and its diffusion (1943). Arrow (1962) linked diffusion of knowledge and growth in the learning-by-doing model. Further research into the dynamics of the knowledge diffusion process and its relationship with growth and inequality was conducted by Davis (1979) and Grossman and Help man

(1991), and Aghion and Howitt (1998) reviewed the analysis of the origins of technological change from endogenous research and development decisions of firms including the impact of increasing returns.

Ultimately, it is the diffusion and accessibility of new information technology to a wider society determines its impact on the development of people. This diffusion process depends on a number of variables including the capacity of people to absorb new technologies and supportive policy environment. Educational levels and human resource development play vital role in this regard. But the educational attainment levels are far low in developing countries compared to industrial countries. There is close link between information and communication systems and human capital. If information system is skill-biased, then successful adoption of it depends on higher-level human capital. This has direct policy implications for developing countries (Patrinos 2000).

There are number of specific benefits that accrue from information and communications systems such as improved functioning of markets through easier and cheaper access to information on goods and services, quality improvements and frequent changes in product and process design; managerial improvements including better decisions through better and faster marshalling of information; savings on material costs, energy and inventories; and a faster and more efficient financial sector. On the face of it, it would stimulate the process of accumulation of human capabilities and thereby reducing the productivity gap between advanced and developing countries.

With some 1.2 billion, or over 20 per cent of the world's population living in absolute poverty at less than US $1 a day, the question is whether humanity can harness the new capabilities of information and communications technology to reduce poverty and generate more equitable growth. While the rapid spread and declining costs of information offers the world's low-income countries a chance to attain a more value-added knowledge-intensive growth and to achieve social and economic equality (ILO 2001). Development of information systems can have a far-reaching impact on the quality of life of marginalized segments of the population by providing more responsive and transparent governance as well as improving the reach and delivery of health, education and other social services. The ability of this information technology to reduce poverty and spur development will be determined by its impact on employment, as well as the creation of productive and remunerative work. Speculation abounds that the new "knowledge economy" will trigger a "paradigm shift" involving new approaches to development (OECD 2001). The role of information systems should therefore be regarded as significant factor in developing economies for growth and poverty alleviation.

Emerging Information Economy

The dramatic acceleration in the development and use of information and communication technologies in recent years has set in motion a worldwide process of transforming the present economies into information economies. As we moved into the third millennium, it is of the utmost importance to understand and to influence the fundamental changes brought about by the communication and information revolution. The complexity and interrelation of today's world problems defy traditional explanations and solutions and require a completely new approach, which must be both comprehensive and interdisciplinary.

Moreover, individuals, groups and communities will need to develop not only new tools of analysis but also very different attitudes in order to meet the challenges of the emerging new economy based on information and knowledge. Markets for new information and interactive services are being aggressively explored and developed, as information providers and carriers seek to expand their activities beyond their traditional borders. The developed countries have an overwhelming lead in all these advances.

Some of the developing countries, using information technology in education and health to help break the vicious circle of poverty and are making rapid progress by creating new sectors of sustainable economic development like software production and data processing. The importance of the information economy has been recognised at the highest political levels in many of these developing countries (Pohoja 2000). The major problems are posed not by the technologies as such, which can be acquired and adapted, but rather by political, social, organisational and gender issues that are involved. However, the benefits derived by the humanity from these opportunities depend on the rate at which the transfer of information technology is possible. This again depends on the efforts of the developing countries in enhancing human capabilities to make the best possible use of the available information infrastructure. Only on this condition, the information economy can attain its ultimate goal-empowerment of all its citizens through access to and use of this new knowledge.

The Information Economy and Empowerment of Women

The emphasis on empowerment of women is found throughout the development cooperation policies. Empowerment is not something that can be done by outsiders to people. Development initiatives should create the conditions whereby women can become the agents of their own development and empowerment. A key aspect of empowerment of women is taking measures to ensure women's equal access to and their full participation in power structures and increasing women's capacity to participate in decision-making.

The segregation of roles according to gender creates barriers that are difficult to overcome, which explains why poverty, which is already more widespread amongst women, is still growing. The development of women will continue to be affected as long as gender discrimination exists in the distribution of work, responsibility and power. Women's empowerment and gender equality is both a matter of justice and a prerequisite for the development of harmonic and sustainable economy.

The crucial element in the empowerment of women is transforming the position of women in such a way that their advancement is sustained. Equally important is that women should themselves feel that they have been the agents of the transformation. Empowerment focuses on strengthening women's economic independence (through increased income and greater individual self-reliance), a more useful approach appears to recognise the multiple roles and interests that women have and the interrelationships between them. In fact, women work longer hours than men in nearly every country. Since the status in contemporary society is so often equated with income-earning power, women suffer a major under valuation of their economic status. If women's unpaid work were properly valued, it is quite possible that women would emerge in most economies as the major breadwinners.

Promoting Women's Empowerment through ICT

Women need not be confined to the lower-skilled ICT jobs related to word processing and data entry. They should make up higher percentages of managerial maintenance and design personal in networks, operating systems and software. Many women are software programmers but very few are in hardware design. Women comprise the majority of those employed in computer and electronic assembly manufacturing jobs. New ICT jobs for women, especially in developing countries, are in the service industries in information processing, banking, insurance, printing and publishing. But women have to reach technical, managerial and decision-making high-level positions in order to reduce the gender gap in human resource development.

The fact is that only a smaller proportion of women in many developing countries have taken advantage of ICT for their economic empowerment as many more are being left out and have not been able to benefit from and contribute to this process. It is necessary to bring women into the ICT mainstream and make them both beneficiaries and contributories to the process of economic growth.

The potential of ICT has to be utilised as a tool for enhancing women's capacities in the area of health and education, as well as their access to basic social services and information. However, in the marginalisation of women due to lack of accessibility and affordability of ICT, women face a variety of barriers from low rates of information literacy to lack of high-skilled ICT training. The dominance of English language in ICT and software fields should not isolate women in non-English developing countries from fully participating and benefiting from the information economy.

The information economy and its rapid pace of continuing change offer enormous potential. If expectations of decline in the cost of this information technology and related infrastructure were realised then the critical factor would be empowering women's ability to make use their creative potential to the utilization of these new technologies. If this can be materialized, countries of the developing world can empower their women and create new value to their human resources.

The information economy is now working as networking economy. This new economy can be a powerful vehicle for transforming radically the world of work and to ensure gender equality. The development of information and communication systems offers many new opportunities for women. But these are to be supported by deliberate policies to ensure their participation, education and training in the information economy with no gender biases (ILO 2001). Recent employment trends show that in spite of progress in some areas, women generally continue to earn lower incomes, suffer higher unemployment, and remain largely restricted to low-skilled, part-time, informal and unstable jobs. At the same time, the proportion of women joining the global labour market is expected to rise rapidly in the coming years. A major challenge of employment policies in the global information economy is the empowerment of women by providing decent work for the female labour force, which is increasingly entering the information workforce.

New Employment Opportunities for Women

Information and communication technologies have created new types of work that favour women. This would facilitate them to carry work to homes and allow for better accommodation of work and family schedules. Women have also been able to capture a large proportion of jobs in information technology enabled services. The most promising potential for women is in the creation of new jobs and work in data processing activities. In India, a quarter of a million jobs during the last five years were created in these activities and a huge proportion of which have gone to women.

In terms ot numbers employed, the role of women in the information economy has become more marked in export-oriented information-processing work. Internationally outsourced jobs, such as medical transcription work or software services are making a considerable difference in the lives and career paths of women in developing countries. In field of software, women enjoy preferences on a scale that they never experienced in any other field of engineering and science. Women in India occupy 27 per cent of professional jobs in the software industry, which is worth 4 billion US dollars annually. Women's share in the total employment in this industry is expected to rise to 40 per cent by 2005 (ILO 2001).

Information systems have enabled women to tap global markets for their products and increased their incomes. New information technologies and networking are new means by which women are empowered to improve their economic and social status. An organisation called 'Sapphire Women', created by a woman in Kampala, Uganda, supports women who have lost family members to AIDS, as well as orphans created by the AIDS epidemic. The Grameen Bank Village Phone project, which provides mobile cell phones to its mostly female members in Bangladesh, demonstrates not only the employment-generating impact of the women who collect fees for the usage of their mobile phones, but other positive spill-over effects as well. Mobile phones and access to the Internet have given rural Bangladeshi women access to learning, created new opportunities for autonomy and improved their position in community and public life. One of the India's non-governmental organisations, self-employed Women's Agency (SEWA), has been involving women in the informal sector since 1972, and has a membership of over 215,000, is one of the first organisations in India to realise the potential of harnessing information infrastructure for the productive growth of the informal sector (ILO 2001). By organising computer awareness programmes and imparting basic computer skills to its team leaders and association members, SEWA has enabled many of its members to launch their own websites and to sell their products inthe global virtual market place. These examples illustrate how information sector can improve the lives of poor women by opening up opportunities they were previously excluded from. The empowerment of women via technology in this way enables them to challenge discrimination and overcome gender barriers.

Despite the enabling potential of information systems to improve women's lives, a digital divide within countries is broadly reflecting in the gender divide. The most striking digital divide relates to Internet use, with women being in the minority of users in both developed and developing countries. It is found that educational differences underlie the different levels of diffusion of information and Internet usage. This leads to the conclusion that the promotion of education in general, and digital literacy in particular is the huge challenge facing all countries (Jovanovich 1989). Equipping workers with information technology related skills would need to be specifically targeted to the needs of women.

But there is possibility that the patterns of gender segregation are being reproduced in the information economy where men hold the majority of high-skilled, high value-added jobs, whereas women are concentrated in the low-skilled, lower value-added jobs. Since the diffusion of the new information has been skill-biased accompanied by wage inequalities, rising pay inequalities between men and women has been the phenomenon. Men are more likely to be found in the high-paying, creative work of software development or Internet start-ups, whereas those in the workforce such as cashiers or data-entry workers are predominantly female and low-paid. While both men and women may be users of the advanced information technology and also share experiences of improving their relative skills, only male groups appear to be occupying the positions in the organisations where use of advanced technology is accompanied by greater discretion and responsibility on the job. But the traditional manufacturing industries that previously employed women are gradually disappearing and more women are now finding jobs in the new information and communications related industries. Although digital globalisation has brought more employment opportunities to young women, new inequalities are therefore emerging between women with information communications relate skilled jobs and those without these skills.

Quality of Work

Many features of the information economy can offer women the potential to strike a better balance between work and family responsibilities, or work and leisure. The increasing knowledge content of work has the potential to favour the equality of women and men in the workforce. Intelligence and creativity are also evenly distributed between men and women, or between able and people with physical disabilities. The potential of the information economy to improve the quality of work and life of people is the genuine concern of the developing countries. However, there are negative effects on the quality of working life of women. Far from adjusting working needs to the requirements of family life, there can be increasing pressure for women to work everywhere and all the time. While teleworking has certainly created new employment opportunities for women, the downside is that women can be excluded from better career possibilities instead of finding a balance. Family responsibilities can be combined with paid work, so that women end up acquiring new tasks on top of the old.

Studies reveal that women in Malaysia and India are reluctant to opt for home-based telework. But they have welcomed the opportunities of employment afforded by call centres because it combines the advantages of interaction with those of being close to home (ILO 2001). Yet they are concerned about possible health hazards brought about by repetitive work in high-pressure working environments. Overall, the work in the information economy can be an effective tool for enhancing gender equality. But the direct intervention of the governments in developing countries is essential to remove the existing inequalities and also to safeguard the needs and rights of the women workers involved. The focus should be on empowerment of women as the creation and loss of jobs for women, the content and quality of their work, the nature of their employment and the skills required for women, the organisation of work and the functioning and effectiveness of worker and employer organisations are affected by the emerging information economy.

Comprehensive Policy for Empowerment of Women

To create an enabling environment that supports women's participation in information economy and thereby to enhance economic empowerment of women through ICT, the following measures have to be incorporated in ICT policy in developing countries.

- Integrating gender perspectives in the development and implementation of national ICT policies, programmes and strategies;
- Allocating resources in the national budgets to support strategies to increase women's participation in the information economy, including funding for Non-Governmental Organisations to strengthen opportunities for women's empowerment through ICT;
- Recognising ICTs as public goods and develop gender-responsive policies and programmes that promote universal access and affordability, especially for rural communities;
- Strengthening national machineries for the advancement of women, particularly through increased financial resources and technical expertise that can facilitate their advocacy role and collaborative action amongst government bodies;
- Increasing existing funding mechanisms to support women's initiatives in ICT-based entrepreneurship and other economic activities;
- Encouraging greater participation of women in the ICT industry by addressing gender-based inequalities and instituting gender-sensitive employment policies;
- Implementing the measures to ensure women's equal access to ICT education, training and literacy;
- Integrating ICT education in school curricula based on gender equality;
- Encouraging the ICT industry to provide ICT education and training, particularly to disadvantaged women and girls, especially in rural areas.

Besides the above policy measures, many economic and institutional arrangements must be revamped to extend more choices to women and men in the work place. Efforts should be made to target the programmes that enable women to gain greater access to economic opportunities through information and communications systems. Remunerative employment opportunities in ICT are the key to empowerment of women. But not all of them need to be in the formal, organised information sectors of the economy. What is most essential in this regard is encouraging women to participate in information economy by creating favourable environment.

Conclusions

At a wider level, the emerging information economy will play an important role in empowering women by transforming the developing countries. With the development of world economic market, the benefits of information economy should reach equally among different sections of people, especially women. The real constraint is the capacity of the developing countries to keep pace with the information revolution and to face the potential repercussions in the labour markets. The gender gap in access to information and communications technology has to be narrowed down in order to ensure the positive impact of information and communications technology on economic growth and development through its linkages with the creation of knowledge.

Government policy is required to contribute to advancing the gender equality through all means of mass communication. This is needed to promote the free flow of ideas, to increase and diffuse knowledge, and to give fresh impulse to spread the new culture. With the advent of the information economy, these tasks of empowering women have to be taken up as a matter of urgency. Once assessible to all, irrespective of gender, occupation or social status, information and communication technologies in developing countries can be instrumental for achieving a truly women centred development.

Developing countries should create an enabling environment to tap the benefits of information economy. An enabling environment includes national ICT policies that promote women's empowerment and gender equality. In most of the countries, the existing national ICT policy frameworks and strategic plans are generally silent on gender and women-focused concerns. This lack of gender analysis in the development of ICT policies results in the failure to realise the potential of ICT to transform gender and power relations as evidenced by successful initiatives of the governments of developing countries. Therefore, in reviewing and developing policies and formulating corresponding strategies and programmes, it is critical to ensure that the issue of empowerment of women is properly addressed.

A new world order that would embrace full equality of opportunity between women and men should emerge to eliminate the prevailing disparities between men and women and create an enabling environment for the full flowering of the productive and creative potential of women.

REFERENCES

Aghion, P and Howitt, P (1998), *"Endogenous Growth in the Global Economy"*, MIT Press, Cambridge, MA.

Arrow, K.J (1962), *"The Economic Implications of Learning by Doing"*, Review of Economics Studies, 29(3): 155-73.

Davies, S (1979), *"The Diffusion Process of Innovations"*, Cambridge University Press, Cambridge.

DOT (2001), *"Digital Opportunities for All: Meeting the Challenge"*, Report of the Digital Opportunities Task Force, New York.

Grossman, G.M and Helpman, E (1991), *"Innovation and Growth in the Global Economy"*, MIT Press, Cambridge MS.

ILO (2002), *"World Employment Report 2001"*, International Labour Organisation, Geneva.

Jovanovic, B and Rob, R. (1989), *"The Growth and Diffusion of Knowledge"*, *Review of Economic Studies*, 56(4): 569-82.

OECD (2001), *"The New Economy: Beyond the Hype"*, Report on the OECD Growth Project, Executive Summary, Organisation for Economic Cooperation and Development, Paris.

Patrinos, H.A (2000), *"The Changing Role of Government Education"*, Paper Presented to the Adam Smith Institute, London.

Pohoja, M. (2000), *"Information Technology and Economic Growth: A Cross-country Analysis"*, Working Paper No. 173, World Institute for Development Economics Research.

Pyramid Research (1999), *"Will the Internet Close the Gap?,"* Report on Info-Development, Washington DC.

UNDP (1995), Human Development Report: *"The Revolution for Gender Equality'*, UNDP, New York.

UNDP (2000), Human Development Report 2000: *"Human Rights and Human Development"*, United Nations Development Program, New York.

Schumpeter, J.A. (1943), *"Capitalism, Socialism and Democracy"*, George Allen and Unwin, London.

UNESCO (2000), *"World Ėducation Report"*, UNCESO, Paris.

13

Views and Perceptions of DWCRA Beneficiaries

A Case Study

**K. Sreelakshmamma*

Though the DWCRA programme was started about one and half decades ago, so far only a few studies were conducted to evaluate its performance and also its socio-economic and political impact on the rural women in Andhra Pradesh. Even the few studies conducted in this area are limited in their scope, as they covered only a few aspects of implementation of the programme at both the macro and micro levels. These studies were conducted on limited aspects of DWCRA despite its prominent nature. Some of the notable studies are those of Asghasi Mohiuddin et al (2000), Hemalatha Prasad et al (1996), Manimekalai (1999), Dwarakanath (1999), Damayanthi (1990), (1999), Suprabha Dahiya (1996), Victoria Nefa and Somehswar (1998), Yerram Raju and Firdousi (1997), Manimekalai and Rajkutti and Pritha Sarkar (1994), Reddy A.R. et al (1994), Suman Singh (1994), Sujatha Prasad (1998), Neeta

* Lecturer in Politics, V.S.R and N.V.R. College, Tenali, Guntur, Andhra Pradesh.

Gautam and Singh (1990). Further, these studies were confirmed to a few districts and no studies were conducted in a major number of districts of Andhra Pradesh. These studies also neglected certain vital aspects of the programme like the composition and information of groups, attitudes and role of Government and Bank Officials, the opinion of different categories of beneficiaries on the implementation of the programme, its impact on the socio, economic and political aspects of beneficiaries and so on. They have not also explored the working of the programme at the micro level. Hence the present study addresses some of these vital aspects of DWCRA in Prakasam District of Andhra Pradesh, which were so far not covered by any research study. Further, there are only few worthwhile studies on the DWCRA programme in Andhra Pradesh, even though this state is among the few states in India where this scheme is successfully implemented and became very popular. As such the present study is expected to fill the gap in the research on this vital programme.

For the purpose of the present study two modals namely Chirala and Vetapalam of situated in Prakasam district of Andhra Pradesh are selected. The villages covered in Chirala mandal are Eepurpalem, Vijayalakshmipuram, Ramakrishnanagar, Gavinivaripalem, Solman Centre and Chirala. Similarly, villages in Vetapalem Mandal covered are Vetapalem, Anmolpeta, Nayenepalli, Desaipeta, Mankenavaripalem, Amodagiripatnam, Katarivaripalem, Ramnagar and Pandillapalli, based on systematic sampling technique the study selected 435 DWCRA beneficiaries for the purpose of the present study.

This paper describes the socio-economic profile of the sample beneficiaries selected for the study and also present the views and perceptions of these beneficiaries on different aspects of DWCRA Programme implemented in Chirala and Vetapalem where the present study is carried out.

The data on the size of beneficiaries and number of groups formed under the DWCRA programme in Chirala Mandal furnished in Table 13.1 indicates that the total number of groups and their membership increased to 132 and 2035 respectively by the end of March, 2001. About 70 per cent of these beneficiaries belong to the Backward Classes, while the Forward Castes and Scheduled Tribes constitute 21 per cent, 6 per cent and 3 per cent respectively. The revolving fund distributed among the DWCRA groups during 1991-2001 was to tune of Rs. 22 lakhs. The activities taken up under the DWCRA programme by the beneficiaries include Weaving, Sale of Fish, Mixed Trade, Vegetable Vending, Dairying handicrafts, preparation of Pickles and Agarbathis etc. Of these activities, only Weaving, Vegetable vending, Fish business and Dairying received major share of the revolving fund.

The second Mandal considered for the study namely Vetapalem is also located on the coastal belt of Prakasam district. Vetapalem is the only small town in this mandal. This Mandal consists of six villages and six hamlets. All the areas are considered in the Mandal for the selection of beneficiaries in the present study. This Mandal extends an area of 84.10 sq. kms. According to 2001 census, this mandal has a total population of 68,037 and the sex ratio is 1005. The percentage of population living in rural areas in the mandal as per the 2001 census is 41.11 while the remaining 58.89 per cent in urban areas. The literacy rate in the Mandal is 57.56 per cent of which men account for 66.23 per cent while women account for 31.20 per cent. Regarding the distribution of workforce in the mandal, the percentage of main workers to total population worked out to 42.45 per cent of which men account for 55.47 per cent and women 29.14 per cent. The dis-aggregated statistics on occupational distribution of workers at the mandal level indicates that about 47 per cent of the workers are engaged in the agricultural operations. Out of the remaining 53 per cent of workers who concentrated on non-agricultural activities, it is the household industry which is providing gainful employment to more than fifty per cent of this category. However, the percentage of workers engaged on livestock activity is not insignificant. The share of labour concentrated on mining, construction activity, trade and commerce and transport sectors in the mandal are, however, not significant.

Table—13.1 Year-wise Particulars of DWCRA Programme in Chirala Mandal

Year	No. of groups	Number of members				Revolving fund released (Rs. in '000s)	Amount per member
		S.C.	S.T.	Others	Total		
1991-92	5	–	–	75	75	75	1000
1992-93	1	–	–	13	13	15	1153
1993-94	3	15	–	32	47	45	958
1994-95	15	45	21	135	201	228	1134
1995-96	16	15	–	215	230	400	1739
1996-97	19	5	1	139	145	342	2358
1997-98	12	1	20	129	150	140	933
1998-99	3	1	–	29	30	30	1000
1999-2000	24	13	4	399	416	433	1040
2000-2001	34	29	12	687	728	578	794
Total	**132**	**124**	**58**	**1853**	**2035**	**2286**	**1192**

Source: Compiled from record of office of M.D.O., Chirala, 2001.

The data on the number of DWCRA groups and beneficiaries of the programme of Vetapalem Mandal are finished in Table 13.2. The data indicates that the number of groups have increased from mere 2 in 1990-91 to 66 by 2001. The total number of groups and membership increased to 224 and 2339 respectively by the end of March 2001. More than 72 per cent of the respondents belong to backward classes, while forward castes, scheduled castes and schedules tribes constitute 10 per cent, 12 per cent and 4 per cent respectively. The revolving fund distributed among the DWCRA groups during 1991-2001 was to the tune of 23 lakhs and the revolving fund given to each number comes to an average amount of Rs. 12,000. The activities covered under DWCRA in Vetapalem Mandal are more or less similar to that of Chirala Mandal.

Socio-Economic Features of Sample Beneficiaries

The distribution of sample beneficiaries by activity in the two mandals under the study is included in Table 13.3. Out of the total 202 sample beneficiaries belonging to Chirala mandal about 20 per cent of them belong to Vijayalakshmipuram and Ramakrishnaagar village each. With regard to the activities it can be seen that Weaving, Fish Business, Mixed Trade and Handicrafts represent about 20 per cent each in the sample. Similarly, in Vetapalem Mandal out of 233 sample beneficiaries 20 per cent hail from Vetapalem and Katarivaripalem villages. As far as the activities of the groups are concerned mixed trade covers about 28 per cent of the total sample while the remaining namely Weaving Fish business, Dairying and Vegetable Vending trades have less than 20 per cent from each mandal.

Table—13.2 Year-wise Particulars of DWCRA Programme in Vetapalem Mandal

Year	No. of groups	Number of members				Revolving fund released (Rs. in '000s)	Amount per member
		S.C.	S.T.	Others	Total		
1990-91	2	29	–	17	46	30	652
1991-92	5	–	–	75	75	75	1000
1992-93	1	–	15	–	15	15	1000
1993-94	6	30	–	60	90	90	1000
1994-95	47	97	13	460	570	589	1033
1995-96	6	–	–	90	90	150	1666
1996-97	21	21	9	95	125	385	3080
1997-98	17	10	31	177	218	216	990
1998-99	31	2	9	371	382	298	1041
1999-2000	22	35	10	160	205	262	1278
2000-2001	66	60	25	438	523	483	923
Total	**224**	**284**	**112**	**1943**	**2339**	**2693**	**1151**

Source: Compiled from record of office of M.D.O., Vetapalem, 2001.

Table—13.3 Distribution of Sample Beneficiaries by Activity Status

Sl. No.	Item	Eepu-rupa-lem	Vijaya Lakshmi Puram	Remak-rishna Nagar	Gavi-nivarip alem	Somon Centre	Old Chirala	Veta-palem	Anumol ipeta	Nayana palli	Desai-peta	Manke navani palem	Amoda giri-patnam	Katari-vari-palem	Ram-nagar	Pandella-palli	Total
Chirala Mandal																	
1.	Weaving	38 (90.44)	–	–	–	–	–	–	4 (9.53)	–	–	–	–	–	–	–	42 (100.00)
2.	Fish business	–	45 (100.00)	–	–	–	–	–	–	–	–	–	–	–	–	–	45 (100.00)
3.	Dairy	–	–	20 (100.00)	–	–	–	–	–	–	–	–	–	–	–	–	20 (100.00)
4.	Mixed trade	–	–	10 (25.00)	20 (50.00)	–	–	–	–	–	–	–	–	10 (25.00)	–	–	40 (100.00)
5.	Vegetables	–	–	–	–	–	11 (100.00)	–	–	–	–	–	–	–	–	–	11 (100.00)
6.	Handi-crafts	–	–	24 (54.55)	–	10 (22.73)	–	–	–	–	–	–	–	–	10 (22.82)	–	44 (100.00)
	Total	38 (18.87)	45 (22.28)	54 (26.73)	20 (9.90)	10 (4.95)	11 (5.45)	–	4 (1.98)	–	–	–	–		10 (4.95)	10 (4.95)	202 (100.00)

(Table Contd…)

Vetapalem Mandal

1	2	3	4	5	6	7	8	9	10	11	12	13	14	15	16	17	18
1.	Weaving	–	–	–	–	–	–	10 (24.39)	21 (51.22)	10 (24.39)	–	–	–	–	–	–	41 (100.00)
2.	Fish business	–	–	–	–	–	–	–	–	–	–	–	–	–	44 (100.00)	–	44 (100.00)
3.	Dairy	–	–	–	–	–	–	–	–	25 (71.43)	–	–	–	–	–	10 (28.57)	35 (100.00)
4.	Mixed trade	–	–	–	–	–	–	14 (21.87)	–	–	10 (15.63)	20 (31.25)	–	–	–	10 (15.3)	64 (100.00)
5.	Vegetables	–	–	–	–	–	–	15 (55.60)	–	–	–	–	12 (44.40)	–	–	–	27 (100.00)
6.	Handi-crafts	–	–	–	–	–	–	10 (45.45)	12 (54.55)	–	–	–	–	–	–	–	22 (100.00)
	Total	–	–	–	–	–	–	**49** **(21.03)**	**33** **(14.16)**	**35** **(15.02)**	**10** **(4.29)**	**20** **(8.59)**	**12** **(5.15)**	**44** **(18.88)**	**10** **(4.29)**	**20** **(8.59)**	**233** **(100.00)**

Source:Figures in parentheses indicate percentages to total.

Age

Regarding the age of sample beneficiaries, about 63 per cent of the beneficaries are young as they are below 40 years (Table 13.4). However, about 30 per cent of them are above 30 years. This indicates that majority of the DWCRA beneficiaries are young and middle aged persons. The prominent feature that can be noticed from the study is that the sample beneficiaries engaged in the Diary, Fish Business, Mixed Trade and weaving activities belong to different age groups.

Religion

Table 13.5 indicates the religion of sample beneficiaries. About 95 per cent of the sample beneficiaries belonging to Chirala Mandal are Hindus by religion and Muslims are only about 4 per cent whereas in Vetapalem Mandal 73 per cent of beneficiaries are Hindus while Muslims and Christians constitute 14 per cent and 12 per cent respectively of the total sample.

Table—13.4 Age of Sample Beneficiaries

Sl. No.	Name of the activity	Chirala Mandal					Vetapalem Mandal				
		15-25	26-40	41-65	66.	Total	15-25	26-40	41-65	66>	Total
1.	Weaving	1 (2.4)	27 (52.4)	18 (42.9)	1 (2.4)	42 (100.0)	2 (4.9)	17 (41.5)	21 (51.2)	1 (2.4)	41 (100.0)
2.	Fish business	5 (11.1)	22 (48.9)	15 (33.3)	3 (6.7)	45 (100.0)	8 (18.2)	25 (56.8)	11 (25.0)	–	44 (100.0)
3.	Dairy	–	10 (50.0)	5 (25.0)	5 (25.0)	20 (100.0)	2 (5.7)	17 (48.6)	18 (45.7)	–	35 (100.0)
4.	Mixed trade	10 (25.0)	18 (45.0)	9 (22.5)	3 (7.5)	40 (100.0)	4 (6.3)	40 (62.5)	20 (31.3)	–	64 (100.0)
5.	Vegetables	2 (18.2)	8 (72.7)	1 (9.1)	–	11 (100.0)	–	20 (74.1)	7 (25.9)	–	27 (100.0)
6.	Handicrafts	10 (22.7)	21 (47.7)	13 (29.5)	–	44 (100.0)	2 (9.1)	12 (54.5)	8 (36.4)	–	22 (100.0)
	Total	**28 (13.9)**	**101 (50.0)**	**61 (30.2)**	**12 (5.9)**	**202 (100.0)**	**18 (7.7)**	**131 (56.2)**	**83 (35.6)**	**1 (0.4)**	**233 (100.0)**

Note: Figures in parentheses indicate percentages to total.

Table—13.5 Distribution of Beneficiaries by Religion

Sl. No.	Item	Chirala Mandal					Vetapalem Mandal				
		Hindu	Muslim	Christian	Others	Total	Hindu	Muslim	Christian	Others	Total
1.	Weaving	42 (100.0)	–	–	–	42 (100.0)	31 (75.6)	10 (24.4)	–	–	41 (100.0)
2.	Fish business	44 (97.8)	1 (2.2)	–	–	45 (100.0)	43 (97.7)	1 (2.3)	–	–	44 (100.0)
3.	Dairy	18 (90.0)	2 (10.0)	–	–	20 (100.0)	24 (68.6)	11 (31.4)	–	–	35 (100.0)
4.	Mixed trade	40 (100.0)	–	–	–	40 (100.0)	25 (39.1)	10 (15.6)	28 (43.8)	1 (1.6)	64 (100.0)
5.	Vegetables	11 (100.0)	–	–	–	11 (100.0)	27 (100.0)	–	–	–	27 (100.0)
6.	Handicrafts	37 (84.1)	6 (13.6)	–	1 (2.3)	44 (100.0)	20 (90.9)	1 (4.5)	1 (4.5)	–	22 (100.0)
	Total	**192 (95.0)**	**9 (4.5)**	**–**	**1 (0.5)**	**202 (100.0)**	**170 (73.0)**	**33 (14.2)**	**29 (12.4)**	**1 (0.4)**	**233 (100.0)**

Note: Figures in parentheses indicate percentages to total.

The caste-wise break up of beneficiaries is presented in Table 13.6. It is evident that about 60 per cent of the beneficiaries in each of the Mandals are backward classes in two mandals. About 15 per cent of sample beneficiaries in Vetapalem Mandal are Scheduled Castes.

Educational Qualifications

The educational qualifications of the sample beneficiaries presented in Table 13.7 reflects that fact that about 57 per cent of the total beneficiaries are illiterates in both the Mandals while the rest are literates studied up to primary (25.7 per cent) or secondary (16.3 per cent) levels. In this respect, the similar position can be noticed from Vetapalem Mandal also. On the other hand, majority of the educated beneficiaries are engaged in Weaving, Mixed Trade, and Handicrafts, which implies that educational background has some impact on selection of trades by the beneficiaries.

Residential Accommodation

It is found that more than 85 per cent of the sample beneficiaries are dwelling in their own houses. With regard to the type of houses, it is evident that more than 47 per cent of the beneficiaries (Table 13.8) live in pucca houses while the remaining reside in Thatched houses. In spite of various rural housing programmes initiated by the Government for the rural houseless, a vast majority of the rural poor still have no houses of their own as disclosed by the present study.

Table—13.6 Distribution of Beneficiaries by Reservation Category

Sl. No.	Item	Chirala Mandal					Vetapalem Mandal				
		O.C.	B.C.	S.C.	S.T.	Total	O.C.	B.C.	S.C.	S.T.	Total
1.	Weaving	1 (2.4)	39 (92.9)	7 (4.8)	–	42 (100.0)	–	41 (100.0)	–	–	41 (100.0)
2.	Fish business	–	44 (7.8)	1 (2.2)	–	45 (100.0)	1 (2.3)	43 (97.7)	–	–	44 (100.0)
3.	Dairy	18 (90.0)	1 (5.0)	–	1 (5.0)	20 (100.0)	–	33 (94.3)	2 (5.7)	–	35 (100.0)
4.	Mixed trade	9 (22.5)	19 (47.5)	–	12 (30.0)	40 (100.0)	8 (12.5)	16 (25.0)	33 (51.6)	7 (10.9)	64 (100.0)
5.	Vegetables	–	11 (100.0)	–	–	11 (100.0)	26 (96.3)	1 (3.7)	–	–	27 (100.0)
6.	Handicrafts	42 (95.5)	–	–	2 (4.5)	44 (100.0)	17 (77.3)	3 (13.6)	1 (4.5)	1 (4.5)	22 (100.0)
	Total	**70** **(34.7)**	**114** **(56.4)**	**3** **(1.5)**	**15** **(7.4)**	**202** **(100.0)**	**52** **(22.3)**	**137** **(58.8)**	**36** **(15.5)**	**8** **(3.4)**	**233** **(100.0)**

Note: Figures in parentheses indicates to total.

Table—13.7 Literacy Level of Sample Beneficiaries

		Chirala Mandal					Vetapalem Mandal				
Sl. No.	Item	Illiterate	Primary	Secondary	Degree	Total	Illiterate	Primary	Secondary	Degree	Total
1.	Weaving	19 (45.2)	12 (28.6)	11 (26.2)	–	42 (100.0)	3 (7.3)	27 (65.9)	9 (22.0)	2 (4.9)	41 (100.0)
2.	Fish business	40 (88.9)	2 (4.4)	3 (6.7)	–	45 (100.0)	36 (81.8)	8 (18.2)	–	–	44 (100.0)
3.	Dairy	10 (50.0)	5 (25.0)	5 (25.0)	–	20 (100.0)	19 (54.3)	12 (34.3)	4 (11.4)	–	35 (100.0)
4.	Mixed trade	21 (52.5)	12 (30.0)	6 (15.0)	1 (2.5)	40 (100.0)	39 (60.9)	13 (20.3)	11 (17.2)	1 (1.6)	64 (100.0)
5.	Vegetables	10 (90.9)	–	1 (9.1)	–	11 (100.0)	23 (85.2)	1 (3.7)	3 (11.1)	–	27 (100.0)
6.	Handicrafts	15 (34.1)	21 (47.7)	7 (15.9)	1 (2.3)	44 (100.0)	14 (63.6)	5 (22.7)	3 (13.6)	–	22 (100.0)
	Total	**115 (56.9)**	**52 (25.7)**	**33 (16.3)**	**2 (1.0)**	**202 (100.0)**	**134 (57.5)**	**66 (28.3)**	**30 (12.9)**	**3 (1.3)**	**233 (100.0)**

Note: Figures in parentheses indicate percentage to total.

Table—13.8 Type of Residential Accommodation

Sl. No.	Item	Chirala Mandal						Vetapalem Mandal					
		Pucca building	Shed	Thatched shed	Hut	Tiled	Total	Pucca building	Shed	Thatched shed	Hut	Tiled	Total
1.	Weaving	15 (35.7)	1 (2.4)	13 (31.0)	7 (16.7)	6 (14.3)	42 (100.0)	22 (53.7)	–	12 (29.3)	–	7 (17.1)	41 (100.0)
2.	Fish business	45 (100.0)	–	–	–	–	45 (100.0)	–	–	44 (100.0)	–	–	44 (100.0)
3.	Dairy	4 (20.0)	2 (10.0)	8 (40.0)	3 (15.0)	3 (15.0)	20 (100.0)	3 (8.6)	2 (5.7)	14 (40.0)	16 (45.7)	–	35 (100.0)
4.	Mixed trade	11 (27.5)	–	29 (72.5)	–	–	40 (100.0)	9 (14.1)	–	34 (53.1)	21 (32.8)	–	64 (100.0)
5.	Vegetables	1 (9.1)	–	10 (90.9)	–	–	11 (100.0)	6 (22.2)	–	18 (66.7)	3 (11.1)	–	27 (100.0)
6.	Handicrafts	20 (45.5)	8 (18.2)	7 (15.9)	5 (11.4)	4 (9.1)	44 (100.0)	7 (31.8)	1 (4.5)	7 (31.8)	7 (31.8)	–	22 (100.0)
	Total	**96 (47.5)**	**11 (5.4)**	**67 (33.2)**	**15 (7.4)**	**13 (6.4)**	**202 (100.0)**	**47 (20.2)**	**3 (1.3)**	**129 (55.4)**	**47 (20.2)**	**7 (3.0)**	**233 (100.0)**

Note: Figures in parentheses indicate percentage to total.

Group Formation and Identification

Group formation is a crucial aspect of DWACRA programme. Pursuit of a common income generating activity has been the basis for formulation of the groups. The officials of DRDA and MDO identify groups from among the economically weaker sections. Since the DWCRA is a sub-scheme of IRDP, identification of women from the families covered under the IRDP will be done at initial stages. Later, the groups are formed on the basis of economic activity such as weaving, leaf making, rock making, preparation of pickles, vegetable business, dairying and fish business etc. By and large identification of groups was done in accordance with the guidelines issued by the Government in the study area. No exigencies and pressure seem to have prevailed in the choice of areas and groups in the two mandals under study.

Group Dynamics

Group dynamics is the prominent feature of DWCRA. The group leaders and second leaders are selected on the basis of suggestions of the VDO/APO (Woman). The basic qualifications looked for such leadership both by the members and VDO/APO are: (a) Communication skills and articulation capabilities; (b) literacy; (c) assistance that could come from the family for maintenance of records and accounts; and (d) the respect that she commands in the community etc.

In the study area the members and officials discuss mainly the issues relating to the activities of the groups. Further issues like welfare of women, childcare, credit activities improvements in production and marketing of goods and services are also discussed. In the study area the position of repayment of revolving fund etc., are also discussed frequently.

Reasons for Joining DWCRA

After presenting the socio-economic background of the sample beneficiaries, it is appropriate to examine the factors, which motivated the sample households for joining the DWCRA group. As can be seen from Table 13.9 a vast majority of the sample has joined this programme to supplement the income of their family. The other reasons, namely to learn new skills, pressure from the family and so on have motivated a small number of beneficiaries who constitute only 15 per cent. Thus the economic factor plays a dominant role in motivating the sample beneficiary for joining DWCRA group as is revealed by the present study.

Motivators

The details of persons who motivated the sample beneficiaries to join the DWCRA group are presented in Table 13.10. Evidently, the family members, APO, Mahila Mandals, students of Agricultural College and Home Science College, Bapatla have played an important role in motivating the sample to join the DWCRA programme. The influence of students is more perceptible in case of groups of Mixed Trade and Vegetable Trade. The influence of others, like Neighbours VAO/VDO, Mahila Mandals is very marginal. However, apart from these factors the self-motivation is a significant motivating factor. With regard to the institutions which assisted the sample beneficiaries to join the DWCRA, it can be noted that Mahila Mandals encouraged about 70 per cent, while the Gram Sabha assisted 20 per cent and the Government Officials about 10 per cent of the total beneficiaries to apply for the assistance from DWCRA. Similarly, the means of knowing other members of the group, it is observed that about 65 per cent of the sample beneficiaries came to know their colleagues through the meeting held by themselves informally while the remaining came to know the other members of the group during the meeting held by the Government Officials before commencing the programme. This position has been noticed in almost all the DWCRA activities.

The sample beneficiaries indicated several reasons for the selection of a particular activity under the DWCRA programme. It is found that about one third of the sample beneficiaries selected a particular activity mainly because of its profitability. There are certain other reasons also like easy sales of their products (28 per cent), prior acquisition of necessary skills through training (26.00 per cent) and finally the simple process involves in the activity (11.0 per cent). It is revealed by about 65 per cent of the sample beneficiaries who are involved in vegetable business selected this specific activity because it is easy to market the vegetables than

Table—13.9 Distribution of Beneficiaries by Reasons for Joining DWCRA

Sl. No.	Name of the activity	Chirala Mandal					Vetapalem Mandal				
		To earn some money	To learn some new skills	Under pressure from family	All the above three	Total	To earn some money	To learn some new skills	Under pressure from family	All the above three	Total
1.	Weaving	41 (97.6)	–	–	1 (2.4)	42 (100.0)	30 (73.2)	–	6 (14.6)	5 (12.2)	41 (100.0)
2.	Fish business	45 (100.0)	–	–	–	45 (100.0)	34 (77.3)	4 (9.1)	5 (11.4)	1 (2.3)	44 (100.0)
3.	Dairy	19 (95.0)	–	–	1 (5.0)	20 (100.0)	32 (91.4)	–	3 (8.6)	–	35 (100.0)
4.	Mixed trade	40 (100.0)	–	–	–	40 (100.0)	36 (54.7)	29 (36.9)	6 (9.4)	–	64 (100.0)
5.	Vegetables	9 (81.8)	–	–	2 (18.2)	11 (100.0)	15 (55.6)	5 (18.5)	6 (22.2)	1 (3.7)	27 (100.0)
6.	Handicrafts	40 (90.9)	–	–	4 (9.1)	44 (100.0)	7 (31.8)	1 (4.5)	10 (45.5)	4 (18.2)	22 (100.0)
	Total	**194 (96.0)**	–	–	**8 (4.0)**	**202 (100.0)**	**153 (65.7)**	**33 (14.2)**	**36 (15.5)**	**11 (4.7)**	**233 (100.0)**

Note: Figures in parentheses indicate percentage to total.

Table—13.10 Motivation Factors to Join DWCRA

S. No.	Item	By self motivation	On advise of family members	A.P.O.	On the advise of sarpanch	Village women	V.D.O/ V.A.O.	Animator	Students	Mahila Mandali	Total
Chirala Mandal											
1.	Weaving	10	13	1	–	–	2	–	12	4	42
		(23.8)	(31.0)	(2.4)			(4.8)		(28.6)	(9.5)	(100.0)
2.	Fish business	10	7	9	5	4	–	–	5	5	45
		(27.2)	(15.6)	(20.0)	(11.1)	(8.9)			(11.1)	(11.1)	(100.0)
3.	Dairy	5	4	3	–	–	2	2	–	4	20
		(25.0)	(20.0)	(15.0)			(10.0)	(10.0)		(20.0)	(100.0)
4.	Mixed trade	5	5	5	–	–	–	–	20	5	40
		(12.5)	(12.5)	(12.5)					(50.0)	(12.5)	(100.0)
5.	Vegetables	4	4	3	–	–	–	–	–	–	11
		(36.4)	(36.4)	(27.3)							(100.0)
6.	Handicrafts	7	6	2	6	3	3	2	13	2	14
		(15.9)	(13.6)	(4.6)	(13.6)	(6.8)	(6.8)	(4.6)	(29.5)	(4.6)	(100.0)
	Total	**41**	**39**	**23**	**11**	**7**	**7**	**4**	**50**	**20**	**202**
		(20.3)	**(19.3)**	**(11.4)**	**(5.4)**	**(3.4)**	**(3.4)**	**(2.0)**	**(24.8)**	**(10.0)**	**(100.0)**

(Table Contd…)

Vetapalem Mandal

1		2	3	4	5	6	7	8	9	10	11
1.	Weaving	9 (21.9)	12 (29.3)	8 (19.5)	2 (4.9)	–	–	–	10 (24.3)	–	41 (100.0)
2.	Fish business	6 (13.6)	–	–	6 (13.6)	14 (31.8)	7 (15.9)	1 (2.3)	10 (22.7)	–	44 (100.0)
3.	Dairy	4 (11.4)	11 (31.4)	3 (8.6)	8 (22.9)	1 (2.9)	–	2 (5.7)	4 (11.4)	2 (5.7)	35 (100.0)
4.	Mixed trade	9 (22.0)	9 (14.1)	5 (7.8)	7 (10.9)	2 (31.1)	2 (3.1)	4 (6.3)	24 (58.5)	2 (3.1)	64 (100.0)
5.	Vegetables	9 (21.9)	–	–	1 (3.7)	1 (3.7)	–	–	16 (59.2)	–	27 (100.0)
6.	Handicrafts	13 (59.1)	3 (13.6)	–	–	–	–	2 (9.1)	2 (9.1)	2 (9.1)	22 (100.0)
	Total	**50 (21.5)**	**35 (15.0)**	**16 (6.9)**	**24 (10.3)**	**18 (7.7)**	**9 (3.9)**	**9 (3.9)**	**66 (28.2)**	**6 (2.6)**	**233 (100.0)**

Note: Figures in parentheses indicate percentage to total.

any other commodities. Similarly, about 50 per cent of the sample members selected their activities on the basis of their castes.

Decision Making Relating to DWCRA

Decision-making regarding the management of activities plays an important role in the success of DWCRA. It is observed in the present study that decisions on all the matters relating to the DWCRA are taken by the group leaders, the group members, concerned officials in consultation with the higher officials. As can be seen from the Table 13.11 the group leaders in consultation with concerned officials take all necessary decisions. This situation is more pronounced in case of activities like Mixed Trade, Weaving and Fish business. With regard to the Vetapalem Mandal more than 40 per cent of the sample groups are participating in taking the necessary decisions relating to their activities. The activities belong to this category are Weaving followed by Vegetable vending, Mixed trade and Fish business.

Disbursement of Revolving Fund

Every group member has to pay Rs. 30/- per months at the rate of Rs. 1/- per day as her contribution to the DWACRA group. The group leader collects this amount from each member and credits it in a local bank. The account is opened in the names of the all group members. Basing on the seniority criteria of the thrift groups, the Government contributes the necessary revolving fund ranging between Rs. 10,000 and Rs. 15,000/- per group except during 1995-96. The revolving fund released during 1995-96 was Rs. 25,000/- per group. It is observed that all the existing groups in the study area were sanctioned the revolving fund. But few of these groups who received revolving found did not start any activity. Later these groups become completely defunct and their number increased gradually.

As can be noticed from the Table 13.12 about 50 per cent of the sample groups were reported to have received the revolving fund from the Government, 12 months after the formation of the thrift groups. As said earlier, some women groups (Weavers) are paid the revolving fund even before the formation of thrift groups as a special case due to the continuous starvation deaths and suicides, occurred in the study area during the last years. Similarly, the assistance was also extended to Scheduled Caste and Scheduled Tribe categories under special drive category for the persons engaged in Mixed Trade and Handicrafts activity with less than one year seniority and in some cases it is even before the formation of thrift groups.

Training to DWCRA Members

The particulars of training undergone by the sample beneficiaries are furnished in Table 13.13. It is observed that about 60 per cent of the sample beneficiaries were undergone training given by the Rural and Urban Development Self-Employment Training Institute (RUDSET) located in Vetapalem. It is sponsored by the nationalised banks of Prakasam district. This institute is the major source to impart training in this locality on variety of activities. Broadly, this institute impacts training on handicrafts, home crafts (phenol, cleaning powder, washing powder, liquid blue, meals leaf plates (etc.,) Agarbathi, dress designing and embroidery, electrical and electronic technology, automobile mechanism, beautician cum health care, plastic and rubber technology, printing technology etc. In addition to this training, about 30 per cent of the sample beneficiaries in Vetapalem Mandal and 10 per cent in Chirala Mandal had undergone training imparted under TRYSEM Programme.

Supervision and Monitoring

As explained earlier, the essential conditions for the effective implementation of any development programme including the DWCRA requires an efficient administrative machinery for exercising, effective supervision control, to take follow-up action and so on. An effective monitoring system is also very much essential to ensure the successful implementation of any programme including the DWCRA.

An assessment of effectiveness of the supervision over the implementation of DWCRA groups is attempted in this study. Table 3.14 reveals that the Mandal officials like M.D.O. and V.D.O. are visiting frequently various groups started in various villages for the purpose of supervising their activities of the beneficiaries. The

Table—13.11 Decisions on Matters Relating to Group Activity

Sl. No.	Item	Chirala Mandal					Vetapalem Mandal				
		Group leader	All the group members	Official concerned	Group leader + officials	Total	Group leader	All the group members	Official concerned	Group Leader + officials	Total
1.	Weaving	13 (31.0)	4 (9.5)	10 (23.8)	15 (35.7)	42 (100.0)	10 (24.4)	31 (75.6)	–	–	41 (100.0)
2.	Fish business	–	–	32 (66.7)	15 (33.3)	45 (100.0)	29 (65.9)	15 (34.1)	–	–	44 (100.0)
3.	Dairy	–	20 (100.0)	–	–	20 (100.0)	15 (42.9)	–	20 (57.1)	–	35 (100.0)
4.	Mixed trade	20 (50.0)	–	–	20 (50.0)	40 (100.0)	10 (15.6)	34 (53.1)	20 (31.3)	–	35 (100.0)
5.	Vegetables	–	–	–	11 (100.0)	11 (100.0)	–	15 (55.6)	12 (44.4)	–	27 (100.0)
6.	Handicrafts	14 (31.8)	–	20 (45.5)	10 (22.7)	44 (100.0)	22 (100.0)	–	–	–	22 (100.0)
	Total	**47 (23.3)**	**24 (11.9)**	**60 (29.7)**	**71 (35.1)**	**202 (100.0)**	**86 (36.9)**	**95 (40.8)**	**52 (22.3)**	–	**233 (100.0)**

Note: Figures in parentheses indicate percentages to total.

Table—13.12 Waiting Period to Receive Revolving Fund

Sl. No.	Item	Chirala Mandal				Vetapalem Mandal			
		<1 year	1-2 years	3 years	Total	<1 year	1-2 years	3 years	Total
1.	Weaving	–	28 (66.7)	14 (33.3)	42 (100.0)	11 (26.8)	20 (48.8)	10 (24.4)	41 (100.0)
2.	Fish business	–	15 (33.3)	30 (66.7)	45 (100.0)	14 (31.8)	15 (34.1)	15 (34.1)	44 (100.0)
3.	Dairy	–	20 (100.0)	–	20 (100.0)	–	35 (100.0)	–	35 (100.0)
4.	Mixed trade	40 (100.0)	–	–	40 (100.0)	–	34 (53.1)	30 (46.9)	64 (100.0)
5.	Vegetables	–	11 (100.0)	–	11 (100.0)	12 (44.4)	15 (55.6)	–	27 (100.0)
6.	Handicrafts	20 (45.5)	25 (54.5)	–	44 (100.0)	12 (54.5)	–	10 (45.5)	22 (100.0)
	Total	**60 (29.7)**	**98 (48.5)**	**44 (21.8)**	**202 (100.0)**	**49 (21.0)**	**119 (51.1)**	**65 (27.9)**	**233 (100.0)**

Note: Figures in parentheses indicate percentages to total.

APO and the officials are also occasionally supervising the activities of these groups. Further Panchayat Raj leaders like the ward members and Surpanches in the village Panchayats, MPTCs and ZPTCs occasionally visit the groups particularly in Vetapalem Mandal for supervising the DWCRA activities. About three fourths of the sample beneficiaries opined that the officials are cooperative and provide necessary guidance and assistance to the group members at various stages of their operations. Further, almost all the sample beneficiaries revealed that the Government officials like the VDOs, MDOs and APOs are frequently visiting the DWACRA groups and attending to their problems. The sample beneficiaries expressed their satisfaction for the prompt attention paid by the VDOs (Women) in solving the problems, which they face while carrying out their activities.

It has been stressed by the Ministry of Rural Development, Government of India, that for regular monitoring of the DWCRA programme, every group member should be contacted by the concerned officials to ascertain their opinions on the entire process of implementation, monitoring and performance of the programme. The present study found that the concerned Officials observe these guidelines as they are regularly and effectively monitoring the DWCRA programme implemented in the study area and also take follow-up action wherever necessary. It was also found that the monitoring cards were provided to all the beneficiaries of DWCRA and they fill the monitoring schedules whenever they visit the group. However, it was noticed that the necessary coordination was absent among the various departments such as ICDS, adult literacy, family welfare etc., as they provide complementary services to the members of DWCRA groups. Another important lapse found during the study is that the numbers of the DWCRA groups do not observe fixed working hours (Table 13.15). Further, the working hours depend upon the nature of activity. The data furnished in the above table reveals that more than 65 per cent of the sample beneficiaries in the study work for about 6-8 hours each in the activities except in the case of weaving. The weavers are working more than 8 hours. They perform weaving activity even in the late night hours.

Table—13.13 Particulars of Training to Participants

S. No.	Item	Chirala Mandal						Vetapalem Mandal					
		RUDSET	Through TRYSEM	Craftsman came to village	Institute/ Polytechnic	Others	Total	RUDSET	Through TRYSEM	Craftsman came to village	Institute Polytechnic	Others	Total
1.	Weaving	14 (33.30)	13 (31.00)	7 (16.70)	5 (11.90)	3 (7.10)	42 (100.00)	10 (24.40)	12 (29.30)	7 (17.10)	3 (7.30)	9 (22.00)	41 (100.00)
2.	Fish business	45 (100.00)	–	–	–	–	45 (100.00)	44 (100.00)	–	–	–	–	44 (100.00)
3.	Dairy	10 (50.00)	10 (50.00)	–	–	–	20 (100.00)	17 (48.47)	9 (25.71)	1 (2.81)	3 (8.57)	5 (28.60)	35 (100.00)
4.	Mixed trade	25 (60.00)	15 (40.00)	–	–	–	40 (100.00)	24 (68.80)	24 (6.30)	6 (9.40)	1 (1.60)	9 (14.29)	64 (100.00)
5.	Vegetables	–	7 (63.60)	–	2 (18.20)	2 (18.20)	11 (100.00)	15 (55.60)	7 (25.90)	–	5 (18.50)	–	27 (100.00)
6.	Handicrafts	24 (54.50)	–	17 (38.60)	1 (2.30)	2 (4.50)	44 (100.00)	5 (22.73)	15 (68.18)	–	–	2 (9.00)	22 (100.00)
	Total	118 (58.42)	62 (30.70)	8 (3.96)	9 (4.45)	5 (2.47)	202 (100.00)	145 (62.2)	25 (10.70)	14 (6.00)	12 (5.20)	37 (15.90)	233 (100.00)

Note: Figures in parentheses indicate percentage to total.

Marketing of Products

The availability of transport facilities to market the products of the groups is very essential for the success of DWCRA programme. The study area is well connected with both road and rail. Apart from the APSRTC Buses, private vehicles are also being used by the members to carry their products to the market places. A vast majority of the sample beneficiaries admitted that generally they do not experience any problems in marketing their products. Generally, the products manufactured by various DWCRA groups are sold in the daily markets and weekly markets held in the locality concerned. Most of the beneficiaries (70 per cent) sell their products in the local markets itself (Table 13.16). As can be seen from the Table 13.17 more than 70 per cent of the DWCRA products are being transported to the nearest markets through road and rail transport.

The striking features noticed during the present study with regard to the marketing of the products like pickles and handicrafts prepared by the DWCRA groups is that the beneficiaries of DWCRA opened a small shop in the main bazaar of Eepurupalem village of Chirala Mandal to market their products. Similarly, the members of DWCRA groups in Vetapalem also opened a shop for selling their products. These beneficiaries reported that they market their products in larger quantities in the DWCRA bazaars frequently conducted by the District Officials at the District Head quarters, namely Ongole. It is also noticed that depending upon the demand from the local people the groups prepare a variety of pickles and sell them in these bazaars. It was also observed during the fieldwork that the marketing of products manufactured by certain groups in the two Mandals had been taken up by the husbands of the members. As a result of the competition from local merchants and traders the DWCRA groups were facing a number of problems in marketing their respective products. Some of the sample respondents reported that some times the market fluctuations are very high which cause heavy loss to them. However, they seemed to be satisfied with the prevailing prices in respect of their products in the market after the introduction of *"Sree Prakasam"* to market the DWCRA products by D.R.D.A. Ongole.

Table—13.14 Details of Supervision Over the Activity

S. No.	Item	Chirala Mandal					Vetapalem Mandal				
		VDO/ MDO	APO	Bank officers	Local politicians	Total	VDO/ MDO	APO	Bank officers	Local politicians	Total
1.	Weaving	42 (100.00)	–	–	–	42 (100.00)	41 (100.00)	–	–	–	41 (100.00)
2.	Fish business	14 (31.10)	10 (22.20)	21 (46.70)	–	45 (100.00)	15 (34.10)	14 (31.80)	–	15 (34.10)	44 (100.00)
3.	Dairy	20 (100.00)	–	–	–	20 (100.00)	15 (45.70)	–	–	20 (51.40)	35 (100.00)
4.	Mixed trade	28 (70.00)	12 (30.00)	–	–	40 (100.00)	16 (25.00)	22 (34.40)	26 (40.60)	–	64 (100.00)
5.	Vegetables	11 (100.00)	–	–	–	11 (100.00)	10 (37.00)	10 (37.00)	7 (25.90)	–	27 (100.00)
6.	Handicrafts	24 (54.50)	20 (45.50)	–	–	44 (100.00)	10 (45.50)	12 (54.50)	–	–	22 (100.00)
	Total	**139 (68.80)**	**42 (20.80)**	**21 (10.40)**	–	**202 (100.00)**	**107 (45.90)**	**58 (24.90)**	**33 (14.20)**	**35 (15.00)**	**233 (100.00)**

Note: Figures in parentheses indicate percentages to total.

With regard to the income from the DWCRA activities, about 87 per cent of the beneficiaries received the amount on account of the sales of their products from the Group leader. The information relating to the number of years of experience of beneficiaries in handling the activity reveals that about one-fourth of the beneficiaries have experience less than one year in their respective trade. This is more pronounced in the case of vegetable vendors. However, about 80 per cent of the sample beneficiaries have three years of experience in their respective activities.

Similarly, with regard to the time gap involved in receiving the cash from the buyers of their products, about 55 per cent of the total sample beneficiaries reported that they get the cash immediately. A considerable number of 17.42 per cent of the total beneficiaries reported that they are paid within a week after they supplied their products to the traders while labour 28 per cent of the beneficiaries complained that they receive their payment only after a month. This fact was reported by the Weaving activity, while the payments are prompt in the case of other activities such as Fish Business, Dairying, Vegetables selling and to certain extent Mixed Trade and Handicrafts.

Opinions and Perceptions of Sample Beneficiaries on Official Procedures of DWCRA

This section discusses broadly the opinions of sample beneficiaries on the official procedures involved in the implementation of the DWCRA programme and the problems involved in this process. The opinion of sample beneficiaries on the behaviour and attitude of Officials involved in the implementation of DWCRA programme are also ascertained. An attempt is also made to probe into the attitude of the family members of the sample beneficiaries and their role in the family matters such as childcare, cooking of food etc.

The opinion of beneficiaries on the procedure involved in the sanction and maintenance of DWCRA activities are presented in Table 13.18. According to this Table about 66 per cent of the sample beneficiaries felt that the procedure involved in the sanction and the maintenance of DWCRA group was simple to a certain extent. But, others felt that understanding of the concept of

Table—13.15 Hours of Work Each Day

S. No.	Item	Chirala Mandal				Vetapalem Mandal			
		Before 6 hours	6-8 hours	8 + hours	Total	Before 6 hours	6-8 hours	8 + hours	Total
1.	Weaving	–	–	42 (100.00)	42 (100.00)	–	–	41 (100.00)	41 (100.00)
2.	Fish business	30 (66.67)	15 (33.33)	–	45 (100.00)	14 (31.82)	30 (68.18)	–	44 (100.00)
3.	Dairy	20 (100.00)	–	–	20 (100.00)	–	35 (100.00)	–	35 (100.00)
4.	Mixed trade	15 (37.50)	25 (62.50)	–	40 (100.00)	39 (60.93)	25 (39.07)	–	64 (100.00)
5.	Vegetables	11 (14.48)	–	–	11 (100.00)	27 (100.00)	–	–	27 (100.00)
6.	Handicrafts	–	44 (52.39)	–	44 (100.00)	–	22 (100.00)	–	22 (100.00)
	Total	**76 (37.62)**	**84 (41.58)**	**42 (20.80)**	**202 (100.00)**	**80 (34.33)**	**112 (48.07)**	**41 (17.60)**	**233 (100.00)**

Note: Figures in parentheses indicate percentage to total.

Table—13.16 Channels of Marketing of Products

S. No.	Item	Chirala Mandal					Vetapalem Mandal				
		In the open market	DWCRA bazar/ riot bazars	Co-operative societies	Consumers	Total	In the open market	DWCRA bazar/ riot bazars	Co-operative societies	Consumers	Total
1.	Weaving	35 (83.33)	2 (4.76)	5 (11.91)	–	42 (100.00)	35 (85.40)	3 (7.31)	3 (7.31)	–	41 (100.00)
2.	Fish business	45 (100.00)	–	–	–	45 (100.00)	36 (81.82)	4 (9.09)	–	4 (9.09)	44 (100.00)
3.	Dairy	20 (100.00)	–	–	–	20 (100.00)	20 (57.14)	–	5 (14.28)	10 (28.58)	35 (100.00)
4.	Mixed trade	29 (72.50)	4 (10.00)	7 (17 50)	–	40 (100.00)	42 (65.62)	5 (7.82)	3 (4.68)	14 (21.88)	64 (100.00)
5.	Vegetables	7 (63.40)	–	–	4 (36.36)	11 (100.00)	11 (40.74)	6 (22.23)	2 (7.40)	8 (29.63)	27 (100.00)
6.	Handicrafts	22 (50.00)	8 (18.18)	4 (9.09)	10 (22.73)	44 (100.00)	16 (72.72)	3 (13.64)	–	3 (13.64)	22 (100.00)
	Total	**158 (78.21)**	**14 (6.93)**	**16 (7.93)**	**14 (6.93)**	**202 (100.00)**	**160 (68.67)**	**21 (9.01)**	**13 (5.58)**	**39 (16.74)**	**233 (100.00)**

Note: Figures in parentheses indicate percentage to total.

Table—13.17 Means of Transport of Products to Market

S. No.	Item	Chirala Mandal				Vetapalem Mandal			
		Bus	Train	Other	Total	Bus	Train	Other	Total
1.	Weaving	19 (45.24)	23 (54.76)	–	42 (100.00)	15 (36.59)	21 (51.22)	5 (12.20)	41 (100.00)
2.	Fish business	–	19 (42.22)	26 (57.78)	45 (100.00)	21 (47.73)	13 (29.35)	10 (22.72)	44 (100.00)
3.	Dairy	12 (60.00)	8 (40.00)	–	20 (100.00)	10 (28.57)	15 (42.86)	10 (28.57)	35 (100.00)
4.	Mixed trade	20 (50.00)	7 (17.50)	13 (32.50)	40 (100.00)	37 (57.81)	25 (39.06)	2 (3.13)	64 (100.00)
5.	Vegetables	11 (100.00)	–	–	11 (100.00)	13 (48.15)	12 (44.45)	2 (7.40)	27 (100.00)
6.	Handicrafts	15 (34.09)	15 (34.09)	14 (31.82)	44 (100.00)	22 (100.00)	–	–	22 (100.00)
	Total	**77 (38.12)**	**72 (35.64)**	**53 (26.24)**	**202 (100.00)**	**118 (50.64)**	**86 (36.91)**	**29 (12.45)**	**233 (100.00)**

Note: Figures in parentheses indicate percentages to total.

DWCRA and procedure are complex and time consuming. However, these beneficiaries understood with these procedures with the help of Officials of Office of M.D.O. and D.R.D.A.

The opinions of the sample beneficiaries on the behaviour of officials concerned are reflected in Table 13.19. It can be seen from the table that about 90 per cent of the total beneficiaries have good opinion on the officials as they considered them honest and efficient. Only a negligible number of beneficiaries revealed that the officials are corrupt.

When the opinion of the respondents on the behaviour of the officials who are implementing in DWCRA, is ascertained it became evident that these officials are responding positively and immediately to the needs and problems of the beneficiaries. An overwhelming majority of the respondent accounting for 94 per cent of the total sample beneficiaries revealed that there was prompt response from the concerned officials to their problems. Apart from this, 80 per cent of the sample beneficiaries (Table 13.20) expressed their satisfaction with the attitude of VDOs (Women) and bank Officials. Further, about 95 per cent of the sample beneficiaries seemed to have been satisfied with the behaviour of the A.P.O. Only three sample beneficiaries were not satisfied with the attitude of the MDO.

It needs no emphasis at the degree of success of DWCRA programme largely depended upon on the attitude of the family members of the beneficiaries towards the programme. About three-fourths of the beneficiaries stated that they are getting constant encouragement from their family members in the activity undertaken under the DWCRA (Table 13.21). However, few of the beneficiaries involved in Weaving, Mixed trade, Fish Business, and Handicrafts and Vegetable selling revealed that they did not get any support and encouragement from their family members. About 5 per cent of the total beneficiaries did not say anything about the cooperation of their family members in their activities. In contrast, about 20 per cent of the total beneficiaries admitted that they are not receiving any co-operation from their family members who considered the activities of the group members are against their traditions and customs. It is also interesting to note that about 95 per cent of the total beneficiaries are satisfied with the support

Table—13.18 **Opinions of Beneficiaries on the Procedure Involved in the Sanction and Maintenance of DWCRA**

S. No.	Item	Chirala Mandal				Vetapalem Mandal			
		Complex and time consuming	Simple	Cannot say	Total	Complex and time consuming	Simple	Cannot say	Total
1.	Weaving	9 (21.40)	32 (76.20)	1 (2.40)	42 (100.00)	7 (17.07)	34 (82.90)	7 (17.10)	41 (100.00)
2.	Fish business	12 (26.70)	31 (68.90)	2 (4.40)	45 (100.00)	13 (29.54)	31 (70.45)	–	44 (100.00)
3.	Dairy	6 (30.00)	10 (50.00)	4 (20.00)	20 (100.00)	10 (28.57)	25 (71.53)	–	35 (100.00)
4.	Mixed trade	6 (15.00)	31 (77.50)	3 (7.50)	40 (100.00)	26 (40.60)	38 (59.40)	–	64 (100.00)
5.	Vegetables	11 (100.00)	–	–	11 (100.00)	5 (18.52)	21 (77.78)	1 (3.70)	27 (100.00)
6.	Handicrafts	11 (25.00)	33 (75.00)	–	44 (100.00)	17 (77.27)	5 (18.52)	–	22 (100.00)
	Total	**55 (27.20)**	**137 (67.80)**	**10 (5.00)**	**202 (100.00)**	**78 (33.47)**	**154 (66.10)**	**1 (0.40)**	**233 (100.00)**

Note: Figures in parentheses indicate percentages to total.

they received from the villagers in their activities relating to the DWCRA programme. These beneficiaries also confessed that they have very cordial relations with the group leaders and with other members of the group (Table 13.22). It is also found during the field work that most of the beneficiaries were satisfied with the behaviour of their husbands and children. It is pointed out by few respondents that their in-laws and other family members did not like the DWCRA programme and are not happy with their involvement in this programme. On the whole, the beneficiaries are very happy with the behaviour of their family members, group leaders and other members in the group.

When the members of DWACRA groups have to spend more time at the work place some one has to look after their children in the house. Interestingly about one third of the total beneficiaries (37.62 per cent) revealed that the children are looked after by their in-laws when they are doing the work relating to the DWCRA programme. While 28 per cent of the beneficiaries reported that their children are taken care by their husbands and elder daughters during their absence from the house. About 25 per cent of the respondents replied that their children are looked after by their friends when they are away (Table 13.23). Only 21 beneficiaries in Chirala and 15 beneficiaries in Vetapalem reported to have availed the facilities provided by the Balwadi/Anganwadi to look after their children during the working hours. On the whole, it can be noted that the children of the beneficiaries of the DWCRA are not properly looked after while they are at work outside.

As the foregoing analysis reveals that a vast majority of the sample beneficiaries considered the attitude of officials involved in the implementation of DWCRA as positive and helpful. Only a negligible number of beneficiaries felt that the officials are indifferent and negative in their approach towards the beneficiaries. About 5 per cent of the total beneficiaries did not say anything about the co-operation of their family members in their activities. Further, it is evident that a vast majority of the beneficiaries are very much satisfied with the behaviour of their family members, group leaders and other members in the group, as they are always helpful and co-operative in all their activities connected with the DWCRA programme.

Table—13.19 Opinion of the Sample Beneficiaries on the Officials

S. No.	Item	Chirala Mandal					Vetapalem Mandal				
		Honest	Efficient	Inefficient	Corrupt	Total	Honest	Efficient	Inefficient	Corrupt	Total
1.	Weaving	6 (14.30)	34 (81.00)	2 (4.80)	–	42 (100.00)	6 (14.60)	32 (78.00)	3 (7.30)	–	41 (100.00)
2.	Fish business	3 (6.70)	42 (93.30)	–	–	45 (100.00)	14 (31.80)	30 (68.20)	–	–	44 (100.00)
3.	Dairy	2 (10.00)	17 (85.00)	1 (5.00)	–	20 (100.00)	26 (74.30)	7 (20.00)	2 (5.70)	–	35 (100.00)
4.	Mixed trade	8 (20.00)	30 (75.00)	2 (5.00)	–	40 (100.00)	15 (23.40)	44 (68.80)	5 (7.80)	–	64 (100.00)
5.	Vegetables	–	3 (27.30)	7 (63.60)	1 (9.10)	11 (100.00)	15 (55.60)	11 (40.70)	1 (3.40)	–	27 (100.00)
6.	Handicrafts	5 (11.40)	39 (88.60)	–	–	44 (100.00)	2 (9.10)	20 (90.90)	–	–	20 (100.00)
	Total	**24 (11.90)**	**165 (81.70)**	**12 (5.90)**	**1 (0.50)**	**202 (100.00)**	**78 (33.50)**	**144 (61.80)**	**11 (4.70)**	**–**	**233 (100.00)**

Note: Figures in parentheses indicate percentage to total.

Table—13.20 Attitude/Behaviour of the Officials Towards Beneficiaries

S. No.	Item	Chirala Mandal				Vetapalem Mandal			
		Positive	Negative	Cannot say	Total	Positive	Negative	Cannot say	Total
1.	Weaving	39 (92.90)	2 (4.80)	1 (2.40)	42 (100.00)	33 (80.50)	3 (7.30)	5 (12.20)	41 (100.00)
2.	Fish business	36 (80.00)	3 (6.70)	6 (13.30)	45 (100.00)	40 (90.90)	4 (9.10)	–	44 (100.00)
3.	Dairy	11 (55.00)	5 (25.00)	4 (20.00)	20 (100.00)	32 (91.40)	–	3 (8.60)	35 (100.00)
4.	Mixed trade	39 (97.50)	1 (2.50)	–	40 (100.00)	52 (81.30)	11 (17.20)	1 (1.60)	64 (100.00)
5.	Vegetables	–	11 (100.00)	–	11 (100.00)	25 (92.60)	2 (7.40)	–	27 (100.00)
6.	Handicrafts	37 (84.10)	3 (6.80)	4 (9.10)	44 (100.00)	20 (90.90)	2 (9.10)	–	22 (100.00)
	Total	**162** **(80.20)**	**25** **(12.37)**	**15** **(7.43)**	**202** **(100.00)**	**202** **(86.70)**	**22** **(9.40)**	**9** **(3.90)**	**233** **(100.00)**

Note: Figures in parentheses indicate percentage to total.

Table—13.21 Attitude of Family Members Towards Beneficiaries

S. No.	Item	Chirala Mandal				Vetapalem Mandal			
		Encouraging	Discouraging	Neutral	Total	Encouraging	Discouraging	Neutral	Total
1.	Weaving	33 (78.10)	8 (19.50)	1 (2.40)	42 (100.00)	37 (90.25)	3 (7.31)	1 (2.44)	41 (100.00)
2.	Fish business	40 (88.90)	4 (8.90)	1 (2.20)	45 (100.00)	28 (63.64)	11 (25.00)	5 (11.36)	44 (100.00)
3.	Dairy	13 (65.00)	6 (30.00)	1 (5.00)	20 (100.00)	22 (62.86)	10 (28.57)	3 (8.57)	35 (100.00)
4.	Mixed trade	30 (72.25)	8 (22.20)	2 (5.55)	40 (100.00)	52 (81.25)	10 (15.63)	2 (3.12)	64 (100.00)
5.	Vegetables	11 (100.00)	–	–	11 (100.00)	17 (62.96)	9 (33.34)	1 (3.70)	27 (100.00)
6.	Handicrafts	32 (72.09)	8 (18.60)	4 (9.30)	44 (100.00)	20 (90.91)	2 (9.09)	–	22 (100.00)
	Total	**159** **(78.71)**	**34** **(16.83)**	**9** **(4.46)**	**202** **(100.00)**	**176** **(75.53)**	**45** **(19.32)**	**12** **(5.15)**	**233** **(100.00)**

Note: Figures in parentheses indicate percentage to total.

Table—13.22 Beneficiaries Relationships with Group Leader

Sl. No.	Item	Chirala Mandal				Vetapalem Mandal			
		Very cordial	Normal	Unsatis-factory	Total	Very cordial	Normal	Unsatis-factory	Total
1.	Weaving	37 (88.10)	5 (11.90)	–	42 (100.00)	33 (80.49)	5 (12.19)	3 (7.32)	41 (100.00)
2.	Fish business	37 (82.22)	3 (6.67)	5 (11.11)	45 (100.00)	40 (90.91)	4 (9.09)	–	44 (100.00)
3.	Diary	9 (45.00)	11 (55.00)	–	20 (100.00)	23 (65.72)	10 (28.57)	2 (5.71)	35 (100.00)
4.	Mixed trade	12 (30.00)	22 (55.00)	6 (15.00)	40 (100.00)	45 (70.31)	16 (25.00)	3 (4.69)	64 (100.00)
5.	Vegetables	5 (45.45)	6 (54.55)	–	11 (100.00)	20 (74.07)	6 (22.22)	1 (3.71)	27 (100.00)
6.	Handicrafts	32 (72.73)	12 (27.27)	–	44 (100.00)	15 (68.19)	6 (27.27)	1 (4.54)	22 (100.00)
	Total	132 (20.30)	59 (71.80)	11 (4.00)	202 (100.00)	176 (75.53)	47 (20.17)	10 (4.30)	233 (100.00)

Note: Figures in parentheses indicate percentage to total.

Table—13.23 Child Care in the Families of DWCRA Beneficiaries

S. No.	Item	Chirala Mandal					Vetapalem Mandal				
		In-law	Husband & elder daughter	Friends	Balwadi/ Angan-wadi	Total	In-law	Husband & elder daughter	Friends	Balwadi/ Angan-wadi	Total
1.	Weaving	21 (50.00)	6 (14.29)	9 (21.43)	6 (14.28)	42 (100.00)	15 (36.59)	11 (26.83)	7 (17.07)	8 (19.51)	41 (100.00)
2.	Fish business	3 (6.67)	14 (31.11)	20 (44.44)	8 (17.78)	45 (100.00)	12 (27.27)	13 (29.55)	19 (43.18)	–	44 (100.00)
3.	Dairy	10 (50.00)	4 (20.00)	5 (25.00)	1 (5.00)	20 (100.00)	12 (34.29)	11 (31.43)	10 (28.57)	2 (5.71)	85 (100.00)
4.	Mixed trade	13 (44.83)	18 (62.07)	7 (24.13)	2 (6.90)	40 (100.00)	29 (45.31)	19 (29.69)	16 (25.00)	–	64 (100.00)
5.	Vegetables	7 (63.64)	2 (18.18)	2 (18.18)	–	11 (100.00)	14 (51.85)	6 (22.22)	5 (18.52)	2 (7.41)	27 (100.00)
6.	Handicrafts	22 (50.00)	12 (27.27)	6 (13.64)	4 (9.09)	44 (100.00)	9 (40.91)	4 (18.18)	6 (27.27)	3 (13.64)	22 (100.00)
	Total	**76 (37.62)**	**56 (27.73)**	**49 (24.25)**	**21 (10.40)**	**202 (100.00)**	**91 (39.06)**	**64 (27.47)**	**63 (27.04)**	**15 (6.43)**	**233 (100.00)**

Note: Figures in parentheses indicate percentages to total.

14

Empowerment of Women Through DWCRA Programme in A.P

A Case Study

**K. Sreelakshmamma*

Most of the women participate in various entire activities but this fact does not find a place in India census reports. Rural women participate in rural agricultural activities like sowing, weeding, transplantation, manuring, harvesting, winnowing, shelling and storing of crops. Though women make a substantial contribution to the family income through have based activities, this is treated as supplementary and hence it goes unnoticed. According to the official statistics the total workforce of 374.39 million in the country in 1993-94 121.63 million (32.5 per cent) are women. This percentage was 35.72 for rural areas and 21.03 for urban areas, which indicates that relatively rural women participate more in work in rural areas than in urban areas. Absolutely the poor and the economic compulsions have forced women particularly the women belonging to the SC and ST, OBC and others economically

* Lecturer in Politics, V.S.R & N.V.R. College, Tenali, Guntur, District, Andhra Pradesh.

weaker sections of the rural society to take up unskilled works requiring more labour hours for which they earn petty section. The Eighth five-year plan (1992-97) shifted the focus from development to empowerment.

The Government of Andhra Pradesh has adopted the achievement of women's empowerment as one of its strategies to tackle the problem of poverty, particularly among the poor. Under this strategy of DWCRA has been conceived as a mass movement by women to improve their living conditions through the means of self-help groups. According to DWCRA was started in 1982 as a sub-scheme of IRDP in Andhra Pradesh. The number of DWCRA groups, membership and financial outlays are increased substantially during 1982-84 to 1998-99. The vision 2020 of Andhra Pradesh Government accords an important place to the self-help group approach to poverty alleviation, particularly among the poor.

The selection of the sample size and the area of the study are discussed in the earlier paper published in this volume. The beneficiaries who are involved in activities such as Weaving, Dairy Vegetable vending, Mixed trade, Fish business, and Handicrafts are purposively selected for the present study. The paper attempts an assessment of the impact of DWCRA Programme on the economic conditions of the sample beneficiaries included in the present study. This paper also examines the extent of the knowledge gained by the beneficiaries on different issues after joining the DWCRA programme. It analyses the employment generated by the DWCRA programme in respect of the sample beneficiaries. Further, an attempt is also made to probe into change in man-days due to SDWCRA, the total family consumption and the share of different items of expenditure. Finally it makes a comparative analysis of the savings of the beneficiaries before and after DWCRA programme.

It has to be noticed that the degree of success of DWCRA Programme depends upon the extent of cooperation extended to the beneficiaries by their family members. When the beneficiaries are enquired about this, three-fourths of them stated that they are getting the support and encouragement of their family members in all the activities that they take up under DWCRA programme.

These beneficiaries also reported this satisfaction with the attitude of their family members, group leaders and other members in the group towards them. About one-third of the beneficiaries revealed that their kids are looked after by their elder daughters during their absence from their house on account of the DWCRA activities, while 38 per cent reported that their children are looked after either by their in-laws or by their husbands. It is also revealed that about 95 per cent of the total beneficiaries opined that DWCRA Programme is highly beneficial in a number of ways, when asked about their impression on the DWCRA Programme.

The present study reveals certain positive trends about the DWCRA programme in the study area. About 94 per cent of the beneficiaries stated that they have cultivated relations with several people in the village and about 60 per cent of the sample beneficiaries reported that they are participating in the implementation of developmental programmes in the village after joining the DWCRA groups.

The extent of knowledge gained by the beneficiaries on different issues after joining the DWCRA group is given in Table 14.1. It is observed from this data that about 62 per cent of the total sample beneficiaries revealed that they have faced problems due to illiteracy in understanding the objectives and benefits of DWCRA and self-help groups and consequently realised the importance of education. After joining the DWCRA about 30 per cent of sample beneficiaries in Chirala Mandal and about 23 per cent in Vetapalem Mandal have come to know their various rights and also about the village politics. Apart from this, 9 per cent of the sample beneficiaries from Chirala Mandal and 6 per cent of these from Vetapalem Mandal have reported that they have come to know about different aspects of health and nutrition only after becoming the members of DWCRA. Some of the groups have also participated in the developmental activities such as educating the village women. About 90 per cent sample beneficiaries from Chirala Mandal and 40 per cent of Vetapalem Mandal have participated in these developmental programmes. And regarding their relations with others in the village, about 95 per cent of the sample women have improved their relations with others in the village.

Table—14.1 Extent of Knowledge Gained by the Beneficiaries

Sl. No.	Item	Name of the Mandal											
		Chirala						Vetapalem					
		Your legal rights	Importance of education	Village politics	Health and nutrition	Any other	Total	Your legal rights	Importance of education	Village politics	Health and nutrition	Any other	Total
1.	Weaving	1 (2.4)	18 (42.9)	23 (54.8)	–	–	42 (100.0)	–	31 (75.6)	2 (4.9)	1 (2.4)	7 (17.1)	41 (100.0)
2.	Fish business	16 (35.6)	13 (28.9)	–	16 (35.6)	–	45 (100.0)	1 (2.3)	40 (90.9)	3 (6.8)	–	–	44 (100.0)
3.	Dairy	8 (40.0)	3 (15.0)	7 (35.0)	2 (10.0)	–	20 (100.0)	1 (2.9)	14 (40.0)	16 (45.7)	4 (11.4)	–	35 (100.0)
4.	Mixed trade	–	40 (100.0)	–	–	–	40 (100.0)	7 (10.9)	42 (65.6)	6 (9.4)	8 (12.5)	1 (1.6)	64 (100.0)
5.	Vegetables	1 (9.1)	10 (90.9)	–	–	–	11 (100.0)	5 (18.5)	19 (70.4)	2 (7.4)	1 (3.7)	–	27 (100.0)
6.	Handicrafts	3 (6.8)	41 (93.2)	–	–	–	44 (100.0)	2 (9.1)	13 (59.1)	7 (31.8)	–	–	22 (100.0)
	Total	29 (14.4)	125 (61.9)	30 (14.9)	18 (8.9)	–	202 (100.0)	16 (6.9)	159 (68.2)	36 (15.5)	14 (6.0)	8 (3.4)	233 (100.0)

Note: Figures in parentheses indicate percentage to total.

Employment Aspects

Majority of the respondents reported that they are continuing their earlier occupation even after joining the DWCRA Programme. Some of them are doing Vegetable business while others are weavers. They stated that they are continuing these activities even after joining the DWCRA programme. About one third of the beneficiaries are agriculturists and two thirds of the respondents who are weavers are continuing their earlier activity. About 94 per cent of the beneficiaries who are pursuing dairying are also continuing the same activity. These respondents hail from Vetapalem Mandal. It can be concluded that, more than 50 per cent of the sample respondents did not leave their earlier occupations in both the Mandals (Table 14.2).

Table 14.3 gives details about the present activities of the beneficiaries. According to this table one fourth of the sample beneficiaries from Chirala Mandal and two thirds of them from Vetapalem Mandal are engaged in two activities. The sample respondents who are vegetable vendors have confirmed to this business only. About two-thirds of the beneficiaries who are in Tailoring and who hail from Chirala Mandal are engaged in other activities besides tailoring. Most of these beneficiaries are working as agricultural labour doing flower business, manufacturing agarbathis, preparing pickle, and in other household activities. All the beneficiaries who have taken up dairying and belong to Chirala mandal are engaged in their activities. All the beneficiaries involved in Fish business activities are not engaged in any other economic activity. Some of the beneficiaries revealed that they are engaged in more than one activity (Table 14.4).

Table—14.2 Classification of Beneficiaries by Activity Before Joining DWCRA

Sl. No.	Item	Weav-ing	Fishe-ries	Dairy	Mixed trade	Tailor-ing	Vege tables	Handi-crafts	Flower busi-ness	Agar-bathi	Pickle	Beedi	Leaf mak-ing	Agri-cul-ture	Total
Chirala Mandal															
1.	Weaving	32 (76.2)	2 (4.8)	2 (4.8)	–	–	1 (2.4)	–	1 (2.4)	1 (2.4)	–	1 (2.4)	–	2 (4.8)	42 (100.0)
2.	Fish business	2 (4.4)	25 (65.6)	–	–	1 (2.2)	1 (2.2)	1 (2.2)	–	–	–	1 (2.2)	–	14 (31.2)	45 (100.0)
3.	Dairy	6 (30.0)	–	12 (60.0)	–	–	–	–	–	–	–	–	–	2 (10.0)	20 (100.0)
4.	Mixed trade	4 (10.0)	–	5 (12.5)	31 (77.5)	–	–	–	–	–	–	–	–	–	40 (100.0)
5.	Vegetables	–	–	–	–	–	11 (100.0)	–	–	–	–	–	–	–	11 (100.0)
6.	Handicrafts	–	–	–	–	34 (77.3)	–	10 (22.7)	–	–	–	–	–	–	44 (100.0)
	Total	**44 (21.8)**	**27 (13.4)**	**19 (9.4)**	**31 (15.3)**	**35 (17.3)**	**13 (6.4)**	**11 (5.4)**	**1 (0.5)**	**1 (0.5)**	–	**1 (.05)**	**1 (0.5%)**	**18 (8.9)**	**202 (100.0)**

(Table Contd...)

Vetapalem Mandal

1	2	3	4	5	6	7	8	9	10	11	12	13	14	15	16
1.	Weaving	41 (100.0)	–	–	–	–	–	–	–	–	–	–	–	–	41 (100.0)
2.	Fish business	–	38 (86.4)	1 (2.3)	–	–	2 (4.5)	–	–	–	–	–	1 (2.3)	2 (4.5)	44 (100.0)
3.	Dairy	–	–	33 (94.3)	–	–	–	–	–	–	–	–	–	2 (5.7)	35 (100.0)
4.	Mixed trade	2 (3.1)	–	2 (3.1)	32 (50.0)	–	–	–	24 (37.5)	4 (6.3)	–	–	–	–	64 (100.0)
5.	Vegetables	2 (7.4)	1 (3.7)	4 (14.8)	–	–	17 (63.0)	–	1 (3.7)	1 (3.7)	1 (3.7)	–	–	–	27 (100.0)
6.	Handicrafts	–	–	–	–	–	–	–	–	12 (54.5)	–	–	–	10 (45.5)	22 (100.0)
	Total	**45 (19.3)**	**39 (16.7)**	**40 (17.2)**	**32 (13.7)**	–	**19 (8.2)**	–	**25 (10.7)**	**17 (7.3)**	**1 (0.4)**	–	**1 (0.4)**	**14 (6.0)**	**233 (100.0)**

Note: Figures in parentheses indicate percentages to total.

Table—14.3 Classification of Beneficiaries by Present Activity

Sl. No.	Item	Weaving	Fisheries	Dairy	Mixed trade	Tailoring	Vegetables	Handicrafts	Flower business	Agarbathi	Pickle	Agriculture	Total
Chirala Mandal													
1.	Weaving	42 (100.0)	–	–	–	–	–	–	–	–	–	–	42 (100.0)
2.	Fish business	–	45 (100.0)	–	–	–	–	–	–	–	–	–	45 (100.0)
3.	Dairy	–	–	19 (95.0)	–	–	1 (5.0)	–	–	–	–	–	20 (100.0)
4.	Mixed trade	–	–	5 (12.5)	35 (87.5)	–	–	–	–	–	–	–	40 (100.0)
5.	Vegetables	–	–	–	–	–	11 (100.0)	–	–	–	–	–	11 (100.0)
6.	Handicrafts	–	–	–	–	34 (77.3)	–	10 (22.7)	–	–	–	–	44 (100.0)
	Total	**42 (20.8)**	**45 (22.3)**	**24 (11.9)**	**35 (17.3)**	**34 (16.8)**	**12 (5.9)**	**10 (5.0)**	–	–	–	–	**202 (100.0)**

(Table Contd…)

Vetapalem Mandal

1	2	3	4	5	6	7	8	9	10	11	12	13	14
1.	Weaving	41 (100.0)	–	–	–	–	–	–	–	–	–	–	41 (100.0)
2.	Fish business	–	44 (100.0)	–	–	–	–	–	–	–	–	–	44 (100.0)
3.	Dairy	–	–	35 (100.0)	–	–	–	–	–	–	–	–	35 (100.0)
4.	Mixed trade	–	–	2 (3.1)	32 (50.0)	–	–	–	30 (46.9)	–	–	–	64 (100.0)
5.	Vegetables	1 (3.7)	–	7 (25.9)	–	–	18 (66.7)	–	–	–	1 (3.7)	–	27 (100.0)
6.	Handicrafts	–	–	–	–	–	–	–	–	12 (54.5)	–	10 (45.5)	22 (100.0)
	Total	**42 (18.0)**	**44 (18.9)**	**44 (18.9)**	**32 (13.7)**	**–**	**18 (7.7)**	**–**	**30 (12.9)**	**12 (5.2)**	**1 (.04)**	**10 (4.3)**	**233 (100.0)**

Note: Figures in parentheses indicate percentage to total.

Man-days Before and After DWCRA

An attempt is made in the study to examine may-days in respect of the sample respondents before and after DWCRA. The relevant data on changes in man-days due to DWCRA is presented in Tables 14.5, 14.6 and 14.7.

Man days before DWCRA by activity and by Mandal is indicated in Table 14.5. It can be observed from this table that about 90 per cent of the respondents from Chirala Mandal had man-days below 120 in a year before they have joined the DWCRA. In Vetapalem Mandal a vast majority of respondents got man-days between 80-160. An analysis on the activity-wise man-days in Chirala Mandal shows that the highest majority of the weavers got below 80 man-days while none got more than 160 man-days. In the case of Fish business, all workers are having less than 120 man-days. In dairying activity, more than 50 per cent workers got between 80-120 man-days and only one respondent of Chirala Mandal got more than 160 man-days before joining DWCRA programme. Regarding the Handicrafts, more than 90 per cent of the workers worked only below 120 days before joining DWCRA programme in the mandal. About 75 per cent of Vetapalem Weavers worked between 120-160 days. About 80 per cent worked between 80-120 days in Fish business as well as Dairy in Vetapalem Mandal. The total picture relating to both the Mandals emphasises the fact that almost all the sample respondents got less than 160 man-days before joining the DWCRA programme. Most of them worked between 80-120 man-days followed by 0-80 and 120-160 man-days before joining DWCRA programme. On the whole weavers and vegetable vendors got more man-days when compared to the other activities. However, it can be said that most of the women in DWCRA had few man-days before they have joined the DWCRA.

Table—14.4 Classification of Beneficiaries Involved in more than One Activity

Sl. No.	Item	Name of the Mandal					
		Chirala Mandal			Vetapalem Mandal		
		Yes	No	Total	Yes	No	Total
1.	Weaving	17 (40.5)	25 (59.5)	42 (100.0)	24 (58.5)	17 (41.5)	41 (100.0)
2.	Fish business	–	45 (100.0)	45 (100.0)	–	44 (100.0)	44 (100.0)
3.	Dairy	20 (100.0)	–	20 (100.0)	15 (42.9)	20 (57.1)	35 (100.0)
4.	Mixed trade	–	40 (100.0)	40 (100.0)	23 (35.9)	41 (64.1)	64 (100.0)
5.	Vegetables	–	11 (100.0)	11 (100.0)	12 (44.4)	15 (55.6)	27 (100.0)
6.	Handicrafts	14 (31.8)	30 (68.2)	44 (100.0)	11 (50.0)	11 (50.0)	22 (100.0)
	Total	51 (25.2)	151 (74.8)	202 (100.0)	85 (36.5)	148 (63.5)	233 (100.0)

Note: Figures in parentheses indicate percentages to total.

Table—14.5 Classification of Beneficiaries by Man-days before DWCRA

Activity	Chirala					Vetapalem					Total				
	Below 80	80-120	120-160	160 and above	Total	Below 80	80-120	120-160	160 and above	Total	Below 80	80-120	120-160	160 and above	Total
Weaving	25 (59.52)	13 (30.95)	4 (9.53)	–	42 (100.00)	2 (4.88)	9 (21.95)	30 (73.17)	0	41 (100.00)	27 (32.53)	22 (26.51)	34 (40.96)	0	83 (100.00)
Fish business	13 (28.89)	32 (71.11)	–	–	45 (100.00)	5 (11.36)	34 (77.27)	5 (11.36)	0	44 (100.00)	18 (20.23)	66 (74.16)	05 (5.60)	0	89 (100.00)
Dairy	3 (15.00)	11 (55.00)	5 (25.00)	1 (5.00)	20 (100.00)	10 (28.57)	21 (60.00)	4 (11.43)	0	35 (100.00)	13 (23.64)	32 (58.18)	09 (16.36)	1 (1.82)	55 (100.00)
Mixed trade	30 (75.00)	10 (25.00)	–	–	40 (100.00)	14 (21.88)	22 (34.38)	25 (39.65)	3 (4.69)	64 (100.00)	44 (42.31)	32 (30.77)	25 (24.04)	3 (2.88)	104 (100.00)
Vegetables	5 (45.45)	6 (54.55)	–	–	11 (100.00)	6 (22.23)	4 (14.81)	17 (62.96)	0	27 (100.00)	11 (28.95)	10 (26.32)	17 (44.73)	0	38 (100.00)
Handicrafts	26 (59.09)	16 (36.36)	2 (4.55)	–	44 (100.00)	4 (18.18)	13 (59.09)	05 (22.73)	0	22 (100.0)	30 (45.45)	29 (43.94)	07 (10.61)	0	66 (100.00)
Total	102 (50.50)	88 (43.56)	11 (5.44)	1 (0.50)	207 (100.00)	41 (17.60)	103 (44.21)	86 (36.90)	3 (1.29)	233 (100.00)	143 (32.87)	191 (43.91)	97 (22.30)	4 (0.92)	435 (100.00)

Note: Figures in parentheses indicate percentages to total.

Table—14.6 Classification of Beneficiaries by Man-days after DWCRA

Activity	Chirala					Vetapalem					Total				
	Below 80	80-120	120-160	160 and above	Total	Below 80	80-120	120-160	160 and above	Total	Below 80	80-120	120-160	160 and above	Total
Weaving	-	4 (9.52)	13 (30.95)	25 (59.52)	42 (100.00)	-	-	23 (56.10)	18 (43.90)	41 (100.00)	-	4 (4.82)	36 (43.37)	43 (51.81)	83 (100.00)
Fish business	-	-	36 (80.00)	9 (20.00)	45 (100.00)	-	9 (20.45)	2 (4.55)	33 (75.00)	44 (100.00)	0	9 (10.11)	38 (42.70)	42 (47.19)	89 (100.00)
Dairy	1 (5.00)	6 (30.00)	11 (55.00)	2 (10.00)	20 (100.00)	1 (2.86)	11 (31.43)	-	23 (65.71)	35 (100.00)	2 (3.64)	17 (30.91)	11 (20.00)	25 (45.45)	55 (100.00)
Mixed trade	-	-	6 (15.00)	34 (85.00)	40 (100.00)	1 (1.56)	15 (23.44)	21 (32.81)	27 (42.19)	64 (100.00)	1 (0.96)	15 (14.43)	27 (25.96)	61 (58.65)	104 (100.00)
Vegetables	-	-	6 (54.55)	5 (45.45)	11 (100.00)	3 (11.11)	3 (11.11)	11 (40.74)	10 (37.04)	27 (100.00)	3 (7.89)	3 (7.89)	17 (44.74)	15 (39.78)	38 (100.00)
Handicrafts	-	4 (9.09)	13 (29.55)	27 (61.36)	44 (100.00)	-	5 (22.73)	-	17 (77.27)	22 (100.00)	-	9 (13.64)	13 (19.69)	44 (66.67)	66 (100.00)
Total	1 (0.50)	14 (6.92)	85 (42.08)	102 (50.50)	202 (100.00)	5 (2.15)	43 (18.45)	57 (24.46)	128 (54.94)	233 (100.00)	6 (1.38)	57 (13.10)	142 (32.64)	230 (52.88)	435 (100.00)

Note: Figures in parentheses indicate percentages to total.

With regard to the man-days after joining the DWCRA programme, the present study indicates that there is considerable growth in man-days in both the Mandals and in different activities. Most of the respondents worked for more than 160 days in a year after joining the DWCRA. In the weaving activity, about half of the beneficiaries worked for more than 200 days in a year. The sample beneficiaries who are engaged in fish business have also increased their man-days. About 80 per cent of these beneficiaries got more than 160 man-days in a year. About 60 per cent of the mixed traders got more than 200 man-days. About 60 per cent of the mixed traders got more than 200 man-days. There is a reasonable variation in the case of the sample that is preparing handicrafts. In Chirala mandal, more than 90 per cent of the sample beneficiaries got man-days of 160 and above. Almost all the beneficiaries in Vetapalem Mandal working as Weavers got 160 man-days and in the case of those respondents in the Dairying and Fish business activities the man-days are 170 and 180 respectively. One beneficiary from Chirala and 5 from Vetapalem got below 120 man days after joining the DWCRA programme.

The change in man-days due to DWCRA (Table 14.7) depicts that there is marginal growth in man-days due to DWCRA for the women of Chirala and Vetapalem Mandals. About 80 per cent of beneficiaries got man-days increased between 20-60 in the study area.

Income of the Beneficiaries

The sample beneficiaries have expressed their satisfaction on the economic benefits desired from the DWCRA programme. More than 95 per cent of them opined that the DWCRA programme improved their economic position. Only 12 beneficiaries out of the total 435 beneficiaries have felt that the programme has not improved their economic condition.

Table—14.7 Classification of Beneficiaries by Increase in Man-days Due to DWCRA

Activity	Chirala						Vetapalem						Total					
	0-20	20-40	40-60	60-80	80-100	Total	0-20	20-40	40-60	60-80	80-100	Total	0-20	20-40	40-60	60-80	80-100	Total
Weaving	7 16.67	21 50.00	14 33.33	–	–	42 100.00	2 4.88	26 63.41	10 24.39	3 7.31	–	41 100.00	9 10.84	47 56.63	24 28.92	3 3.61	–	83 100.00
Fish business	3 66.67	16 35.56	26 57.78	–	–	45 100.00	1 2.27	19 43.18	20 45.45	2 4.55	2 4.55	44 100.00	4 4.49	35 39.33	46 51.69	2 2.25	2 2.25	89 100.00
Dairy	3 15.00	7 35.00	8 40.00	2 10.00	–	20 100.00	1 2.86	23 65.71	11 31.43	–	–	35 100.00	4 7.27	3 54.55	19 34.55	2 3.64	–	55 100.00
Mixed trade	11 27.50	20 50.00	8 20.00	1 2.5	–	40 100.00	5 7.81	28 43.75	22 34.38	6 9.38	3 4.69	64 100.00	16 15.38	48 46.15	30 28.85	7 6.73	3 2.88	104 100.00
Vegetables	1 9.10	6 54.55	4 36.36	–	–	11 100.00	7 25.93	14 51.85	5 18.52	1 3.70	–	27 100.00	8 21.05	20 52.63	9 23.68	1 2.63	–	38 100.00
Handicrafts	14 31.82	23 52.27	3 6.82	3 6.82	1 2.27	44 100.00	1 4.55	7 31.82	10 45.45	3 13.64	1 4.55	22 100.00	15 22.73	30 45.45	13 19.70	6 9.10	2 3.03	66 100.00
Total	39 19.31	93 46.04	63 31.12	6 2.97	1 0.50	202 100.00	17 7.30	117 50.21	78 33.48	15 6.44	6 2.58	233 100.00	56 12.87	210 48.29	141 32.41	21 4.83	7 1.61	435 100.00

Note: Figures in second line indicate percentage to total.

All the sample beneficiaries of the first group revealed that they are getting regular income due to the DWCRA programme. Regarding the overall improvement of the family conditions after joining the DWCRA, less than 1 per cent sample beneficiaries from Chirala Mandal and about 4 per cent of the Vetapalem Mandal stated that the impact of the programme on these family positions is only marginal. About 48 per cent of them felt that there is substantial improvement in their family economic position and for 30 per cent there is no considerable improvement in these conditions. About 20 per cent of beneficiaries revealed that there is moderate improvement in their family economic position (Table 14.8).

It is attempted to make a comparative analysis of the income of sample beneficiaries before and after DWCRA in the two Mandals selected for the study. Table 14.9 reflects the income of the beneficiaries of the two Mandals before joining DWCRA programme. About 80 per cent of these beneficiaries in Chirala Mandal used to earn between Rs. 200-400 before joining the DWCRA programme while about 90 per cent of these from Vetapalem Mandal beneficiaries got an income between Rs. 200-400 before joining the DWCRA programme. No beneficiary got more than Rs. 500 in Vetapalem Mandal. Only four beneficiaries in the study area got more than Rs. 500 before joining the DWCRA programme whereas 9 beneficiaries got less than Rs. 100/-.

These increase in the income of the sample beneficiaries can be seen from the table 14.10. It is evident from this Table that there is a minimum increase of Rs. 300/- income of these respondents after they joined the DWCRA programme. About 60 per cent of the sample beneficiaries of the two Mandals selected for the study derived an income between Rs. 300-600 while the remaining sample beneficiaries are earning more than Rs. 600/-. About half of respondents belonging to the Chirala Mandal and three fourths of them from Vetapalem Mandal are earning between Rs. 300-600 from the DWCRA activities. All most all the sample beneficiaries who are selling vegetables are earning more than Rs. 600.

Table—14.8 Classification of Beneficiaries by Increase in Family Economic Position

Sl. No.	Item	Name of the Mandal									
		Chirala Mandal					Vetapalem Mandal				
		Substantial	Considerable	Moderate	Marginal	Total	Substantial	Considerable	Moderate	Marginal	Total
1.	Weaving	6 (14.3)	18 (42.9)	8 (19.0)	10 (23.8)	42 (100.00)	–	17 (41.5)	8 (19.5)	16 (39.0)	41 (100.0)
2.	Fish business	32 (71.1)	13 (28.9)	–	–	45 (100.0)	23 (52.3)	2 (4.5)	10 (22.7)	9 (20.5)	44 (100.0)
3.	Dairy	13 (65.0)	6 (30.0)	1 (5.0)	–	20 (100.0)	26 (74.3)	6 (17.1)	3 (8.6)	–	35 (100.0)
4.	Mixed trade	14 (35.0)	12 (30.0)	3 (7.5)	11 (27.5)	40 (100.0)	13 (20.3)	28 (43.8)	13 (20.3)	10 (15.6)	64 (100.0)
5.	Vegetables	–	–	5 (45.5)	6 (54.5)	11 (100.0)	23 (85.2)	3 (11.1)	1 (3.7)	–	27 (100.0)
6.	Handicrafts	15 (34.1)	11 (25.0)	11 (25.0)	7 (15.9)	44 (100.0)	–	12 (54.5)	10 (45.5)	–	22 (100.0)
	Total	**80** **(39.6)**	**60** **(29.7)**	**28** **(13.9)**	**34** **(16.8)**	**202** **(100.0)**	**85** **(36.5)**	**68** **(29.2)**	**45** **(19.3)**	**35** **(15.0)**	**233** **(100.0)**

Note: Figures in parentheses indicate percentages to total.

Table—14.9 Income of Beneficiaries Before Joining DWCRA Programme

Activity	Chirala						
	Below 100	100-200	200-300	300-400	400-500	500-+	Total
Weaving	–	11	20	10	–	1	42
		26.19	47.62	23.81		2.38	100.00
Fish business	1	9	17	17	–	1	45
	2.22	20.00	37.78	37.78		2.22	100.00
Dairy	–	2	5	–	13	–	20
		10.00	25.00		65.00		100.00
Mixed trade	1	6	16	17	–	–	40
	2.5	15.00	40.00	42.50			100.00
Vegetables	–	–	6	5	–	–	11
			54.55	45.55			100.00
Handicrafts	2	1	12	17	10	2	144
	4.55	2.27	27.27	38.64	22.73	4.55	100
Total	**4**	**29**	**76**	**66**	**11.39**	**4**	**202**
	1.98	**14.36**	**37.62**	**32.67**		**1.98**	**100.00**

(Table Contd…)

	Vetapalem						
Activity	**Below 100**	**100-200**	**200-300**	**300-400**	**400-500**	**500-+**	**Total**
Weaving	–	3	13	22	3	–	41
		7.31	31.71	53.65	7.32		100.00
Fish business	–	1	26	17	–	–	44
		2.27	59.09	38.64			100.00
Dairy	1	–	14	20	–	–	35
	2.85		40.00	57.14			100.00
Mixed trade	1	6	30	26	1	–	64
	1.56	9.38	46.88	40.63	1.56		100.00
Vegetables	–	4	5	18	–	–	27
		14.81	18.52	66.67			100.00
Handicrafts	–	2	6	13	1	–	22
		9.09	27.27	59.09	4.55		100.00
Total	**2**	**16**	**94**	**116**	**5**	–	**233**
	0.86	**6.87**	**40.34**	**49.79**	**2.15**		**100.00**

(Table Contd…)

	Total						
Activity	Below 100	100-200	200-300	300-400	400-500	500-+	Total
Weaving	–	14	33	32	3	1	83
		16.86	39.76	38.55	3.61	1.20	100.00
Fish business	1	10	43	34	–	1	89
	1.12	11.24	48.31	38.20		1.12	100.00
Dairy	1	2	19	20	13	–	55
	1.82	3.64	34.55	36.36	23.64		100.00
Mixed trade	2	12	46	43	1	–	104
	1.92	11.54	44.23	41.35	0.96		100.00
Vegetables	–	4	11	23	–	–	38
		10.53	28.95	60.53			100.00
Handicrafts	2	3	18	30	11	2	66
	3.03	4.55	27.27	45.45	16.67	3.03	100.00
Total	**6**	**45**	**170**	**182**	**28**	**4**	**435**
	1.38	**10.34**	**39.08**	**41.84**	**6.44**	**0.92**	**100.00**

Note: Figures in second line indicate percentages to total.

An attempt is also made in this study to examine total family income of the sample before and after they have joined DWCRA to analyse the share of income from DWCRA in the total family income. It can be understood from the Table 14.11 that, only 8 sample beneficiaries out of the total of 435 samples earned below Rs. 900 per month before joining the DWCRA programme. These respondents are the only earning members in their families. Another 5 members are getting an income of Rs. 1600. But in the case of these respondents, some of the family members are also employed and got income. About 65 per cent of the respondents had an income that was less than Rs. 1200 per month before joining DWCRA.

The data relating to the total family income of the sample beneficiaries from various sources after joining the DWCRA is presented in Table 14.12. According to this Table only four of the sample respondents are getting an income below Rs. 1400 per month. More than half of the beneficiaries belonging to Chirala mandal are earning Rs. 1500 and above while about the same number of beneficiary families from Vetapalem Mandal are having an income more than Rs. 1500 per month after joining the DWCRA. It can be concluded from the forgoing analysis that, there is substantial increase in the family income of the sample beneficiaries after they have joined the DWCRA Programme. It can also be observed from the data that some of the husbands of the sample beneficiaries are employed as agricultural labour and also own cattle.

The increase in the income of the families of the sample beneficiaries due to the DWCRA programme is presented in Table 14.13. As the Table reveals about three fourths of the beneficiaries families hailing from Chirala Mandal and about 80 per cent of them from Vetapalem Mandal earned an additional income between Rs. 201-400 due to DWCRA programme while about 90 per cent of the sample beneficiaries derived between Rs. 200-600 per month as additional income. This indicates that the DWCRA is assisting the rural women to cross the poverty line.

Table—14.10 Income of the Beneficiaries after Joining DWCRA Programme

Activity	Chirala				
	Below 300	**301-600**	**601-900**	**901-+**	**Total**
Weaving	–	30 (71.43)	12 (28.57)	–	42 (100.00)
Fish business	–	31 (68.89)	14 (31.11)	–	45 (100.00)
Dairy	–	6 (30.00)	14 (100.00)	–	20 (100.00)
Mixed trade	–	28 (70.00)	12 (30.00)	–	40 (100.00)
Vegetables	–	1 (9.09)	10 (90.91)	–	11 (100.00)
Handicrafts	–	20 (45.45)	23 (52.27)	1 (2.27)	44 (100.00)
Total	–	**116 (57.43)**	**85 (42.08)**	**1 (0.50)**	**202**

(Table Contd...)

Activity	Vetapalem				
	Below 300	**301-600**	**601-900**	**901-+**	**Total**
Weaving	–	16 (39.02)	25 (60.97)	–	41 (100.00)
Fish business	–	30 (68.18)	14 (31.82)	–	44 (100.00)
Dairy	1 (2.85)	17 (48.57)	17 (48.58)	–	35 (100.00)
Mixed trade	–	47 (73.44)	17 (26.56)	–	64 (100.00)
Vegetables	–	18 (66.67)	9 (33.33)	–	27 (100.00)
Handicrafts	–	17 (77.27)	5 (22.73)	–	22 (100.00)
Total	**1** **(0.43)**	**145** **(62.23)**	**87** **(37.33)**	**–**	**233** **(100.00)**

(Table Contd...)

Activity	Total				
	Below 300	301-600	601-900	901-+	Total
Weaving	–	46 (55.42)	37 (44.58)	–	83 (100.00)
Fish business	–	61 (68.54)	28 (31.46)	–	89 (100.00)
Dairy	1 (1.82)	23 (41.82)	31 (56.36)	–	55 (100.00)
Mixed trade	–	75 (72.12)	29 (27.88)	–	104 (100.00)
Vegetables	–	19 (0.50)	19 (0.50)	–	38 (100.00)
Handicrafts	–	37 (57.58)	28 (42.42)	1 (1.15)	66 (100.00)
Total	**1** **(0.23)**	**261** **(60.03)**	**172** **(39.54)**	**1** **(0.23)**	**435** **(100.00)**

Note: Figures in parentheses indicate percentages to total.

Table—14.11 Total Family Income Before DWCRA

Activity	Chirala				
	Below 900	**901-1200**	**1201-1500**	**1500-+**	**Total**
Weaving	–	8 (19.05)	32 (76.19)	2 (4.76)	42 (100.00)
Fish business	3 (6.67)	7 (60.00)	15 (33.33)	–	45 (100.00)
Dairy	–	17 (85.00)	3 (15.00)	–	20 (100.00)
Mixed trade	–	18 (45.00)	22 (55.00)	–	40 (100.00)
Vegetables	–	9 (81.82)	2 (18.18)	–	11 (100.00)
Handicrafts	–	28 (63.64)	16 (36.36)	–	44 (100.00)
Total	**3 (1.49)**	**107 (52.97)**	**90 (44.55)**	**2 (1.00)**	**202 (100.00)**

(Table Contd…)

Activity	Vetapalem				
	Below 900	901-1200	1201-1500	1500-+	Total
Weaving	1 (2.43)	26 (63.40)	12 (29.26)	2 (4.55)	41 (100.00)
Fish business	–	41 (93.18)	2 (4.55)	1 (2.27)	44 (100.00)
Dairy	–	23 (65.71)	11 (31.43)	1 (2.85)	35 (100.00)
Mixed trade	1 (1.56)	55 (85.94)	7 (10.94)	1 (1.56)	64 (100.00)
Vegetables	3 (11.11)	20 (74.07)	3 (11.11)	1 (3.70)	27 (100.00)
Handicrafts	–	17 (77.27)	5 (22.73)	–	22 (100.00)
Total	**5 (21.46)**	**182 (78.11)**	**40 (17.17)**	**6 (2.58)**	**233 (100.00)**

(Table Contd...)

Activity	Total				
	Below 900	**901-1200**	**1201-1500**	**1500-+**	**Total**
Weaving	1 (1.20)	34 (40.96)	44 (53.01)	4 (4.82)	83 (100.00)
Fish business	3 (3.36)	68 (76.40)	17 (19.04)	1 (1.12)	89 (100.00)
Dairy	–	40 (72.73)	14 (25.45)	1 (1.82)	55 (100.00)
Mixed trade	1 (0.96)	73 (70.19)	29 (27.88)	1 (0.96)	104 (100.00)
Vegetables	3 (7.89)	29 (76.32)	5 (13.16)	1 (2.63)	38 (100.00)
Handicrafts	–	45 (68.18)	21 (31.82)	–	66 (100.00)
Total	**8** **(1.84)**	**289** **(66.44)**	**130** **(29.89)**	**8** **(1.84)**	**435** **(100.00)**

Note: Figures in parentheses indicate percentages to total.

It is also noticed from the data presented in this Chapter that more than three fourths of the sample beneficiaries are contributing upto 30 per cent of the family income before they joined the DWCRA programme. The same is evident in the case of all categories of sample beneficiaries from the two mandals. It can also be noted that about 60 per cent of the sample beneficiaries are contributing 30 per cent to their family total income after they have joined the DWCRA programme. It may be concluded that the DWCRA has considerable impact on the economic position of the sample beneficiaries.

Regarding the per capita income of the sample beneficiaries before and after joining DWCRA, there is a significant growth in their per capita income during the Post-DWCRA period. The average increase of per capita income of the sample respondents has risen by Rs. 250 per month in both the mandals.

An attempt is also made to examine the savings of the sample beneficiaries. There is positive relation between growth of income and savings in the sample beneficiaries covered under the present study area. About 50 per cent of the total sample beneficiaries did not have any savings before they joined to DWCRA programme. About 90 per cent of the sample respondents admitted that they have inculcated the habit of saving effectively only after they are cover by the DWCRA programme. The sample beneficiaries are saving the amounts in different ways. It is revealed that about 58 per cent of the respondents from Chirala Mandal are saving between Rs. 200 and Rs. 400 per month while in Vetapalem Mandal only 50 per cent of the sample beneficiaries are saving the same amount. About 95 per cent of the total respondents are saving about Rs. 400 (Table 14.14). The savings of the sample beneficiaries after they have joined the DWCRA programme are presented in Table 14.15. As per the Table about 50 per cent of the respondents saved about Rs. 3000 so far. In the activities like Weaving, Fish business, more than half of the beneficiaries saved Rs. 3000-5000 in Chirala Mandal whereas in Vetapalem mandal 14 beneficiaries saved more than Rs. 5000.

Table—14.12 Total Family Income After DWCRA

Activity	Chirala				
	Below 500	501-1000	1001-1500	1501-+	Total
Weaving	1 (2.38)	–	10 (23.81)	31 (73.81)	42 (100.00)
Fish business	–	–	21 (46.67)	24 (53.33)	45 (100.00)
Dairy	–	–	4 (20.00)	16 (80.00)	20 (100.00)
Mixed trade	–	–	13 (32.50)	27 (67.50)	40 (100.00)
Vegetables	–	–	–	11 (100.00)	11 (100.00)
Handicrafts	–	–	20 (45.45)	24 (54.55)	44 (100.00)
Total	**1** **(0.50)**	–	**68** **(33.66)**	**133** **(65.84)**	**202** **(100.00)**

(Table Contd…)

Activity	Vetapalem				
	Below 500	501-1000	1001-1500	1501-+	Total
Weaving	1 (0.43)	–	14 (34.84)	26 (63.41)	41 (100.00)
Fish business	–	–	29 (65.91)	15 (34.09)	44 (100.00)
Dairy	–	1 (2.85)	17 (48.57)	17 (48.58)	35 (100.00)
Mixed trade	–	5 (7.81)	39 (60.94)	25 (39.06)	64 (100.00)
Vegetables	–	2 (7.41)	12 (44.44)	13 (48.15)	27 (100.00)
Handicrafts	–	–	13 (59.09)	9 (40.91)	22 (100.00)
Total	**1 (0.43)**	**3 (1.29)**	**119 (51.07)**	**105 (45.06)**	**233 (100.00)**

(Table Contd...)

Activity	Total				
	Below 500	501-1000	1001-1500	1501-+	Total
Weaving	2 (2.40)	–	24 (28.92)	57 (68.67)	83 (100.00)
Fish business	–	–	50 (56.18)	39 (43.82)	89 (100.00)
Dairy	–	1 (1.82)	21 (38.18)	33 (0.60)	55 (100.00)
Mixed trade	–	–	52 (0.50)	52 (0.50)	104 (100.00)
Vegetables	–	2 (5.26)	12 (31.58)	24 (63.16)	38 (100.00)
Handicrafts	–	–	33 (50.00)	33 (50.00)	66 (100.00)
Total	**2 (0.46)**	**3 (0.69)**	**192 (44.14)**	**238 (54.71)**	**435 (100.00)**

Note: Figures in parentheses indicate percentages to total.

Table—14.13 Growth of Income due to DWCRA

Activity	Chirala				
	Below 200	201-400	401-600	601-+	Total
Weaving	3 (7.14)	32 (76.19)	7 (16.67)	–	42 (100.00)
Fish business	2 (4.44)	35 (77.78)	8 (17.78)	–	45 (100.00)
Dairy	–	9 (45.00)	8 (40.00)	3 (15.00)	20 (100.00)
Mixed trade	2 (5.00)	32 (80.00)	6 (15.00)	–	40 (100.00)
Vegetables	–	6 (54.55)	3 (27.27)	2 (18.18)	11 (100.00)
Handicrafts	2 (4.55)	35 (79.55)	7 (15.90)	–	44 (100.00)
Total	**9** **(44.55)**	**149** **(73.76)**	**39** **(19.31)**	**5** **(2.4)**	**202** **(100.00)**

(Table Contd...)

Activity	Vetapalem				
	Below 200	201-400	401-600	601-+	Total
Weaving	–	30 (73.17)	10 (24.39)	1 (2.44)	41 (100.00)
Fish business	4 (9.09)	33 (75.00)	6 (13.64)	1 (2.27)	44 (100.00)
Dairy	3 (8.57)	29 (82.86)	3 (8.57)	–	35 (100.00)
Mixed trade	4 (6.25)	49 (76.56)	11 (17.19)	–	64 (100.00)
Vegetables	1 (3.70)	21 (77.78)	4 (14.81)	1 (3.70)	27 (100.00)
Handicrafts	3 (13.64)	16 (72.72)	3 (13.64)	–	22 (100.00)
Total	**15 (6.49)**	**178 (76.39)**	**37 (15.88)**	**3 (1.29)**	**233 (100.00)**

(Table Contd...)

Activity	Total				
	Below 200	201-400	401-600	601-+	Total
Weaving	3 (3.61)	62 (74.70)	17 (20.48)	1 (1.20)	83 (100.00)
Fish business	6 (6.74)	68 (76.40)	14 (15.73)	1 (1.12)	89 (100.00)
Dairy	3 (5.45)	38 (69.09)	11 (0.20)	3 (5.45)	55 (100.00)
Mixed trade	6 (5.77)	81 (77.88)	17 (16.35)	–	104 (100.00)
Vegetables	1 (2.63)	27 (71.05)	7 (18.42)	3 (7.89)	38 (100.00)
Handicrafts	5 (7.58)	51 (77.27)	10 (15.15)	–	66 (100.00)
Total	**24** **(5.52)**	**327** **(75.17)**	**76** **(17.47)**	**8** **(1.84)**	**435** **(100.00)**

Note: Figures in parentheses indicate percentage to total.

Table—14.14 Savings of the Family Per Month

Activity	Chirala				Vetapalem				Total			
	Below 200	201-400	401-600	Total	Below 200	201-400	401-600	Total	Below 200	201-400	401-600	Total
Weaving	14 (33.33)	27 (64.29)	1 (2.38)	42 (100.00)	11 (26.83)	26 (63.41)	4 (9.76)	41 (100.00)	25 (30.12)	53 (63.55)	5 (6.02)	83 (100.00)
Fish business	13 (28.89)	30 (66.67)	2 (4.44)	45 (100.00)	23 (52.27)	20 (45.45)	1 (2.27)	44 (100.00)	36 (40.45)	50 (56.18)	3 (3.37)	89 (100.00)
Dairy	3 (15.00)	13 (65.00)	4 (20.00)	20 (100.00)	15 (42.86)	19 (52.29)	1 (2.85)	35 (100.00)	18 (32.73)	32 (58.18)	5 (0.90)	55 (100.00)
Mixed trade	15 (37.50)	25 (62.50)	–	40 (100.00)	27 (42.19)	35 (54.69)	2 (3.13)	64 (100.00)	42 (40.38)	60 (57.69)	2 (1.92)	104 (100.00)
Vegetables	–	10 (90.91)	1 (9.09)	11 (100.00)	12 (44.44)	13 (27.00)	2 (7.41)	27 (100.00)	12 (31.58)	23 (60.53)	3 (7.89)	35 (100.00)
Handicrafts	15 (34.09)	28 (63.64)	1 (2.27)	44 (100.00)	16 (72.72)	6 (27.27)	–	22 (100.00)	31 (46.97)	34 (51.52)	1 (1.52)	66 (100.00)
Total	**60 (29.70)**	**133 (65.84)**	**9 (4.46)**	**202 (100.00)**	**104 (44.64)**	**119 (51.07)**	**10 (4.29)**	**233 (100.00)**	**164 (37.70)**	**252 (57.93)**	**19 (4.37)**	**435 (100.00)**

Note: Figures in parentheses indicate percentages to total.

Table—14.15 Total Personal Savings of Beneficiaries

S. No.	Item	Chirala Mandal				
		Below Rs. 1000	Rs. 1000-3000	Rs. 3000-5000	Rs. 5000 +	Total
1.	Weaving	17 (40.5)	4 (9.5)	21 (50.0)	–	42 (100.0)
2.	Fish Business	5 (11.1)	13 (28.9)	27 (60.0)	–	45 (100.0)
3.	Dairy	12 (60.0)	1 (5.0)	7 (35.0)	–	20 (100.0)
4.	Mixed trade	16 (40.0)	24 (60.0)	–	–	40 (100.0)
5.	Vegetables	1 (9.1)	–	10 (90.9)	–	11 (100.0)
6.	Handicrafts	23 (52.3)	21 (47.7)	–	–	44 (100.0)
	Total	73 (36.6)	73 (36.1)	55 (27.2)	–	202 (100.0)

(Table Contd...)

S. No.	Item	Vetapalem Mandal				
		Below Rs. 1000	Rs. 1000-3000	Rs. 3000-5000	Rs. 5000 +	Total
1.	Weaving	5 (12.2)	36 (87.8)	–	–	41 (100.0)
2.	Fish Business	3 (6.8)	41 (93.2)	–	–	44 (100.0)
3.	Dairy	4 (11.4)	20 (57.1)	–	11 (31.4)	35 (100.0)
4.	Mixed trade	5 (7.8)	38 (59.4)	18 (28.1)	3 (4.7)	64. (100.0)
5.	Vegetables	3 (11.1)	24 (88.9)	–	–	27 (100.0)
6.	Handicrafts	4 (18.2)	7 (31.8)	11 (50.0)	–	22 (100.0)
	Total	**24 (10.3)**	**166 (71.2)**	**29 (12.4)**	**14 (6.0)**	**233 (100.00)**

Note: Figures in parentheses indicate percentages to total.

Consumption Pattern

Since consumption is an important economic indicator of development, an attempt is made to examine the level of consumption of the sample beneficiaries (Table 14.16). The data on variables like expenditure on food, children education, entertainment, liquor, religious and social ceremonies and, other miscellaneous items are taken into consideration to examine the expenditure-pattern of the sample beneficiaries.

The data presented in the relevant Table reflects that there is substantial change in the consumption pattern of the sample beneficiaries selected from the two mandals covered under this study. About three-fourth of the sample beneficiaries have been spending more on various food items. It can be inferred that there exists a relationship between the increase in income and increase in the expenditure on food. It can also be observed from this table that about 20 per cent of the sample beneficiaries have been incurring more expenditure on their children education than in the past. In the case of 12 respondents the expenditure on entertainment has increased considerably. These respondents have acquired cable connection for their televisions, which manifests the economic empowerment of the beneficiaries of the DWCRA in the study area. The family members of the DWCRA beneficiaries have admitted that the economic empowerment of these women. They revealed that they have given up drinking following the words of their women. Only less than 2 per cent of the sample respondents revealed that is an increase in their expenditure on liquor. The other respondents reported that the expenditure on other items has increased to a certain extent.

Table—14.16 Change in the Consumption Pattern of Beneficiaries

S. No.	Item	Chirala Mandal					
		Food	Children Education	Entertainment	Liquor	Others	Total
1.	Weaving	38 (90.5)	2 (4.8)	1 (2.4)	1 (2.4)	–	42 (100.0)
2.	Fish business	27 (60.0)	13 (28.9)	2 (4.4)	–	3 (6.7)	45 (100.0)
3.	Dairy	9 (45.0)	11 (55.0)	–	–	–	20 (100.0)
4.	Mixed trade	24 (60.0)	14 (35.0)	2 (5.0)	–	–	40 (100.0)
5.	Vegetables	9 (81.8)	–	–	–	2 (18.2)	11 (100.0)
6.	Handicrafts	40 (90.9)	–	3 (6.8)	1 (2.3)	1 (2.3)	44 (100.0)
	Total	**147 (72.8)**	**40 (19.8)**	**8 (4.0)**	**2 (1.0)**	**5 (2.5)**	**202 (100.0)**

(Table Contd...)

S. No.	Item	Vetapalem Mandal					
		Food	Children Education	Entertainment	Liquor	Others	Total
1.	Weaving	24 (58.5)	14 (34.1)	3 (7.3)	–	–	41 (100.0)
2.	Fish business	35 (79.5)	6 (13.6)	–	–	3 (6.8)	44 (100.0)
3.	Dairy	25 (71.4)	8 (22.9)	–	2 (5.7)	–	35 (100.0)
4.	Mixed trade	49 (76.6)	3 (4.7)	6 (9.4)	3 (4.7)	3 (4.7)	64 (100.0)
5.	Vegetables	13 (48.1)	9 (33.3)	–	–	5 (18.5)	27 (100.0)
6.	Handicrafts	11 (50.0)	11 (50.0)	–	–	–	22 (100.0)
	Total	**157 (67.4)**	**51 (21.9)**	**9 (3.9)**	**5 (2.1)**	**11 (4.7)**	**233 (100.0)**

Note: Figures in parentheses indicate percentages to total.

It can be inferred from the above analysis that the DWCRA programme has improved the economic position of the sample beneficiaries and also of their families to a considerable extent. It can also be stated that the DWCRA programme has created social and economic awareness among the beneficiaries to certain extent. The contribution of beneficiaries of DWCRA programme to their families income is significant which has resulted in overall improvement in the levels of living of these families.

Political Empowerment of Beneficiaries

It is evident from the data presented in the Table 14.17 that about 20 per cent of the beneficiaries have membership in different political parties before joining the DWCRA group. These beneficiaries have also participated in various activities of their respective parties. The distribution of these respondents by activity and by political party indicates that about 56 per cent of them belong to the Telugu Desam party, which is at present the ruling party in the State while the next highest numbers of respondents constituting 30 per cent of the respondents belong to the Congress (I) party. The beneficiaries belonging to other parties like CPM, etc., are insignificant in number. The position is same in the two Mandals covered under study. With regard to the participation of sample respondents in political activities before joining the DWCRA, out of these sample respondents 83 beneficiaries are attending the meeting of ruling party. About one third of them are canvassing in favour of ruling party in various elections. It can also be seen from the Table 9.18 that two respondents, one from each Mandal, had ever contested in the village panchayat elections as the ward members.

Table—14.17 Distribution of Beneficiaries Belonging to Various Political Parties Before Joining DWCRA

	Chirala				Vetapalem				Total			
Activity	T.D.P.	Congress	Others	Total	T.D.P.	Congress	Others	Total	T.D.P.	Congress	Others	Total
Weaving	15 (71.43)	6 (28.53)	–	21 (100.00)	10 (43.48)	9 (39.13)	4 (17.39)	23 (100.00)	25 (54.55)	15 (34.09)	4 (0.90)	44 (100.00)
Fish business	8 (66.67)	4 (33.33)	–	12 (100.00)	8 (66.67)	4 (33.33)	–	12 (100.00)	16 (6.44)	8 (33.33)	–	24 (100.00)
Dairy	4 (40.00)	3 (30.00)	3 (30.00)	10 (100.00)	7 (58.33)	5 (41.67)	–	12 (100.00)	11 (50.00)	8 (36.36)	3 (13.64)	22 (100.00)
Mixed trade	2 (40.00)	2 (40.00)	1 (20.00)	5 (100.00)	7 (70.00)	3 (30.00)	–	10 (100.00)	9 (60.00)	5 (33.33)	1 (6.66)	15 (100.00)
Vegetables	2 (66.67)	1 (33.33)	–	3 (100.00)	5 (62.50)	3 (37.50)	–	8 (100.00)	7 (63.64)	4 (36.36)	–	11 (100.00)
Handicrafts	1 (25.00)	3 (75.00)	–	4 (100.00)	2 (50.00)	2 (50.00)	–	4 (100.00)	3 (37.50)	5 (62.50)	–	8 (100.00)
Total	**32** **(58.18)**	**19** **(34.55)**	**4** **(7.27)**	**55** **(100.00)**	**39** **(56.52)**	**26** **(37.68)**	**4** **(5.80)**	**69** **(100.00)**	**71** **(57.26)**	**35** **(28.29)**	**8** **(6.45)**	**124** **(100.00)**

Note: Figures in parentheses indicate percentages to total.

Table—14.18 Political Participation Before DWCRA

Activity	Chirala			
	Attending party meeting	Participation in canvassing	Contesting elections	Total
Weaving	14 (66.67)	07 (33.33)	–	21 (100.00)
Fish business	8 (66.67)	3 (25.00)	1 (8.33)	12 (100.00)
Dairy	7 (70.00)	3 (30.00)	–	10 (100.00)
Mixed trade	4 (80.00)	1 (20.00)	–	5 (100.00)
Vegetables	2 (66.67)	1 (33.33)	–	3 (100.00)
Handicrafts	3 (75.00)	1 (25.00)	–	4 (100.00)
Total	**38 (69.10)**	**16 (29.10)**	**1 (1.80)**	**55 (100.00)**

(Table Contd...)

Activity	Vetapalem			
	Attending party meeting	Participation in canvassing	Contesting elections	Total
Weaving	17 (73.91)	06 (26.09)	–	23 (100.00)
Fish business	8 (66.67)	4 (33.33)	–	12 (100.00)
Dairy	7 (58.33)	5 (41.67)	–	12 (100.00)
Mixed trade	6 (60.00)	3 (30.00)	1 (10.00)	10 (100.00)
Vegetables	5 (62.50)	3 (37.50)	–	8 (100.00)
Handicrafts	2 (50.00)	2 (50.00)	–	4 (100.00)
Total	**45 (65.22)**	**23 (33.34)**	**1 (1.44)**	**69 (100.00)**

(Table Contd...)

Activity	Total			
	Attending party meeting	Participation in canvassing	Contesting elections	Total
Weaving	31 (70.45)	13 (29.55)	–	44 (100.00)
Fish business	16 (66.67)	7 (29.17)	1 (4.16)	24 (100.00)
Dairy	14 (63.64)	8 (36.36)	–	22 (100.00)
Mixed trade	10 (66.67)	4 (26.67)	1 (6.66)	15 (100.00)
Vegetables	7 (63.64)	4 (36.36)	–	11 (100.00)
Handicrafts	5 (62.5)	3 (37.5)	–	8 (100.0)
Total	83 (66.94)	39 (31.45)	2 (1.61)	124 (100.00)

Note: Figures in parentheses indicate percentages to total.

Regarding the distribution of sample respondents among various political parties after joining DWCRA are furnished in Table 14.19. The data shows that the membership of the sample beneficiaries in various political parties has increased by more than 3 times. It is also interesting to mention that about 80 per cent of the total respondents are members of TDP which is the ruling party in the State while the number of respondents who are members of Congress, CPI, CPM etc., parties is negligible. The participation of the respondents in various political activities has been increasing after they have joined the programme. As is evidenced from Table 14.20, the sample of beneficiaries have reported that they have been regularly attending the meetings of their political party. Further, they are actively involving in the other activities such as election canvassing and also contesting the local bodies elections. Most of these respondents are involved in the weaving activity and fish business. The respondents have contested as the panchayat ward members, and also as MPTC members in the local body elections held in 2001. Interestingly all the respondents are members of TDP.

The comparative picture about the political activities of the respondents before and after joining the DWCRA can be seen from Table 14.17 and 14.20. These tables reveal that the highest number of sample beneficiaries belong to the ruling TDP. It can be assumed that in the formation of the DWCRA groups, the party affiliation is playing an important role in the identification of beneficiaries of DWCRA. It is also found during the field work that the DWCRA members are directed by the party leaders to attend meeting of the party whenever they are held in their villages. Further they are also involved in propagating the various developmental programmes lunched by the present Government like the Janmabhoomi, Adarana and Deepam and so on.

Table—14.19 Distribution of Beneficiaries Belong to Various Political Parties After Joining DWCRA

Activity	Chirala				Vetapalem				Total			
	T.D.P.	Congress	Others	Total	T.D.P.	Congress	Others	Total	T.D.P.	Congress	Others	Total
Weaving	28 (80.00)	7 (20.00)	–	35 (100.00)	26 (66.67)	9 (23.08)	4 (10.25)	39 (100.00)	54 (72.97)	16 (21.62)	4 (5.41)	74 (100.00)
Fish business	37 (90.24)	4 (9.76)	–	41 (100.00)	37 (88.10)	5 (11.90)	–	42 (100.00)	74 (89.16)	9 (10.84)	–	83 (100.00)
Dairy	11 (61.11)	4 (5.41)	3 (2.70)	18 (100.00)	26 (83.87)	5 (16.13)	–	31 (100.00)	37 (75.51)	9 (18.37)	3 (6.12)	49 (100.00)
Mixed trade	34 (91.89)	2 (5.41)	1 (2.70)	37 (100.00)	50 (95.16)	3 (4.84)	–	53 (100.00)	84 (93.33)	5 (5.56)	1 (1.11)	90 (100.00)
Vegetables	8 (80.00)	1 (10.00)	1 (10.00)	10 (100.00)	21 (84.00)	4 (16.00)	–	25 (100.00)	29 (82.86)	5 (14.29)	1 (2.85)	35 (100.00)
Handicrafts	41 (93.18)	3 (6.82)	–	44 (100.00)	20 (90.00)	2 (10.00)	–	22 (100.00)	61 (92.42)	5 (7.58)	–	66 (100.00)
Total	**159 (85.95)**	**21 (11.35)**	**5 (2.70)**	**185 (100.00)**	**180 (84.91)**	**28 (13.20)**	**4 (1.89)**	**212 (100.00)**	**339 (85.39)**	**49 (12.34)**	**9 (2.27)**	**397 (100.00)**

Note: Figures in parentheses indicate percentages to total.

Table—14.20 Political Participation of Beneficiaries After Joining DWCRA

Activity	Chirala			
	Attending party meeting	Participation in canvassing	Contesting elections	Total
Weaving	30 (85.71)	3 (8.57)	2 (5.72)	35 (100.00)
Fish business	30 (73.17)	6 (14.63)	5 (12.20)	41 (100.00)
Dairy	12 (66.67)	6 (33.33)	–	18 (100.00)
Mixed trade	28 (75.68)	9 (24.32)	–	37 (100.00)
Vegetables	6 (50.00)	5 (41.67)	1 (8.33)	12 (100.00)
Handicrafts	33 (75.00)	9 (20.45)	2 (4.55)	44 (100.00)
Total	139 (74.33)	38 (20.32)	10 (5.35)	187 (100.00)

(Table Contd…)

Activity	Vetapalem			
	Attending party meeting	Participation in canvassing	Contesting elections	Total
Weaving	25 (64.10)	12 (30.77)	2 (5.13)	39 (100.00)
Fish business	29 (69.05)	13 (30.95)	–	42 (100.00)
Dairy	16 (51.61)	13 (4.94)	2 (6.45)	31 (100.00)
Mixed trade	41 (77.36)	12 (22.64)	–	53 (100.00)
Vegetables	22 (80.00)	3 (12.00)	–	25 (100.00)
Handicrafts	10 (45.45)	12 (54.55)	–	22 (100.00)
Total	**143 (67.45)**	**65 (30.68)**	**4 (1.89)**	**212 (100.00)**

(Table Contd…)

Activity	Total			
	Attending party meeting	Participation in canvassing	Contesting elections	Total
Weaving	55 (74.32)	15 (20.28)	4 (5.40)	74 (100.00)
Fish business	59 (71.08)	19 (22.89)	5 (6.02)	83 (100.00)
Dairy	28 (57.14)	19 (38.78)	2 (4.08)	49 (100.00)
Mixed trade	69 (76.67)	21 (33.33)	–	90 (100.00)
Vegetables	28 (80.00)	8 (22.86)	1 (2.86)	35 (100.00)
Handicrafts	43 (65.15)	21 (31.82)	2 (3.03)	66 (100.00)
Total	**282 (71.03)**	**103 (25.94)**	**14 (3.53)**	**397 (100.00)**

Note: Figures in parentheses indicate percentages to total.

It is also evident that about 80 per cent of the sample respondents have membership in women's organisation started in their villages. It is also observed that about three fourths of them are actively participating in public awareness programmes like the literacy campaigns, AIDS control, sanitation, improvement, child care programmes and such other programmes.

Apart from the membership in various Mahila Mandals, all these beneficiaries are also having membership in various other organisations like education committees, water users' associations etc. As seen from the Table 14.21, about 50 per cent of the beneficiaries are having membership in the education committees constituted in their respective villages. Similarly, about one-third of the sample beneficiaries have reported that they have membership in various voluntary organisations started by their friends and relatives in their villages.

Political Contacts of the Sample Beneficiaries

Further, an attempt is also made to study the political contacts of the sample beneficiaries with the leaders of different political parties. As observed during the field survey only about 35 per cent of the sample respondents have close contacts/relations with the party leaders of their area. Similarly, it can also be noticed that about 40 per cent of the total respondents are approached by the leaders of various political parties for their support and cooperation in various elections.

Table—14.21 Membership of Beneficiaries in Various Organisations

Activity	Chirala				
	Education committee	Water users association	Voluntary organisations	Not a member	Total
Weaving	25 (59.52)	–	14 (33.34)	3 (7.14)	42 (100.00)
Fish business	18 (40.00)	–	23 (51.11)	4 (8.89)	25 (100.00)
Dairy	9 (45.00)	2 (10.00)	7 (35.00)	2 (10.00)	20 (100.00)
Mixed trade	18 (45.00)	–	17 (42.50)	5 (12.50)	40 (100.00)
Vegetables	4 (33.36)	4 (33.36)	3 (27.28)	–	11 (100.00)
Handicrafts	27 (61.36)	–	10 (22.73)	7 (15.91)	44 (100.00)
Total	101 (50.00)	9 (4.46)	74 (36.63)	21 (10.40)	202 (100.00)

(Table Contd...)

Activity	Vetapalem				
	Education committee	Water users association	Voluntary organisations	Not a member	Total
Weaving	32 (78.05)	–	9 (21.95)	–	41 (100.00)
Fish business	18 (40.91)	–	22 (50.00)	4 (9.09)	44 (100.00)
Dairy	19 (54.29)	4 (11.43)	9 (25.71)	3 (8.57)	35 (100.00)
Mixed trade	27 (42.19)	–	26 (40.63)	11 (17.18)	64 (100.00)
Vegetables	11 (40.74)	3 (11.11)	10 (37.04)	3 (11.11)	27 (100.00)
Handicrafts	9 (40.91)	4 (18.18)	7 (31.82)	2 (9.09)	22 (100.00)
Total	**116 (49.79)**	**11 (4.73)**	**83 (35.61)**	**23 (9.87)**	**233 (100.00)**

(Table Contd...)

Activity	Total				
	Education committee	Water users association	Voluntary organisations	Not a member	Total
Weaving	57 (68.67)	–	23 (27.71)	3 (3.61)	83 (100.00)
Fish business	36 (40.45)	–	45 (50.56)	8 (8.99)	89 (100.00)
Dairy	28 (50.91)	6 (10.91)	16 (29.09)	5 (0.91)	55 (100.00)
Mixed trade	45 (43.27)	–	43 (41.35)	16 (15.38)	104 (100.00)
Vegetables	15 (39.47)	7 (18.42)	13 (34.21)	3 (7.89)	38 (100.00)
Handicrafts	36 (54.55)	4 (6.06)	17 (25.76)	9 (13.63)	66 (100.00)
Total	**217 (49.89)**	**20 (4.60)**	**157 (36.09)**	**44 (10.11)**	**435 (100.00)**

Note: Figures in parentheses indicate percentages to total.

DWCRA Members and Party Positions

As has been discussed earlier, it is observed during this present study that the priority is given to the DWCRA members in the selection of candidates for contesting various local bodies elections. Out of the total, 14 sample respondents have contested for different offices in the local body elections. Of them five members were elected as the ward members of village panchayat, one member as to MPTC and another as the village Sarpanch.

In addition to this, nine sample respondents were elected to the village/urban committees and women committees of the TDP. These facts reflect that considerable number of the women become politically active after joining the DWCRA programme and involving in various activities. This ultimately indicates that DWCRA women gained political empowerment after becoming the beneficiaries of this Programme.

Motivation to Join Politics

It is observed that some of the members of DWCRA group, family members, members of Mahila Mandals etc., are motivating the beneficiaries to join in politics. Out of the total 435 beneficiaries only 36 are not members of any political party, because of various reasons. The reasons stated by them include lack of interest in politics, old age, pre-occupation with their own activities and so on. Majority of the beneficiaries who have joined in the politics are aspiring for political positions in politics like ward membership and Sarpanches of village panchayats, members of MPTCs, ZPTCs and official positions in their party organisations. Similarly about 96 of the sample beneficiaries expressed the opinion that involvements in the DWCRA programme the leadership qualities among the rural women. However, only 3 per cent of the total respondents felt that the DWCRA provides political training to its members. About 63 per cent of the sample beneficiaries admitted that this programme was introduced by the Government of Andhra Pradesh to gain certain political end.

DWCRA Members' Participation in Elections

The present study reveals that DWCRA members are influencing their family members as well as other rural women in exercising their votes in different elections. They are motivating the illiterate women to cast their votes in the elections.

It can be concluded from the above discussion that about 90 per cent of sample beneficiaries from Chirala Mandal and 40 per cent of Vetapalem Mandal have been actively participating in all programmes undertaken in their villages such as Pulse Polio, Janmabhumi, Mass Literacy campaign, anti AIDS campaign etc. Its can be seen about 90 per cent of the sample beneficiaries were benefited by the DWCRA programme as there is a significant growth in their man-days. As a result, these beneficiaries were expressed their satisfaction with the DWCRA as an employment generation programme.

As these respondents are assured of regular income from the activities they have undertaken under this programmes which was not the case before. The study also revealed that a vast majority of the sample beneficiaries are able to contribute considerably to their family total income after they have joined the DWCRA programme. Further, the programme also increased their saving capacity of the beneficiaries as they are saving regularly out of the income they earned from their activities. DWCRA beneficiaries also realised the benefits of the programme as they felt that the programme has led to the empowerment of their women. There is also ample evidence of the political empowerment of DWCRA beneficiaries as these women are non-actively involved in various political activities at the grass root level.

15

Empowerment of Women

SWOT Analysis

**Dr. P. Venugopal*

The constitution of India provided adequate safeguards of the socio-economic development of the disadvantaged sections such as women. SC's and ST's and other backward communities. The level of development of these sections is not in desired extent and direction despite plethora of developmental programmes implemented during the past five decades. More than fifty per cent of these sections have been living in the vicious circles of poverty due to skewed distribution of developmental opportunities on one side and low levels of motivation and aspirations for better future on the other. Over a period of time most of the assert less families of these disadvantaged sections have developed a dependency syndrome, expecting Government to do everything for their development.

Women are mostly considered as weaker than men and hence they require social and economic protection. This attitude has

* Lecturer in the Department of Economics, Hindu College, Guntur; Andhra Pradesh.

constrained their mobility and consequently lack of opportunities for development of their personalities. So women have lagged behind in the fields of education, skill development and employment and hence their work is greatly undervalued in economic terms. Therefore, women need to be empowered economically, socially and politically.

Women and Empowerment

The primary task of the development is initiating a process of awareness building of education, of people farming their own organisations to define and create and demand what they need to lead a decent life. People's participation in rural development, particularly by rural women, will not automatically flow. Concrete efforts are needed to empower women to get involved in all aspects of development. Development should ultimately become a process of empowerment.

Components of Women Empowerment

The empowerment process encompasses severally mutually reinforcing components but begins with and is supported by economic independence which implies access and control over production resources.

* Awareness Building: About
  - Situation of women
  - Discrimination of women
  - Rights of women
  - Opportunities to the women
  - Importance of gender equality
* Organising a Group
  - Collectively
  - Group identity and
  - Group pressure
* Capacity building and skill development
  - Ability to plan

— To decide

— To organise

— Ability to manage

— Ability to carry out activities

— Ability to deal with people/institutions in the world around them

* Participation

— Participation in decision making at home

— Participation in decision making in the community

— Participation in decision making in the society

* Access and Control

— Over resources

— Over means of productivity and

— Over distribution

Categories of Empowerment

There are three major categories of empowerment of women

— Social empowerment

— Economic empowerment

— Political empowerment

Agents of Empowerment

Agents of empowerment can be classified into two namely external and self motivation.

External Agents

The external agents are government/semi-government agents and non-governmental organisation. The external agents empower women through

— Legislation

— Policy

— Special programmes and

— Positive discrimination for women

Self motivation: Self motivation (with or without NGO's) includes

— Self-help groups
— Thrift and credit groups

Constrains of Empowerment

- Low education of the women;
- Poor skills of the women;
- Poor information base to the women;
- Poor exposure of the women;
- Available time to the women;
- Transfer of technology causes replacement of women;
- Women won't have any protection in informal sector; and
- No relief due to drudgery.

SWOT Analysis on Empowerment of Women in India

Worthiness of the empowerment of women in India has to be judged in the light of the following SWOT analysis. Strength and weakness are the internal and opportunities and threats are external problems.

Strength

1. Women folk constitute a significant part of total labour force;
2. The employment in the organised sector requires certain minimum qualifications and most of the educated women are drawn from middle classes and richer sections;
3. Employment of women in unorganised sector has been increasing for the last few decades;
4. Education and social status of the women has also been increasing;

5. In many cases, the spouses and the family members support the lead of women in finding solutions to various problems and consequently the women gain equal opportunity to take part in the decision making on both domestic and community matters.

Weakness

1. In the male dominated society, women are supposed to remain in the four walls of their households or help in husband jobs particularly at farm. Women has been subject to inequalities and subsidiary status related to man, within the family and outside in the society;
2. Today, nobody may deny the need for women's education. But still, there is a feeling that providing education for women is a luxury which the rich may afford for their girls and poor do not bother to provide the facilities of education for their girl children.

Opportunities

1. When India began to plan for its future development, it was clearly understood that upliftment of women is an equally important factor for the nations development. Welfare was the earliest policy approach for women which is still the most prevalent one.
2. The first Five Year Plan (1951-56) envisaged various welfare schemes for women. It planned for the development of material and child health and family planning services.
3. In 1953, the Central Social Welfare Board (CSWB) was set to chalk out various welfare programmes for the development of women.
4. The Community Development Programme (1952) for the first time, enphasized the need for mobilisation of women through Mahila Mandals.
5. The International Women's decade (1975-85) in India, however, witnessed unprecedented efforts from various quarters to reassess the role of women, to enlarge the

information base, to search for alternative strategies for women's equality and development and to develop policies and programmes addressed to the specific needs and problems of women.

6. In 1982 the National Commission for Women was set up as a nation apex statutory level body to review the constitutional and legal safeguards for women, recommended remedial legislative measures, facilitate redressal of grievances and advise the Government on all policy matters affecting women.
7. Several efforts have been made through various plans and programmes to improve the status of women.
8. The Eight Plan (1992-97) shifted the focus from development to empowerment.
9. In 1990, The National Commission for Women Act was enacted.
10. In 1991, a National Plan of Action for SAARC Decade of the Girl Child (1991-2000) was formulated by the Department of Women and Child Development.
11. In 1996, the Draft of National Policy for Empowerment of Women was finalised.

Threat

1. In most of the cases, employers in private sector adopt policy of biasedness in providing employment to the women. Even having some academic and technical qualification, women are not offered the employment equal to the status of the men.
2. It can be observed in unorganised sector that in wage payments, discrimination exists on the basis of sex.
3. Regarding the kind of work opportunities open to urban women working in unorganised sector, very often the choice is made for them in the sense that they go for the type of work of their parents or relatives are involved in what even the occupation they manage to enter, their work is generally unskilled, low paying and physically exhausting.

4. Although government has launched a number of schemes for providing financial assistance for self-employment of the unemployed irrespective of sex, education and rural background, hardly few rural women could have availed this opportunity due to lack of incentive from the Government and the society as well as lack of education, vocational training and entrepreneurship, etc.

Conclusion

It may be concluded that to empower the women steps are to be taken to implement adult education programme among the women workers of unorganised sector. Women should be educated with labour legislations and welfare measures to promote awareness among them to avoid all types of exploitations.

The Labour Department should introduce a special wing to prevent socio-economic, physical, mental and sexual exploitations of women.

The violation of 'Minimum Wages Act' and 'Payment of Wages Act' has not been observed in many of the unorganised sector activities. For effective implementation of the Act, all possible efforts should be strengthened to safeguard the interest of Women and to promote the welfare of the women.

16

Welfare and Empowerment of Women in India

Some Reflections

**Prof. M. Bapuji*

***Dr. M. Koteswara Rao*

Welfare and empowerment in the context of women are different but interrelated and overlapping concepts. The words welfare or development came to mean exclusively as economic development or betterment measured in terms of income, literacy, health, savings, employment, etc. In contrast, empowerment connotes strengthening of groups and individuals through interaction in all levels of social organisations. It is a social psychic and to certain extent and external process. It has to grow over a period of time in the case of socially and economically poor and disadvantaged groups at the individual, family and community levels and among both the sexes. Empowerment of women results from women

* Professor in the Department of Political Science and Public Administration, Nagarjuna University.

** Associate Professor and Head of the Department of Adult Continuing Education Extension Work and Field Outreach, Nagarjuna University.

assessing what they are and where they are. It is not wrong to use these two terms synonymously in the context of women. In the case of women empowerment, both attitudinal empowerment and material advancement are necessary. The latter may not, and often does not automatically lead to the former. It is to be noted that economic betterment is a necessary but not sufficient condition for women empowerment. Besides economic or material advancement, attitudinal change along with awareness about their inherent potentialities and capacities is necessary for empowering women.

In India, welfare of women has become one of the nation's primary goals right from the independence while empowerment has come to forefront in the country's political agenda only in 1980s. Ever since there has been growing concern for the empowerment of women, ever since it is realised that the real development of the country can not take roots if the women who constitute nearly half of the country's total population remain backward and are denied equal rights and participation in the political as well as development processes. Even though, the Government has been making concerted efforts for the upliftment of women in all the fields ever since the beginning of independence in accordance with the directives of the constitution, not much was delivered in this direction. It is against this background that the Government realised the need to empower women in order to enable them to play their role in the on-going development process and also to get their due share in the benefits of this process. Of course, there are a host of factors inhibiting the women from taking active part in the development process. In fact, the efforts for women's development were started with the conventional approach that poverty was the basic problem of women and economic betterment would not only improve their position but also empower them to enjoy the benefits of planned development. In reality, however such a sequence of improvement in the conditions of women did not take place even after the implementation of several programmes and schemes under various strategies during various Five Year Plans. Apart from this, the position of rural and tribal women living in the remote areas became still worse. It was only during 1980s that the Government realised that the conventional strategies implemented for the development of women have failed and hence needed reshaping and reassessment. The results of five decades of planning also has shown that the provision of economic assistance alone cannot improve the conditions of women. This fact has changed the mind set of the policy makers which led to the evolution of a new strategy during 1980s that promises to deliver a new life to the women, especially to those millions who live below the poverty line by empowering them socially, economically and politically.

Dismal Position of Women

It is within this conceptual framework that the issue of welfare and empowerment of women in India is examined in this chapter. In terms of any set of developmental indicators and living conditions the Indian women are always in a dismal state of affairs. Needless to mention that in no period in the history of India women lived a decent life and enjoyed equal rights and status with men. Even after independence and adoption of a constitution promising a welfare state, there is no improvement in the conditions of women, more particularly, those belonging to the depressed sections, the SCs and STs living in the rural and tribal areas. They lag far behind the men in terms of every socio-economic indicators in spite of the gender equality mandated by the constitution. Out of the 428 million literates in the country, women account for 275 millions constituting 39.4% while it is 63.8% among the men, as per the 1991 census. The school enrolment figures for girls are also less than those of boys at all stages and ages and dropout rates are also higher for girls compared with the boys. In the case of utilization of various health services also the gap between the women and men is glaring. Further, in the field of employment and earnings the women occupy a position far below the men. Even though the women constitute 95% of workforce in the unorganised sector their earnings are very meagre. In the political sphere, the situation of women is glaringly dismal. It is estimated that the number of women among the total members in the Parliament as well as the State Legislatures never exceeded 7% after independence. Women's representation in the higher echelons of decision-making positions has been consistently and extremely negligible.

Women Welfare in Various Plans

In the earlier plans, women development efforts were guided by welfare orientation. Development in the conditions of women was conceived as advancement in different fields through the implementation of various programmes and schemes. During the First and Second plan period few welfare measures were undertaken with the association of voluntary organisations while the governmental agencies were not involved seriously. In line with the strategy adopted during the First Five Year Plan the Central Social Welfare Board was established in 1953 to assist and coordinate the activities of the various voluntary organisations working in the area of development of women, particularly, the rural women. It was latter felt that unless education and health levels among the women are improved, they could not make any progress in their conditions. Accordingly, the Third and Fourth Five Year Plans laid stress on the promotion of health and education among the women. In the sphere of health, a number of schemes were taken up to promote maternal health services to women along with general health facilities in these Plans. Similarly, schemes aiming at the provision of scholarships, establishment of schools exclusively for girls, free supply of text books, grant of fee concessions etc., were implemented on a massive scale for improvement of education among the women. The Fifth Plan made a shift from welfare to development of women to increase their capabilities for playing an active rolc in the development process. Accordingly, several developmental programmes were implemented for improving the socio-economic status to improve the earning capacity of women by providing them employment opportunities in the agriculture and allied sectors like dairying etc. This plan emphasised on the integration of developmental and welfare programmes to improve the overall position of women, particularly, the rural women. The Sixth Plan adopted a multi-disciplinary approach with focus on health, education and economic betterment of women. The main thrust of this Plan was to enhance the social and economic position of women in order to help them to cross the poverty line. In the Seventh Plan beneficiary-oriented programmes were taken up in different sectors for providing employment and income generation opportunities for women so that their economic position would be improved resulting in their overall development.

The Eighth Five Year Plan strengthened the strategy already laid down in the Sixth and Seventh Plans for the development of women. It focused on the empowerment of women to make them equal partners and participants along with men in the development process. The plan adopted a holistic approach towards the development of women as opposed to the restricted approach adopted by the earlier plans. This plan gave top priority to the economic empowerment through the provision of employment opportunities and skill training to the women, particularly, for the rural areas. The provision of proper nutrition and health facilities to the poor women was also stressed in this Plan. The Ninth Plan (1997-2002) evolved certain new and novel strategies for the promotion of welfare as the agents of social change and development is adopted as the main strategy for the development of women. The Plan advocated that empowerment of the women first starts with awareness and confidence and their transformation would follow in due course. In accordance with this strategy, the Plan suggested the reservation of certain seats for women in the Parliament and legislative assemblies of various States. The Plan also proposed the reservation of jobs for them in public sector including higher civil services. This plan also proposed several new initiatives for the health and educational development of women. The plan emphasised on free education to girls upto the college level and also greater vocational training to them. The plan ensured participation of women in industrial development, and proposed the setting up of development banks for women entrepreneurs for providing them assistance to start small scale industries. However, the most novel feature of this Plan is the incorporation of special component to ensure the flow of 30% of the total Plan funds to the women development programmes. By earmarking 30% of funds in all the programmes for the development of women it is hoped that "trickling down" from the above would take place resulting in the socio-economic betterment of the women and ultimately their empowerment.

An analysis of the women welfare schemes incorporated in different plans reveals that these plans have rightly accorded highest priority to the health and educational development among the women in order to improve their social and familial status and make them aware of their rights guaranteed by the constitution and also play their role as mothers and wives effectively. These Plans have also rightly gave top priority to the provision of various services for the protection of health of mothers and children. The first five Plans had almost continued the same strategy of concentrating more on education and health programmes. The Sixth plan broke a new ground by shifting the focus from welfare to development as it realised that even after the implementation of five Plans the women remained backward and the goal of gender equality was far away, and also the share of women in the benefits of planned development was very meagre. From this plan onwards economic prosperity for empowering the women for bringing them into national activity as equal partners along with men has become the main objective of the Five Year Plans in so far as the women are concerned. In accordance with this objectives the subsequent Plans focused on the empowerment of the women, both political and economic and introduced several initiatives in this direction.

Various Rural Development Schemes and Women

Apart from the general sector programmes the women development received priority in all the poverty eradication programmes launched during the Fifth Plan and subsequent Five Year Plans. The emphasis of these programmes is on the economic betterment of women by providing them employment and income generating assets. The prominent poverty eradication programmes like the Integrated Rural Development Programme (IRDP), the Programme for Training of Rural Youth and Self-Employment (TRYSEM) and the National Rural Employment Programme (NREP), the Rural Land less Employment Guarantee Programme (RLEGE), The Jawahar Rojgar Yojana (JRY) etc., were included special components for the women and they are viewed as special targeted group for providing assistance for undertaking various activities. A special and innovative programme named as the Women and Child in Rural Areas, (DWACRA) was launched in April, 1981 as a component of IRDP to accelerate the process of integrating the rural women into the development process through economic empowerment. Initially started in about 50 districts in different states, this scheme was extended to almost all the districts in India. By the end of Eighth Five Year Plan under the DWACRA several thousands of selected women were encouraged to form self-help groups to undertake various economic activities with the funding provided by the central and state governments along with their own contribution as seed money. During the last few years the DWCRA has met with considerable success in several States, particularly Andhra Pradesh where the DWCRA groups have increased from 400 in 1982-83 to 4,000 in 1993-94 and 12,000 in 1994-95. Its success is largely due to the formation of thrift and credit societies in large numbers which facilitated the mobilization of funds for undertaking productive activities without depending upon the outside agencies like private money lenders, Banks etc., this programme also helped the women to realise their inherent potential for taking up income generating the activities on their own.

Policy Initiatives and Documents

To back up its various schemes and programmes initiated for the development of women in various Plans, the government prepared several policy instruments to guide its efforts of women development in the form of action-plans and policy documents. The National Plan for Action for Women (1976) was drafted to guide the women development efforts. In 1988, the National Perspective Plan for Women was adopted which suggested a long term holistic approach (1988-2000) for women's development. The National Commission on Self-Employed Women and Women in Informal Sectors appointed in 1988 made a number of recommendations for the development of women in the informal sector by providing them legislative protection, training for skill development, marketing and credit facilities. The National Policy of Action Plan for Women (1991-2000) adopted in 1991 suggests a plan of action for ensuring protection and promoting development of children, with special gender sensitivity aimed for the girl children and adolescent girls. In addition to these women specific policy initiatives, several general National Policies contain women welfare component. These Policies include: the National Policy on Education (1986), the National Policy on Adult Education (1983) the National Population Policy (1993) etc., which proposed several measures for the development of women in the respective fields.

With an idea of creating a national level autonomous body to address the women's issues and to act as a watch dog of their interests, the National Commission on Women was instituted in 1991 with an objective to watch and monitor the implementation of various constitutional and legal safeguards provided for women and also to make necessary suggestions for their effective implementation. Further, it also looks into the complaints regarding the violation of rights of women. The commission has taken up a number of activities like the formulation of expert committees to advise on issues related to women, to look into the complaints made by them against the violation of their rights, to promote awareness among the women about the various legal measures enacted for the protection of their rights and so on. The legal literacy manuals (1992) were prepared to educate the women about their rights and safeguards and also about the provisions of various enactments existing for their protection, including the marriage laws, anti-dowry acts, rights to property acts, and also those providing them protection against rape, various types of harassments including sexual abuses and so on. These manuals were written in various regional languages in very simple style and were distributed among the women through various governmental and voluntary agencies.

Another innovative initiative taken by the Government is the creation of the Integrated Child Development Services, (ICDS) which provides a package of services to the children and mothers living in the most backward rural and tribal areas and in urban slums all over the country to improve their health and nutritional status. Started in 1975, the ICDS was gradually expanded to cover the entire country. By 1997, this programme implemented 5164 projects in about 3663 blocks and 260 urban slums in different States, which benefited around 20 million children and 3.50 million women through their services. The ICDS Projects located in certain States like Orissa, Bihar, Madhya Pradesh, Andhra Pradesh etc., are getting financial aid from the World Bank for taking up several innovative schemes.

Apart from the special policy initiatives the Government has created several agencies and also initiated certain measures to strengthen the administrative mechanism for the effective implementation of all those initiatives. The Central Government had set up in 1992 the Department of Women and Child Development (DECD) in the Ministry of Human Resource Development exclusively for attending the development of women and children. The Department is conceived as a nodal agency for formulating policies and programmes for the development of women and children. It coordinates the activities of various governmental agencies and NGOs engaged in the development of women. The department concentrates on the implementation of programmes in the area of employment and income generation, gender sensitization, welfare and support services and so on. These programmes supplement and complement various women welfare programmes implemented under various schemes. In accordance with the Eighth Plan strategy the Department laid emphasis on the employment and income generation activities for the economic empowerment of women.

The Central Government has launched the Indira Mahila Yojana (IMY) in August 1995 as a mechanism to coordinate and integrate all the on going sectoral programmes of women development and to facilitate their convergence for the improvement of the economic conditions of the women. The Employment Guarantee Scheme was introduced in 1990 to provide employment to at least 50 women each day who belong to the SCs, and STs living below the poverty line. In 1993, the Mahila Samrudhi Yojana was launched for the social empowerment of rural women. The Support for Empowerment of Women Programme (STEP) is another similar programme undertaken by the Central Government for the economic empowerment of women by providing them employment in different sectors.

All these policy initiatives and administrative measures have attained mixed success in achieving their goal of improving the conditions of women in the country. They have achieved certain level of development in their socio-economic conditions, which of course, is marked by unevenness. While the women among certain sections are fully benefited by various state sponsored initiatives and achieved significant progress in different fields, the women belonging to the weaker sections, particularly, the SCs and STs are still backward and are not in a position to utilise the benefits of various developmental programmes and schemes. Hence not only the economic betterment but also the expected socio-cultural changes did not take place in their lives. Of course, there are several reasons for the chasm between the stated goals and actual achievements in the field of women development.

Political Empowerment

Political participation of women in India has been continuously neglected ever since independence, even though the country is wedded to the democratic system and the women constituted nearly half of its total population. For a long time, the participation of women in the political process at different levels is very marginal. Due to various constraints they could not occupy the positions of power and assume leadership roles. They were also denied opportunities to participate in the administration, even in the making of decisions that affect their life and welfare. In all the thirteen Parliamentary elections held so far (1952-1999) the number of women candidates contesting the elections is extremely low when compared with the men. Further, the number of women candidates who have won the Parliamentary elections held so far is also very megre as it varies between 2 per cent and 8 per cent. This reflects the very low participation of women in the political process throughout the period after independence. This position aroused deep resentment among women and their organisations who started agitating for greater participation women in politics. There is a growing demand to secure women their rightful place in all aspects of the Governance of the country. In view of these developments during 1980's the political empowerment of women has become the main commitment of the Government. It is conceded that there can never exist a true democracy unless there is active participation of women in the governance and development process. This realisation on the part of the policy makers and planners led to the adoption of a new strategy known as the political empowerment of women which is considered crucial to their emancipation in all directions. Thus political empowerment of women came to the fore in the National agenda. Subsequently, women's empowerment became a buzz-word in different circles.

The Rajiv Gandhi Government attempted to translate this strategy into reality through the initiation of 64th and 65th Constitutional Amendment Bills in the Parliament which became the 73rd and 74th Constitutional Amendment Acts in 1992. These two Acts are rightly considered as the watershed in the lives of Indian women. These Acts ensured the reservation of 1/3rd of the total seats for women in all the elected offices in both the rural and urban local bodies. The reservation of seats for the women in the political offices in these grassroots institutions is expected to strengthen the democracy by way of providing an opportunity to them to play an active role in policy making as well as development process at the lowest level. It is also hoped that this step would create a new paradigm of political participation and a new situation would emerge in the country's political system by creating critical mass. The reservation of 30 per cent of the elected positions for women in all the representative bodies would certainly go a long way in empowering them. As decision makers they shall be able to sensitize other women of their legitimate rights and to lay down developmental priorities focus of problem which they pace in their life. After the implementation of these two Acts, it was estimated that about 8 lakh women came to occupy different positions in the Panchayati Raj and Urban Local bodies across the country. Even though it is too early to assess the impact of these Acts, several studies conducted in different States came out with several findings on the implications of these Acts for the political empowerment of women. These studies have exposed the nature and quality of women representatives elected to various offices in the rural and urban local bodies in different States. On the whole, the findings of the studies suggest that there is a significant change in the position of women after they have assumed positions in the local bodies. There is greater awareness among the women about their rights and also the development concerns. As the representatives of the local bodies they are actively participating in the development process at the grassroots level. They become assertive and demanding for gender equality in the provision of various facilities provided by the Government under different schemes. These studies also highlighted that there is tremendous increase in the position of women inside and outside their families.

These studies, however, did expose the failure of the 73rd and 74th Amendments in realising their objective of political empowerment of women to the desired extent. These studies pinpointed that the system of reservation of seats for women in the local bodies worked well in some states and not well in other states. It was held that even after the introduction of 73rd and 74th Amendments Acts Political power is still far away from them as their proxies are exercising power in actual practice. Even though they are occupying seats of power in the governance at the local level and have become the decision makers legally, in practice their participation in decision making process, is limited. Evidently, the elected women representatives are treated as puppets and are dominated by the males even though officially they have no official positions. Some of the findings of the studies are even more distressing and disheartening. They concluded that the elected women themselves are not yet considering themselves politically empowered. They lack confidence to assert themselves as the leaders. Most of them, even do not know what to do and hence simply doing what the male leaders wanted them to do. The main reason for this dismal position is lack of education and consequent ignorance among the women, particularly, the rural woman. However, the position is some what encouraging in the case of women leaders in urban local bodies.

Not withstanding the findings of these studies, it is true that it is too early to assess exactly the impact of 73rd and 74th Amendments at this stage, as only a decade has passed after these Acts were brought into existence. Ten years period is not enough to alter the situation drastically. At this point it is also pertinent to emphasis that the reservation of certain number of positions in the grassroots governance alone could not politically empower the women. There should be reservation of seats for women in the national and states level representative bodies i.e., Parliament and State Legislatures. Then only they can truly become politically empower. Unless and until this has been done political empowerment of women remains as an empty slogan. The 73rd and 74th Amendment Acts are merely starting points. Even though the Government which is in power at the Centre at present has contemplated this idea long back, so far it could take the final shape. A bill reserving 30% of seats in both the Parliament and State Legislative Assemblies for women was introduced in the Parliament as 81st Constitution Amendment almost a decade ago, is still pending due to the indifferent attitude of the political parties in the country.

Conclusion

Promoting the welfare of women and also empowering and enabling them to participate in the development process are complex and complicated tasks, in view of their differential rights and status and the role assigned to them in the Indian society. It is a task that needs a multi dimensional approach, well designed and pragmatic strategies and policies, concerted and committed efforts and the involvement of Government, NGOs, media, enlightened public and so on. Particularly the women organisations and their leaders have a vital role to play in empowering women. Above all, awareness among women themselves and a thorough change in their value orientation and psyche are essential for their empowerment. The strategy for women empowerment should focus far beyond economic prosperity to restructuring social relations and value systems in the society which restrained and constrained women and their leaders for a very long time.

As an activist of women movement in India aptly pointed out on the part of women confrontationist approach campaigning against men for what they are lacking and indulging in the rhetoric of holding the male chanvinism responsible for all their backwardness handicaps would hinder their efforts for the achievement of their goal of equality and empowerment. Such an attitude would arouse resistance among men who tend to look them as a menacing force rather than equal partners. Hence the women have to play their role subtly and with tolerance to achieve what they aim without upsetting the social relations in the society. Indian society can claim itself as a civilized society and its democracy as a perfect democracy only when gender equality is achieved in all the spheres of society.

REFERENCES

Mira Seth, *Women and Development—The Indian Experience*, New Delhi: page, 2002.

Sakuntala Narasimhan, *Empowering Women: An Alternative Strategy from Rural India*, New Delhi: Sage, 1999.

John G. Sommer, *Empowering the Oppressed*, New Delhi: Sage, 2001.

UNDP, *Human Development Reports*, New York: Oxford University Press, 1999-2000.

K. Shanti, *Empowerment of Women*, New Delhi: Anmol Publishers, 1998.

Sangeetha Puruphottaman, *The Empowerment of Women in India: Grossroots Women Networks in the States*, New Delhi: Sage, 1998.

Nelson Barbara and Najma Choudary, *Women and Politics*, New Delhi: Oxford University Press, 1997.

Government of India, Planning Commission, *The Five Year Plan Documents, 1952-1997*.

17

Conditions of Scheduled Caste Women in Social Sector

A Case Study of Ujjain Division of M.P.

**Dr. Mrs. S. Murty*

Scheduled Caste is one of the most neglected sections of Indian Economy and society. Their economic and social conditions need special attention. This paper concentrates on a study of conditions of S.C. women in social sector of the economy. The results are the outcome of 2000 women of Ujjain division having 5 districts before 1st November 2001. The districts of Ujjain, Dewas, Shajapur, Mandsaur and Ratlam. In each district 400 S.C. women were surveyed at random, 200 each in rural as well as urban areas of the 5 districts of Ujjain Division with the help of neatly drawn questionnaires. The resultant data is classified according to the nature of the data and tabulated in 9 tables which are appended to the paper. The study is presented in three sections.

1. Educational status of S.C. women;
2. Health status of S.C. women;
3. Housing conditions of S.C. women.

---

* Retd. Professor of Economics, Vikram University, Ujjain (MP).

The analysis of the different tables according to the sections given above is as under—

EDUCATIONAL STATUS OF S.C. WOMEN IN UJJAIN DIVISION OF M.P.

1. Introduction

Today all nations want development. The less developed countries, poor and stagnant for centuries, want to revolt against poverty, diseases and illiteracy. The advanced countries likewise are committed to growth. The slogan of this world wide revolution is development and like other revolutionary slogans, it has various meanings to different groups.

The need for an urgency of building human capital for the attainment of accelerated and self sustained economic growth in a developing country needs no stress. A country may have abundant natural and physical resources, machinery and capital equipment but unless there are men and women to mobilise, organise and utilise natural beautiful resources for progress and development, the country cannot make rapid strides towards advancement. Human resource development is the process of increasing literacy and education, skills and capacity of all the people in the society and this is possible through investment in education of people.

This paper takes into consideration the level of education of surveyed women, their type of educational institution—school or college, total expenditure on education by surveyed women on school education and on college education, opinion of S.C. women about reservation of seats—in educational institutions and in service, attitude of surveyed women towards education—towards men education, women education, children education, higher education of children, towards adult education and liking for education.

2. Educational Position and Type of Educational Institutions of Surveyed S.C. Women

Educational Position

Table 17.1, there are ten levels of educational category. Uneducated primary, middle, high school, higher secondary, graduate, post-graduate, medical, engineering and other, 62% in urban and 79% rural women are illiterate. 17% urban and 10% rural women are educated till primary school. 9% urban and 4.4% rural women are educated till middle school, 3 to 4% urban women and 1 to 2% rural women are educated till high school and higher secondary, 3.4% urban women only are graduate and 0.8% urban women only are post-graduate, 0.1% urban is doctor and 0.1% rural is engineer, which is a nominal percentage. Rest viz. 0.2% and 3.7% respectively are educated in other disciplines. Almost same is the picture of different districts.

Thus it is clear that most of the S.C. women are illiterate, only some are low educated and only a few are highly educated.

Association of attributes was calculated between urban and rural residency and education. The hypothesis is that education is more popular in urban people. The degree of association is +0.396 say 0.4. This is a moderate degree of positive relationship and thus the hypothesis proves.

Type of Educational Institutions

As regards school education 35.2% urban and 15.7% rural women are educated in Government schools, whereas 18 and 10% respectively are made literate in private schools, other are either not educated, educated at home or are drop outs. Some joined the school but dropped out before the examination. As regards college education, 3-8% urban and 0.1% rural women are educated in Govt. Colleges and 0.4% and 0.1% are educated in private college. Others either did not go to college or studied privately at home. Some also dropped out after joining the college.

3. Expenditure on Education of Surveyed Women

On School Education

As shown in Table 17.2 the expenditure on school education of women is distributed in five ranges like, less than 1000, 1 to 2, 2 to 3, 3 to 4 and more than 4 thousand per annum, 0.2% urban and 0.3% rural women spent less than one thousand, 0.1 urban and 0.1 rural spent 2 to 3 thousand, 0.1 urban spent 3 to 4 thousand, 0.5 urban and 0.2 rural spent more than 4 thousand. 20.8% urban women and 11.8% rural could not tell about their expenditure, rest either spent nil or this was not applicable on they as them are illiterate.

Thus there is very little expenditure on school education of women during their life time and even then they are uneducated. The trend of rise in school education in urban and rural areas has a positive correlation of the degree of +0.062.

On College Education

Expenditure on college education is also not much. In urban areas 0.1% spent less than 1000, 0.1% spent between 1 to 2 thousand, 0.4% spend 2 to 3 thousand, 0.3% spent 3 to 4 thousand, 0.5% spend more than 4 thousand, 6.6% do not know, 62.6% are not concerned and 29.2% spent nil. In rural areas 0.1% spent less than 1000, 4.7% do not know, 83.8% are not concerned and 11.4% spent nil.

Thus the expenditure of women on college education is also not much and even very few S.C. women are taking college education. The trends of rise in college education in urban and rural areas have a correlation of –0.56 i.e. it is negative. This may be because there are only few or no colleges in rural areas.

4. Opinion Regarding Reservation of Surveyed S.C. Women

Reservation in Education

Table 17.3 shows the opinion of surveyed women on reservation policy in education and in services. About reservation of self in education in urban areas 31% are in favour of reservation of self in school and 12% are against it, 57% did not say anything. Of rural women 22% are for it, 25% are against it and 53.3% are quiet.

The urban women when asked about reservation of others in education, 34% said yes, 8.3% said no and 58% said nil. In rural areas 37% said yes, 7% said no and 56% said nil.

The hypothesis was tested that S.C. women want reservation in education for self and also others. The degree of association is +0.65. Thus the hypothesis does prove.

Reservation in Service

When enquired about reservation in service, for self, 35% urban women said yes, 9% said no and 56% did not say anything.

In rural areas 29.3% said yes for self, 16.7% said no for self, 54% said nil. About reservation in service for others in urban areas 35% women said yes, 8% said no, and 57% said nil. In rural areas, 38.4% said yes, 5.8% said no and 55.8% said nil.

Thus most of the urban and rural women are in favour of reservation for self and for others in education and in services.

The hypothesis was that the S.C. women want reservation in service for self and for others. The degree of association is –0.30. Thus the hypothesis proves. They want reservation for self as well as for others.

5. Attitude Towards Education of Surveyed S.C. Women

Table 17.4 shows the attitude of surveyed women towards education. Questions were asked about essentiality of education, essentiality of women education, essentiality of child education, attitude towards adult education and liking towards education.

95% to 99.5% women in urban sectors are in favour of men, women and children's education 86 to 96% rural women are in favour of men, women and children education. Rest do not believe in education or did not speak. Their percentage is mostly about 4%. 68.8% urban and 55.1% rural women are in favour of higher education of children. Rest are either against it or kept quite. Attitude towards adult education is comparatively less enthusiastic. Only 20% urban and 32% rural women favour it. Rest say no or do not say anything. As regards liking for education or liking for service, about 5 to 7% in rural and urban areas said yes for both but rest did not commit anything.

If we look at the total of attitude in favour of education, it is 77% in urban and 73% in rural areas. 15% are not in favour of education in urban areas and 25% in rural areas. 8% in urban and 2% in rural are quiet about this enquiry.

HEALTH STATUS OF S.C. IN UJJAIN DIVISION OF M.P.

1. Introduction

Development activities in the post-independence India has resulted into multiphased socio-economic, scientific and technical progress in all fields. The share of health and medical sciences activities has also increased in our country. The people have witnessed development of large infrastructure for providing health care to them. Effectiveness of this health care establishment, build up with vast investment of efforts and finances in men and material in the form of doctors and hospitals, depends largely on the smooth flow of their services to those who most need them as the most weak, poor, diseased, deprived and distressed. In the contest of our commitment to provide health for all by 2000, it has been a challenging job. On the other hand, the facilities, no doubt, are increasing but the population is also increasing on the other hand. As a result, the efforts made so far have not been sufficient and we have to go much further.

This chapter concentrates on the study of health condition of families of surveyed S.C. women, prevalent diseases in the families of these women, type of treatment which they go for, treatment awareness of S.C. women, use of treatment by S.C. women, health awareness of S.C. women, use of rest and nutrition by S.C. women etc.

2. Health Condition of Families of Surveyed S.C. Women

Table 17.5 given at the end of this chapter shows the health condition of the families of surveyed S.C. women. Questions were asked about the health of self, health of husband and health of children of surveyed women. The answers were in four categories—good, medium, bad and no answer or, not applicable.

90% urban and 89.5% rural women are in good health. 8.1% urban and 7% rural women are in medium health and 19% urban and 3.5% rural women's health is bad. Thus most of the women said that their health is good. The health is better in urban areas. This may be because the urban women are on the one hand more conscious about their health and on the other hand, health facilities are available more in urban areas.

As regards the health of husband's of surveyed women, about 85% urban and 87% rural men have good health, 3.1% urban and 6.6% rural men have medium health and 1.8% urban and 1.9% rural men have bad health. 10.2% urban and 4.8% rural men's information did not come. Thus in urban areas the health of men is worse than in rural areas just vice versa of women's health. This may mean that women take more care of their husbands in rural areas.

When the questions were asked about the health of children of surveyed S.C. women, 87% children in urban areas and 90.4% children in rural areas have good health. 1.7% in urban and 4.8% in rural areas have medium health and 0.7% urban and 1.8% rural children have bad health. 11% urban and 2.9% rural children's health condition is not reported. Thus children are more healthy in rural areas. This may be because of better milk, better air, better care, less strains of education in rural areas.

On the whole 98% in urban and 97% in rural areas have good health and 2% urban and 3% rural people have bad health. Thus most of the people have good health.

Association of attributes was calculated between good health and urban residence. It was found that the association between the good health of children and urban residence is +0.45. Association between the good health of self and urban residence is +0.02 and association between the good health of husbands and urban residence is +0.26. Thus the association for grown up people is nominal and positive whereas for children it is moderate and positive.

3. Prevalent Diseases in Families and Type of Treatment of Surveyed S.C. Women

As shown in Table 17.6, women were asked about the type of prevalent diseases that they suffer from, diseases such as headache, paralysis, blood pressure, leprosy, appendix, asthma and other. 186 families in urban areas and 61 families in rural areas are suffering from one or the other disease. The most common diseases in urban areas is asthma and high blood pressure. This may be because of the polluted atmosphere and tense life of urban areas.

When asked about the type of treatment they take, 85.5% urban and 87.7% rural families take allopathic treatment. Next prevalent treatment if indigenous followed by Ayurvedic, Unani and then Homoeopathic. Thus allopathic is the most popular type of treatment both in urban and rural areas.

Karl Pearson's coefficient was calculated between diseases and rural–urban residence. It was +0.76. The hypothesis was that the urban and rural women have similar ailments. The hypothesis proved as it is of a positively high degree.

Another hypothesis was that allopathic treatment is more prevalent in urban areas. This hypothesis does not prove as it's degree is -0.094. Thus the correlation between the two factors is negative, though of a low degree.

4. Treatment Awareness and Use of Treatment by Surveyed S.C. Women

Table 17.7 shows the treatment awareness of S.C. women and use of treatment by them. The treatment awareness has been shown by the parameters such as per month number of visits to doctor or hospital, average monthly expenditure on treatment, first aid facilities available in the house, first aid facilities available in the office, immunisation of children, immunisation in pregnancy etc.

53.8% urban and 45.4% rural people visit a doctor or hospital less than 5 times in a month. 3.1% urban and 4.6% rural visit for 5 to 10 times. 0.6% urban and 0.3% rural visit doctor or hospital for more than 10 times in a month. Rest of the women did not say anything. As regards average monthly expenditure on treatment, 18.7% urban women spend less than 200 rupees in a month and 10.8% urban and 5.7% rural women spend more than 200 rupees on treatment every month. Rest could not give the figure.

As regards first aid facilities at home 11.5% urban and 5.2% rural women have it in their own house. The rest do not have it. So far as first aid in office is concerned, 20.6% urban and 14.1% rural women enjoy it. 70.4% urban and 85.9% rural women do not have it at their work place or they have not replied.

People are careful about the immunisation of children and immunisation during pregnancy. 88.9% urban and 91.9% rural women immunise their children. Rest either do not do or did not say. 85.8% urban and 90.3% rural women had immunised during pregnancy and the rest did not, or spoke not.

Thus more women and children are immunised in both urban and rural areas, the number of un-immunised is very low. Surprisingly more rural children and pregnant women are immunished in comparison to urban areas. This may be possible due to more consciousness of Government machinery in rural areas.

The association of attributes between urbanisation and ruralisation on the one side and immunisation and no-immunisation on the other hand has been + 0. This shows that there is no association between these two sets of factors.

5. Health Awareness and Use of Rest and Nutrition by Surveyed S.C. Women

Table 17.8 has presented the health awareness situation and use of rest and nutrition by S.C. women. Women were asked whether during sickness, their domestic work is done by themselves, or their husband or neighbours or children or relatives. 50.7% urban and 55.8% rural women do house work in sickness also. Rest viz 49.3% urban and 44.2% rural women's work is done by others (such as husband or children or relatives or neighbours), if they are sick.

About leave from office or outside work during sickness, 4.2 urban and 2.5 rural women take leave whereas 55.3% urban and 73.7% rural women do not take leave. 40.6% urban and 31.9% rural women did not answer this question, may be because some of them do not work outside house or because they did not want to say anything.

Questions were also asked about the regular vegetable consumption, regular fruit consumption, regular milk consumption and sufficient food consumption. Total of these four categories showed the condition of total good nutrition and total bad nutrition 66% urban and 56% rural women fall in the category of good nutrition and 34% urban and 44% rural women fall in the category of bad nutrition. Thus through more women are getting good nutrition, the percentage of those having bad nutrition is very high and should go down by proper health awareness, proper treatment and proper nutrition and proper advice.

Association of attributes was calculated between residence and nutrition. The hypothesis was that the S.C. women take better nutrition in urban areas. The two sets of attributes were urban and rural areas on one side and good and bad nutrition on the other side. The association was of the degree of +0.21. It is a positive association but its degree is low. So we can say that the hypothesis proves but not remarkably.

HOUSING PROFILE OF S.C. WOMEN IN UJJAIN DIVISION OF M.P.

1. Introduction

Housing is one of the basic but one of the most important and expensive needs of mankind. Though a national need, it has a local market. Poverty, unemployment, multiplicity of authorities dealing in housing, defective land policies and patta system, lack of proper housing policies, increasing cost of production due to defective tax system, defective building industry, delay in completion of projects, imbalanced role of private and public sector have made housing an unplanned and disorganised industry at many places in India. It is more so in rural areas.

Housing besides serving the purpose of providing shelter, plays an important role of helping the achievement of some of the socio-economic development objectives of a country. A certain minimum standard of housing is essential for healthy and civilized existence. The development and planning of housing, therefore must have a high priority in a poor and backward society. Proper housing does not only provide shelter but it also raises the quality life, health conditions, conducive to good health, education, sanitation, additional employment (for construction of houses) and generation of additional voluntary savings. A healthy and comfortable living provides incentives and generates efficiency, energy, zeal and strength on which depend the agricultural, industrial, infrastructual and intellectual property of a nation. Thus besides a consumer good, a house is also a source of human capital formation.

The Housing Profile of Surveyed S.C. Women is given in Table 17.9.

2. Type of Ownership of House

Type of ownership of a house is divided into three, self owned, rented or free of rent. 87% urban and 96.5% rural women have their own house, 12.5% urban and 2.6% have it on rent and 0.5% urban and 0.9% rural live free of rent in somebody's annexe or garage or room or under a tree. Self owned, house is a good indicator but how much good it is, depends on some other factors as under.

3. Type of House

Type of house is the actual indicator of living style. Type of houses is also divided into three. Kachcha, Pakka and Tin Shed. 55.2% urban and 83.6% rural women have a Kachcha house, 41% urban and 14.5% rural have a pakka house and 3.8% urban and 1.9% rural have a house with tin walls and tin roof or other type. Thus more than half have a kachcha house and more so in rural areas.

4. Number of Rooms

The type of house also depends on its accommodation and number of rooms. 17% urban and 28% rural women have one room only or no room. 52% urban and 44% rural women have two rooms. 16% urban and 19% rural have three rooms, and about 15% urban and 9% rural have more than 3 rooms. Thus more than half have two rooms and above.

5. Rent of Houses

Rent of houses is the actual rent that they are paying for the house and expected rent that they would get if they rent their house if the house is self owned. Rent has been classified in slabs of Rs. 200/- each. 92.6% urban and 98.8% rural women pay or expect a rent of Rs. 200/- per month. 4% urban and 1% rural of 200/- to 400/- and about 1% or even less for other slabs. Rent does not exceed Rs. 600/- per month in rural areas.

6. Facilities in Houses

Only four walls of a house are not enough. A house should have the facilities of electricity, water, fan, bathroom and toilet. Garden may be a luxurious facility. 92% houses in urban areas and 89% in rural areas are electrified. 80% in urban and 29% in rural houses have water facility. 76% in urban and 31% in rural have fans. 56% in urban and 17% in rural have the amenity of a bathroom and 51% urban and 12% rural houses have latrines. 4.8% urban and 1.8% rural have a small kitchen garden also. Those who do not have water, latrine and bathroom facilities use public taps or facilities for their purpose.

7. Amplicity of Space in Houses

House should have ample place for all members of the family. 60.9% in urban areas and 47% in rural areas feel that their house does not have ample space for all members. Only 39.1% in urban and 53% in rural have enough place to live.

8. Airiness of the House

House should be airy for the good health of family members. If house is airy, absence of fan also does not matter. 80% houses in urban and 74% in rural areas are airy but 20% in urban and 26% in rural areas are not airy according to the respondents.

9. Sunlight in House

Sunlight in the house and outside the house is also essential for the disinfection process, for drying clothes, and for drying many other things. 70% urban women get it and 30% do not, whereas 80% of the rural women get it and 20% do not.

10. Play Ground Near the House

All work and no play makes Tom a dull boy. S.C. Women's children mostly work. They must get some time and place to play. Women were asked whether they have play ground nearby. In urban areas 68.7% have and 31.3% do not have play ground near the residence. In rural areas 52.2% have and 47.8% do not have a play ground near about.

11. Other Facilities Near the House

Women were asked whether other facilities like school, hospital, market, street etc. are near to their house. In urban areas 85.5% and in rural areas 74.2% said that school is near. As regards hospital, 82.3% in urban and 43.3% in rural areas said yes. 84.2% in urban and 45.5% in rural areas accepted that market is quite close to their house. 70% urban and 35% rural women feel that street is not away from their house. Thus most of the women have these facilities nearby but more in urban areas than in rural areas.

Table—17.1 Educational Position and Type of Educational Institution of Surveyed Scheduled Caste Women in Ujjain Division

S. No.	Educational position & type of educational institution	Ujjain district				Dewas district				Shajapur district			
		Urban		Rural		Urban		Rural		Urban		Rural	
		No.	%	No.	%	No.	%	No.	%	No.	%	No.	%
1	2	3	4	5	6	7	8	9	10	11	12	13	14
01.	**Level of Education**												
1.1	Uneducated	55	27.5	171	85.5	140	70	143	71.5	145	72.5	176	88
1.2	Primary	30	15	22	11	29	14.5	26	13	40	20	14	7.0
1.3	Middle	24	12	05	2.5	23	11.5	18	9.0	14	7.0	06	3.0
1.4	High school	20	10	01	0.5	06	03	07	3.5	01	0.5	–	–
1.5	Higher secondary	31	15.5	01	0.5	01	0.5	06	03	–	–	03	1.5
1.6	Graduate	29	14.5	–	–	01	0.5	–	–	–	–	–	–
1.7	Post-graduate	08	4.0	–	–	–	–	–	–	–	–	–	–
1.8	Medical	01	0.5	–	–	–	–	–	–	–	–	–	–
1.9	Engineering	–	–	–	–	–	–	–	–	–	–	–	–
1.10	Other	02	1.0	–	–	–	–	–	–	–	–	01	0.5
1.11	Total	200	100	200	100	200	100	200	100	200	100	200	100

(Table Contd...)

I	II	III	IV	V	VI	VII	VIII	IX	X	XI	XII	XIII	XIV
02	**Type of School**												
2.1	Government	137	68.5	27	13.5	59	28.5	54	27	50	25	20	10
2.2	Private	06	3.0	02	1.0	01	0.5	02	1.0	05	2.5	–	–
2.3	None/NA	56	28	171	85.5	140	70	144	72	145	72.5	180	90
2.4	Study at home	01	0.5	–	–	–	–	–	–	–	–	–	–
0.3	**Type of College**												
3.1	Government	36	18	–	–	02	1.0	–	–	–	–	–	–
3.2	Private	04	2.0	–	–	–	–	–	–	–	–	01	0.5
3.3	None/NA	159	79.5	200	100	168	84	200	100	200	100	199	99.5
3.4	Study at home	01	05	–	–	30	15	–	–	–	–	–	–

(Table Contd...)

S. No.	Educational position & type of educational institution	Ratlam district				Mandsour district				Total of all			
		Urban		Rural		Urban		Rural		Urban		Rural	
		No.	%	No.	%	No.	%	No.	%	No.	%	No.	%
		15	16	17	18	19	20	21	22	23	24	25	26
01.	Level of Education												
1.1	Uneducated	140	70	191	95.5	138	69	108	54	618	61.8	789	78.9
1.2	Primary	36	18	05	2.5	38	19	33	16.5	173	17.3	100	10.0
1.3	Middle	17	8.5	02	1.0	11	5.5	13	6.5	89	8.9	44	4.4
1.4	High school	03	1.5	–	–	04	2.0	05	2.5	34	3.4	13	1.3
1.5	Higher secondary	01	0.5	02	1.0	08	4.0	04	2.0	41	4.1	16	1.6
1.6	Graduate	03	1.5	–	–	01	0.5	–	–	34	3.4	–	–
1.7	Post-graduate	–	–	–	–	–	–	–	–	08	0.8	–	–
1.8	Medical	–	–	–	–	–	–	–	–	01	0.1	–	–
1.9	Engineering	–	–	–	–	–	–	01	0.5	–	–	01	0.1
1.10	Other	–	–	–	–	–	–	36	18	02	0.2	37	3.7
1.11	Total	200	100	200	100	200	100	200	100	1000	100	1000	100

(Table Contd...)

I	II	III	IV	V	VI	VII	VIII	IX	X	XI	XII	XIII	XIV
02	**Type of School**												
2.1	Government	56	28	08	4.0	50	25	48	24	352	35.2	157	15.7
2.2	Private	04	2.0	–	–	02	1.0	06	3.0	18	1.8	10	1.0
2.3	None/NA	140	70	192	96	148	74	108	54	629	62.9	795	79.5
2.4	Study at home	–	–	–	–	–	–	38	19	01	0.1	38	3.8
0.3	**Type of College**												
3.1	Government	–	–	–	–	–	–	01	0.5	38	3.8	01	0.1
3.2	Private	–	–	–	–	–	–	–	–	04	0.4	01	0.1
3.3	None/NA	200	100	200	100	200	100	199	99.5	927	92.7	998	99.8
3.4	Study at home	–	–	–	–	–	–	–	–	31	3.1	–	–

04 Association between urban residence and education and rural residence and illiteracy = + 0.396

Note: NA = No answer.

Source: Based on survey.

Table—17.2 Total Expenditure on Education of Surveyed Scheduled Caste Women in Ujjain Division

S. No.	Expenditure on education	Ujjain district				Dewas district				Shajapur district			
		Urban		Rural		Urban		Rural		Urban		Rural	
		No.	%	No.	%	No.	%	No.	%	No.	%	No.	%
1	2	3	4	5	6	7	8	9	10	11	12	13	14
01.	**Expenditure on school education**												
1.1	Less than 1000	–	–	01	0.5	–	–	–	–	02	1.0	–	–
1.2	1000-2000	–	–	–	–	–	–	–	–	–	–	–	–
1.3	2000-3000	01	0.5	–	–	–	–	–	–	–	–	–	–
1.4	3000-4000	01	0.5	–	–	–	–	–	–	–	–	–	–
1.5	More than 4000	03	1.5	–	–	–	–	–	–	–	–	–	–
1.6	Don't know	84	42	27	13.5	61	30.5	29	14.5	17	8.5	13	6.5
1.7	Not applicable	98	49	170	85.0	139	69.5	120	60	161	80.5	173	86.5
1.8	Nil	13	6.5	02	1.0	–	–	51	25.5	20	10	14	7.0
02.	**Expenditure on college education**												
2.1	Less than 1000	–	–	–	–	–	–	–	–	01	0.5	–	–
2.2	1000-2000	01	0.5	–	–	–	–	–	–	–	–	–	–
2.3	2000-3000	04	2.0	–	–	–	–	–	–	–	–	–	–
2.4	3000-4000	03	1.5	–	–	–	–	–	–	–	–	–	–
2.5	More than 4000	04	2.0	–	–	–	–	–	–	–	–	–	–
2.6	Don't know	41	20.5	–	–	03	1.5	01	0.5	16	8.0	03	1.5
2.7	Not applicable	141	75.5	200	100	196	98.0	149	74.5	163	81.5	184	92
2.8	Nil	06	3.0	–	–	01	0.5	50	25.0	20	10	13	6.5

(Table Contd...)

S. No.	Expenditure on education	Ratlam district				Mandsour district				Total of all			
		Urban		Rural		Urban		Rural		Urban		Rural	
		No.	%	No.	%	No.	%	No.	%	No.	%	No.	%
		15	16	17	18	19	20	21	22	23	24	25	26
01.	Expenditure on school education												
1.1	Less than 1000	–	–	–	–	–	–	02	0.5	02	0.2	03	0.3
1.2	1000-2000	–	–	–	–	–	–	–	–	–	–	–	–
1.3	2000-3000	–	–	–	–	–	–	01	0.5	01	0.1	01	0.1
1.4	3000-4000	–	–	–	–	–	–	–	–	01	0.1	–	–
1.5	More than 4000	02	1.0	–	–	–	–	02	1.0	05	0.5	02	0.2
1.6	Don't know	25	12.5	01	0.5	21	10.5	48	24	208	20.8	118	11.8
1.7	Not applicable	72	36	199	99.5	14	7.0	99	49.5	484	48.4	761	76.1
1.8	Nil	101	50.5	–	–	165	82.5	48	24	299	29.9	115	11.5

(Table Contd...)

I	II	III	IV	V	VI	VII	VIII	IX	X	XI	XII	XIII	XIV
02.	**Expenditure on college education**												
2.1	Less than 1000	–	–	–	–	–	–	01	0.5	01	0.1	01	0.1
2.2	1000-2000	–	–	–	–	–	–	–	–	01	0.1	–	–
2.3	2000-3000	–	–	–	–	–	–	–	–	04	0.4	–	–
2.4	3000-4000	–	–	–	–	–	–	–	–	03	0.5	–	–
2.5	More than 4000	01	0.5	–	–	–	–	–	–	05	0.5	–	–
2.6	Don't know	01	0.5	01	0.5	05	2.5	42	21	66	6.6	47	4.7
2.7	Not applicable	97	48.5	199	99.5	29	14.5	106	53	626	62.6	838	83.8
2.8	Nil	101	50.5	–	–	166	83	51	25.5	292	29.2	114	11.4

03 Correlation between expenditure on school education in rural and urban areas = + 0.62.

04 Correlation between expenditure on college education in rural and urban areas = - 0.56

Note: NA/NA = Not applicable and no answer

Source: Based on survey.

Table—17.3 Opinion Regarding Reservation by Surveyed Scheduled Caste Women in Ujjain Division

S. No.	Opinion on reservation	Ujjain district				Dewas district				Shajapur district			
		Urban		Rural		Urban		Rural		Urban		Rural	
		No.	%	No.	%	No.	%	No.	%	No.	%	No.	%
1	2	3	4	5	6	7	8	9	10	11	12	13	14
01	**Reservation of self in education**												
1.1	Yes	137	66.5	172	86	159	79.5	51	25.5	11	5.5	15	7.5
1.2	No	27	13.5	21	10.5	02	1.0	21	10.5	81	40.5	66	33
1.3	Don't know/NA	36	18.0	27	13.5	39	19.5	148	74.0	108	54.0	139	69.5
02	**Reservation of other in education**												
2.1	Yes	134	67.0	153	76.5	162	81	53	26.5	39	19.5	29	14.5
2.2	No	34	17.0	01	0.5	–	–	–	–	39	19.5	28	14
2.3	Don't know/NA	32	16.0	46	24	38	19.0	147	73.5	122	61.0	143	71.5
03	**Reservation of self in service**												
3.1	Yes	163	81.5	179	89.5	160	80	53	26.5	19	9.5	16	8.0
3.2	No	20	10.0	01	0.5	–	–	–	–	61	30.5	38	19
3.3	Don't know/NA	17	08.5	20	10	40	20.0	147	73.5	120	60.0	146	73.0
04	**Reservation of other in service**												
4.1	Yes	155	77.5	172	86.0	159	79.5	53	26.5	32	16.0	22	11.0
4.2	No	22	11.0	01	0.5	–	–	–	–	46	23.0	26	13
4.3	Don't know/NA	23	11.5	27	13.5	41	20.5	147	73.5	121	61	152	76.0

(Table Contd...)

S. No.	Opinion on reservation	Ratlam district				Mandsour district				Total of all			
		Urban		Rural		Urban		Rural		Urban		Rural	
		No.	%	No.	%	No.	%	No.	%	No.	%	No.	%
		15	16	17	18	19	20	21	22	23	24	25	26
01	Reservation of self education												
1.1	Yes	03	1.5	–	–	–	–	41	20.5	310	31.0	219	21.9
1.2	No	01	05	115	57.5	13	6.5	27	13.5	124	12.4	250	25.0
1.3	Don't know/NA	196	98	85	42.5	187	93.5	132	66.0	566	56.6	531	53.1
02.	Reservation of other in education												
2.1	Yes	03	1.5	96	48	01	0.5	38	19.0	339	33.9	369	36.9
2.2	No	01	0.5	11	5.5	09	4.5	27	13.5	83	8.3	67	6.7
2.3	Don't know/NA	196	98	93	46.5	190	95	135	67.0	578	57.8	564	56.4

(Table Contd...)

I	II	III	IV	V	VI	VII	VIII	XI	X	XI	XII	XIII	XIV
03.	**Reservation of self in service**												
3.1	Yes	02	1.0	–	–	06	3.0	45	22.5	350	35.0	293	29.3
3.2	No	02	1.0	97	48.5	07	3.5	31	15.5	90	9.1	167	16.7
3.3	Don't know/NA	196	98	103	51.5	187	93.5	124	62.0	560	56.0	540	54.0
04	**Reservation of other in service**												
4.1	Yes	03	1.5	96	48	–	–	41	20.5	349	34.9	384	38.4
4.2	No	01	0.5	01	0.5	12	6.0	30	15.0	81	8.1	58	5.8
4.3	Don't know/NA	196	98	103	51.5	188	94.0	129	64.5	570	57.0	558	55.8

05. Association between attitude towards reservation in education for self and others = + 0.65

06. Association between attitude towards reservation in service for self and others = - 0.30

Note: NA/NA = Not applicable and no answer

Source: Based on survey.

Table—17.4 Attitude Towards Education of Surveyed Scheduled Caste Women in Ujjain Division

S. No.	Attitude towards education	Ujjain district				Dewas district				Shajapur district			
		Urban		Rural		Urban		Rural		Urban		Rural	
		No.	%	No.	%	No.	%	No.	%	No.	%	No.	%
1	2	3	4	5	6	7	8	9	10	11	12	13	14
01.	Essentiality of eduation												
1.1	Yes	199	99.5	196	98	198	99.0	199	99.5	199	99.5	187	93.5
1.2	No	–	–	04	2.0	02	1.0	01	0.5	–	–	06	3.0
1.3	Don't know/NA	01	0.5	–	–	–	–	–	–	01	0.5	07	3.5
02	Essentiality of children education												
2.1	Yes	198	99.0	193	96.5	198	99	199	99.5	199	99.5	185	92.5
2.2	No	01	0.5	07	3.5	02	1.0	01	0.5	–	–	08	4.0
2.3	Don't know/NA	01	0.5	–	–	–	–	–	–	01	0.5	07	3.5
03.	Essentiality of children education												
3.1	Yes	197	98.5	149	74.5	184	92	193	96.5	196	98.0	163	81.5
3.2	No	–	–	38	19	10	5.0	06	3.0	03	1.5	29	14.5
3.3	Don't know/NA	03	1.5	13	6.5	06	03	01	0.5	01	0.5	08	4.0

(Table Contd...)

I	II	III	IV	V	VI	VII	VIII	IX	X	XI	XII	XIII	XIV
04.	**Higher education of children**												
4.1	Yes	140	70.0	27	13.5	50	25	110	55	158	79	100	50
4.2	No	58	29	167	83.5	145	72.5	89	44.5	41	20.5	92	46
4.3	Don't know/NA	02	1.0	06	3.0	05	2.5	1.0	0.5	01	0.5	08	4.0
05.	**Attitude towards adult education**												
5.1	Yes	08	4.0	01	0.5	07	3.5	62	31	49	24.5	27	13.5
5.2	No	70	35	179	89.5	114	57	138	69	148	74	164	82
5.3	Don't know/NA	122	61	20	10	79	39.5	–	–	03	1.5	09	4.5
06.	**Liking**												
6.1	For education	31	15.5	41	20.5	05	2.5	07	3.5	14	7.0	05	2.5
6.2	For service	19	9.5	–	–	03	1.5	–	–	35	17.5	21	10.5
6.3	Don't know/NA	150	75	159	79.5	192	96	193	96.5	151	75.5	174	87
07	**Total of attitude**												
7.1	Yes	742	74.2	566	56.6	637	63.7	763	76.3	801	80.1	662	66.2
7.2	No	129	12.9	395	39.5	273	27.3	235	23.5	192	19.2	299	29.9
7.3	NA	129	12.9	39	3.9	90	9.0	02	0.2	07	0.7	39	3.9

(Table Contd…)

S. No.	Attitude towards education	Ratlam district				Mandsour district				Total of all			
		Urban		Rural		Urban		Rural		Urban		Rural	
		No.	%	No.	%	No.	%	No.	%	No.	%	No.	%
		15	16	17	18	19	20	21	22	23	24	25	26
01.	Essentiality of eduation												
1.1	Yes	200	100	193	96.5	197	98.5	187	93.5	993	99.3	962	96.2
1.2	No	–	–	07	3.5	03	1.5	07	3.5	05	0.5	25	2.5
1.3	Don't know/NA	–	–	–	–	–	–	06	03	02	0.2	13	1.3
02	Essentiality of children education												
2.1	Yes	200	100	188	94	200	100	186	93	995	99.5	951	95.1
2.2	No	–	–	12	6.0	–	–	07	3.5	03	0.3	35	3.5
2.3	Don't know/NA	–	–	–	–	–	–	07	3.5	02	2.0	14	1.4
03.	Essentiality of children education												
3.1	Yes	184	93.5	176	88	198	99	183	91.5	962	96.2	864	86.4
3.2	No	09	4.5	24	12	02	1.0	10	5.0	24	2.4	107	10.7
3.3	Don't know/NA	04	2.0	–	–	–	–	07	3.5	14	1.4	29	2.9

(Table Contd...)

I	II	III	IV	V	VI	VII	VIII	IX	X	XI	XII	XIII	XIV
04.	**Higher education of children**												
4.1	Yes	151	75.5	158	79	189	94.5	156	78	688	68.8	551	55.1
4.2	No	45	22.5	42	21	11	5.5	33	16.5	300	30.0	423	42.3
4.3	Don't know/NA	04	2.0	–	–	–	–	11	5.5	12	1.2	26	2.6
05.	**Attitude towards adult education**												
5.1	Yes	63	31.5	141	70.5	68	34	88	44	195	19.5	319	31.9
5.2	No	107	53.5	59	29.5	82	41	102	51	521	52.1	642	64.2
5.3	Don't know/NA	30	15	–	–	50	25	10	5.0	284	28.4	39	3.9
06.	**Liking**												
6.1	For education	02	1.0	–	–	06	3.0	22	11	58	5.8	75	7.5
6.2	For service	–	–	01	0.5	04	2.0	28	14	61	6.1	50	5.0
6.3	Don't know/NA	198	99	199	99.5	190	95	150	75	881	88.1	875	87.5
07	**Total of attitude**												
7.1	Yes	801	80.1	856	85.6	852	85.2	800	80.0	3833	77	3647	73
7.2	No	161	16.1	144	14.4	98	9.8	159	15.9	753	15	1232	25
7.3	NA	38	3.8	–	–	50	5.0	41	4.1	414	8.0	121	2.0

Note: NA/NA = Not applicable and no answer

Source: Based on survey

Table—17.5 Health Condition of the Families of Surveyed Scheduled Caste Women in Ujjain Division

S. No.	Health condition	Ujjain district				Dewas district				Shajapur district			
		Urban		Rural		Urban		Rural		Urban		Rural	
		No.	%	No.	%	No.	%	No.	%	No.	%	No.	%
1	2	3	4	5	6	7	8	9	10	11	12	13	14
01	**Health of self**												
1.1	Good	165	82.5	193	96.5	185	92.5	192	96	177	88.5	156	78
1.2	Medium	33	16.5	06	3.0	13	6.5	07	3.5	12	6.0	18	9.0
1.3	Bad	02	1.0	01	0.5	02	1.0	01	0.5	11	5.5	26	13
02	**Health of Husband**												
2.1	Good	108	54.0	175	87.5	183	91.5	195	97.5	181	90.5	159	79.5
2.2	Medium	14	7.0	08	4.0	03	1.5	01	0.5	07	3.5	26	13
2.3	Bad	03	1.5	01	0.5	–	–	01	0.5	08	4.0	10	5.0
2.4	NA/NA	75	37.5	16	8.0	14	7.0	03	1.5	04	2.0	05	2.5
03	**Health of children**												
3.1	Good	113	56.5	189	94.5	184	92.0	197	98.5	176	88.0	167	83.5
3.2	Medium	10	5.0	02	1.0	02	1.0	–	–	04	2.0	21	10.5
3.3	Bad	01	0.5	02	1.0	01	0.5	–	–	04	2.0	08	4.0
3.4	NA/NA	76	38	07	3.5	14	7.0	03	1.5	16	8.0	04	2.0
04.	**Total health**												
4.1	Good	386	98	557	99	552	99	584	99.7	534	96.0	482	92
4.2	Bad	06	2.0	04	1.0	03	01	02	0.3	23	4.0	44	08
4.3	Total	392	100	561	100	555	100	586	100	557	100	526	100

(Table Contd...)

S. No.	Health condition	Ratlam district				Mandsour district				Total of all			
		Urban		Rural		Urban		Rural		Urban		Rural	
		No.	%	No.	%	No.	%	No.	%	No.	%	No.	%
		15	16	17	18	19	20	21	22	23	24	25	26
01	**Health of self**												
1.1	Good	191	95.5	196	98	182	91	158	79	900	90.0	895	89.5
1.2	Medium	06	3.0	04	2.0	17	8.5	35	17.5	81	8.1	70	7.0
1.3	Bad	03	1.5	–	–	01	0.5	07	3.5	19	1.9	35	3.5
02	**Health of Husband**												
2.1	Good	186	93	176	88	191	95.5	162	81	849	84.9	867	86.7
2.2	Medium	–	–	02	1.0	07	3.5	29	14.5	31	3.1	66	6.6
2.3	Bad	07	3.5	03	1.5	–	–	04	2.0	18	1.8	19	1.9
2.4	NA/NA	07	3.5	19	9.5	02	1.0	05	2.5	102	10.2	48	4.8
03	**Health of children**												
3.1	Good	195	97.5	195	97.5	197	97.5	156	78	865	86.5	904	90.4
3.2	Medium	–	–	03	1.5	01	0.5	22	11.0	17	1.7	48	4.8
3.3	Bad	01	0.5	–	–	–	–	08	4.0	07	0.7	18	1.8
3.4	NA/NA	04	2.0	02	1.0	02	1.0	14	7.0	110	11.0	29	2.9

(Table Contd...)

I	II	III	IV	V	VI	VII	VIII	IX	X	XI	XII	XIII	XIV
04.	**Total health**												
4.1	Good	572	98	567	99	570	99.8	476	96	2614	98	2666	97
4.2	Bad	11	02	03	01	01	0.2	19	4.0	44	2.0	72	3.0
4.3	Total	583	100	570	100	571	100	495	100	2658	100	2738	100

05. Association between good health of children and urban residence = + 0.45

06. Association between good health of self and urban residence = + 0.02

07. Association between good health of husband and urban residence = + 0.26

Note: NA/NA = Not applicable and no answer

Source: Based on survey.

Table—17.6 Prevalent Diseases in the Families of and Type of Treatment Taken by Surveyed Scheduled Caste Women in Ujjain Division

S. No.	Name of disease & type of treatment	Ujjain district				Dewas district				Shajapur district			
		Urban		Rural		Urban		Rural		Urban		Rural	
		No.	%	No.	%	No.	%	No.	%	No.	%	No.	%
1	2	3	4	5	6	7	8	9	10	1	12	13	14
01.	Name of diseases												
1.1	Headache	–	–	–	–	–	–	–	–	01	0.5	–	–
1.2	Paralysis	–	–	–	–	–	–	–	–	01	0.5	–	–
1.3	Blood Pressure	08	4.0	–	–	–	–	–	–	–	–	–	–
1.4	Leprosy	–	–	–	–	–	–	01	0.5	–	–	–	–
1.5	Appendix	–	–	–	–	–	–	–	–	–	–	–	–
1.6	Axema	–	–	–	–	–	–	–	–	35	17.5	–	–
1.7	Other	108	54.0	25	12.5	22	11	24	12	03	1.5	09	4.5
1.8	Total of diseases	116	58.0	25	12.5	22	11	25	12.5	40	20	09	4.5
1.9	NA/NA	84	42.0	175	87.5	178	89	175	87.5	160	80	191	95.5
1.10	Total	200	100	200	100	200	100	200	100	200	100	200	100

(Table Contd...)

I	II	III	IV	V	VI	VII	VIII	IX	X	XI	XII	XIII	XIV
02	**Type of treatment**												
2.1	Ayurvedic	11	5.5	–	–	–	–	–	–	–	–	06	3.0
2.2	Homoeopathic	05	2.5	–	–	–	–	–	–	–	–	01	0.5
2.3	Allopathic	176	88.0	200	100	200	100	200	100	167	83.5	176	88
2.4	Unani	06	3.0	–	–	–	–	–	–	–	–	01	0.5
2.5	Indegenious	–	–	–	–	–	–	–	–	–	–	05	2.5
2.6	Others	02	1.0	–	–	–	–	–	–	33	16.5	11	5.5
2.7	Total	200	100	200	100	200	100	200	100	200	100	200	100

(Table Contd…)

S. No.	Name of disease & type of treatment	Ratlam district				Mandsour district				Total of all			
		Urban		Rural		Urban		Rural		Urban		Rural	
		No.	%	No.	%	No.	%	No.	%	No.	%	No.	%
		15	16	17	18	19	20	21	22	23	24	25	26
01.	Name of diseases												
1.1	Headache	–	–	–	–	02	1.0	01	0.5	03	0.3	01	0.1
1.2	Paralysis	01	0.5	–	–	01	0.5	–	–	03	0.3	–	–
1.3	Blood Pressure	01	0.5	–	–	–	–	–	–	09	0.9	–	–
1.4	Leprosy	–	–	–	–	–	–	–	–	–	–	01	0.1
1.5	Appendix	–	–	–	–	–	–	–	–	–	–	–	–
1.6	Axema	–	–	–	–	–	–	–	–	35	3.5	–	–
1.7	Other	02	1.0	–	–	01	0.5	01	0.5	136	13.6	59	59.0
1.8	Total of diseases	04	2.0	–	–	04	2.0	02	1.0	186	18.6	61	6.1
1.9	NA/NA	196	98	200	100	196	98	198	99	814	81.4	939	93.9
1.10	Total	200	100	200	100	200	100	200	100	1000	100	1000	100

(Table Contd...)

I	II	III	IV	V	VI	VII	VIII	IX	X	XI	XII	XIII	XIV
02	Type of treatment												
2.1	Ayurvedic	01	0.5	–	–	–	–	19	9.5	12	1.2	25	2.5
2.2	Homoeopathic	–	–	–	–	–	–	25	12.5	05	0.5	26	2.6
2.3	Allopathic	113	56.5	193	96.5	199	99.5	108	54	855	85.5	877	87.7
2.4	Unani	01	0.5	–	–	–	–	–	–	07	0.7	01	0.1
2.5	Indegenious	85	42.5	07	3.5	–	–	18	9.0	85	8.5	30	3.0
2.6	Others	–	–	–	–	01	0.5	30	15.0	36	3.6	41	4.1
2.7	Total	200	100	200	100	200	100	200	100	1000	100	1000	100

03. Correlation between diseases and rural—urban residence = + 0.76

04. Correlation between urban residence and allopathic treatment and rural residence and other treatments = - 0.094

Note: NA/NA = Not applicable and no answer

Source: Based on survey.

Table—17.7 Treatment Awareness and Use of Treatment by Surveyed Scheduled Caste Women in Ujjain Division

S. No.	Treatment Awareness and use of treatment	Ujjain district				Dewas district				Shajapur district			
		Urban		Rural		Urban		Rural		Urban		Rural	
		No.	%	No.	%	No.	%	No.	%	No.	%	No.	%
1	2	3	4	5	6	7	8	9	10	11	12	13	14
01.	**Per month visit to doctor/hosp.**												
1.1	Less than 5	196	98	149	74.5	86	43	98	49	125	62.5	103	51.5
1.2	5 to 10	02	1.0	–	–	–	–	–	–	21	10.5	46	23
1.3	10 to 15	01	2.5	–	–	–	–	01	0.5	02	1.0	01	0.5
1.4	More than 15	–	–	–	–	–	–	01	0.5	–	–	–	–
1.5	NA/NA	01	0.5	51	25.5	114	57	100	50	52	26	50	25
02.	**Average monthly expenditure on treatment**												
2.1	Less than Rs. 100	45	22.5	05	2.5	02	1.0	03	1.5	–	–	06	3.0
2.2	Rs. 100 to 200	49	24.5	85	42.5	60	30	26	13	3.0	1.5	14	7.0
2.3	Rs. 200 to 300	38	19.0	25	12.5	10	5.0	02	1.0	06	03	12	6.0
2.4	More than Rs. 300	14	7.0	11	5.5	02	1.0	–	–	09	4.5	01	1.0
2.5	Don't know	54	27	74	37	126	63	169	84.5	182	91	166	83

(Table Contd...)

I	II	III	IV	V	VI	VII	VIII	IX	X	XI	XII	XIII	XIV
03.	**First Aid at Home**												
3.1	Available	28	14.0	01	0.5	04	2.0	08	4.0	46	23	12	6.0
3.2	Not available	172	86	199	99.5	196	98	192	96	154	77	188	94
04.	**First aid in office**												
4.1	Available	17	8.5	02	1.0	01	0.5	52	26	72	36	14	7.0
4.2	Not available/NA	183	91.5	198	99	199	99.5	148	74	128	64	186	93
05.	**Immunisation of children**												
5.1	Yes	119	59.5	190	95	187	93.5	196	98	191	95.5	181	90.5
5.2	No	04	2.0	06	3.0	02	1.0	–	–	04	2.0	13	6.5
5.3	NA/NA	77	38.5	04	2.0	11	5.5	04	2.0	05	2.5	06	3.0
06.	**Immunisation in pregnancy**												
6.1	Yes	100	50.0	191	95.5	175	87.5	196	98	191	95.5	178	89
6.2	No	23	11.5	06	3.0	14	7.0	–	–	05	2.5	16	8.0
6.3	NA/NA	77	38.5	04	2.0	11	5.5	04	2.0	04	2.0	06	3.0
07.	**Total immunisation**	219	89.0	381	97	362	96	392	100	382	98.0	359	93
7.1	Total No. immunisation	27	11.0	12	3.0	16	4.0	–	–	09	2.0	29	7.0
	Total	246	100	393	100	378	100	392	100	391	100	388	100

(Table Contd…)

S. No.	Treatment Awareness and use of treatment	Ratlam district				Mandsour district				Total of all			
		Urban		Rural		Urban		Rural		Urban		Rural	
		No.	%	No.	%	No.	%	No.	%	No.	%	No.	%
		15	16	17	18	19	20	21	22	23	24	25	26
01.	**Per month visit to doctor/hosp.**												
1.1	Less than 5	87	43.5	50	25	44	22	54	27	538	53.8	454	45.4
1.2	5 to 10	–	–	–	–	08	4.0	–	–	31	3.1	46	4.6
1.3	10 to 15	–	–	–	–	03	1.5	–	–	06	0.6	02	0.2
1.4	More than 15	–	–	–	–	–	–	–	–	–	–	01	0.1
1.5	NA/NA	113	56.5	150	75	145	72.5	146	73	425	42.5	497	49.7
02.	**Average monthly expenditure on treatment**												
2.1	Less than Rs. 100	01	0.5	–	–	02	1.0	–	–	50	5.0	14	1.4
2.2	Rs. 100 to 200	17	8.5	–	–	08	4.0	–	–	137	13.7	125	12.5
2.3	Rs. 200 to 300	19	9.5	–	–	02	1.0	–	–	75	7.5	39	3.9
2.4	More than Rs. 300	04	2.0	04	2.0	04	2.0	01	0.5	33	3.3	18	1.8
2.5	Don't know	159	79.5	196	98	184	92	199	99.5	703	70.3	804	80.4

(Table Contd…)

I	II	III	IV	V	VI	VII	VIII	IX	X	XI	XII	XIII	XIV
03.	**First Aid at Home**												
3.1	Available	04	2.0	–	–	33	16.5	31	15.5	115	11.5	52	5.2
3.2	Not available	196	98	200	100	167	83.5	169	84.5	885	88.5	948	94.8
04.	First aid in office												
4.1	Available	41	20.5	35	17.5	75	37.5	38	19	206	20.6	141	14.1
4.2	Not available/NA	159	79.5	165	82.5	125	62.5	162	81	794	79.4	859	85.9
05.	**Immunisation of children**												
5.1	Yes	195	97.5	194	97.0	197	98.5	158	79.0	889	88.9	919	91.9
5.2	No	–	–	02	1.0	–	–	24	12	10	1.0	45	4.5
5.3	NA/NA	05	2.5	04	2.0	03	1.5	18	9.0	101	10.1	36	3.6
06.	**Immunisation in pregnancy**												
6.1	Yes	195	97.5	193	96.5	197	98.5	145	72.5	858	85.8	903	90.3
6.2	No	–	–	03	1.5	–	–	34	17	42	4.2	59	5.9
6.3	NA/NA	05	2.5	04	2.0	03	1.5	21	10.5	100	10.0	39	3.9
07.	**Total immunisation**	390	100	387	99	394	100	303	84	1747	97	1822	97
7.1	Total No. immunisation	–	–	05	1.0	–	–	58	16	52	3.0	58	3.0
	Total	390	100	392	100	394	100	361	100	1799	100	1880	100

8. Association between immunisation and urban residence, no immunisation and rural residence = 0.

Note: NA/NA = Not applicable and no answer

Source: Based on survey.

Table—17.8 Health Awareness and Use of Rest and Nutrition by Surveyed Scheduled Caste Women in Ujjain Division

S. No.	Awareness facilities and their use	Ujjain district				Dewas district				Shajapur district			
		Urban		Rural		Urban		Rural		Urban		Rural	
		No	%	No	%	No	%	No	%	No	%	No	%
1	2	3	4	5	6	7	8	9	10	11	12	13	14
01.	**Domestic work during sickness**												
1.1	Self	71	35.5	109	54.5	99	49.5	123	61.5	109	54.5	64	32
1.2	Husband	25	12.5	21	10.5	12	6.0	19	9.5	37	18.5	32	16
1.3	Neighbour	02	1.0	–	–	–	–	–	–	02	1.0	09	4.5
1.4	Children	36	18	33	16.5	12	6.0	42	21	47	23.5	55	27.5
1.5	Relatives	66	33	37	18.0	77	38.5	16	8.0	05	2.5	40	20
02.	**Leave during sickness**												
2.1	Yes	34	17.0	–	–	01	0.5	–	–	07	3.5	01	0.5
2.2	No	25	12.5	149	74.5	136	68	66	33	153	76.5	190	95
2.3	No answer	141	70.5	51	25.5	64	32	134	67	40	20	90	45

(Table Contd...)

I	II	III	IV	V	VI	VII	VIII	IX	X	XI	XII	XIII	XIV
03	**Regular vegetable consumption**												
3.1	Yes	155	77.5	136	68	148	74	119	59.5	68	34	04	2.0
3.2	No	16	8.0	53	26.5	12	6.0	05	2.5	08	4.0	03	1.5
3.3	Sometimes	29	14.5	11	5.5	44	22	76	38	124	62	193	96.5
04.	**Regular fruit consumption**												
4.1	Yes	36	18	07	3.5	09	4.5	09	4.5	45	22.5	–	–
4.2	No	89	44.5	181	90.5	134	67	103	51.5	53	26.5	91	45.5
4.3	Sometimes	75	37.5	12	6.0	57	28.5	88	44	102	51	109	54.5
05.	**Regular milk consumption**												
5.1	Yes	73	36.5	43	21.5	31	15.5	61	30.5	26	13	55	27.5
5.2	No	63	31.5	144	72	121	60.5	99	49.5	121	60.5	128	64
5.3	Sometimes	64	32.0	13	6.5	48	24	40	20	53	26.5	17	8.5
06.	**Sufficient food consumption**												
6.1	Yes	163	81.5	176	88	159	79.5	186	93	186	93	195	97.5
6.2	No	06	3.0	12	6.0	02	1.0	–	–	10	5.0	01	0.5
6.3	Sometimes	31	15.5	12	6.0	39	19.5	14	7.0	04	02	04	02
07.	**Total**	597	100	752	100	616	100	582	100	517	100	477	100
7.1	Total good nutrition	423	71.0	362	48	347	56	375	64	325	63	254	53
7.2	Total bad nutrition	174	29.0	390	52	269	44	207	36	192	37	223	47

(Table Contd...)

S. No.	Awareness facilities and their use	Ratlam district				Mandsour district				Total of all			
		Urban		Rural		Urban		Rural		Urban		Rural	
		No	%	No	%	No	%	No	%	No	%	No	%
		15	16	17	18	19	20	21	22	23	24	25	26
01.	**Domestic work during sickness**												
1.1	Self	83	41.5	110	55	145	72.5	152	76	507	50.7	558	55.8
1.2	Husband	25	12.5	12	6.0	21	10.5	29	14.5	120	12.0	113	11.3
1.3	Neighbour	01	0.5	-	-	-	-	08	4.0	05	0.5	17	1.7
1.4	Children	17	8.5	19	9.5	-	-	01	0.5	112	11.2	150	15.0
1.5	Relatives	74	37	59	29.5	34	17	10	5.0	256	25.6	162	16.2
02.	**Leave during sickness**												
2.1	Yes	-	-	-	-	-	-	24	12	42	4.2	25	2.5
2.2	No	89	44.5	200	100	150	75	132	66	553	55.3	737	73.7
2.3	No answer	111	55.5	-	-	50	25	44	22	406	40.6	319	31.9
03	**Regular vegetable consumption**												
3.1	Yes	99	49.5	96	48	121	60.5	65	32.5	591	59.1	420	42.0
3.2	No	-	-	-	-	03	1.5	27	13.5	39	3.9	88	8.8
3.3	Sometimes	101	50.5	104	52	76	38	108	54	374	37.4	492	49.2

(Table Contd...)

I	II	III	IV	V	VI	VII	VIII	IX	X	XI	XII	XIII	XIV
04.	**Regular fruit consumption**												
4.1	Yes	32	16	–	–	11	5.5	35	17.5	133	13.3	51	5.1
4.2	No	63	31.5	93	46.5	57	28.5	51	25.5	396	39.6	519	51.9
4.3	Sometimes	105	52.5	107	53.5	132	66	114	57	471	47.1	430	43.0
05.	**Regular milk consumption**												
5.1	Yes	49	24.5	–	–	64	32	30	15	243	24.3	189	18.9
5.2	No	107	53.5	125	62.5	105	52.5	83	41.5	517	51.7	579	57.9
5.3	Sometimes	44	22	75	37.5	31	15.5	87	43.5	240	24.0	232	23.2
06.	**Sufficient food consumption**												
6.1	Yes	196	98	198	99	195	97.5	140	70	899	89.9	895	89.5
6.2	No	03	1.5	01	0.5	03	1.5	18	9.0	24	2.4	32	3.2
6.3	Sometimes	01	0.5	01	05	02	01	42	21	77	7.7	73	7.3
07.	**Total**	549	100	513	100	559	100	449	100	2838	100	2773	100
7.1	Total good nutrition	376	68	294	57	391	70	270	60	1862	66	1555	56
7.2	Total bad nutrition	173	32	219	43	168	30	179	40	976	34	1218	44

8. Association between urban residence and good nutrition, and rural residence and bad nutrition = + 0.21

Source: Based on survey.

Table—17.9 Housing Condition of Surveyed Scheduled Caste Women in Ujjain Division

S. No.	Housing condition	Ujjain district				Dewas district				Shajapur district			
		Urban		Rural		Urban		Rural		Urban		Rural	
		No.	%	No.	%	No.	%	No.	%	No.	%	No.	%
1	2	3	4	5	6	7	8	9	10	11	12	13	14
01.	**Type of ownership**												
1.1	Self	157	78.5	196	98	189	94.5	193	96.5	183	91.5	197	98.5
1.2	Rented	41	20.0	03	1.5	11	5.5	07	3.5	16	8.0	–	–
1.3	Free	02	1.0	01	0.5	–	–	–	–	01	0.5	03	1.5
02.	**Type of house**												
2.1	Kachha	60	30	159	79.5	134	67	144	72	71	35.5	192	96
2.2	Pakka	136	68	41	20.5	66	33	50	25	95	47.5	03	1.5
2.3	Tin shed, other	04	2.0	–	–	–	–	06	3.0	34	17	05	2.5
03.	**Number of rooms**												
3.1	One or nil	16	8.0	29	14.5	44	22	92	46	34	17	61	30.5
3.2	Two	95	47.5	110	55	120	60	78	39	94	47	56	28
3.3	Three	49	24.5	48	24	20	10	30	15	18	9.0	44	22
3.4	Above three	40	20	13	6.5	16	3.0	–	–	43	21.5	39	19.5

(Table Contd…)

I	II	III	IV	V	VI	VII	VIII	IX	X	XI	XII	XIII	XIV
04.	**Rent**												
4.1	0 to 200	171	85.5	199	99.5	193	96.5	193	96.5	191	95.5	200	100
4.2	200 to 400	01	0.5	01	0.5	06	3.0	06	3.0	06	3.0	–	–
4.3	400 to 600	10	5.0	–	–	01	0.5	01	0.5	03	1.5	–	–
4.4	600 to 800	10	5.0	–	–	–	–	–	–	–	–	–	–
4.5	800 to 1000	03	1.5	–	–	–	–	–	–	–	–	–	–
4.6	More than 1000	05	2.5	–	–	–	–	–	–	–	–	–	–
05.	**Facilities**												
5.1	Electricity	195	97.5	196	98.0	151	75.5	172	86	179	89.5	181	90.5
5.2	Water	180	90.0	14	7.0	85	42.5	113	56.5	157	78.5	15	7.5
5.3	Fan	180	90.0	23	11.5	106	53	129	64.5	154	77.0	44	22
5.4	Bathroom	169	84.5	20	10.0	46	23	121	60.5	118	59.0	–	–
5.5	Toilet	168	84.0	17	8.5	48	24	47	23.5	94	47	01	0.5
5.6	Garden	14	7.0	–	–	04	2.0	14	7.0	13	6.5	–	–
5.7	Others	04	2.0	–	–	–	–	–	–	04	2.0	12	6.0
06.	**Amplicity of space**												
6.1	Yes	137	68.5	158	79	111	55.5	87	43.5	93	46.5	88	44.0
6.2	No	63	31.5	42	21	89	44.5	113	56.5	107	53.5	112	56

(Table Contd...)

I	II	III	IV	V	VI	VII	VIII	IX	X	XI	XII	XIII	XIV
07.	**Whether Airy**												
7.1	Yes	161	80.5	146	73	101	50.5	95	47.5	193	96.5	169	84.5
7.2	No	39	19.5	54	27	99	49.5	105	52.5	07	3.5	31	15.5
08.	**Whether sunlight**												
8.1	Yes	136	68	150	75	108	54	105	52.5	108	54	189	94.5
8.2	No	64	32	50	25	92	46	95	47.5	92	46	11	5.5
09.	**Play ground**												
9.1	Yes	98	49	85	42.5	71	35.5	99	49.5	191	95.5	179	89.5
9.2	No	102	51	115	57.5	129	64.5	101	50.5	09	4.5	21	10.5
10.	**Other facilities**												
10.1	School	179	89.5	185	92.5	157	78.5	131	65.5	121	60.5	106	53
10.2	Hospital	172	86.0	184	92.0	136	68.0	34	17	120	60.0	52	26
10.3	Market	171	85.5	181	90.5	159	79.5	75	37.5	119	59.5	46	24
10.4	Street	120	60.0	18	9.0	63	31.5	73	36.5	114	57	60	30
10.5	Others	02	1.0	–	–	18	9.0	52	26	26	13	90	45

(Table Contd...)

S. No.	Housing condition	Ratlam district				Mandsour district				Total of all			
		Urban		Rural		Urban		Rural		Urban		Rural	
		No.	%	No.	%	No.	%	No.	%	No.	%	No.	%
		15	16	17	18	19	20	21	22	23	24	25	26
01.	**Type of ownership**												
1.1	Self	183	91.5	198	99	158	79	181	90.5	870	87.0	965	96.5
1.2	Rented	15	7.5	02	1.0	42	21	14	7.0	125	12.5	26	2.6
1.3	Free	02	1.0	–	–	–	–	05	2.5	05	0.5	09	0.9
02.	**Type of house**												
2.1	Kachha	135	67.5	183	91.5	152	76	158	79	552	55.2	836	83.6
2.2	Pakka	65	32.5	17	8.5	48	24	34	17	410	41.0	145	14.5
2.3	Tin, Shed, Other	–	–	–	–	–	–	08	4.0	38	3.8	19	1.9
03.	**Number of rooms**												
3.1	One or nil	28	14	22	11	48	24	77	38.5	170	17.0	281	28.1
3.2	Two	108	54	129	64.5	99	49.5	65	32.5	516	51.6	438	43.8
3.3	Three	33	16.5	39	19.5	38	19	25	12.5	158	15.8	186	18.6
3.4	Above three	31	15.5	10	5.0	15	7.5	23	11.5	145	14.5	85	8.5

(Table Contd...)

I	II	III	IV	V	VI	VII	VIII	IX	X	XI	XII	XIII	IV
04.	**Rent**												
4.1	0 to 200	193	96.5	200	100	178	89	196	98	926	92.6	988	98.8
4.2	200 to 400	06	3.0	–	–	21	10.5	03	1.5	40	4.0	10	1.0
4.3	400 to 600	–	–	–	–	–	–	01	0.5	14	1.4	02	0.2
4.4	600 to 800	01	0.5	–	–	01	0.5	–	–	12	1.2	–	–
4.5	800 to 1000	–	–	–	–	–	–	–	–	03	0.3	–	–
4.6	More than 1000	–	–	–	–	–	–	–	–	05	0.5	–	–
05.	**Facilities**												
5.1	Electricity	195	97.5	194	97	200	100	143	71.5	920	92.0	886	88.6
5.2	Water	174	87	72	36	199	99.5	72	36	795	79.5	286	28.6
5.3	Fan	153	76.5	57	28.5	162	81	60	30	755	75.5	313	31.3
5.4	Bathroom	110	55	08	4.0	119	59.5	17	8.5	562	56.2	166	16.6
5.5	Toilet	114	57	32	16	84	42	15	7.5	508	50.8	112	11.2
5.6	Garden	06	3.0	–	–	11	5.5	04	2.0	48	4.8	18	1.8
5.7	Others	01	0.5	–	–	03	1.5	14	7.0	12	1.2	26	2.6
06.	**Amplicity of space**												
6.1	Yes	107	53.5	47	23.5	161	80.5	87	43.5	609	60.9	467	46.7
6.2	No	93	46.5	153	76.5	39	19.5	113	56.5	391	39.1	533	53.3

(Table Contd...)

I	II	III	IV	V	VI	VII	VIII	IX	X	XI	XII	XIII	XIV
07.	**Whether Airy**												
7.1	Yes	150	75	196	98.0	197	98.5	136	68	802	80.2	742	74.2
7.2	No	50	25	04	2.0	03	1.5	64	32	198	19.8	258	25.8
08.	**Whether sunlight**												
8.1	Yes	152	76	197	98.5	200	100	153	76.5	704	70.4	794	79.4
8.2	No	48	24	03	1.5	–	–	47	23.5	296	29.6	206	20.6
09.	**Play ground**												
9.1	Yes	152	76	142	71	175	87.5	17	8.5	687	68.7	522	52.2
9.2	No	48	24	58	29	25	12.5	183	91.5	313	31.3	478	47.8
10.	**Other facilities**												
10.1	School	198	99	188	94	200	100	132	66	855	85.5	742	74.2
10.2	Hospital	197	98.5	71	35.5	198	99	92	46	823	82.3	433	43.3
10.3	Market	197	98.5	64	32	196	98	89	44.5	842	84.2	455	45.5
10.4	Street	193	96.5	106	53	189	94.5	91	45.5	679	67.9	348	34.8
10.5	Others	01	0.5	03	1.5	13	6.5	11	5.5	60	6.0	156	15.6

NA/NA = No answer and not applicable.

Source: Based on survey.

18

Strategies for Empowerment of Women in India

A Review

**Dr. K. Chandra Kumar*

Poverty and chronic deprivation of certain sections have long been a tragic aspect of human society. Globally 1.5 billion people live in extreme poverty. Roughly more than two thirds of them are in Asia and more particularly in South Asia alone. Three quarters of these poor live and work in rural areas, while more than half of them are expected to do so by 2025. Seventy per cent of the Dollar—poor work and live in rural areas. Recent projections suggest that over 60 per cent of the population will continue to so even by 2025. Most of them in this category are women and they are considered on per with other sex. In India in spite of several welfare programmes and poverty alleviation programmes which have been implemented even since the launching of development planning in 1950s, even the trickle down effect is not visible among the

* Professor, Dept. of Political Science & Public Administration, Acharya Nagarjuna University, Nagarjuna Nagar.

women particularly rural women. Gender related human development index lags behind the general human development index. Gender discrimination and gender gaps and ubiquitous.

Most of the rural women participate in various economic activities but this fact does not find place in the Indian Census Reports. Rural women participate in agricultural activities like sowing, weeding, transplantation, manuring, harvesting, winnowing, shelling, shelling and storing of crops. According to official statistics out of the total work force of 374.39 million in the country in 1993-94, 121.63 million (32.5%) are women. The rural work force has increased by more than 50 per cent during the last two decades from 69.2 million in 1972-73 to 104.29 million in 993-94, while the rural female population has increased at a much lower rate by 43 per cent during the period. The same is reflected in the work participation rate also. Absolute Poverty—and economic compulsions have forced, women particularly belonging to Scheduled Caste, Scheduled Tribe, other backward classes and economically weaker sections of the rural society to take up unskilled and menial works requiring more labour hours for which they earn a petty sum.

The Indian National Commission on Self-employment (1987) in its report envisaged that in wage employment, more than half of the rural women labour receives wages below the subsistence level. It further reveals that the jobs in which they are usually appointed generally irregular, uncertain, seasonal and discretionary and characterised by malpractices in payment, non-payment of wages on times, signature on inflated amount and exertion of commission on payment. In 1991 the World Bank remarked that participation in such activities is not increased women control over family resources. An attempt is made in this chapter to review the shifts in the approach women welfare in India during the last five decades of Indian economic planning.

Government Policies Towards Women Welfare After Independence

More than 30 programmes for rural development have been implemented for the alleviation of poverty and well being of rural poor. When India adopted planned strategy for future development it was already understood that the upliftment of women was an equally important factor in the nations development. The principle of welfare was the earliest policy approach towards the women.

When India adopted planned development as the strategy for its future development, it was clearly understood that the upliftment of women was an equally important factor for the nation development. The principle of welfare was the earliest policy approach towards women, which is still the most prevalent in all the welfare policies of the Government. The First-Five-Year Plan (1951-56) envisaged various welfare schemes for women. It planned for the development of maternal and child health and family planning services. In 1953, the Central Social Welfare Board (C.S.W.B.) was set up to chalk out various welfare programmes for the development of women. It symbolised the approach of the Government towards the welfare of women. The community development programmes (1952), for the first time, emphasised the need for mobilisation of women through Mahila Mandals or Women's clubs. In 1956, the CSWB started a scheme of Condensed courses of Education for adult Women and a scheme for Socio-Economic Programmes for Women. The Second Five-Year Plan (1956-61) while emphasing the overall development of rural women it mainly focused on the protection of women against various types of atrocities. It also stressed that women should be provided maternity benefits and creates for their children. It also suggested speedy implementation of the principle of equal pay for equal work and provision be set up, for training women to enable them to compete even for higher level jobs. The Maternity Benefits Act, 1961 was enacted at the end of this plan. The Third Five-Year Plan (1961-66) pinpointed the female education as a major welfare strategy. In social welfare, largest share was provided for expanding rural welfare services and condensed courses of education. The Fourth Five-Year Plan (1969-74) continued the emphasis on women's education. It gave high priority to the immunisation of pre-school children and provision of supplementary feeding for children, expectant and nursing mothers. In 1972, the central scheme of Assistance for Construction of Hostel Buildings for Working Women was introduced by the Central Government. The scope of the scheme was widened in 1980 by including a provision for day care centres for children.

It was in the early 1970s that Crash Schemes for rural Employment, Food for Women Programme, Drought Prone Area Programme, and Desert Development Programme, were initiated, aiming at strengthening the rural base of the economy. Though these schemes seemed to be gender neutral, they were male biased. They were targeted at men at the head/earners of the families, with the assumption that benefits to men will trickle down to the rest of the family members. The Fifth Five-Year Plan (1974-79) continued the emphasis, the need to train women who in need of income and protection. A major thrust at the beginning of 70s was women's employment and this was seen as the "critical entry point" for women's integration into the process of the nation development. The International Women's Decade (1975-85) in India, however, witnessed unprecedented efforts, various agencies to reassess the role of women, to enlarge the information base, to search for alternative strategies for women's equality and development and to develop policies and programmes addressed to women's specific needs and problems. The Fifth Plan (1974-79) showed a shift from welfare to development. It emphasised the need to train women whom in need of women and protection. In 1975, the CSWB started the Scheme of Assistance to Voluntary Organisation for Creches for Working and Ailing Women's Children and the Scheme for Vocational Training and Adult Women. The Ministry of Social Welfare started a massive scheme, called as the of Functional Literacy for Adult Women in the same year and a Scheme for setting up women's training centres for rehabilitation of women in distress in 1977-78. In 1976, Welfare and Development Bureau was set up in the Ministry of Social Welfare. In the same year, the equal Remuneration Act was enacted.

The various development schemes launched parallel to the welfare schemes were again gender neutral. Initiating the Integrated Rural Development Programme (IRDP), the Government launched a direct attack on the poverty in 1978-79. Credit from banking institutions and subsidy from the government were given to rural families below the poverty line for self-employment and income generation. Under the IRDP, a special place was accorded for Training Rural Unemployment Youth for Self-Employment (TRYSEM). Further the National Rural

Employment Programme (NREP) was introduced in 1980 and also the Rural Landless Employment Guarantee Programme (RLEGP) in 1983. But in all these employment programmes rural women were only marginally helped, as they were mainly targeted for men.

The National Plan of Action (NPA) was an immediate consequence of the CSWB Report. It identified the areas of health, family planning, nutrition, education, employment, legislation and social welfare for the formulation and implementation of action programme for women and called for planned intervention to improve the conditions of women. The National Machinery for Women was set up in 1975 consisted of: (a) a national committee; (b) a steering committee of the national committee; (c) an inter-dependent coordination committee; and (d) a women's welfare and development bureau.

The programmes the sixties and the seventies made no discrimination among the urban and rural women, among the rich, and also among the not so poor and extremely poor. As a result, most of the benefits of all these schemes were cornered for the urban middle class women. In the late 70s, it was realised that the improvement in the conditions of women remains confined to the urban and economically affluent families. In the rural areas there was minimum impact of various schemes, and women belonging to socially backward and poor classes were further relegated to the background.

Right from the beginning of 1980s, there has been a change in the administrative framework for planning and monitoring of women-based programmes implemented by the Central Government. In 1985, the Department of Women and Child Development was set up based on the appreciation of women's productive role in the development process rather than as mere beneficiaries of various Government's programmes. In the Sixth Five-Year Plan, a shifter was made from welfare to development approach in the case of women. The Plan recognised the inaccessibility of women to resources as a critical factor impeding their development. Hence it adopted a three-pronged thrust on the wealth, education and employment of women in accordance with the sub-themes of the International Decade for Women. This approach led to the initiation of several schemes for women beneficiaries, such as the Employment and Income Generating Training-cum Production Centres for Women and Non-formal Education for Girls. As the coverage of Women in the main Anti-poverty Programme of IRDP was very poor, a sub-scheme was launched in IRDP called 'Development of Women and Children in Rural Areas' (DWCRA), 1982, in 1985, a separate Department in India. This Department now funds the CSWB that sponsors welfare and developmental schemes for women.

The Seventh Five-Year Plan (1985-90) operationalised the concern for equity and employment for women as articulated by the international Decade for Women. For the first time, the emphasis was focused on including confidence among women; generating awareness about their rights and privileges and providing them training in various economic activities and employment. The National Policy on Education, 1986 truly began the women's empowerment phase in India. In the subsequent years access of women to critical inputs and productive resources such as land was expanded to include support through credit, marketing, training in skills/management and technology. Directions were given priority to women headed households and enhance the share of women in the fruits of development process under the anti-poverty programmes of IRDP, TRYSEM, NREP and RLEGP. In 1982, the National Commission for women was set up as a national apex level statutory body to review the constitutional and legal safeguard for women. It recommended several remedial legislative measures, facilitate redressal of grievances and advice the Government on all policy matters affecting women.

The Eighth Plan (1992-97) shifted the focus from development to empowerment. In 1990, the National Commission for Women Act was enacted. In 1991, a National Plan of Action for SAARC Decade for the Girl Child (1991-2000) was formulated by the development of women and Children. In 1996, the Draft of the National Policy for the Empowerment of Women was finalised. The Ninth Five-Year Plan, (1997-2002) has its objectives evolved from the Common Minimum Programme (CMP) of the Government and the Chief Minister's Conference and basic minimum services. Based on the objectives of this programme emphasis has been laid on the empowerment of women and socially disadvantaged groups like the Scheduled Castes, Scheduled Tribes, Backward Class and Minorities.

The Ninth Five-Year Plan attempted to consolidate the women empowerment strategic adopted by the earlier plans through creating a enabling environment which provide the women ample opportunities to realise their potential through exercising their rights as equal partners with men. The Ninth Plan adopted specific strategies for empowering women to play their role as the agents of socio-economic development. These strategies include:

(i) to create an enabling environment to exercise their rights equally with men;

(ii) to provide reservation for women to the extent of 33 per cent in the Lok Sabha as well as in the State Legislative Assemblies to ensure them adequate role in the decision making process;

(iii) to adopt an integrated approach to for empowering women through effective convergence of the services, resources, structures and man power in related sectors;

(iv) to organise women into self-help groups for empowering them;

(v) to accord high priority to the child health services;

(vi) to equip women with modern skills in modern ventures to make them economically independent and self reliance;

(vii) to take steps to provide equal access to for women to claimant gender basis in the field of education.

The Central Government initiated several steps to translate its strategy of women empowerment into a concrete reality. It has constituted a committee on empowerment of women in March 1997 to review the progress of various programmes taken up for the empowerment of women from time to time. The Planning Commission required the various Ministries of Central and State Governments to draw up special component plans exclusive for women in the programmes of their respective Ministries. Further, the nodal Department of Women and Child Development responsible for women welfare has initiated several innovative programmes for the promotion of women welfare. These programmes are in the fields of: (i) empowerment; (ii) employment generation; (iii) welfare and support services; (iv) awareness generation and gender sensitisation; and (v) creating enabling environment.

Conclusions

The various development strategies, schemes and programmes which were implemented during different plan periods with huge outlays for the all round development of women produced substantial results which improved their socio-economic conditions to a largest extent. Particularly, the women welfare interventions have brought about radical transformation in the conditions of women. The over-arching strategy of special component Plan for women development in the programmes and programmes resulted in the mobilisation and convergence orchestrated by the women's groups. The mobilisation of women under this strategies is expected to empower them and provide them a forum for articulating their felt needs and contribution of their perspectives to development. This will also enable them to participate in the decision-making process which will result in the building grassroot leadership capable to participating in the governance at the local level.

Needless to point out that the women specific development interventions over the last 5 decades have created enabling atmosphere which sensitised the women about their rights and responsibilities and also increased awareness about their inherent potential capabilities. A consequently the participation of women in the development process has increased and now they are playing a role equal to the men in indifferent spheres of national life. In particular, the political empowerment of women consequent of the 73rd and 74th Constitutional Amendment Acts along with the social and economic empowerment resulted from the Self Help Groups and other innovative strategies have greater impact on the economic position and psychological outlook of women.

As a result, the Indian women are now standing at the cross roads of their destiny. There has been tremendous urge among them for empowerment, development and emancipation in all spheres of life. They are considering the space now they occupy in politics as the space in development. They are equipped to play their role in the society as equal partners with men. They are prepared to take up any responsibility or challenge and convert these challenges and responsibilities into opportunity for the achievement development in their life as well as the society as a whole.

REFERENCES

Mira Seth, *Women and Development*, New Delhi: Sage, 2001.

Sakuntala Narasimhan, *Empowering Women*, New Delhi: Sage, 2001.

Asha Das, "*Child Development and Empowering Women in India*", The Indian Journal of Public Administration, Vol. XVII, No. 3, July, September, 1997.

Government of India, Five-Year Plan Documents, 1950-1997, New Delhi: *Planning Commission*.

Sahay, Sushma, *Women and Empowerment: Approaches and Strategies*, New Delhi, Discovery Publishing House, 1998.

Bipin Chandra et al, *India After Independence 1947-2000*, New Delhi, Penguin Books, 2000.

19

Problems of Girl Child Labour in India

Some Issues

**Dr. K. Chandra Kumar*

Child labour is a global phenomena. Millions of children are engaged in various types of activities world wide, which hinders their education, health, development and future. Most of them are engaged in worst forms of child labour that causes physical and psychological damage. Globalisation processes have played a major role in pushing the issue of child labour as a priority issue in the international debate. In India, several empirical studies carried out in the post liberalisation period tend to substantiate this eventuality. The International Programme on the Elimination of Child Labour (EPEC) and Statistical Information and Monitoring Programme on Child Labour (SIMPOC) of the International Labour Organisation (ILQ) have for the first time, prepared the global estimates of incidence of child labour. They also estimated the magnitude of children employed in hazardous work in other worst

* Professor, Dept. of Political Science and Public Administration, Nagarjuna University, Nagarjuna Nagar, Guntur (A.P.)

forms of child labour. The global estimates on the child labour prepared by the international agencies are given in Table 19.1. The ratio of boys and girls of various age groups is worked out to 23 per cent. Similarly the regional estimates of economically active children in the age group of 5-14 years furnished in Table 19.2 show that more number of children are found in Asia and Pacific, while their work ratio is more in Sub-Saharan Africa also.

The existing statistics suggest that wide variations exist across the States in India in the incidence of child labour and its rates of decline over the last three decades. States like Kerala, Tamil Nadu, Himachal Pradesh and Punjab are leading in subsequently reducing the incidence of child labour while others like Uttar Pradesh, Bihar, Rajasthan, Madhya Pradesh and Andhra Pradesh continue to have a rather sluggish progress in the elimination of child labour. Substantial variations are also reported among these states that are in the category of sluggish progress in this aspect. Among all the states of India, Andhra Pradesh ranks first with more than 14 per cent incidence of child labour. Broadly child labour concentrates on the activities such as fishing, manufacturing, tourism, domestic work, construction, mining and quarrying, and in the urban informal economy. It is identified that multiplicity of factors causing pervasive and high incidence of child labour in India; Poverty, unemployment, illiteracy, high fertility and infant mortality rate are the major reasons for high rate of incidence of child labour in the developing economies like India.

Highlighting the circumstance leading to the child labour scholars point out that it is a fact that girls and boys abandon their education when they are forced to work despite their tender age or the hazards of their labour, when armed conflicts and other emergencies disrupt their lives, when poverty surrounds them or when adults exploit them sexually or buy and sell them like commodities. Further, they argue that evils of Child labour has more disasters impact on the girls than boys.

They emphasis that to be a girl born into poverty is to endure discrimination many times over pervasive and insidious patterns. From the moment of conception, the rights of girls are in peril. About 30 million children mostly girls are found as unpaid family labour. Unlike boys, girls have far less control over their wages. Parents often take away these wages. The option between school and work, simply does not exist. In fact the girls enter the job markets much earlier than boys. The girls are also vulnerable to various types of harassment and crime. There has been increasing number of suicides of girls between age 15-19 years of their age. According to the UNICEF, 12 million, 12 million girls are born in India every year of which 25 per cent do not survive beyond the age of 15. About 3 lakhs more girls die annually than boys. The number of girl children deaths per 1000 live births upto the age of 5 years is higher than that of the male children. The respective figures are 172 and 160 in rural areas and 93 to 92 in urban cities.

Every year about 12 million girls are born in India and 3 million or 25 per cent of them do not survive to see their 15th birthday, one-third of these deaths take place in the very first year itself. Apart from this, the girl child labourers face various occupational hazards: rag pickers collect rusted metals and pieces of glass in the garbage, domestic workers suffer body aches from washing clothes and swabbing floors and agricultural labourers have to face heat-stokes and stomach cramps.

Sexual molestation is also a constant threat to the girl labour. A recent data related to 19 states from 1992-93 compiled by the National Family Health Survey of India reveals that girls are breast-fed for shorter periods than boys, are less likely to be vaccinated than boys and are less likely to receive treatment for diseases like diarrhoea, fever and a cute respiratory infections. Child mortality in the age group of 0-14 is 43 per cent higher for girls than for male children. The study also revealed that it is 42 per 1000 for girls while it is only 29 per 1000 for male children.

Girls are found in large number in a wide range of industries such as the gem polishing trade in Jaipur, the coir industry in Kerala, the lock-making industry in Aligarh, the Brassware industry in Moradabad and Zari (Gold thread), embroidery industry of Varanasi and so on. In the stifling rooms in the slums of Nagpur, women and girls sit rolling agarbattis throughout the day for earning Rs. 5 for 1000 pieces. According to a study, at least 5,00,000 children under 15 years of age in India are sex workers.

Most girl child labourers in Mumbai live in slums or on the pavement, in such worst conditions that spoil their health. In the multitude of fields across India, girls under age 14 toil from dawn to dusk. According to available official statistics boys and girls, constitute 85 per cent of the child labour force in the country. But because the work done at home is non-remunerative and labour in the field forms part of the vast unorganised sector, they are not included as child labourers in the official estimates.

Magnitude of Girl Child Labour in India

The estimation of the magnitude girl child labour varies from institute to institute. The International Labour Institute estimated the children who are neither in school nor at work, called them no where as children. As per the 1991 Census, nearly 5 million are working either as main or marginal workers. Of the 76 million girls in the country in the age group 5-14 years, there will be many more silent workers. Among the main workers, there are more than 3 million girls and nearly 5 million boys at the all-India level. Another 1.6 million girls are categorised as marginal workers, while only half a million boys fall in this category. The child work participation rate in India as a proportion of the total population in the age group 5-14 years is 7 for males and 6 for females. Variation in the female work participation rate (FCWPR) is more than that of the male children across the states. The relevant statistics are furnished in Table 19.3. It is evident from this table that it is very significant in Kerala and Punjab while it ranges up to 14 per cent in Andhra Pradesh. The other states where the FCWPR is reported to be high are Mizoram, Madhya Pradesh, Karnataka, Maharashtra and Rajasthan.

It is reported that girls are mostly marginal workers. According to the data presented in Table 19.4 the states where girls predominate as main workers over boys are: Arunachal Pradesh, Manipur, Himachal Pradesh, Goa, Nagaland, Maharashtra, Mizoram, Sikkim, Andhra Pradesh and Tamil Nadu. Further among the marginal workers, girls exceed boys in all states except for Kerala and Nagaland.

The sex ratio among total workers state-wise are furnished in Table 19.5. The data in this Table show that the sex ratio among total workers ranges from a low of 160 in Punjab to as high as 1,521 in Himachal Pradesh. Large variations are found across the Districts in these States. The burden of work on girls is higher in the districts where the participation of girls in work exceeds that of the boys. Out of the 440 districts belong to 24 states, 218 districts have a higher number of girls working than boys in the age group of 5-14 years, either as main or marginal workers.

Girl Child Labour in Unorganised Sector

In spite of their significant contribution to the family income, the girl participate in economic activities often goes un-noticed as they are employed either in family or domestic work or in the unorganised sector. The predominance of girls in the total labour population is also manifested in the finding of the various studies conducted on the garment industry of India, match industry in Tamil Nadu or in the bangle industry of Ferozabad. The findings of these studies indicate that more than 60 per cent of girl children are deprived of their childhood comforts struggling between their workplace and domestic chores at home. According to the estimates of certain agencies more than 60 per cent of the working children in Asia belong to the rural areas and work in the unorganised primary sector. They enter the labour market to help their poverty-stricken families, because of sudden death of the breadwinner of the family or sometimes they run away from the families due to personal or caste exploitation.

In most economically disadvantaged families, the greater the poverty, the more aggravated is the situation of the girl child labour. Denied educational and nutritional opportunities and healthcare, her growth and development are rather restricted by the process of socialisation. In certain communities the rules of permission and restriction of girl children are mor stringent, which paves the way for greater exploitation and discrimination.

Similarly, there is disparity in the education of girls, which is evident from various reports and surveys conducted from time to time. Table 19.6 and Table 19.7 show that in almost all states in India there exists a gender gap with regard to education of children particularly in the lower income brackets. UP presents the case of highest per cent of gender gap (29.4 per cent), followed by Maharashtra (28.3 per cent).

It may be concluded that the efforts to eradicate girl child labour require strategies both at the level of individual agents as well as in terms of interaction among the different agents. The perception and attitude of parents towards girls child need to be urgently changed. Similarly, greater awareness about the rights of the girls and equal treatment across the gender should be promoted on priority basis. However, the Government's efforts to improve literacy among girls and identify and remove children from involvement in hazardous occupations, being implemented through the Five-Year Plans, still have to go a long way.

Table—19.1 Global Estimates of Economically Active Children Ages 5-17 in 2000, by Gender and Age-Group

Gender and Age Group	Total Population ('000s)	Number at Work ('000s)	Work Ratio (%)
Boys			
5-9	308500	38100	12.3
10-14	307900	70900	23.0
5-14	616400	109000	17.7
15-17	170200	75100	44.1
Total	786600	184100	23.4
Girls			
5-9	291800	35000	12.0
10-14	291300	66800	22.9
5-14	583100	101800	17.5
15-17	161800	65800	40.7
Total	744900	167600	22.5
Both Genders			
5-9	600200	73100	12.2
10-14	599200	137700	23.0
5-14	1199400	210800	17.6
15-17	332100	140900	42.4
Total	1531100	351700	23.0

Source: Every Child Counts: Now Global Estimates on Child Labour, IPEC and SIMPOC International Labour Office, Geneva, April, 2002.

Table—19.2 Regional Estimates of Economically Active Children Ages 5-14 in 2000

Region	Number of Children ('000s)	Work Ratio (%)
Developed economies	2.5	2
Transition economies	2.4	4
Asia and the pacific	127.3	19
Latin America & Caribbean	17.4	16
Sub-Saharan Africa	48.0	29
Middle East and North Africa	13.4	15
Total	211	18

Source: Every Child Counts: New Global Estimates on Child Labour, IPEC and SIMPOC International Labour Office, Geneva, April, 2002.

Table—19.3 State-wise Work Participation Rates (1991 Census)

State	Person	Male	Female
Andhra Pradesh	12	11	14
Arunachal Pradesh	6	5	7
Assam	6	7	4
Bihar	4	5	3
Goa	2	2	2
Gujarat	7	6	8
Haryana	3	4	2
Himachal Pradesh	5	4	6
Karnataka	11	11	11
Kerala	1	1	1
Madhya Pradesh	10	9	11
Maharashtra	8	7	10
Manipur	5	4	5
Meghalaya	9	10	8
Mizoram	11	10	12
Nagaland	6	5	7
Orissa	6	7	6
Punjab	4	6	1
Rajasthan	8	6	10
Sikkim	5	5	5

(Table Contd...)

1	2	3	4
Tamil Nadu	6	5	7
Tripura	2	3	2
Uttar Pradesh	4	5	3
West Bengal	5	7	3
India	6	7	6

Source: Calculated from Census of India, 1991.

Table—19.4 State-wise Sex Ratios Among Total Population, Main and Marginal Workers

State	Total Population (5-14 Years)	Main Workers	Marginal Workers
Andhra Pradesh	948	1040	3300
Arunachal Pradesh	933	1328	2958
Assam	964	336	3095
Bihar	880	335	3554
Goa	968	1201	1966
Gujarat	925	586	7960
Haryana	860	300	4120
Himachal Pradesh	966	1273	1892
Karnataka	981	830	3338
Kerala	983	751	985
Madhya Pradesh	926	758	3066
Maharashtra	941	1156	2746
Manipur	966	1281	1736
Meghalaya	983	702	1674
Mizoram	986	1125	1090
Nagaland	955	1165	962
Orissa	987	494	3799
Punjab	883	80	5453
Rajasthan	888	827	4413
Sikkim	980	1058	1516
Tamil Nadu	955	1033	6100
Tripura	960	512	2521
Uttar Pradesh	858	269	2777
West Bengal	963	323	1710
India	918	638	3281

Source: Calculated from Census of India, 1991.

Table—19.5 Sex Ratio Among Child Works and Numbers of Districts with Higher Number of Girls Working

State	Sex ratio among child workers (SRCW)	No. of districts with SRCW>1000	Total No. of districts
Andhra Pradesh	1127	19	23
Arunachal Pradesh	1391	11	11
Assam	563	4	23
Bihar	522	6	42
Goa	1343	2	2
Gujarat	1129	13	19
Haryana	536	3	16
Himachal Pradesh	1521	12	12
Karnataka	1039	13	20
Kerala	792	3	14
Madhya Pradesh	1075	27	45
Maharashtra	1426	29	30
Manipur	1344	8	8
Meghalaya	776	–	5
Mizoram	1107	3	3
Nagaland	1159	6	7
Orissa	866	6	13
Punjab	160	–	12
Rajasthan	1443	24	27
Sikkim	1081	3	4
Tamil Nadu	1205	18	21
Tripura	697	–	3
Uttar Pradesh	465	7	63
West Bengal	456	1	17
All India	879	218	440

Source: Calculated from Census of India, 1991.

Table—19.6 Gender Gap in Education Among the Lower 40 Per cent Income Brackets in Different States

States	Male	Female	Gender gap
Andhra Pradesh	25.4	7.2	18.1
Assam	28.0	18.3	9.7
Bihar	31.8	6.5	25.3
Gujarat	30.9	10.0	20.9
Haryana	30.3	5.6	24.6
Himachal Pradesh	–	13.6	–
Karnataka	32.2	9.8	23.4
Kerala	47.4	57.9	10.5
Madhya Pradesh	27.4	5.3	22.1
Maharashtra	42.1	13.8	28.3
Orissa	29.6	9.5	20.1
Punjab	19.3	8.9	10.4
Rajasthan	24.6	1.7	23.0
Tamil Nadu	37.9	17.7	20.2
Uttar Pradesh	37.4	8.1	29.4
West Bengal	18.4	9.4	9.1
All India	31.3	9.5	21.8

Table—19.7 Gender Gap in Education Among the Upper 20 Per cent Income Brackets in Different States

States	Male	Female	Gender gap
Andhra Pradesh	90.6	82.0	8.6
Assam	90.4	81.9	8.5
Bihar	87.5	85.1	2.5
Gujarat	88.7	80.4	8.3
Haryana	74.1	71.5	2.6
Himachal Pradesh	82.8	80.8	2.0
Karnataka	83.6	79.7	3.9
Kerala	90.9	93.7	-2.8
Madhya Pradesh	87.3	78.8	8.5
Maharashtra	87.0	79.9	7.1
Orissa	93.3	88.1	5.2
Punjab	78.2	77.3	0.9
Rajasthan	82.6	71.0	11.6
Tamil Nadu	85.9	82.1	3.8
Uttar Pradesh	84.7	82.6	2.1
West Bengal	83.8	64.8	19.1
All India	85.2	79.6	5.6

20

Women Empowerment

A Theoretical Perspective

**Dr. M. Koteswara Rao*

Poverty and chronic deprivation of certain sections have long been a tragic aspect of human society. Most of the persons in this category are women and they are not considered on par with the other sex. Ironically, development planners and policy makers all over the world have often failed to consider women's needs and their viewpoint in designing the programmes for their development. Nevertheless women form central focus for development of any society. Everywhere women discharge two roles: at home as housewives and outside as wage earners. Both are important for the progress of any society and nation as a whole. Further, they carry out several vital socio-economic activities like bearing and rearing of children, providing much of the Labour for household maintenance and subsistence, agriculture and so on. Women make an important contribution to the economy through working in both the formal and informal sectors. Ironically,

* Professor, Dept.of Economics, Acharya Nagarjuna University, Nagarjuna Nagar, Guntur. (Anhdra Pradesh).

women's work is generally undervalued and the additional development it promotes is usually unrecognized. As a result, their work suffers and development is held back.

According to the analysts, Indian woman has a multi-faceted personality. She is the pivot around whom the whole household revolves. Hard working and dedicated, she shares most of the duties and responsibilities of a family. Housekeeping, child-rearing, assisting in agriculture and industry, cattle rearing are part of her duties. She strongly influences the moral, social and creative development of her children. But she, herself continues to be under-developed and oppressed[1]. The Labour Bureau's publications on the socio-economic status of workers in India focused their attention on the legislative measures initiated for the protection and welfare of women workers, male and female differences in wages and earnings, working conditions, social conditions, health care etc., in the case of women workers for the period ending 1950. Gadgil made several observations on the nature and extent of women's participation in economic activity in India and the impact of state sponsored development on them[2].

Women and Workforce

Most of the rural women participate in various economic activities but this fact does not find a place in the Indian Census Reports[3]. Rural women participate in several agricultural activities like sowing, weeding, transplantation, manuring, harvesting, winnowing, shelling and storing of crops. Though women make a substantial contribution to the family income through home-based activities, this is treated as supplemental and hence it goes unnoticed. According to the Official statistics the total workforce of 393.19 million in the country in 1999-00, 123.00 million (31.3 per cent) are women. This percentage was 35.90 for rural areas and 24.60 for urban areas, which indicates that relatively more women participate in work in rural areas than in urban areas. The rural female workforce has increased by more than 50 per cent during the last two decades, from 69.2 million in 1972-73 to 123 million in 1999-00, while the rural female population has increased at a much lower rate, by 43 per cent during the period. The same is reflected in their Work Participation Rate (WPR) also. About 31 per cent of rural females participate in the workforce against a mere 12 per cent of urban females. This WPR of rural women has shown the highest increase, among all the components of labourforce during 1991-2001. Though women's participation in the labour market is much lower than that of males, rural females have a much higher WPR compared to urban females, and the rural female-workforce has shows a much faster increase in the recent decade. This higher percentage of rural women, however, is not accompanied by any positive characteristics of the workforce. At the same time the rural female workforce enjoys much lower occupational diversification, very poor employment status and high unemployment raters. With regard to the occupational diversification of rural women, it is found that 92.2 million (75 per cent) of rural women workers are in the primary sector in 1999-2000. This proportion was slightly lower (77.4 per cent) in 1993-94, implying a marginal increase in their share of women workers in the primary sector during the decade. This indicates that rural women are in worst position in the labour market in terms of occupational diversification, employment status and wages. The changes in their position in the labour market during the last two decades were also not very encouraging. Their diversification is almost stagnant, their employment status is not improving and their wages are increasing at much lower rates. The only positive aspects are (a) their slow increase in the labour market, (b) the small improvement in their share in the manufacturing sector and (c) the decline in their unemployment rate. These changes, however, are very small. The overall scene is very grim and does not lead one to expect a very bright future for rural women in the labour market[4].

Absolute poverty and economic compulsions have forced women, particularly belonging to the Scheduled Castes, Scheduled Tribes, Other Backward Classes and other economically weaker sections of the rural society to take-up unskilled and menial works requiring more labour hours for which they earn a petty sum.

The Indian National Commission on Self-Employed Women (1987) in its Report envisaged that, in wage employment, more than half of the sample women labour receives wages below the subsistence level. It further reveals that the jobs in which they are usually appointed are generally irregular, uncertain, seasonal and discretionary and characterized by malpractices in payment, non-payment of wages on time, signature on inflated amount and exertion of commission on payment. In 1991, the World Bank remarked that participation in such activities does not increase women's control over family resources.

Women and Education

Social and economic development of a country depends on its high literacy rates and better educational facilities. In India, though the general literacy rate has been increasing steadily, female literacy is lower than male literacy. According to the 1991 Census, the literacy percentage is 63.86 per cent whereas in women it is 39.42. These figures on the literacy levels of women in our country amply reflect the disparities in the literacy rate prevailing between both the sexes.

Lack of education is a potential hindrance for the socio-economic development of women. As 1991 Census shows the literacy rate among the women in rural areas is 31.87 per cent as against 64.05 per cent in urban areas. The literacy rate of Scheduled Castes and Scheduled Tribes in rural areas is only 19.46 and 21.62 per cent respectively as against women literacy among the Scheduled Castes and Scheduled Tribes in urban areas are 42.29 per cent and 45.66 per cent respectively. During 1951-91, the female literacy rate went up from a mere 7.93, percent in 1951 to 31.87 percent in 1991. It may be inferred that with the increasing access of women to the educational facilities in recent times there has been some improvement in literacy rate among them.

Short Falls in Poverty Alleviation Programmes

Due to the failure of trickle down effect, several direct poverty reduction programmes are undertaken in India and elsewhere exclusively for women. The planners and administrators identified many pitfalls in the micro level interventions of poverty alleviation in this country along with other operational deficiencies. The maladies of earlier Poverty Alleviation Programmes (PAPs) in India were exposed by several government and non-governmental agencies concerning with these programmes[5]. Scholars like

Copestake[6] and Dantwala[7] also analyzed the operational and deficiencies of these programmes. Thus, a large volume of literature is available now, which depicts very clearly the series of inadequacies in the PAPs. These inadequacies range from possession of unproductive assets, the high cost of the available assets, the high rates of interest on bank loans, absence of forward and backward linkages, lack of co-ordination among the various departments concerned, absence of innovativeness in the departmental interventions, failure in providing marketing support, unrealistic repayment schedules, inadequacy of managerial and technical skills and absence of urge for development among the poor women. It was also brought out that the IRDP provided an opportunity for making political capital out of the patronage potential inherent in the subsidized credit delivery. On the employment generation front also in the case of programmes such as JRY introduced in 1989-90, the evaluation by the PEO concludes that average number of days a person got wage-employment was 11.44 days, 15.68 days and 12.81 days during 1989-90, 1990-91 and 1991-92 respectively. The evaluation report also identifies many weaknesses such as low participation of women, disparity in the wage structure between male and female unskilled workers, execution of works by contractors, inappropriate timing, corruption, adhocism in project implementation, delayed and poor participation of the people in all these programmes.

Further, the World Bank's Project Appraisal Document on Andhra Pradesh Districts Poverty Initiatives Project[8] has also recognized and pointed out several limitations of the earlier micro-interventions in which the poor households/persons are the direct beneficiaries. Among the limitations identified, mention is to be made of the following:

(i) Programmes like Employment Assurance Programme (EAS) and Swarna Jayanti Grama Samridhi Yojana (SGSY) are centrally sponsored with limited State contributions and control. Besides, these programmes encounter deficiencies such as:

(a) low beneficiary involvement in planning, implementation and monitoring,

(b) supply driven implementation, primarily by numerical targets,

(c) poor targeting; and

(d) inefficient management.

(ii) Political and social structures at the local levels tend to prevent adequate attention to the poorest of the poor.

With a view to overcome the foregoing constraints and deficiencies and to facilitate direct participation of the beneficiaries from the stage of project design to the stage of performance appraisal, a self-help group approach is being evolved by the State Government.

DWCRA: A Tool for Women Empowerment

The fact has been recognized that women were benefited only marginally under various rural development schemes implemented after Independence. This leads to the realization that since reaching women in isolation was considered to be very difficult, it was decided to adopt a group approach to reach them in large numbers. Hence a programme, which facilitates the groups of about 15-20 women belonging to families below the poverty line to get organized under self-employment, was visualized in 1982 and it was named after the Development of Women and Children in Rural Areas (DWCRA). The groups are provided financial assistance in the forms of loan and subsidy and technical assistance including training, marketing linkages and other follow up support to take up the selected enterprise successfully. The specific objectives of the DWCRA are to improve women's participation in rural development by making them self-reliant and to establish meaningful linkages between this programme and various other programmes designed for the development of rural and backward sections of the society.

The Development of Women and Children in Rural Areas (DWCRA) Programme, a sub-scheme of the IRDP, was started in 1982-83. The Programme focuses on the women members of rural families, which are below the poverty line, with a view to providing them opportunities for self-employment on a substantial basis. It is also supposed to provide other services to improve the quality of their life, and also to assist in improving childcare. Through such social and economic empowerment, the programme seeks to improve the access of rural women to health, education, safe drinking water, sanitation, nutrition etc., thereby bringing about an improvement in the quality of life and general well being of the women and children.

Under the DWCRA Programme the women form groups of 10-15 members each for taking up economic activities suited to their skills, aptitude and local conditions. A revolving fund amounting to Rs.15,000 is given to each group to meet their working capital requirements etc. Expenditure on revolving fund was being shared equally by the Central Government, State Government and UNICEF till 1994-95. From 1995-96 the revolving fund has been increased from Rs.15,000 to 25,000 per group to be shared by the Central, State Governments and UNICEF in the ratio of 40:40:20. The UNICEF support was, however, withdrawn from 1st January, 1996. The Vision-2020 of Andhra Pradesh Government accords an important place to the self-help group approach to poverty alleviation, particularly among the poor.

Approaches to Women Welfare

In the women's studies several perspectives have been followed by various scholars to analyze the position of women in relation to the developmental process. The important ones are: (a) Cultural Dualism; (b) Social Evolution Approach; (c) Developmentalism; (d) Dependency Theory; and (e) Target Group Approach; and (f) Empowerment Approach. The common assumption of all these five perspectives is that the position of women has not registered significant improvement despite the efforts at their development and modernization.

(a) Perspective of Cultural Dualism

Simone de Beauvoir is one of the chief protagonists of the perspective towards women's development, which is based on cultural dualism. This perspective holds the perception that the secondary status of women is universalistic[9]. Beauvoir treated the origins of women's subordination in part, in their relationship to nature and nature's relationship to culture. Woman is identified with nature. Man controls nature through culture. So, he is superior to nature or woman, yet, man can neither abolish nature nor live without woman. Elaborating the perspective of cultural dualism Whyte and Whyte note that what is certain is that today it is very difficult for women to manifest their autonomous individuality and their destiny lies in the source of their awkwardness and discomfort[10]. They also suggested that Western women seek liberation as an individual, while the Asian woman seeks greater satisfaction by the improvement of her family's economic situation and of her status within the family. A Latin American study notes that since women are socialized from childhood to view their primary roles--wife and mother--involving sacrifices, they experience ambivalence when they become wage-earners[11]. Though the theory of cultural dualism lacks coherence it provides an useful analysis by supplying a sophisticated view of the internal dynamics of culture relating to the position of women.

(b) Social Evolutionary Theory

Social evolutionary theory concerns with the issue whether women's position becomes better or worse as societies undergo change. This perspective has considerable influence on those who study the role of women in developing societies. It provides them with an explanation of the dynamic of social change and evaluation of its directions. The social evolutionary perspective asserts that societies are affected by the changes in the population as well as resource balance and also competition from neighbors to move along the scale of increasing division of labour and differentiation[12]. Basing on the notion of division of labour, the social evolutionary theory provides an explanation for the inequality, existing both among and within societies. Boserup demonstrates that women have been relegated to jobs in the backward sectors of the economy involving low levels of specialization. Because they fail on the lower side of the "productive gap" they suffer inequality[13]. It is held that they lost the opportunity to participate in decision-making in the public domain. The growth of centralization and bureaucratization had also increased the scope for subordination of women.

(c) Developmentalism

The perception that modernization will have differential effects on men and women has led planners to identify the obstacles, which prevent women's participating in development. The United Nations Conference on women held in Mexico City in 1975, focused world-wide attention on the need for intensified action to ensure the full integration of women in the development process[14]. The developmentalist perspective emerged at this Conference presented three different notions about social change that differ from the assumptions of conventional modernization theory. They are (1) changes introduced in one sector may not generate corresponding changes in various other sectors of society. New technologies introduced to increase productivity many remain encapsulated, just as development Programmes of a general nature or those addressed to men do not often generate benefits for women. (2) There are contradictions in the process of social change. Policies targeted to increase women's employment may accentuate the problem by increasing their exploitation if wages and working conditions are not improved at the same time. (3) National elites and external forces play major roles in launching new Programmes aimed at social change among women.

(d) Dependency Theory

Dependency theory focuses attention on constraints placed on development by international forces. It gained some currency as the modernization theorists had difficulty in explaining the reasons for the persistence of under-development in Third World Countries. Dependency theory attempts to locate systemic connections among the contradictions noted by the develop mentalists by pursuing the linkage through the socio-economic infrastructure of the countries concerned[15].

An important variant of dependency theory pertaining to women was conceptualized by Marxist feminists with an international orientation. The Dependency theory alters the classical Marxist explanation of women's subordination, by asserting that women are relegated to the domestic economy and denied the opportunity to participate in production of goods for exchange in the larger society. According to the dependency theory women's subordination in development is due to the backwardness of the household.

(e) Target Group Approach

The target group approach is based on the assumption that disadvantaged sections of society need special programmes for their advancement. In several developing countries such as India immediately after independence little or no effort was made by the planners to integrate women into the main stream of development process. The Government made provision for industrialization, rural development, education and health programmes, etc., and the women were expected to benefit from this overall development effort. However, the results were not at all encouraging. The Scholars like Barbara Rogbers[16] felt that special schemes should be designed and targeted for specific groups like women. The United Nations puts the current status of women in stark perspective in the following way:

While they (women) represent 50 per cent of the world population and one-third of the official labour force, they account for nearly two-thirds of all working hours, receive only one-tenth of the world income and own less than one per cent of the world income and own less than one per cent of world property. Almost two out of every three illiterates in the world are women[17].

In many developing countries, improvement in the economic status of a class is reported to have led to more unequal treatment of women[18]. It is also held that failure to give full access to women to employment opportunities actually defeats the national development plans in a number of ways[19]. Where improvements did not take place in the conditions of women it involves a consequence of imperfect integration of women into the process of development.

Another important debate generated by the Scholars of this approach is the relationship between gender equality and socio-economic inequalities in stratified societies. Many researchers infer that social stratification strengthens or increases sexual inequality[20]. These studies stressed the increasingly adverse impact of the processes of change among women. The macro-indicators in this regard include the adverse decline in the sex-ratio, the differentials in mortality, literacy, access to health care and the accelerated decline in women's employment since 1941[21].

Responding to this situation the Indian Planners have designed new policy instruments for women's development. These are basically target-group oriented schemes aimed at the diversification and expansion of opportunities for education and training of women, provision of credit facilities for self-employment and small-scale sector employment and strengthening the existing agencies or creating new agencies to identify and promote Programmes for women.

Patriarchy has been used by feminist scholars as a theoretical construct to explain the structure underlying the subordination of women and as one hindering the development of women. The structure of patriarchy has been conceived of at psychological, cultural and material levels. Indian society is basically patriarchal in nature. Therefore, the status of women in various spheres is subordinate to that of men. Any improvement desired in the women's status may be viewed in societies like India as a threat to the existing balance. It is argued by a few analysts that it is, therefore, not easy to actually fully integrate women into the development process or projects, without preparing the ground sufficiently for it.

Development is, by definition a historical process moving forward from one stage to another or a preferred situation. According to Samuel Beer "the concept of development recognizes the importance of the time dimension" and so should be studied in keeping with that perspective. The past behavior of an individual or a group has to be carefully studied as it provides the basic data, which determines the future shape of events. The cultural and social mores that structure the subordinate position of women need a careful and systematic analysis in the context of gender-specific policies and programmes.

(f) Empowerment Approach

This approach gained currency only in 1990s but became a very important theme in the academic circles in the West as well as non-west. Block assumes that empowerment goes hand-in-hand with politics[22]. It implies the process of exchange of power. People empower themselves by discovering a positive way of being political. They become political without being manipulative. Thus, empowerment involves the development of positive political skills among the people. In another way, people can be empowered by involving them in their work through a process of participation. Accordingly, it is defined as a process, which enhances their intrinsic work motivation by positively influencing impact, competence, meaningfulness and choice[23]. Empowered people believe that they are competent and valued, that their jobs have meaning and impact and that they have opportunities to use their talents. Likewise, from the standpoint of assumption that powerlessness gives rise to low self-efficacy, an attempt has been made to define it as a process of identifying and removing the conditions which cause powerlessness while increasing feelings of self efficacy[24].

As a basis for the redistribution of power in work settings, Brown and Brown define empowerment as the reorientation of all forces, values and beliefs which determine human behavior in organizations so that they support and liberate the individual rather than reduce their range of thought and action[25]. This process releases the full potential of every individual to contribute to the common enterprise. Randolph18 believes that empowerment is not just 'giving people the power to make decisions. He defines empowerment as recognizing and releasing into the organization the power, which the people already have in their wealth of useful knowledge and internal motivation. Likewise, Bowen and Lawler III[26] conceive empowerment as a process of providing information, rewards, knowledge and power to people in work settings. They emphasize the need to share information and develop teams, which have decision-making power. They also emphasize the importance of training and reward. People require relevant training and knowledge about how to be empowered. Empowered people must be rewarded for their increased responsibility and accountability.

Quinn and Spreitzer[27] classify the various definitions of empowerment as mechanistic and organic. The definitions provided by Randolph and Bowen and Lawler III belong to the mechanistic category. This perspective of empowerment assumes that managers tend to empower people by sharing information, providing structure, developing a team-based alternative to hierarchy, offering relevant training opportunities and rewarding them for the risks and initiatives they are expected to take. The definitions provided by Conger and Kanungo and Thomas and Velthouse are considered organic. From this perspective, empowerment is a process of risk taking, trusting and personal growth; it is a mind-set, which people have about their role in the organization. While management can create a context, which is more empowering, people must choose to be empowered. They must see themselves as having freedom and discretion. Both perspectives are incomplete. It is only by juxtaposing these two perspectives that we can begin to fully understand the concept of empowerment. Quinn and Spreitzer suggest a set of four levers to integrate these perspectives: a clear vision and challenge; openness and teamwork; discipline and control; and support and a sense of security.

Importance of Empowerment

A central issue for the twenty-first century organizations will be how to balance top-down control with bottom-up empowerment[28]. Empowerment has currently emerged as one of the most popular business words. The immensely decreasing costs of information technology (IT) are changing the economics of organizational decision making with the result that decentralized control is becoming imperative in several situations. The increasing extent of decentralization is not merely a fad but responds to fundamental changes in the economics of decision making caused by the new information technologies. In the knowledge-based emerging economy, which is globally connected, decentralized decision-making is likely to play increasingly significant roles. Figuring out how to design effective control systems and how to manage the constantly shifting balance between empowerment and control will not be an easy task. However, mastering this challenge will be one of the most important differences between organizations which succeed in the next century and those which fail[29].

It has been evidenced that power and effectiveness increase with sharing power and control[30] Likewise, several studies have also demonstrated that empowerment is positively associated with organizational effectiveness[31]. Empowerment facilitates fuller application of advanced technology[32]. It forms a source of intrinsic motivation and a determinant of fairness perception of supervisory leadership among subordinates[33]. It is a prerequisite to quality-focused organizations[34] a core value the TQM effort[35] has congruence with TQM[36]. This is true because intrinsically motivated people make continuous improvement possible[37] by resolving the systematic problems and preventing better customer service[38]. In general, there is a synergy among the themes of TQM, empowerment, learning organizations, horizontal organizations and high performance work systems[39].

As a growing concern, empowerment facilitates fuller application of human potential, spontaneous commitment of people to organisational goals and innovative response to unexpected organisational problems[40]. Therefore, it is not surprising that empowerment is considered an 'elixir' for the 1990s and a prerequisite to the survival of the business in the emerging market place and an indispensable device for accomplishing a competitive edge in a globalised and a liberalized economy[41].

Notwithstanding its utmost importance and all the efforts which have gone into fostering it, empowerment remains very much like the emperor's new clothes; it is praised loudly in public but cannot be tolerated privately; there has been neither any transformation in the workplace nor any sweeping metamorphosis[42].

Empowerment of Women in Indian Context

In most South Asian countries, the status of women is low and their socio-economic conditions are much more depressed than that of men[43]. Regionally variations and disparities make them even more vulnerable. Poverty, infact, is one of the aspects of their deprived condition. Low earning, lower wages, low level of skills, limited access to the factors of production, low literacy, malnutrition, poor standard of health, greater exposure to domestic violence and vulnerability to sexual crimes are some of the other dimensions of their low status. Women's movements and feminist thinkers have even questioned the existing models of development, which provide the parameters within which we think and act. They advocate structural and cultural transformation of the society, thereby creating a more egalitarian relationship between men and women. For this empowerment of women is most essential condition.

It is important to note that in India it was only in the 70s that the shift in approach from welfare to development has emerged with reference to the weaker sections of the society including women. The VI Plan clearly emphasized the potential of women to become against of development. In the 80s, the IRDP that takes the family as a unit of development and stands for integrated development of those living below the poverty line was improved and refined in order to make it more effective, particularly in the case of rural women. The VIII Plan, which corresponded the beginning of liberalization and market-friendly economy, marks a major shift in the developmental strategy. It emphasized people-oriented perspective of development grounded in local realities. It calls for a "certain degree of flexibility built into the programmes leaving the choice to the people based at the local level, regarding their needs and priorities". The voluntary organizations are encouraged to mobilize and organize the people to play their role in the promotion of self-reliant development rather than limit their activities to relief works, charity and welfare.

The Government, with a view to make the constitutional mandate a reality, has also been trying to create a policy environment in which women's concerns can be reflected, articulated and redressed in the society. The most important policy initiative in this regard has been the introduction of the National Plan of Action for Women (1976), and a National Perspective Plan for Women (1998-200), which advocates a holistic approach for the development of women. The National Plan of Action for the Children and Girl Child (1991-2000) aims at for ensuring survival, protection and development of children with a special gender sensitivity built for girl children and adolescent girls. In addition to the above women specific policy initiatives, various national policies like the National policy on Education 91986), National

Health Polity (1983), National Nutrition Policy (1993) have identified women as vulnerable groups requiring support for their welfare and development. It was in this context that national machinery for the advancement of women in India has been set up in the form of Department of Women and child Development[44].

The Draft National Policy on Empowerment of Women envisages:

(i) To set up councils at the national and state levels to review the implementation of the recommendations of the national and state commissions for women;

(ii) The centre and state to draw-up time-bound action plans to translate this policy into concrete action in consultation with the central and state commissions for women; and

(iii) Every ministry at the centre and in the state is obliged to ensure equal flow of benefits in physical and financial terms to women, including the disadvantaged among them through different programmes and plans. The Government of India also reiterated its commitment of women empowerment of International Women's Day on March 6th 1997 for setting up of Commissioner for Women Rights and National Resources Centre for Women in order to create a conducive environment for the advancement of women.

A few important areas which calls for empowerment of women in rural India are:

(a) Women and their workforce participation

(b) Women and their education

(c) Women and their health and,

(d) Women and their political participation at the grassroots to deal with atrocities on women and other development issues of rural women[39].

Despite several welfare schemes and poverty alleviation programmes which are implemented during the era of planned development started during the post independence period, the trickle down effect is not visible. The rural women are doubly disadvantaged as they are being located in the rural society and were not considered separately for poverty alleviation programmes until recently. They are often victims of traditions, social and domestic violence. Despite all the developmental measures and constitutional guarantee, women have lagged behind men in almost all walks of life. The irony is that man is born of a woman and get the latter is dominated in every field. Effective measures should be taken in a developing country like India apart from the efforts initiated by the Government through SHGs so far to increase the participation of female workforce in economic activities.

REFERENCES

1. For an Excellent Detailed Discussion on these Very Vital Issues See Also Ghadially, Rehana (eds.) (1985). *Women in Indian Society*, New Delhi; Sage Publications.

Government of India (1974). *Towards Equality, Report of the National Commission on the Status of Women in India*, New Delhi.

Government of India (1980). *'Shramshakti', Report of the National Commission on the Self-employed Women in Informal Sector*, New Delhi.

Government of India (1988). *National Perspective Plan for Women: 1988-2000*, Report of the Core Group Set Up by the Department of Women and Child Development, New Delhi.

Jeffery, P. (1979). *Frogs in a Well: 'Indian Women in Purdah,'* Zed Press, London.

Usha Rao, N.J. (1981). *Women in a Developing Society*, Ashish Publishing House, New Delhi.

Ramola M. Boxamusa and Sobha Joshi (1976). *Assistance for Women Development from National Agencies*, Popular Publications, Bombay.

Kulkarni (1962). *Social Policy in India*, Tata Institute of Social Sciences, PISS, Bombay.

George Zeidenstuen (1987). *Women and Development*, World Development Report, No. 6 and 7.

Raksha Saran (1987). *Welfare of Women in India*, S.Chand Publications, New Delhi.

Duvvury Nata, (1987). "Women in Agriculture: A Review of the Indian Literature", *Economic and Political Weekly*, October 28.

Kalpagam U. (1994). *Labour and Gender*, Sagar Publications, New Delhi.

2. Gadgil, D.R. (1938). The Industrial Evolution of India in Recent Times, Oxford University Press, Bombay.

3. The Role of Women in Development has been Extensively Discussed by Acharyda, S, (1984). Women and Rural Development in Third World, Report Prepared for International Centre for Public Enterprises, Lujbljana,

   See also:

   Boserup, E. (1970). *Women's Role in Economic Development*, St. Martins's Press, New York.

   Rogers, B. (1979). *The Domestication of Women: Discrimination in Developed Societies*, St. Martin Press, New York.

   OECD (1985). *Integration of Women in the Economy*, Paris, OECD.

   Ramanamma, A.(1999). "Globalization, Women and Economic Development', in Raj Mohini Sethi (eds.), *Globalisation, Culture and Women's Development*, Rawat Publications, Jaipur, pp. 110-118.

   Sunit Gupta and Mukta Gupta (eds. 2000). *Role of Women in 21st Century*, Anmol Publications, New Delhi.

   Bhalla, Sheila (1994). ' Globalisation Growth and Employment", in G.S. Bhalla and Manmohan Aggarwal (eds.), *World Economy in Transition*, Har Anand Publications, New Delhi, pp.124-125.

   Shah, N. et al (1994). "Structural Adjustment, Feminization of Labour Force and Organisational Strategies", *Economic and Political Weekly*, April 30 pp. 39-48.

   UNDP (1991). *Human Development Report*, United Nations Development Programme, New York.

   UNDP (1992). *Human Development Report*, United Nations Development Programme, New York.

   UNDP (1993). *Human Development Report*, United Nations Development Programme, New York.

   UNDP (1995). *Human Development Report*, United Nations Development Programme, Oxford Economic Press, New York.

   Bhagavan Prasad Singh (1987). Role of Women in Economic Development, *Conference Volume of Indian Economic Association*.

4. Indira Hirway and Anil Kumar Roy, "Women in Agriculture and Rural Development" *Indian Journal of Agricultural Economics*, Vol. 54, No.3, July- September 1999, pp. 251-271.

   See also:

   Chadha, G.K. and P.P. Sahu (2002). "Post Reform Setbacks in Rural Employment, Issues that Need Further Scrutiny", *Economic and Political Weekly*, Vol. 37, No. 21, May 25-31, pp. 1998-2096.

Indira Hirway (2002). "Employment and Unemployment Situation in 1990's: How Good are NSS Data?" *Economic and Political Weekly*, Vol. 37, No. 21, May 25-31, pp. 2027-2036.

Reena Jhabvala and Shalini Sinha, "Liberalisation and Women Workers", *Economic and Political Weekly*, Vol. 37, No. 21, May 25-31, pp.2037-2044.

Acharya, Sarthi and Vinalini Mathew (1991). "Women in Indian Labour Force: A Sectoral and Regional Analysis", *The Indian Journal of Labour Economics*, Vol. 34, No. 3, July-September.

Agarwal, Sarita (1993). "General Discrimination in the Labour Market: A Review of Literature", *Indian Jounral of Labour Economics*, Vol. 36, No. 2, April-June.

Dev, Mahendra (1997). "State Intervention and Women's Employment", *The Indian Journal of Labour Economics*, Vol. 40, No. 3, July-September.

Gopalan, Sarala (1995). Women and Employment in India, Har-Anand publications, New Delhi.

Vargese, V.N. (1991). "Women and Work: An Examination of the Female Marginalisation Thesis in the Indian Context," *The Indian Journal of Labour Economics*, Vol. 34, No. 3, July-September.

Visaria, Pravin (1996). "Structure of Indian Labour Force, 1961-1994", *The Indian Journal of Labour Economics*, Vol. 39, No. 4, October-December.

Visaria, Pravin (1999). "Level and Pattern of Female Employment, 1911-1994", in T.S. Papola and Alakh N. Sharma (eds. 1999), Gender and Employment in India, Indian Society of Labour Economics and Institute of Economic Growth in Association with New Delhi: Vikash Publishing House.

5. IFMR (1984). *An Economic Assessment of Poverty Eradication and Rural Unemployment Alleviation Programme and their Prospects*, Madras.

See Also:

NABARD (1984). *Study of Implementation of IRDP* (mimeo), Bombay.

RBI (1984). *Implementation of Integrated Rural Development Programme - A Field Study*, Bombay.

Planning Commission (1985). *Evaluation Report on Integrated Rural Development Programme*, New Delhi, PEO.

6. Copertake James G. (1996). "The Resilience of IRDP: Reform and Perpetuation of an Indian Myth," *Development Policy Review*, 14.

7. Dantwala, M.L. (1996). *'Dilemmas of Growth: The Indian Experience'*, New Delhi: Sagar Publication.

8. APDPIP (2000). *On Andhra Pradesh District Poverty Initiatives Project Appraisal Document (PAD)*, Report No. 20089, South Asia Regional Office.

9. For An Excellent Detailed Discussion on these Very Vital Issues See

Ghadially, Rehana, (eds.) (1985). *Women in Indian Society*, New Delhi: Sage Publications.

Government of India, (1974). *Towards Equality, Report the National Commission on the Status of Women in India*, New Delhi.

Government of India, (1980). *'Shramshakti'*, Report of the National Commission on the Self-employed Women and in Informal Sector, New Delhi.

Government of India (1988). *National Perspective Plan for Women: 1988-2000*, Report of the Core Group Set Up by the Department of Women and Child Development, New Delhi.

Jeffery, P. (1979). *Frogs in a well: Indian Women in Purdah*, London, Zed Press.

10. Gadgil, D.R. (1938). *The Industrial Evolution of India in Recent Times*, Bombay: Oxford University Press.

11. Government of India, (1975). *Report of the Committee of Status of Women*, New Delhi.

Mitra, A (1980). *India's Population: Aspects of Quality Control*, New Delhi: Abhinav Publications.

Jain, D and Chand M, (1980). 'An investigation into the time allocation of men, women and children in selected rural households", paper presented in a seminar on Women in the Indian Labour Force, BANKOK; ILO, ARTEP.

RRI, (eds.) (1985). *Women and Rice Farming*, London, Gower.

Agarwal, B, (1981), *Agricultural Modernization and Third World Women*, Working Paper No.WEP10/WFZI/ILO, Geneva.

12. The Role of Women in Development has been Extensively Discussed by Acharyda, S. (1984). *Women and Rural Development in Third World*, Report Prepared for International Centre for Public Enterprises, Lujbljana Boserup, E, (1970), 'Women's Role in Economic Development', New York, St Martins's press.

Rogers, B. (1979), *The Domestication of Women: Discrimination in Developed Societies*, New York, St. Martin Press.

OECD (1985), Integration of Women in the Economy, Paris, OECD.

1. Simone de Beauvoir, (1952). The Second Sex, New York,. Alfred A. Knopf Inc.

2. See Whyte, Rebert O., and Pauline Whyute,(1982), *The Women of Rural Asia*, Boulder, Colorado, Westview Press, p. 9.
3. Rohrlich-Leavitt, Ruby,(1975). "Women in Latin America: Introduction" in Ruby Rohrlich-Leavitt (eds.), *Women Cross Culturally Change and Challenge*, The Hague, Monton Publiushers, p. 55.
4. Parsons, Talcott, (1966). *Societ es: Evolutionary and Comparative Perspectives*, Englewood Cliffs, N.J., Prentice-Hall.

13. Boserup, Ester, (1970). *Women's Role in Economic Development*, London, Allen and Unwin.

14. United Nations (1975). *Report of the World Conference of the International Women's Year* (Mexico City, June 19-July 2), New York, United Nations, p. 9.

15. Elliott, Carolyn M., (1977), "Theories of Development: An Assessment", in Wellesley Editorial Committee 'Women and National Development', Chicago, The University of Chicago Press.

16. Rogers, Barbara,(1980). *The Domestication of Women: Discrimination in Developing Societies*, London, Tavistock Publications. See also Tade T. (1984). 'Studies on Rural Women in Africa: An Overview', in International Labour Organization, Rural Development in Africa, Geneva, pp. 65-73.

17. Asian and Pacific Centre for Women and Development, *Report of the International Workshop on Feminist Ideology and Structures in the First Half of the Decade for Women* (24-30 June, 1979), Bangkok, 1979, p. 3. See also, Mazumdar, Vina, (1979), "Women Development and Public Policy". in Rounaq Jahan and Hanna papanek (eds.), Women and Development, Dacca, Bangladesh Institute of International Affairs, pp. 39-54.

18. *Ibid*.

19. Boserup, Ester and Christian Liljencrantz, (1975), *Integration of Women in Development: Why When and How?*, New York, United Nations, Department of Public Information, United Nations.

20. ICSSR, (1977), *Report of the Advisory Committee on Women's Studies, Critical Issues on the Status of Women*, New Delhi, The Indian Council of Social Science Research.

21. Mitra, A,L. Pathak and S. Mukherji, *The Status of Women-shifts in occupational Participation* 1961-71, New Delhi, Abhinav Publications.

    Nayyar, Rohini, (1987), 'Female Participation Rates in Rural India', *Economic and Political Weekly*, 19 December, Vol. XXII, No. 51, pp. 2207-16.

    Ramu G.N. (1989), *Women, Work and Marriage in Urban India: A Study of Dual and Single-earner Couples*, New Delhi, Sage, pp. 25-29.

Boulding et. al. (1976), *Handbook on International Data on Women*, London, Sage Publications.

Sharma, Kumud, (1979), 'Women and Development: Research and Policy Perspectives' in A.K. Gupta, (eds.), *Women and Society, The Developmental Perspective*, New Delhi, Criterion Publications, pp. 101-22.

22. Barrett, M., (1980), *Women's Oppression Today*, London, Verse.

Beechey V. "On Patriarchy", (1979), *Feminist Review*, No. 3, pp. 66-82.

Kandivati, D, (1988), "*Bargaining with Patriarchy*", Gender and Society, Vol. 2, No. 3, pp. 274-90.

23. Thomas, K.W. and Velthouse, B.A. (1990), "Cognitive Elements of Empowerment: An Interpretative Model of Intrinsic Task Motivation", *Academy of Management Review*, October, pp. 661-681.

24. Coger, J.A. and Kanungo, R.N. (1988), "The Empowerment Process: Integrating Theory and Practice", *Academy of Management Review*, 13 (3), pp. 471-482.

25. Brown, R. and Drown, M. (1995), *Empowered*, Research Press, New Delhi.

26. Randolph, R.A., (1995), "Navigating the Journey to Empowerment", Organisational Dynamics, Spring, pp. 19-32.

27. Brown, D.E. and Lawler, III, E.E., (1992), "The Empowerment of Service Workers: What, Why, How and When", *Sloan Management Review*, pp. 36-39.

28. Quinn, R.E. and Spreitzer, (1997), "The Road to Empowerment: Seven Questions Every Leader Should Consider", *Organisational Dynamics*, Autumn, pp. 37-49.

29. Johansen, B, Saveri A, and Schmid, G. (1995), "21st Century organizations: Reconciling Control and Empowerment. Institute for future, Menlo Park, California.

30. Malone, Thomas W. (1997), "Is Empowerment Just a Fad? Control, Decision Making and IT", *Sloan Management Review*, Winter, pp. 23-35.

31. Kanter, R.M.(1983), "The Change Master", Basic Books, New York.

32. Mc.Cllelland, D.C., (1975), "Power: The Inner Experience", Irvington Press, New York.

Bennis, W. and Nanus, B. (1985), *Leaders*, Harper & Row, New York.

33. Zuboff, S. (1988), cited in Crainer, S (eds.) (1995), op. cit.

34. Keller, T. and Dansereau, F. (1995), "Leadership and Empowerment: A Social Exchange Perspective", *Human Relations*, 42, (2), pp. 127-146.

35. Robbins, T.L. and Fredendall, L.D. "The Empowering Role of Self-Directed Work Teams in the Quality Focussed Organisations", *Organisational Development Journal*, 13, (1), pp. 33-42.

36. Gobor.C. and Meunier, G. (1993), "Organisational Development, Leadership and Vision in Higher Education: Putting Power in to Empowerment", *The Journal of Quality and Participation*, 16, pp. 98-101.

37. Freed, J.E. and Burack, E.H. (1996), "Employees Involvement and TQM: Clarifying the Mixed Messages", *Organisation Development Journal*, 14 (2), pp. 19-29.

38. Aguayo, R. (1990), Dr. Deming, Carol Publishing Group, New York.

39. Wilkinson, A, Marchington, M. and Dale, B. (1993), "Enhancing the Contribution of the Human Resource Function to Quality Improvement", *Quality Management Journal*, October, pp. 35-46.

40. Hodgetts, R.M., Luthans, F. and Lee, S.M. (1994), "New Paradigm Organisations: from Quality to Learning to World Class", *Organisational Dynamics*, Spring, pp. 5-19.

41. Brown and Brown *op.cit*.

42. Burdett, J.O. (1991), "What is Empowerment Anyway", *Journal of European Industrial Training*, 15 (6), pp. 23-30.

43. Gosky, K.L. and Belfry, m. (1991), "Achieving Competitive Advantage Through Employee Empowerment", *Employees Relations Today*, 18, pp.213-220.

44. Argyris, C. (1998), "Empowerment: The Emperor's New Clothes", *Harvard Business Review*, May-June, pp. 98-108.